Praise for *Hitler's British Traitors*

'Tim Tate, in *Hitler's British Traitors*, [explores] the entire grimy
landscape of British treachery during the Second World War and the
astonishing rogues' gallery of traitors working to help Nazi Germany
win. [He makes] excellent use of the vast trove of material declassified
by MI5 in recent years.'
Ben Macintyre, *The Times*

'The extent to which the British far right supported Hitler, even after
the outbreak of the second world war, has largely been suppressed.
Now Tim Tate's absorbing study offers a bracing reappraisal of their
sympathies. ... Tate reveals the widespread existence of a fifth column in
Britain, using hitherto unseen archival material.'
The Observer

'A brilliant book'
Dan Snow, History Hit podcast

'A superb book ... absolutely gripping'
Iain Dale, Iain Dale's Book Club podcast

'Fascinating'
The Herald

'Tate explores many engrossing accounts of espionage and
counter-espionage uncovered in the archives, as well as the
jaw-dropping ineptitude and complacency of the authorities who,
though all too keen to imprison and execute petty criminals recruited by
German intelligence, displayed a characteristic restraint when dealing
with far more threatening and powerful traitors. ... Tate's formidable
scholarship paints a picture of Britain during the war that is a far cry
from the reassuring story told about our collective heroism of a nation
united under the banner of Keep Calm and Carry On.'
Morning Star

HITLER'S
BRITISH
TRAITORS

HITLER'S BRITISH TRAITORS

The Secret History of Spies, Saboteurs and Fifth Columnists

TIM TATE

ICON

This edition published in the UK in 2019 by
Icon Books Ltd, Omnibus Business Centre,
39–41 North Road, London N7 9DP
email: info@iconbooks.com
www.iconbooks.com

First published in the UK in 2018 by Icon Books Ltd

Sold in the UK, Europe and Asia
by Faber & Faber Ltd, Bloomsbury House,
74–77 Great Russell Street,
London WC1B 3DA or their agents

Distributed in the UK, Europe and Asia
by Grantham Book Services, Trent Road,
Grantham NG31 7XQ

Distributed in Australia and New Zealand by
Allen & Unwin Pty Ltd, PO Box 8500,
83 Alexander Street, Crows Nest, NSW 2065

Distributed in India by Penguin Books India,
7th Floor, Infinity Tower – C, DLF Cyber City,
Gurgaon 122002, Haryana

Distributed in South Africa by
Jonathan Ball, Office B4, The District,
41 Sir Lowry Road, Woodstock 7925

ISBN: 978-178578-561-0

Typeset in Adobe Text by Marie Doherty

Printed and bound in Great Britain
by Clays Ltd, Elcograf S.p.A.

Contents

For my children and grandchildren.

*May they never have to choose between
an existential threat and a moral evil.*

ABOUT THE AUTHOR

Tim Tate is an award-winning documentary film-maker, investigative journalist and author of fifteen previous books of non-fiction, including the best-selling *Slave Girl* (John Blake, 2009) and *Hitler's Forgotten Children* (Elliott & Thompson, 2015) telling the story of the largely-secret Nazi Lebensborn programme through the life of one of its victims. He lives in Wiltshire.

List of Illustrations

Jessie Jordan, Scottish hairdresser and centre of a pre-war Nazi espionage network.

Edwin Heath, a conman who sold British military secrets to the Germans.

Donald Adams, a journalist and racing tipster who spied for the German Secret Service.

Serocold Skeels, who was jailed for four years for conspiring to assist the enemy.

Oliver Conway Gilbert, interned for communicating with German and Japanese spies.

Admiral Sir Barry Domvile, interned for disseminating Nazi propaganda.

The 12th Duke of Bedford, a fascist who tried to negotiate peace terms with Germany.

Lord Sempill, who sold military secrets to Japanese Intelligence for more than fifteen years.

Anthony Ludovici, a leading conservative intellectual and friend of Nazi leaders.

Captain Archibald Ramsay, Conservative MP, fascist and founder of The Right Club.

Anna Wolkoff, who was jailed for sending British military secrets to Nazi Germany.

Tyler Kent, a cipher clerk at the US Embassy who smuggled British military secrets to Berlin.

John Beckett, a fascist who was interned for planning a revolutionary coup d'état.

Leigh Vaughan-Henry, interned for leading a highly-organised plot for an armed coup d'état.

Molly Hiscox and Norah Briscoe, fascists caught in an undercover MI5 sting operation.

George Johnson Armstrong, the first British man to be hanged for treachery during the war.

Dorothy O'Grady, condemned to death for treachery, though her sentence was commuted.

Duncan Scott-Ford, convicted of treachery and executed in November 1942.

Irma Stapleton, caught in an MI5 sting operation and jailed for ten years.

Hermann Simon, who set up a network of 'Fifth Column' sub-agents for German Intelligence.

Josephine 'My' Eriksson, a cook in aristocratic houses who led a double life as a Nazi spy.

Sir John Anderson, the Home Secretary responsible for internment policy.

Alexander Maxwell, Permanent Under Secretary at the Home Office, who clashed with MI5.

Norman Birkett, head of the Home Office Advisory Committee on internments.

Sir Vernon Kell, MI5's first Director, who was sacked on Churchill's orders in June 1940.

Guy Liddell, Director of B Branch of MI5, the section responsible for counter-espionage.

Colonel William Hinchley-Cooke, MI5's most effective spycatcher for more than a decade.

Maxwell Knight, who ran a string of often amateurish undercover agents for MI5.

Marjorie Amor, a middle-class housewife who became a highly effective undercover agent.

Joan Miller, whose memoirs offered revealing insights into Maxwell Knight and his agents.

John Bingham, who ran one of MI5's entrapment operations against Nazi sympathisers.

Victor Rothschild, who masterminded MI5's elaborate 'Jack King' *agent provocateur* scheme.

Eric Roberts, the former bank clerk who became MI5's most successful undercover agent.

Eric Roberts' Gestapo officer's identity card in the name of 'Jack King', created by MI5.

A nation can survive its fools, and even the ambitious. But it cannot survive treason from within. An enemy at the gates is less formidable, for he is known and carries his banner openly.

But the traitor moves amongst those within the gate freely, his sly whispers rustling through all the alleys, heard in the very halls of government itself.

For the traitor appears not a traitor; he speaks in accents familiar to his victims, and he wears their face and their arguments ...

MARCUS TULLIUS CICERO, 106–43 BC

Prelude

Notting Hill, West London

On the evening of Tuesday, May 28, 1940, a succession of men and women rang the bell at No. 36 Stanley Crescent, a quiet, upmarket enclave of tall, stone-faced terraces just three miles to the north of Buckingham Palace and the Houses of Parliament. They arrived one at a time and, to an attentive observer, might have seemed a little furtive.

The visitors were met at the door by a softly-spoken middle-aged man sporting a monocle, who quickly escorted them inside. He, too, seemed nervous. Each new arrival was given elaborate instructions for escaping via a back exit in the event of a raid; each time the doorbell rang, those inside the elegant drawing room moved quickly into the gardens behind the house.

The guests were a curious mixture: representatives of London's political class mixed with members of high society and a Japanese journalist-turned-spy. When the last visitor was ushered inside, their host began issuing orders which, as their Leader, he expected to be obeyed to the letter. This was to be their final gathering: from then on each man or woman would meet only within one of eighteen 'watertight' cells: each had 25 members. Communication was to be limited and careful; members were to speak only with the two immediate 'contacts' in their own cell. Phone calls were discouraged, but if unavoidable, passwords were to be used by both parties to the conversation.

The Leader told his followers that a network of safe houses had been prepared to accommodate cell members' dependent wives and children; none was further than ten minutes' travel from the various headquarters.

In the event of serious trouble, members were to make their way to a temporary rendezvous point outside London, from where they would be escorted out of the country to Ireland, via south Wales. This route had already been successfully tested: over the previous two weeks six people had separately used it to leave Britain without attracting the attention of the authorities.

Meanwhile, the Leader himself was working hard on the next stage of the plan: the infiltration of mainstream political parties. He warned his guests that if this met opposition or proved problematic, key individuals were either to be intimidated by threats against their wives and children or 'bumped off'.

'The Leader' was Dr Leigh Francis Howell Wynne Sackville de Montmorency Vaughan-Henry. To the public he was known as a celebrated composer, music critic and author; he featured regularly on the wireless, had been director of music at the Theatre Institute in Florence and had conducted orchestral performances for the royal family.

To the British Security Service, MI5, however, Leigh Vaughan-Henry was better known as a diehard fascist and violent anti-Semite. It had been monitoring him and his organisation for five years – and for good reason.

The followers he had gathered round him that evening were to be the vanguard of an imminent fascist revolution: a violent coup d'état to replace the British government and the King with an authoritarian pro-Nazi regime, just as soon as German troops landed in Britain.

These men and women were part of Hitler's British Fifth Column. And they were far from alone.

Introduction

This book tells a story which has been suppressed for more than 70 years. It is the story of Hitler's British Traitors – hundreds of men and women who betrayed their country to Nazi Germany during the Second World War.

They did so not on the battlefield, or within the Third Reich, but from the safety of their own homes and offices throughout Britain. They were an 'enemy within', willing and able to spy, commit acts of sabotage and provide information to Berlin during some of the most uncertain days of the war, when Hitler's armies were poised to invade.

Most – though not all – were fascists who held the same rabidly anti-Semitic beliefs as the leaders of National Socialism. Most sold out their country in the hope that Germany would win the war; some expected to receive their reward once the longed-for invasion arrived, while others sought – and received – more immediate payment for their treachery.

This is, however, a secret history. The official account of the Second World War dismisses the idea of a Fifth Column in Britain as either press-driven scaremongering or a diversionary tactic by the Security Service MI5 to justify an unquestionably shameful period in which thousands of 'enemy aliens' – Italian and German nationals, many of whom were Jewish refugees from Nazi persecution – were interned en masse.

Papers by academic historians and legal scholars have argued – in the words of the late Professor A.W.B. Simpson, one of the foremost authorities on internment – that the Fifth Column was a 'myth' and that those who believed in it during the Second World War were 'credulous'.[1] Richard Thurlow, a veteran chronicler of British fascism, went further; his 1999 paper for Oxford University Press's internationally-distributed *Twentieth Century History* series charged, bluntly, that 'the supposed existence of the fifth column became a means by which MI5 came to justify its growth, existence and importance'.[2]

Even the two authorised 'biographies' of MI5 have adopted this version of events. The first, published by Her Majesty's Stationery Office (the government's own press) in 1994, dismissed the threat of domestic 'enemies within' as 'a panic';[3] the second – Professor Christopher Andrew's exhaustive 2009 history of the Security Service from its inception to the present day – pronounced that: 'None of the reports sent to MI5 led to the discovery of any real fifth column or the detection of a single enemy alien.'[4]

And yet, files held by MI5, the Home Office and the Treasury Solicitor's department tell a very different story. Those files, released piecemeal and in a remarkably haphazard manner to the National Archives between 2000 and 2017, show that between 1939 and 1945 more than 70 British men and women were convicted – mostly in secret trials – of working to help Nazi Germany win the war. Among them were Dorothy O'Grady, who sabotaged military communications on the Isle of Wight and drew up detailed plans of south coast defences; George Armstrong and Duncan Scott-Ford, who passed military secrets to German Intelligence; William Gutheridge and Wanda Penlington, who cut telephone wires to obstruct the emergency services during air raids; and besides them, a small army of hardened fascists who volunteered their loyalty and their assistance to Germany's intelligence services. Four of these traitors were sentenced to death – two were executed – while most of the others received lengthy prison sentences.

In the same period, hundreds of other British fascists were interned without trial on specific and detailed evidence that they were spying for, or working on behalf of, Germany. Some of these men and women were lone wolves or members of small, localised networks, but others were very much more dangerous. The declassified intelligence files document three separate, if occasionally overlapping, conspiracies to launch a violent 'fascist revolution'. That the plots, led by Captain Archibald Ramsay, John Beckett and Dr Leigh Vaughan-Henry, occurred during the nation's 'darkest hour' – the months when Britain was bracing itself for invasion – emphasises the reality of the threat. This was no manufactured myth.

Why then has this history remained secret, and for so long? Part of the answer must lie in the inexplicable delay in releasing for public scrutiny the files which document them. Even under the original '50 year rule' – Whitehall's post-war insistence that the records of its various departments should be hidden from view for half a century following their creation – the dossiers should have been turned over to the National Archives before the new millennium. But that waiting period was reduced to 30 years in 1967 and abolished altogether by the Freedom of Information Act in 2000, making the delay even more curious. The sole exemption which might have been used to keep the files under lock and key – that their release might 'damage the country's image, national security or foreign relations' – seems hard to justify.

Whatever the explanation (none has ever been given), the result of this secrecy has been to deny previous researchers – whether academics or journalists – access to the facts. Certainly, when Simpson and Thurlow wrote their papers denying the existence of a substantial pool of British traitors, none of the files which proved their existence had been released.

There are, however, other factors which helped create the dominant – but false – narrative that the Fifth Column was no more than a chimera – a myth dreamed up by Fleet Street or MI5. The first is the unease surrounding Britain's policy of internment without trial, and its application to domestic fascists as well as 'enemy aliens'.

Wartime Defence Regulations bestowed on the Home Secretary a draconian executive power, not subject to review by the courts, to detain anyone believed to pose a threat to public safety or the war effort. The round-ups of thousands of Germans and Italians – many of whom were entirely innocent of any Nazi taint – was unquestionably a shameful period; that hundreds of them died, when the ship transporting them to camps in the Dominions was sunk by a U-boat, compounded this tragedy.

But what emerges from the declassified dossiers is clear evidence that Whitehall's own dithering and incompetence was the deciding factor in the chaos of alien internment. Similarly, they reveal a bitter and long-running feud between the Home Office and MI5 over the problem posed by thousands of British fascists – a feud which erupted into a secret war between the Security Service and civil servants. Given this picture, it is not hard to understand why the Home Office was reluctant to release the files.

That, however, is only one half of the picture. MI5 must also bear a significant share of the blame. Its operations – particularly in the early days of the war – were amateurish and disorganised. Thereafter, although technically groundbreaking for the era, some of its efforts to control the Fifth Column, and to defuse the threats it posed, were ethically questionable to say the least.

But beneath these practical issues lies a more fundamental question concerning the story Britain has told itself about the Second World War. Over the decades since then newspapers, television and the cinema have portrayed the years between 1939 and 1945 as the country's finest hours: the spirits of Dunkirk, the Blitz and a nation bonded by the rubrics of 'Keep Calm and Carry On', 'Make Do and Mend', are repeatedly invoked to create an all-powerful narrative of brave stoicism.

This narrative is not false. It is simply not the whole story. For all the genuine unity and determination of the vast majority of the population to defeat Hitler, there was also a small – but dangerous – sub-stratum which yearned for the day when his troops could goose-step down Whitehall amid an orgy of swastika flags.

Challenging a dominant narrative – especially one which speaks to a nation's image of itself – is not easy. When the research for this book began there were those who argued that Britain was 'not ready' to hear the evidence emerging – belatedly – from official files. But history, if sometimes uncomfortable, is not binary: the existence of a large group of traitors, committed to transforming Britain into a fascist dictatorship, does not negate the equally-factual heroism of a country which fought – sometimes on its knees – to prevent that catastrophe. As the embodiment of the nation's wartime spirit, Winston Churchill, told the House of Commons during the First World War: 'Truth is incontrovertible.

Malice may attack it, ignorance may deride it, but in the end, there it is.'[5]

This, then, is the history – the secret history – of Hitler's British Traitors: a Fifth Column of men and women who committed crimes including espionage, sabotage, and communicating with enemy intelligence agents in the hope of delivering a German victory during the Second World War.

But it begins three years before the war started, and with a small, unremarkable woman in a drab Scottish town.

CHAPTER ONE

A Wake-up Call

'Jessie Jordan. The least sentence I can impose
upon you, having regard to the grave nature of the
offences to which you have pleaded guilty, is that
you be detained in penal servitude for four years.'
Lord Justice Clerk Aitchison, trial judge

High Court, Edinburgh, Monday, May 16, 1938
Jessie Jordan did not look like a spy.

The 51-year-old, twice-married grandmother was still pretty, but tending towards fat. Her clothes were plain, not haute couture, and as befitted the owner of a small hairdressing salon in a working-class district of Dundee, her blonde hair was curled but not stylish. She was, in short, unremarkable. Yet, according to the evidence presented in court, for two years the outwardly-respectable woman in the dock had sold military information to Nazi Germany and was the central figure in a major espionage ring stretching throughout Europe and across the Atlantic to New York and Washington, DC.

The discovery of Jessie Jordan's network should have sounded an alarm inside the British government and its intelligence services, for it revealed both the extent to which Hitler's spymasters had planted agents in the nations with which Germany would shortly be at war

– and the willingness of otherwise unexceptional men and women to betray their country.

*

The Abwehr – Germany's military intelligence service – began life in 1920 as an unfavoured department within the Reichswehr, the country's first national army since its defeat in the First World War. The upper echelons of the Reichswehr were dominated by remnants of the Prussian military caste, who viewed espionage as a dishonourable profession; for the first years of its life the Abwehr was staffed by only three regular army officers and seven brought out of retirement.

Despite this unpromising start, by the end of the 1920s, bolstered by an amalgamation with the naval intelligence division of the Reichsmarine, it had grown substantially and had sufficient resources to operate three separate divisions; one began seeking out potential agents in both the United States and Britain. But the first British spy to join the Abwehr's payroll walked, quite literally, in off the street.

In August 1932, a 21-year-old British Army lieutenant checked into the Hotel Stadt Kiel on Berlin's Mittelstrasse. A few days later he obtained the address and telephone number of the German War Office from the hotel porter and, from a phone box on the tree-lined Unter den Linden boulevard, called the number he had been given. He was quickly connected to a 'Major Mueller' and a rendezvous was arranged under the left-hand arch of the Brandenburg Gate.

The Abwehr officer said he would be easy to recognise: he would be carrying a newspaper and 'the lower part of his face was covered with scars ... caused by the explosion of a hand grenade'.[1]

The British officer was Norman Baillie-Stewart, the son of a lieutenant colonel in the British Indian Army who had served with distinction during the First World War. Baillie-Stewart had followed family tradition and entered the Royal Military College at Sandhurst, where as a cadet he was appointed as an orderly to Prince Henry, son of King George V. In 1929 he was commissioned as a subaltern with the Seaforth Highlanders and posted to India's north-west frontier; here, according to notes in his Army file, he earned a reputation as 'conceited, bombastic and self-important'[2] and was unpopular among his men for provoking unnecessary conflict with the Afridi tribesmen ranged against them.

Baillie-Stewart returned to England early in 1932, and requested a transfer to the Royal Army Service Corps. While waiting for orders to report to his new regiment he put in for leave to visit Germany, ostensibly for a holiday. He received War Office approval on August 1, and left Harwich the same day.

His arrival in Berlin attracted attention – not least because his chosen hotel, the Stadt Kiel, was seedy, had a reputation for what MI5 delicately termed 'ill repute' and was 'one at which no British officer should stay'.[3] A Russian informant passed the titbit of news on to the British Air Attaché in Berlin, who prepared a report for his masters at the War Office in London.

Baillie-Stewart, meanwhile, kept his appointment with Major Mueller. Over a light lunch the Abwehr officer handed Baillie-Stewart a 'questionnaire' and a list of detailed questions about British military organisation and weapons under development for the Army. The latter was, Mueller admitted, a test: if the young subaltern was, as he claimed, willing to betray his country, he should return home, obtain the information and bring it to a second meeting in Holland.[4]

On his return to England Baillie-Stewart set about collecting the documents Mueller had asked for: a list of British 'War Establishments' and a handbook on the tactics of modern Army formations. On August 28 he took a ship from Harwich to the Hook of Holland and delivered them to his Abwehr handler, receiving £10 in Bank of England notes – equivalent to almost £500 today – for his trouble. They agreed to meet again in the middle of October; at that rendezvous in Rotterdam, Baillie-Stewart handed over the latest War Establishments list and a manual of British military small arms. Mueller was evidently pleased, paying his spy another £10 – and requesting further military information.

Back in England, Baillie-Stewart motored down from London to the Army's military library in Aldershot. On the pretext of studying for Staff College exams, he borrowed a sheaf of top-secret documents, including the technical specifications and photographs of an experimental tank, details of a new automatic rifle, and mobilisation tables for the Aldershot Command. He delivered these to Mueller on October 30, and pocketed another £10 note in payment.

The Abwehr handler also provided his agent with the address of a German Secret Service accommodation flat in Berlin where Baillie-Stewart was to send further documents, and instructions to sign all his letters with the codename 'Alphonse Poiret'. Between November 1932 and January the following year, Baillie-Stewart posted to Germany a succession of secret papers, including rough sketches of two more experimental tanks and a list of Army officers Baillie-Stewart believed were employed by MI5 or MI6. For these he was rewarded with two payments totalling £50[5] – equivalent to £3,000 today.

By this time, the report from the Air Attaché had arrived in Room 505 of the War Office in Whitehall. Its occupant was a tubby 46-year-old major, notionally employed as a staff officer with the 55th Anti-Aircraft Brigade of the Royal Artillery; in reality, William Edward Hinchley-Cooke was MI5's most senior spycatcher.

He had been born in 1894; his father was British, his mother German, and he had spent the first twenty years of his life in Dresden. On the outbreak of war in 1914 he was repatriated to England where, on the recommendation of a senior diplomat, he was recruited by Sir Vernon Kell, head of the nascent Security Service. Because 'Cookie', as he was universally known within the War Office, spoke English with a discernible German accent, Kell found it necessary to inscribe his official pass with the words: 'He is an Englishman.'[6]

On November 30, 1932, Hinchley-Cooke obtained a Home Office warrant to monitor letters sent from (and to) Baillie-Stewart's address in Southsea: the intercept revealed a continuing exchange of correspondence with the German Secret Service; on January 23, 1933 Baillie-Stewart was arrested and charged with ten counts of espionage. In April, two months after Hitler seized power in Germany, Norman Baillie-Stewart was sent to prison for five years.[7]

His case attracted enormous press and public attention. For the first few months of his sentence, Baillie-Stewart was held in the Tower of London; while MPs filed parliamentary questions,[8] sightseers flocked to watch him take his daily exercise in the Tower's grounds. After his transfer to more mundane accommodation in Maidstone prison,

Baillie-Stewart cashed in on his celebrity status as 'The Officer in the Tower', selling a serialisation of his life story to the tabloid *Daily Sketch*.

His motives for treachery appear to have been both financial and political: his Army records indicate that he left India in considerable debt – the result of attempting to maintain an aristocratic polo-playing lifestyle on the relatively meagre pay of a junior subaltern. But more important, according to MI5's account of his eventual confession, was a desire for revenge.

> His life with his regiment had been an unhappy one, especially in India, where ... he felt that as he had always been treated as 'dirt' he might just as well turn himself into 'dirt'.[9]

He was also a genuine – if misguided – admirer of German military and cultural life. His great-grandmother was German and, despite his father's successful army career, Norman Baillie-Stewart believed that the peace terms imposed by Britain and her allies under the Treaty of Versailles were grossly unjust. He was, on all counts, an ideal Abwehr recruit.

Prison evidently did nothing to dim his ardour for Germany. When he was released on licence in 1937 he promptly emigrated, first to Austria, before moving to Germany; in Berlin, he once again volunteered to betray his country to the Nazi regime.

While Baillie-Stewart served out his sentence, the German Foreign Ministry and the Abwehr were growing rapidly. In 1934, the Abwehr drew up a four-year plan to expand its Etappenorganisation – the umbrella designation for its country bureaus in Britain, Scandinavia, Central America and North Africa.

The budget for this intensification of intelligence-gathering was, according to a US intelligence report based on captured German documents, 20,000 Reichsmarks – the equivalent of a distinctly modest £80,000 today. The bulk of this was to be spent on the recruitment and training of new agents, and 'special attention was to be directed towards the building up of *Etappe* England'.[10]

It was against this backdrop that, in February 1937, Jessie Jordan landed at the Port of Leith on the Firth of Forth.

*

She had been born in Glasgow in 1887, the illegitimate and unloved daughter of a housemaid, who abandoned her child for the first four years of her life to the care of her grandmother. When Elizabeth Wallace eventually married she reclaimed Jessie, but from then on, the girl's childhood was scarred by violence – her stepfather was a brutal and abusive man – and by the stigma of her birth. At the age of sixteen, Jessie ran away from home and found work as a housemaid, 60 miles away in Perth.

In 1907, according to her own subsequent ghost-written account,[11] she met Frederick Jordan, a German waiter working in a Dundee hotel. He took her home to meet his family in Hamburg, where they settled, and five years later the couple married; Jessie Jordan, *née* Wallace, became a German citizen.

In the spring of 1914 she gave birth to her first child: the couple named their daughter Marga Frieda Wilhelmina – the last name being 'given out of loyalty to Kaiser Wilhelm'.[12] Three months later Frederick was called up for military service: within a year he was fatally wounded on the Western Front.

After Frederick's death, the widow Jordan established a successful hairdressing business in Hamburg before marrying Baur Baumgarten, her late husband's cousin and a wealthy local merchant, in 1920. Although she later claimed the marriage was unhappy and her new husband faithless,[13] the couple stayed together, jointly raising Marga and supporting her budding career as a moderately successful singer and actress.

In January 1937, Jessie Baumgarten applied for a divorce, citing her husband's alleged infidelity. A month later, she booked a one-way ticket in her maiden name on the German liner, SS *Europa*: twenty years after she emigrated, Jessie Jordan was returning to Scotland.

Ostensibly, she was on family business. When she landed in Leith on February 14 she told immigration officials that she had come home in the hope of tracking down details of her birth father. She explained that the Nazis' obsession with blood and race meant that for Marga to continue with her career she had to obtain an Ahnenpass – a certificate, based on church records, demonstrating that her family tree contained no Jewish heritage. It was a plausible story, but completely untrue. In reality Jordan had spent the week before her departure being briefed by her Abwehr handler, Joanna Hoffman, alias Jennie Schluetter. As she later admitted:

> With regard to what transpired during these eight days I need not say more than this ... Certain requests were made to me to render services to Germany ... as a friend I was asked to verify certain information that was already in the hands of the Germans ... I was now approaching the most dangerous and exciting period of my life. I was about to become a spy in the interests of Germany.[14]

Hoffman's job as the *Europa*'s on-board hairdresser provided perfect cover for her role as an intelligence agent. It involved regular voyages to Britain and the United States – trips she used to hand-deliver orders to German agents based in both countries.[15]

On the dockside in Hamburg she gave Jordan final instructions for her first mission: to make a sketch of the Royal Naval Armament Depot at Crombie on the Firth of Forth, as well as the details of a post office box in Hamburg to which she was to send the drawing.

Jordan took lodgings in Perth, 40 miles away from Crombie, and soon made the first of several nervous visits to the naval base.

> It was a secret Government factory and well watched ... I was more than a little scared and it was some time before I managed to make the sketch ... I had a rough idea of the kind of information that was needed by Germany, and this I tried to put into the sketch ...[16]

Jordan knew that her drawing was intended to guide future German bombers to the most vulnerable and inflammable parts of the depot: the munitions stores, electrical generating station, oil tanks and the area in which cordite was cut to fill shells.[17] But, by her own account, she felt no remorse at betraying the country of her birth.

> I did not take this step because I bore Britain any ill-will or had become pro-German. Nothing could be further from the truth. I only did it to oblige friends in Germany and because I felt it would afford some excitement ...

I did receive payment, but the amount was so small as to be immaterial ... I was neither an unrepentant offender against the laws of my country nor a whining penitent. My eyes were open all through.[18]

By June 1937 the sketch was complete. Jordan folded it into an envelope, on which she carefully wrote 'Sanders, PO Box 629, Hamburg'. She sent it from a post office near her lodgings in Perth, but deliberately did not include either her name or a return address. She then set off on a trip around Britain, staying initially with her aunt in Wales, then travelling down to Southampton, where she bought two picture postcards, marking on them and an accompanying sheet of paper the position of the local barracks and officers' mess. On her return to Wales, she posted these to 'Sanders'.

MI5 had been monitoring correspondence to the address in Hamburg for more than a year, after its overseas sister service, MI6, warned that PO Box 629 'was being used as a cover address by the Head Agency of the Secret Service of a foreign power for communications from agents operating in the United Kingdom'.[19] A Home Office warrant, obtained by MI5 in early 1936, ensured that all letters sent there from Britain were discreetly opened and copied by the Post Office.

Photostats of Jordan's letters landed on the desk of William Hinchley-Cooke. A year earlier he had played a central role in the arrest of Hermann Goertz, a German agent collecting information on RAF bases in East Anglia; the case[20] cemented his reputation as a spycatcher and had earned him a promotion to the rank of Colonel.

Hinchley-Cooke's initial assessment of Jordan's correspondence was that the drawings and postcards 'appeared to be a very feeble attempt at espionage ... It was absolutely the attempt of a beginner'.[21] He allowed the original letters to go forward, but added the photostats to his growing files on the Hamburg address.

By early July, Jordan realised that her cover story was beginning to wear thin. Using her aunt's address in Wales, she wrote to the Department of Alien Registration, explaining that she was a German national, although Scottish by birth, and asking how to obtain official permission – required by all 'aliens' – to 'set up in business' in Britain. There is no record of any reply in her files, but within a week she began negotiations to buy a hairdressing salon in a shabby, working-class district of Dundee.

In the meantime copies of intercepted letters addressed to 'Sanders, PO Box 629, Hamburg' continued to be forwarded to MI5. The sender's address had plainly been either omitted or erased, so although the contents led Hinchley-Cooke to conclude that 'there is no doubt whatever that [the writer] is a member of the German Espionage Organisation at Hamburg', he was unable to pinpoint the location of the spy.[22]

At the end of summer a careless mistake provided the first clue. One intercepted envelope bore the imprint of a sender's address which had been only partially obliterated. Police enquiries revealed that it was – or had been – a room in Perth rented by Jessie Jordan. But by the time the Home Office granted a warrant for the interception of letters arriving there, Jordan had moved on: she had purchased the salon in Kinloch Street, Dundee, and found new accommodation nearby.

The trail might have ended there. But, as Hinchley-Cooke had suspected, Mrs Jordan was an amateur in the game of spying and her behaviour aroused local suspicion. On November 17, 1937, Mary and John Curran, the former owners of the hairdressing business, walked into Dundee police station to report their belief that Mrs Jordan was not the respectable businesswoman she claimed to be.

She had, they claimed, been 'unusually keen to get the shop', offering double its market value of £25. She had paid this in cash, and then spent a further £300 renovating the premises and installing 'the latest appliances'.[23] Since the salon was in an economically-deprived area, Jordan's willingness to spend far more than the business was worth[24] appeared suspicious. Nor did she seem unduly concerned about its success: she took a great deal of time off, touring Britain as well as making eight lengthy trips back to Germany. Each time she left the shop in the hands of Mrs Curran.

The following month, the Currans surreptitiously searched Jordan's handbag: inside they found a map of Scotland on which the location of military barracks had been marked in pencil. They showed it to the police before slipping it back in place.[25] At this stage, Hinchley-Cooke still believed Jordan was no more than a low-level and largely ineffective spy. But towards the end of December the Home Office warrants on the Kinloch Street salon began intercepting evidence of something more troubling.

Letters, posted in New York, began arriving from a man signing himself 'Crown'. Although the envelopes were addressed to Jordan, their contents were plainly meant for someone else; a few days after each letter arrived, Jordan folded it inside a new envelope and sent it on to PO Box 629, Hamburg.

In London, Hinchley-Cooke studied the copies made by the Post Office of each arriving letter and reached the conclusion that Jordan was acting as 'an intermediary between German Secret Service Agents operating in U.S.A. and the Hamburg Head Office'. 'Crown' appeared to be the head of the ring: his letters requested technical espionage equipment, including a Zeiss micro camera, forged White House stationery and blank American passports, as well as substantial sums of cash: all were to be routed via the Dundee hairdresser.[26]

Then, on January 17, 1938, 'Crown' sent Jordan a lengthy new letter for onward delivery to Hamburg: it set out details of a plot to kidnap Colonel Henry Eglin, commander of the US Army base at Fort Totten, New York, and to steal from him – by force – 'details regarding coastal defence operations and bases' on the north-eastern seaboard.

> I shall order the gentleman to appear before a supposed Emergency Staff Meeting to be held in the Hotel McAlpin in New York on Monday, January 31st ... giving myself out as the aide de camp of the commanding general of the second corps area ... I shall stress the importance of obeying the given instructions in detail ... [Colonel Eglin] will not be able to check on the message because I will advise him that it would be useless, since the planned meeting is a military secret.
>
> Upon his arrival at the hotel, I shall then ... take him to a room for which arrangements have been previously made. There we shall attempt to overpower him and to remove papers that he will have been ordered to fetch along.[27]

The discovery of 'Crown's' plot posed a diplomatic problem for MI5 and the British government. Much of America was then strongly isolationist: a combination of the financial devastation caused by the Great

Depression and the memory of more than 100,000 US soldiers killed during the First World War ensured that public opinion was hostile to any involvement in the looming conflict between Britain and Germany. In public, Washington and London maintained a pose of careful independence, while behind the scenes MI5 pressed the FBI to investigate German Secret Service operations. In this uncertain climate, a public revelation that Nazi spies were operating on American soil with the assistance of a Scottish agent – and that British spies were secretly opening American mail – would be politically incendiary.

But given the seriousness and immediacy of the kidnap plan, MI5 could not afford to withhold the information. On January 29 it cabled a lengthy memo to the US Military Attaché in London setting out the details of the conspiracy, but stressing that 'it is of the utmost importance that in any action which is taken on this information, no indication whatever should be given of the fact that it was obtained in Great Britain'.[28]

One month later, FBI agents arrested the leaders of the spy network. 'Crown' turned out to be Guenther Rumrich, a 37-year-old US Army deserter who admitted supplying German Intelligence with details of fleet movements and ship-to-shore signalling systems. He had received his instructions from a familiar name: Joanna Hoffman, the hairdresser on the SS *Europa* who had recruited Jessie Jordan. She was held along with two other Nazi spies.[29]

MI5 hoped that the arrests would be made in secret since Hinchley-Cooke wanted to continue monitoring correspondence between the Dundee hairdressing salon and PO Box 629 in Hamburg. But on February 28 newspapers across the United States published sensational accounts of the uncovering of a major German spy-ring. London papers carried the story the next day. On March 3, Dundee City Police, accompanied by Hinchley-Cooke, raided the salon in Kinloch Street and arrested Jessie Jordan under the espionage sections of the Official Secrets Act.

Two months later, at the High Court in Edinburgh, she pleaded guilty to four counts of spying. In a fifteen-minute mitigation speech, her defence counsel helpfully pointed out that the laws governing such cases – the Official Secrets Acts of 1911 and 1920 – were outdated and not fit for purpose.

'The powers which the authorities ... exercise in times of peace could not have prevented the agents of a foreign power from obtaining the information', A.P. Duffes KC told the judge. 'A case of this type might suggest that the authorities perhaps ought to have greater powers.'[30] Given the circumstances, he suggested, the law – such as it was – could be 'vindicated ... without involving [my] client in any ... serious penalty'.[31]

The judge, Lord Clerk Aitchison, was unimpressed. Imposing a sentence of four years' penal servitude,[32] he told Jordan:

'You possessed yourself of certain information, and you did certain things which, in the words of the indictment, were 'calculated to be useful to an enemy', and you did this at a time when you were in communication with the agents of a foreign power, and, again the words of the indictment, 'for purposes prejudicial to the safety and interests of the State'. It is impossible to take a light view of offences of that kind.'[33]

Jessie Jordan, however, seemed unconcerned at the prospect of spending the next four years doing hard labour.[34] In her sole statement before being taken down to the cells, she said: 'The sentence is my medicine and I can take it.'[35]

Pleading guilty to what, in peacetime, were serious but not capital crimes served German Intelligence well. It precluded the opportunity for a thorough investigation of the full extent of the Hamburg network: the British Security Service complained that Jordan 'was never interrogated with the object of obtaining from her all the information in her possession about her employers'. MI5 also noted that during her limited interviews with the police 'it was obvious that Mrs Jordan was lying throughout ... She could give us a great deal of information if she desired ... [but] she is a clever and determined woman.'[36]

Politically, too, the truncated nature of Jordan's court appearance had been a disaster, since this 'prevented details about German espionage in the U.S. becoming public property at a time when their publication would have been of immense value from the point of view of political relations between this country and the U.S.'[37] But the British government was, to an extent, the architect of its own misfortune.

Determined to maintain the highest standards of 'fair play', it actively obstructed any wider examination of the case, deliberately preventing the US attorney prosecuting Rumrich and his co-conspirators from interviewing Jordan.

The Crown Office in Edinburgh pronounced loftily that this 'would be quite contrary to British law and practice'.[38] The decision was precise, neatly argued and legally correct, but it was also a troubling example of the government's complacency in the dwindling days of peace, and its inability to grasp the nature of the foe Britain now faced. As Hitler plotted a 'total war' and the Abwehr schemed, Whitehall seemed content to slumber.

But while ministers and their mandarins appeared unaware of the severity of the threat that Britain – and its allies – faced from domestic Nazi spies, the first rumblings of public unease began to emerge in the press: in an editorial commenting on the lessons of the Jessie Jordan case, the *Dundee Courier* accurately prophesied the most likely source of danger:

> There must be a very considerable number of British women in a position closely akin to that of Mrs Jordan, and we get a hint here that the German Secret Service has its eyes upon them as possible serviceable tools.[39]

Within a year, that prediction would – to the considerable disquiet of the Security Service – come repeatedly to pass.

CHAPTER TWO

Target Britain

'The German Intelligence Service has us at a great disadvantage'
MI5 memo, November 1938

The death, on March 4, 1938, passed largely unremarked. Perhaps because it was a suicide – then technically a crime to attempt and one which was habitually punished by the denial of a Christian burial to those who succeeded – no notices appeared in the classified columns of local or national newspapers and no obituaries were written or published.[1]

One organisation did, however, note the passing of an otherwise unremarkable London woman, and did so with some regret. The Security Service had been monitoring the mail arriving at 90 Broadhurst Gardens, West Hampstead, since August 1937 because the occupant, Mrs Else Klara Duncombe (*née* Bolternstern), a 49-year-old widow, 'was known to be acting as a post-box for the German Secret Service'.[2] As predicted, Jessie Jordan had not been the only British woman willing to betray her country to Nazi Germany.

*

The Abwehr's efforts to build up its Etappe England intelligence network had initially been hampered by an order issued by the Fuehrer.

In June 1935, signature of the Anglo-German Naval Agreement (which fixed the size of the Kriegsmarine at 35 per cent of the total tonnage of the Royal Navy) hinted at the prospect of a tentative improvement in relations between London and Berlin. Anxious – for tactical reasons – not to damage this slender hope, Hitler temporarily banned new attempts at espionage. But by the summer of 1937, the prohibition was rescinded, and German Intelligence once again targeted Britain.

While the Abwehr began rebuilding the network of agents which had atrophied during the years of the Fuehrer's injunction, other organs of the Nazi state turned to less conventional channels. Cultural organisations, journalists and – above all – transnational companies were drafted in to provide intelligence and offer cover for spying. As MI5 noted, 'from 1936 onwards the Nazi regime had made it clear that service to the Fatherland was obligatory on the part of Germans living and working abroad. This service was deemed likely to include acts of espionage.'[3]

The biggest and most important of these companies was Siemens Schuckert GB, a wholly-owned subsidiary of the vast Siemens electrical manufacturing combine which had established a presence in countries throughout the world; all reported back to the head office in Germany and, as a 1941 MI5 memorandum noted, all were involved in spying:

This ... firm runs a vast espionage organisation for the German Government. This espionage ranges from the ordinary industrial spying that all German firms do in peace time, distribution of pro-Nazi propaganda in foreign countries, the organisation of fifth column activities, economic and political espionage, the reporting of data about prominent individuals in foreign countries, espionage regarding armament programmes, to the setting up and servicing of illicit wireless stations.

The British subsidiary was largely staffed by Germans or dual nationals before the war and without exaggeration it can be said to have been entirely pro-Nazi, to have indulged in most of the forms of espionage mentioned above and to have had as an employee at least one member of the German Secret Service.[4]

What made this particularly troubling was that many of the firm's technical specialists worked on its military contracts; as a result they 'had access to British armaments factories and service establishments in the course of their business'.[5] In the complacent atmosphere of the interwar years, Siemens' strategic position effectively allowed its roster of undercover spies free rein to report back to Berlin.

The Abwehr was also finding Britain remarkably easy to penetrate. By the end of 1938 its Etappenorganisation was up to full strength: 200 undercover agents worked directly for it, travelling from their bases in Hamburg, Frankfurt or Berlin to Scandinavia, southern Europe, the Low Countries of Holland and Belgium and, in particular, England.[6] But these salaried spies – each received between 300 and 500 Reichsmarks[7] per month (in addition to their business income) – were only the tip of the network: each was expected to recruit sub-agents within their given territories. According to an American intelligence service assessment, there were strict requirements for recruitment.

> The agents of the organisation were mainly reliable German businessmen and shipping agents established in ports all over the world. *Etappen* orders stressed that Germans should be well-established in business and respected by the authorities of the country.[8]

Rudolph Rosel, for instance, landed in Britain in the early 1930s (there is no landing card marking the date of his arrival in the seven volumes of his file compiled by MI5[9]), ostensibly as the London diplomatic correspondent of the *Essener National Zeitung* – a newspaper owned and controlled by Hermann Goering.

In reality, this was no more than a cover story for his true role as one of the leading Nazi Party officials in England; by June 1936 he was officially listed as the 'Schulungsleiter' – training manager – of the NSDAP's* Landesgruppe, Great Britain and Ireland.[10] The following month he rented an office in Parliament Street, SW1, and set up the Anglo-German Information Service. A Special Branch report observed

---

* Nationalsozialistische Deutsche Arbeiterpartei (National Socialist German Workers' Party).

that its ostensible objective was 'to disseminate information regarding internal conditions and social services in Germany, and to endeavour to bring about a better understanding between the peoples of Germany and England'.

In practice this meant identifying pro-German contacts, who were signed up to receive NSDAP propaganda. 'Articles are sent out to subscribers at frequent, but irregular, intervals', the report noted. 'The articles are forwarded to the offices of the Conservative Party in London, Edinburgh and Glasgow; influential members of the British Legion who are interested in affairs in Germany, and Members of Parliament.' Rosel also cultivated Oswald Mosley's British Union of Fascists (BUF), becoming one of its key links with Berlin[11] and sending reports back to the Reich Chancellery on its membership – both sympathisers and opponents of the Nazi regime. According to an MI5 informer within the BUF: 'one of the principal tasks [of the Anglo-German Fellowship] was to collect all the anti-Hitler speeches made in England and also collect information about anti-Hitler activities and send these to Berlin regularly. All Rosel's reports are sent to Hitler himself who reads them.'

Rudolph Rosel was not the only 'journalist' dispatched to England to work as an undercover informer. On October 3, 1936 Arnold Littmann landed at Harwich and made his way to London. He described himself, variously, as a 'banking student at the London School of Economics' and an assistant to the London representative of the *Hamburger Fremdenblatt* newspaper. After a brief stay at the YMCA on Tottenham Court Road he presented himself at Toynbee Hall in the East End, then the base of a community of German exiles, posing as a refugee from Nazism, and soon applied for permanent resident status in Britain.

Arnold Littmann was not, however, the innocent expatriate he professed to be. As well as a string of aliases, he had a lengthy history of involvement with the NSDAP. In 1935 he had been the Cologne district leader of the Deutsche Freischar youth group and an official of the overall German youth movement, including the Hitler Jugend. The following year he was arrested for homosexual offences and sent briefly to a concentration camp. Here, according to an MI5 account of his life, '[after] he received a good deal of maltreatment, he was released on the condition that he should work for the Gestapo', sending details of opponents of the Nazi regime back to Berlin.[12] Littmann remained free to spy in London until April 1938 when he left Britain to set up an Abwehr-controlled news agency in France.

There were two particularly troubling aspects to the Littmann case. The first was the ease with which his claim to be a genuine refugee had been accepted without any real scrutiny by MI5; the second was that his true identity was uncovered only when another asylum seeker recognised him as a former interrogator at the German Interior Ministry and passed the information to the British government. These lapses pointed to significant gaps in British intelligence and the extent to which it was reliant on amateur informants to detect enemy agents, and both problems would soon come to haunt the Security Service.

On the night of April 8, 1939, a 27-year-old petty criminal and occasional informer walked into New Scotland Yard with a friend and asked to see an officer from Special Branch. He explained that he had recently met a Nazi spy who, amid the teacups and sandwiches of the Lyons Corner House near Piccadilly Circus, had expressed interest in obtaining military secrets.

The informer, Michael Peres, was himself at least partly German. He had been born in Shoreditch but was taken to Germany by his parents in 1912 and had stayed there until 1928; after his return to London he accumulated three entries on his criminal record – for theft, burglary and for the rather less specific offence of being 'a suspected person'.

According to a report of their meeting by Special Branch Inspector Charles Allen, Peres had encountered the spy earlier that day and initially taken him to be an easy 'mark' who could be conned into parting with his money.

> Peres stated that on his way to visit friends this afternoon he enquired of a stranger at Notting Hill the way to Bayswater. This person answered him in German and Peres, who was educated in Germany, thinking that there was an opportunity of making easy money, told this stranger that he was a German communist refugee and illegally landed here.

The stranger invited him into a Lyons tea shop and during the course of the conversation Peres, to impress this stranger, told him that he had been fighting in Spain with the Spanish Air Force (all false). The merits of various aircraft were discussed and Peres said that he had a friend in a factory at Bristol that manufactured 'Spitfire' machines (all false) and also that his friend had in his possession plans of this machine, which he believed he was willing to dispose of for about £30. The stranger then said that he was quite willing to pay up to £50,000* if the plans were genuine and gave Peres his card bearing the name Carl Erich Kullmann.[13]

On its face, the story was distinctly unpromising, a point which Allen stressed, noting with casual prejudice that both Peres and the friend who accompanied him to New Scotland Yard 'are Jews and unemployed'. Nonetheless, he passed the information on to MI5 the same day, and followed it by forwarding updates on Peres' subsequent meetings with Kullmann.

At these, the apparent spy had repeatedly pressed for copies of the Spitfire blueprints; with no response from MI5, Peres stalled for as long as he could before finally bowing out.

Had the Security Service followed up the lead, it would have discovered that there was – despite its source – a genuine espionage threat within Peres' account. Carl Kullmann – alias Carlos Kogan-Mandoza and Carlos Enrique Ullmann – was a 32-year-old Abwehr officer working in Britain under commercial cover. He had landed at Croydon aerodrome on March 23, 1939, telling immigration officers that he was employed as a representative of J.C. Knefel, a Berlin-based telephones and cables company. He took rooms in a boarding house in Ladbroke Gardens, but failed to register his presence with the local police.**

---

* Equivalent to £2.2 million today – an astronomical sum which suggests either exaggeration by Peres or the Abwehr's realisation of the importance of the Spitfire in the looming war.

** Despite the growing realisation in 1938 and 1939 that war with Germany was coming, Britain retained a surprisingly relaxed attitude to the arrival of German visitors: entry regulations for 'alien' nationals only required them to report to police within three months of landing.

At the end of May he slipped out of Britain, bound, ostensibly, for Spain. In reality, he travelled immediately on to the United States and joined a German espionage ring being run out of Siemens' offices in Washington, DC.[14] It would not be the only occasion that failures in British intelligence enabled an Abwehr spy to slip out of England and operate freely in America.

Paul Borchardt arrived in London in April 1939. He was 55 years old and bore impeccable credentials: he was a Fellow of the Royal Geographical Society and, by his own account, a Jewish refugee from Nazi oppression. He took lodgings in Brunswick Square, WC1, and, as war with Germany came ever closer, approached the Foreign Office to volunteer his services to MI6. The offer was evidently taken seriously, since MI5 was asked to vet him. A memo, dated December 9, inserted on the Registry Minute Sheet of Borchardt's file, recorded the Security Service's reluctant decision not to recommend his appointment.

He is no doubt genuine when he says he is anti-Nazi, but it is clearly impossible to mediate the employment who is also pro-German, and I do not think it worth submitting to SIS [the Secret Intelligence Service, i.e. MI6]. A polite letter of refusal seems to be indicated.[15]

Had MI5 looked a little more closely at its own files, it would not have been quite so sanguine about Paul Borchardt's story and his offer of assistance. Notes earlier in the Registry Minute Sheet recorded him as having been identified 'as a German spy ... in September 1917'. Operating under the pseudonym Abdel Hamid Batoota, he had worked for the Abwehr's predecessor organisation throughout the First World War. Not only was he not a genuine Jewish refugee, he had never stopped being a German agent.

'Borchardt's primary job [was] the penetration of British Intelligence Services', MI5 subsequently – and ruefully – noted in its files. 'It seems therefore that he came to this country to get into one of our Intelligence Services [and] was prevented from doing so, though otherwise not investigated ...'

In December 1939 Borchardt applied for – and was granted – clearance to emigrate to America, where he quickly became the central figure in an Abwehr spy network based in New York.[16]

Paul Borchardt's arrival in England coincided with the departure of Rudolph Rosel. For some months MI5's informants had warned that beneath his layers of cover, Rosel had been tasked with an additional mission: his MI5 file noted that 'It was ... reported that he had admitted that his express purpose in Britain had been to organise a reliable Fifth Column'.[17] By April 1939 his activities were sufficiently troubling to push Whitehall into action: he was given notice to leave Britain immediately.

It was too little, too late. By then MI5 had ample evidence of the Abwehr's ability to dispatch its agents to spy on military facilities, and of the willingness of British citizens – a domestic 'Fifth Column' – to support and assist them.

On July 25, 1937, a tall German sea captain landed at Harwich. Hermann Walter Christian Simon was 57, a Kriegsmarine veteran who been captured at sea in 1914 and interned in Australia for the remainder of the First World War. He was also a fully trained and salaried Abwehr spy, bearing orders to obtain 'information about aerodromes and to vet a number of individuals who were apparently considered as candidates for employment by the German Secret Service'.[18]

In the fortnight after his arrival Simon travelled freely, from Stroud in Gloucestershire to Portsmouth and Lee-on-Solent; at each location he made notes and sketches of local air force bases, apparently without ever attracting police suspicion. In the middle of August he took these back to 'Nest Bremen', the Abwehr intelligence division in north-west Germany, before being deployed to Britain on a new mission the following month.

Although he was being paid the standard intelligence agent stipend of 200 Reichsmarks per month, Simon needed cash to operate in England, and the Abwehr had set up a network of local sub-agents through whom it funnelled his expenses. One was the unfortunate Mrs Duncombe in Hampstead. MI5 had been warned – probably by MI6 – that she was 'acting as a post-box for the German Secret Service', and had obtained a Home Office warrant to monitor correspondence sent from, and arriving at, her home in Broadhurst Gardens.

In August 1937 this yielded an intercepted letter from the Hamburg Abwehrstelle instructing Duncombe to pay £15[19] to Simon; a new file was opened on the German sea captain and the Security Service began the laborious process of tracing his movements and contacts across the country. The effort yielded evidence of two more expenses payments – both in cash – sent to Simon via the German Consul and then directly to his temporary lodgings in a Salvation Army hostel at Aldgate.

More importantly, MI5 discovered the next of Simon's British contacts, and the way he was now sending his intelligence reports out of the country: the trail led to Gloucester Lodge, an aristocratic address on the edge of Regent's Park and the London home of Arthur and Elizabeth Guinness, Viscount and Lady Elveden.

In November, Lady Elveden hired a new cook. Josephine 'My' Eriksson was ostensibly a Swedish divorcee – in reality she was German – who had arrived in England in 1930 on a twelve-month visa to work as a domestic servant for a middle-class family in Roehampton. Although her employment permit was cancelled in 1934, no attempt appears to have been made to deport her and she spent the next four years being passed between a succession of increasingly wealthy and aristocratic employers.[20]

Despite her (theoretically) precarious residency status, Eriksson was sufficiently confident to boast of her connections to Nazi Party leaders in Germany, telling Lady Elveden 'that she knew Field Marshal Goering, saying that his first wife, a Swedish woman, lived near her family in Sweden'.[21] She was also able to move freely between Britain and the Continent: transit stamps in her passport showed that between 1934 and 1938 she had made six trips to Europe, returning with between 50 and 100 Reichsmarks each time. On one of these trips she was recruited by Dr Nikolaus Ritter, alias Dr Reinhardt and Dr von Rantzau, one of the Abwehr's most senior spymasters.[22] Her duties were to distribute expenses to his agents in England, and to courier their intelligence reports back to Hamburg.

Four days before Christmas 1937, Eriksson met Hermann Simon at Marylebone Underground station; Simon handed over a letter for 'Dr R' which Eriksson agreed to deliver the following day. From then onwards she seems to have supplanted Mrs Duncombe as his chief contact and paymistress.[23] For two months Simon travelled extensively throughout the south-east. On February 5, 1938 he was seen outside an RAF bar-rage balloon section at Kidbrooke in Kent, where he appeared to be making notes of the station's layout. He left before being challenged and was later spotted close to Hendon aerodrome in north London.

But for an accomplished spy, he had made an unaccountably care-less mistake. During one of his earlier trips to Kent he had failed to sign the register at his hotel; on his return to the YMCA hostel he found police officers waiting to arrest him.

The charge he faced was relatively minor: contravening the Aliens Order 1920 would normally have yielded little more than a warning or – at most – a fine. But the officers were unusually diligent and insisted on examining the contents of his room: what they discovered was clear evidence of espionage. According to Simon's MI5 file:

> When his belongings were searched a survey map, a small black book containing rough sketches of an aerodrome [were found] ... He was also in possession of material for sending and receiving messages which were invisible to the naked eye. This material consisted of buff coloured wax paper between two sheets of writing paper (similar to carbon paper) and writing the message on the top sheet with a reason-ably blunt pencil. The 'carbon copy' was then actually sent through the post. The messages were made visible by shaking fine graphite powder over them, the graphite adhering to the wax and revealing the writing. Messages to Simon were sent in the same manner but typewritten.[24]

Kent Constabulary took Simon into custody and interrogated him late the same evening. He tried to spin a story that he was an innocent com-mercial agent of two German doctors, based in Hamburg, who had been impressed with his seafaring expertise and had commissioned him to purchase an ocean-going yacht on their behalf. It was a somewhat desperate tale, particularly because the police had also recovered his diaries, listing a series of names and addresses throughout England: none had any discernible involvement with yachts or yachting.

The diaries were sent to Room 505 at the War Office, marked for the attention of Colonel William Hinchley-Cooke. At his direction, police forces in London, Kent and the home counties eventually visited nine addresses Simon had noted down.* What they discovered proved beyond doubt that the Abwehr agent had successfully recruited British citizens who were willing to betray their country to the German intelligence service; two of the names were particularly troubling.

George Billings was a seventeen-year-old schoolboy and ardent member of 'the Fascist Youth organisation'** in Tonbridge. When Hinchley-Cooke interviewed him, Billings admitted that for several years he had, at his own request, been sent Nazi propaganda literature from Germany; this appeared to have prompted contact from the Abwehr.

> Billings ... stated that early in 1937 he had received a letter from Hamburg signed 'Huber' asking whether he would be willing to carry letters from London to various places on the Continent with a promise of very good pay. As he was then a schoolboy of 17 the excitement appealed to him, though he knew it was not on the level, and so he replied that he was agreeable. He did not receive an answer and so he burnt the letter.
>
> The next he heard about it was when Simon came to Tonbridge and met him at The Chequers Inn, and he was told to prepare a list of routes to the Continent with details of times, costs etc. Early in January he received an unsigned letter from Liverpool House and on February 2nd a letter signed H.W. Simon which was in the same handwriting. In this letter he was asked if he was prepared to take risks, and he replied that he would not mind.[25]

There is no record of what – if any – missions Billings undertook on behalf of his Abwehr controllers, and his initial arrest seems to have deterred him from any further 'excitement'. An MI5 memo following Hinchley-Cooke's interrogation noted that 'Billings got the fright of his life when he was pulled in by the police and it was decided that

---

* MI5 officers – then, as now – do not hold warrant cards allowing them to make arrests. For that reason they usually work with or through police officers.
** It is, perhaps, an indication of MI5's limited pre-war understanding of fascist groups that this 'youth organisation' is not identified by name. It was probably a section of the British Union of Fascists.

he was unlikely to ever undertake such work again and no further action was taken'.[26] But the willingness of a card-carrying British fascist to work for German intelligence was a warning of the potential threat from domestic traitors.

The second contact, Bernard Durrant, had proved a rather more active convert to the Nazi cause. After Simon had visited his home in Westcliff-on-Sea, the former soldier travelled to Germany for Abwehr training as an undercover agent. In the summer of 1939 he was smuggled into Cairo in the uniform of a ship's officer; Abwehr contacts met him on the dockside and took him to the German Consulate. He was given clothes, cash and instructions to gather intelligence on British military strength in Egypt.

MI5 did not catch up with Durrant until October 1939 – and then not due to its own efforts. Shortly after the war began, Durrant developed cold feet; he walked into the British Consulate, confessed to his role as a German spy and was promptly sent back to England where he was interned for much of the war.[27]

The sketches of airfields, the secret message-writing equipment and the entries in his diary were, on the face of it, strong evidence that Hermann Simon was a German spy, controlling – or at least in contact with – a network of British sub-agents. But throughout his police interview he stuck to his implausible story of being in search of an ocean-going yacht, and a decision on whether to charge him with espionage was passed up to the government's Law Officers, whose sanction was needed for a trial involving the Official Secrets Act.

There is no clear indication in the file when, or why, permission was refused, but it notes that his initial British contact, the mysterious Mrs Duncombe, committed suicide immediately after Simon's arrest and implies that this was among the 'various reasons' which persuaded the Attorney General not to back an espionage prosecution.

This seems an improbable explanation. Mrs Duncombe's role in assisting Simon had been taken over by Josephine 'My' Eriksson – whose activities were amply documented in intercepted correspondence. More likely, MI5 did not discover the extent of Simon's intelligence work, and his contact with British sub-agents, until some time later: fragmented or mislocated documents in the file suggest that his case may have escaped any substantive attention until the outbreak of war. Whatever the reason, Hermann Simon was tried only for the relatively minor offence of failing to sign the hotel register. In March 1938 he was convicted and sentenced to two consecutive three-month prison terms; five months later he was released on licence and deported back to Hamburg. His arrest and imprisonment do not, however, seem to have harmed his career with the Abwehr. Shortly after the outbreak of war it sent him, by submarine, on a new espionage mission to the Republic of Ireland; he was eventually arrested near Dublin and spent the next six years in an Irish prison.[28]

There was a similar unexplained delay in dealing with Josephine Eriksson. Despite the evidence gleaned by monitoring of her correspondence, neither the police nor MI5 interviewed her in the wake of Simon's prosecution and she spent the next eighteen months working in the houses of prominent aristocrats including Sir Walter Wyndham, Baronet Burrell, and Timothy Eden, brother of the recently-resigned Foreign Secretary, Sir Anthony Eden.

Two months after the war began, Eriksson successfully applied to the Foreign Office for an exit visa. Permit No. 122303 was issued on December 11, 1939, and authorised her to make a single journey between the UK and Holland. Eriksson's application stated that she wanted to travel to The Hague. But four days later, when she reported, as now required of all alien nationals, to Bow Street police station, she gave her intended destination as Sweden. The discrepancy led the police to place a 'watch' notice on her passport; on December 16 immigration officers arrested her at Harwich docks just as she was about to board a steamship.

The following day she was brought to New Scotland Yard to be interrogated by Hinchley-Cooke. A verbatim transcript of the police shorthand notes of the interview shows that MI5's veteran spycatcher began by warning Eriksson she had been under observation for several months.

'I know a good deal about you ... I have kept an eye on you and I have been waiting for you for a long time', Hinchley-Cooke told her. 'You have been the paymaster of German agents in this country ... I know all about you and all about Dr Rantzau ... Dr Rantzau runs German spies in this country ... You have been abusing the hospitality of this country.'[29]

Eriksson admitted that she knew and had regularly met Rantzau – alias Ritter – and that she had posted Hermann Simon's letters to his Hamburg address. But she denied receiving money from him, even when shown the intercepted correspondence detailing their transactions, and insisted that she had done nothing wrong. Unable to break her down, Hinchley-Cooke handed her back to Special Branch; on December 19 Eriksson was charged at Westminster Police Court with a single count of making a false statement in her application to the Foreign Office, contrary to article 18 of the 1920 Aliens Order, and sentenced to three months in prison, with a £100 fine – the equivalent of almost £4,500 today.

Despite its clear evidence of German espionage, and a shadowy network of Nazi spies being aided by British – or at least British-resident – citizens, 'My' Eriksson's trial was not reported. According to a memo from an MI5 agent sitting on the spectators' benches, presiding magistrate Ronald Powell 'requested the representatives of the press to refrain from publishing the proceedings in the interests of the State'.[30]

The Security Service had good reason to be grateful for the newspapers' discretion. It knew – and had recorded in an internal memo in November 1938 – that 'the German Intelligence Service has us at a great disadvantage'.[31] According to the account of this admission in the official history of Britain's wartime intelligence services, MI5 realised that Nazi espionage chiefs were 'in a position to obtain information not only from a professional spy organisation, but also from the organ of the Nazi Party in the United Kingdom and from some of the considerable number of people of German origin who served in the British armed forces and industry'.[32] By contrast, MI5's information was so inadequate that, on the outbreak of war both it and MI6 'remained unaware even of the name of the German espionage organisation, the Amtsgruppe Auslandsnachrichten und Abwehr [Office of Foreign Intelligence and Defence]'.[33]

This substantial gap in intelligence was not an isolated problem; as war with Germany loomed, every aspect of the British government's preparation was dangerously inadequate.

CHAPTER THREE

A Nation Unprepared

'During the vital years between 1935 and 1939 ... there were
not more than 12 agents employed by the Department.'
Internal MI5 Report on the Recruitment and Operation of Agents, 1945

On October 5, 1936 a new phrase entered the English lexicon via the
columns of the *Daily Express* – then, with a circulation of 2.25 million, the largest selling daily newspaper in the world. William Forrest,
a 34-year-old Scottish journalist, was covering the Spanish Civil War
from the Republican side (he was, himself, a card-carrying Communist
Party member) and filed a sympathetic report on its struggle to resist
the forces of the 'Nationalist' (in reality, fascist) forces led by Francisco
Franco.

> Insurgent general Franco has said that in addition to his four columns
> in the field he has a column in Madrid ... How strong is this fifth col-
> umn? No-one knows. But its numbers must run to many thousands.
> Insurgent spies – they are everywhere – agents provocateur, rumour
> mongers, grumblers in the food queues; all these are members of that
> fifth column.[1]

A fortnight after Forrest's story, the *New York Times* picked up the
phrase, reporting on a radio broadcast by Nationalist General Emilio

Mola in which he boasted of the efficacy of his fascist 'fifth column' inside the beleaguered Republican capital.[2] Then, in October 1938, Ernest Hemingway boosted its recognition by publishing a play written from inside Madrid as the Nationalist forces laid siege. *The Fifth Column*[3] received poor notices from critics, but the phrase attained global currency as shorthand for the dangers of the hidden 'armies' of pro-fascist spies, saboteurs and traitors who were ready and willing to assist Hitler and his dreams of European domination.

*

Britain was slow to grasp the implications of the rise of Nazi Germany. Still dreaming of past glory, and seemingly oblivious to the shifting tectonic plates of European power which followed the First World War, the Committee of Imperial Defence clung to the Ten Year Rule – a 1919 doctrine, formulated by the then-Secretary of State for War, Winston Churchill, which insisted that 'the British Empire would not be involved in any great war during the next ten years'. Military spending was successively reduced – from £766 million in 1919 to £102 million twelve years later. In April 1931, the First Sea Lord warned that the Royal Navy's capabilities had declined alarmingly by comparison with other European powers and that the country was facing an existential threat.

'Owing to the operation of the "ten-year-decision" and the clamant need for economy', Sir Frederick Field advised the Committee on Imperial Defence, 'our absolute strength also has ... been so diminished as to render the fleet incapable, in the event of war, of efficiently affording protection to our trade.'

The doctrine was formally abandoned in late 1932, but it took until October 1933 – nine months after Hitler became Chancellor and three months after the country became a one-party state – for the Committee to begin examining the likely consequences of Nazism and Britain's ability to fight another war with Germany.

That such a war would be very different to past conflicts should have been evident. Shortly after Hitler seized the reins of power, one of Germany's leading theoreticians propounded the fundamental principle on which it would conduct its affairs, both domestic and international.

In a pamphlet entitled 'The Total State' Ernst Forsthoff argued that to assure the survival of the nation, the state must control every element of society.[4] His view was prophetic: the Nazi Party quickly set about creating laws and paramilitary organisations which enthusiastically persecuted perceived internal 'enemies' in order to create a *seelische Geschlossenheit*, or 'psychological unity', within the new Reich.

The same underlying theory was also to be applied to Germany's armed forces, in preparation for what the state's leading National Socialist military tactician described as a coming 'total war'. General Erich Ludendorff had witnessed (and effectively presided over) the defeat of Kaiser Wilhelm's forces in the First World War; in December 1935 he published 'Der Totale Krieg', arguing the need to harness every aspect of German civilian life – social, political, economic and cultural – to the demands of military success over the enemy, and to do so free of the legal codes of conduct which had characterised the previous practice of war. 'Total war is not only aimed against the armed forces', Ludendorff insisted, 'but also directly against the people.'[5] The book was an instant bestseller at home and by 1936 was widely republished throughout Europe and Britain.[6]

The threat posed to Britain by the Nazi state was recognised by at least some of the political class. In January 1936, Foreign Secretary Anthony Eden warned the Cabinet about Germany's plans to expand into and then control large swathes of Continental Europe.

Hitler's foreign policy may be summed up as the destruction of the [Versailles] peace settlement and re-establishment of Germany as the dominant power in Europe.

The means by which this policy is to be effected are two-fold: (a) Internally through the militarisation of the whole nation in all its aspects; (b) externally by economic and territorial expansion so as to absorb as far as possible all those of German race who are at present citizens of neighbouring States, to acquire new markets for German industry and new fields for German emigration, and to obtain control of some of the sources of raw materials at present lacking in Germany. The form and direction of this expansion is the one still doubtful factor in Germany's plans for the future.[7]

In 1938 Hitler resolved that uncertainty. In March, German troops marched into Austria; in September he annexed Czechoslovakia. Despite the Chamberlain government's attempts at appeasement, it was clear that war with Germany was coming; but it was equally evident to Britain's military leaders that the country's armed forces would not be ready to fight for another year. On September 20, General Hastings Ismay, Secretary of the Committee of Imperial Defence, presented a report to the Cabinet warning that: 'German absorption of Czechoslovakia will enhance her military prestige, increase her war potential and probably enable her to dispose of stronger land forces against France and ourselves than she can do at present.' By contrast, Britain lagged behind the Reich – particularly in air power – and 'if war with Germany has to come, it would be better to fight her in, say, 6–12 months time'.[8]

On the Home Front, Britain's security laws, and the intelligence services on which the country's defence against German spies or British collaborators depended, were equally unfit for purpose.

The most glaring evidence of this was the absence of any legislation against foreign espionage. Between 1914 and 1918, 35 spies had been caught; 22 were convicted and sixteen executed under an emergency law passed immediately after the outbreak of war. But the Defence of the Realm Act had lapsed with the Armistice, without any attempt at a peacetime replacement. The only other possible provision – the various Treason Acts dating back almost 250 years – required the perpetrator to owe allegiance to the Crown;* since German intelligence operatives had no such duty of loyalty, there could be no statutory basis for trying, let alone putting to death, any Abwehr agent who did not hold a UK passport. Even British sub-agents faced little danger of treason proceedings, since the Acts required prosecutors to produce two witnesses to an alleged offence – an unlikely prospect given the necessarily clandestine nature of spying.

---

* Sir Edward Coke's *Institutes of the Lawes of England* (1628–44) – the foundation stone of British common law – explicitly excluded foreign nationals from the provisions of the Treason Acts: 'An enemy coming in open hostility into England ... cannot be indicted of treason, for that he was never within the protection or ligeance of the king.'

But beyond the lack of a functioning anti-espionage law was a more fundamental – and more fundamentally thorny – problem: what should be done about enemy aliens when war, as seemed inevitable, began?

During the First World War, Defence Regulations had granted the Home Secretary executive power to order the detention of anyone – foreign nationals or British citizens – he deemed to be of 'hostile origins ... or associations'.[9] However, despite widespread public 'spy fever', the provision was used sparingly; between 1914 and 1918 only 342 enemy aliens were interned under Defence Regulation 14B, and at the war's end the prerogative lapsed.

From the mid-1920s, Whitehall began considering whether to prepare legislation for a future conflict. It is a testament to the sporadic and leisurely nature of the discussions between the Home Office and MI5 that they rumbled on from 1923 to 1936 without ever reaching a definitive decision on the dilemma underlying the question of internment: was it morally right – let alone legal – to imprison people without trial? Centuries of English law held that it was wrong both ethically and constitutionally, and a succession of habeas corpus cases dating back to the reign of Henry II had established a clear right of anyone lawfully resident in the United Kingdom not to be detained on the unchallengeable order of either government or monarch.

'Of great importance to the public is the preservation of this personal liberty', William Blackstone wrote in *Commentaries on the Laws of England* (1765–69) – the bedrock for all English jurisprudence – 'for once it were left to the power of any ... magistrate to imprison arbitrarily whomever he or his officers thought proper ... there would soon be an end of all other rights and immunities.'[10]

The view of the Security Service was that, however distasteful, war trumped personal freedom; by contrast, the Home Office, traditionally – and with some historical justification – viewed as the guarantor of individual rights within Whitehall, was resistant to any measure which gave ministers untrammelled power over the people.

But by the end of 1936, as Hitler's actions laid increasingly bare the threat posed by Nazi Germany, a consensus was reached. On December 11 a Home Office memorandum set out the principle to be adopted in new Defence Regulations if, or when, war came.

It would be necessary that the Defence Bill should confer on the Home Secretary an arbitrary power to intern, without trial and for an indefinite period, persons (whether British or alien) whose sympathies were such that if they were allowed to remain at large they would be likely to impede the war effort.[11]

In July the following year the Committee of Imperial Defence accepted the broad brushstrokes of this policy, but left the details to be ironed out by yet another inter-departmental Whitehall sub-group; this spent the next two years bickering about who could be interned – aliens or British citizens – and the bureaucratic checks and balances to be built into the legislation.

None of this was disclosed to, let alone discussed with, the public or its representatives. Nor did Whitehall share its final draft of the new regulations with Parliament until the last days of peace. On August 24, 1939, Parliament was recalled from its summer break and the Emergency Powers (Defence) Bill, endowing the Home Secretary with the executive power of internment – was ushered through the voting lobby.

The law was primarily intended to target enemy aliens, whose numbers had risen dramatically in the years during which Whitehall laboriously pondered. In 1930 there were approximately 20,000 German nationals living in Britain, as well as an uncounted number of dual nationals and exiles who had taken on British citizenship by marriage or naturalisation. From 1933, as Hitler's regime imposed increasingly repressive laws and political as well as religious oppression on German citizens, an exodus began. Over the next five years 300,000 refugees fled the country, almost a quarter of them arriving in Britain. Many – almost certainly the vast majority – were genuinely seeking asylum, but although there were economic controls aimed at preventing them from being a drain on the state, as the numbers increased in direct correlation with Nazi persecution there was little effective political or intelligence screening of those claiming sanctuary. By September 1939, approximately 70,000 non-naturalised Germans and Austrians were living within the territorial borders of the United Kingdom.

From 11.15am on Sunday, September 3, 1939 – the moment Britain formally declared war on Nazi Germany – all of those men and women became enemy aliens and subject to possible internment.[12]

The new Defence Regulations instituted a system of classifying the level of threat they posed. Those deemed the greatest risk were designated Category A, to be rounded up as a matter of urgency; those in Category B were to have restrictions imposed on their movements and association, while Category C aliens would be left largely undisturbed. The responsibility for providing the information on which these decisions rested was handed to the Security Service. Assessing 70,000 men and women was a Herculean task which would have troubled even the most efficiently-organised and well-resourced intelligence department; unfortunately, MI5 was neither.

At the end of 1918, the Home Section of the War Office Directorate of Military Intelligence – the formal title under which the Security Service operated – had more than 800 staff, all focused on counter-espionage inside Britain. The department had proved its worth during the First World War; by 1916 its actions had – according to the official history of British Intelligence – made it 'virtually impossible for Germany to maintain agents in Britain'.[13] But in the years that followed, funding and manpower were cut as part of a succession of turf wars with MI6 and with the Metropolitan Police Special Branch.

Even MI5's departmental parentage – the Ministry which controlled it – became obscure; after a remarkably ill-documented series of reorganisations neither the War Office nor the Home Office was sure which was in charge, resulting – as a subsequent secret review caustically noted – that by the outbreak of war the Security Service was 'something of a lost child'.[14] By September 1938, the total staff complement at its Thames House HQ on London's Millbank was 150: of these, only 30 were intelligence officers, the remainder being secretaries or clerks who painstakingly posted entries – often handwritten – on the suspect index files in the Thames House basement.

This vast Registry, as the collection of intelligence was known, had once provided the Security Service with a state-of-the-art system of recording and accessing information gleaned on individuals and organisations perceived as a danger to the country. By the end of the First

World War it held 250,000 punch cards and 27,000 specific name files on individuals deemed to be 'suspicious' or dangerous'.[15] In the lean years of the 1920s and 1930s, however, it was – according to MI5's official history – allowed to 'fall behind ... with serious consequences when the war broke out in 1939'.[16]

Even the diminished overall staffing levels were slightly deceptive and disguised the extent to which meagre resources were thinly spread. By 1939 MI5 was divided into four sections. A Branch was responsible for personnel, finance and administering the Registry; C Branch was tasked with vetting political appointments, while D Branch handled the security of the munitions industry and worked alongside immigration officials at ports and aerodromes. MI5's primary raison d'être – investigating threats to the nation's security – was the purview of B Branch, yet it was kept remarkably short of both money and staff. A 1945 memorandum, written for internal consumption, noted that 'there were not more than 12 agents employed by the Department [B Branch] as a whole'.

> It will probably come as a surprise – even to the personnel of the Security Service – to learn that during the vital years between 1935 and 1939 such a small number of agents was available to cover a vast field of work of the first importance; but it is fair to say that this was not due to any lack of foresight on the part of the Department. It was entirely due to financial starvation for which the Department was in no way to blame.[17]

The report's author, Maxwell Knight, was symptomatic of both the Service's strength in fiscal adversity and, simultaneously, the fundamental problems at its heart. Born in 1900 and a youthful midshipman in the Royal Naval Reserve during the final years of the First World War, Knight had gone to work as a teacher in a boys' preparatory school and as a freelance journalist before being recruited to join a shadowy private industrial espionage unit run by Sir George Makgill, an ultra-conservative business leader with a visceral dislike of trade unions. The Industrial Intelligence Bureau was financed by the Federation of British Industries and the Coal Owners' and Shipbuilders' Federations.

Its self-appointed and somewhat sinister mission was to seek out intelligence on industrial unrest fomented – allegedly – by communists, anarchists and the Irish Republic Army.

Because MI5 had few, if any, agents of its own, in the early 1920s its head, Sir Vernon Kell, formed an alliance with the IIB, allowing the Service to reap the benefit of its information. In 1924, Knight was sent on an undercover mission on behalf of both organisations.

> At the request of Sir George Makgill, Bt., who was then running agents on behalf of Sir Vernon Kell, I joined the first of the Fascist Movements in this country, The British Fascisti. I remained with this organisation until 1930 when it more or less became ineffectual.
>
> My association with this body was at all times for the purposes of obtaining information for H.M. Government and also for the purposes of finding likely people who might be used by this department for the same purposes.[18]

Knight's account of his involvement with the British Fascisti (rebranded as The British Fascists in 1924) is a little disingenuous: at the time he was, politically and emotionally, far closer to fascist beliefs than he later cared to admit. MI5's authorised history quotes the recollections of an (unnamed) young officer, who served under Knight, that he 'had no time for democracy and believed the whole country should be ruled by the social élite'.[19]

In December 1929 Knight was recruited by MI6 to investigate communist groups throughout Britain.* He was apparently picked for his willingness to break the law in the service of his employers.

> [Knight] makes an excellent impression, is clearly perfectly honest, and at need prepared to do anything, but is at the same time not wild.
>
> When required by his previous masters, he and two friends burgled, three nights running, the premises of the local committee of the

---

* Despite a notional injunction against operating inside the United Kingdom, MI6's financial and political supremacy over MI5 allowed it to do so throughout the late 1920s and early 1930s.

Communist Party in Scotland, the branch of the Labour Research department there and the YCL [Young Communist League].[20]

Two years later, in a widespread reorganisation of all three intelligence-gathering services (MI5, MI6 and Special Branch), he transferred to the Security Service, bringing with him a collection of informants and unpaid amateur 'agents', to which he gave the codename 'M.S.'.* Together they infiltrated the Communist Party and exposed the willingness of some of its luminaries to spy on behalf of Moscow.[21]

Much less attention was devoted to the growing fascist movement in Britain. In the month that Hitler assumed power in Germany – January 1933 – Knight wrote an internal policy study which took a benign view of the groups then in existence and, in particular, of the one to which he had belonged.

> It can be confidently said that at no time between 1923–1927 was there any intention on the part of the British Fascisti to act in any unconstitutional manner, nor to usurp the functions of the properly constituted authorities.[22]

Five years later B Branch had belatedly realised that Knight and his team had been focused too greatly on the lesser enemy of communism – albeit that they had also managed to infiltrate the official British fascist parties – and too little on the wider problem of pro-Nazi sympathisers. As his own post-war account noted:

> In 1938 it was obviously necessary to pay some attention to the desirability of having agents who could be used in connection with that branch of German espionage which had an affinity with either the NSDAP Organisation in Great Britain, or pro-German societies and groups which did not properly fall under the heading of fascist bodies. And between 1938 and the outbreak of war, a small group of agents was developed to deal with such matters.[23]

---

* Short for 'M Section', with the initial presumed to stand for Maxwell.

Unfortunately, Knight's efforts were hampered by two major obstacles. The first was money: until the last days before war was declared, very little additional government funding reached B Branch, much less the 'M.S.' operation – a short-sightedness which would, very shortly, cause severe problems. 'Had the Government of the day taken a more courageous attitude', Knight complained in 1945, 'and had they loosened the purse-strings in time, it is certain that the administration of agents during the later years of the war could have been more efficient.'[24]

The accusation was just, if tinged with a degree of hypocrisy: Knight's own inefficiencies and shortcomings were the second fundamental problem which would, in time, undermine MI5's efforts against Hitler's sympathisers in Britain.

Knight was – either by nature or affectation (accounts differ)* – an eccentric and defiantly independent figure. According to Joan Miller, his secretary, mistress (of sorts) and sometime 'M.S.' agent:

> M was enigmatic and debonair ... The range of his accomplishments was extraordinary. He'd played drums in a jazz band at the Hammersmith Palais and more impressively was equally proficient on the clarinet ... He published a couple of thrillers ... knew more about the Occult than anyone I've ever met ... was a crack shot and a collector of antique guns.[25]

Knight operated from his own, habitually chaotic flat in Sloane Street (and later Dolphin Square) rather than from MI5's offices. Visitors would frequently be greeted by one of his succession of exotic pets – from grass snakes to a bush-baby or a baboon. He was, in the words of the Service's official history, 'a law unto himself'.

---

* Alone of all MI5's wartime counter-espionage officers, Maxwell Knight has been the subject of two biographies. While these have detailed some of his serious flaws as an intelligence agent, both have promoted a distinctly shaky myth that he was the Service's 'greatest spymaster' and the model for 'M' in the MI6 of James Bond. There is little to justify either claim.

He was probably the last officer who, as one who served under him later recalled, 'would burgle premises without authority and recruit whomever he wished.'[26]

With no money to pay his team, Knight recruited largely from his own set of acquaintances: an impoverished minor aristocrat, a crime novelist, and the son of his close friend, the thriller writer Dennis Wheatley. He also found at least one agent from within London's gay community. (Knight was himself a probable homosexual, at a time when this was illegal; his marriage was unconsummated and he was estranged from his wife, who ran a small hotel on Exmoor.)

If this was, of necessity, a distinctly unprofessional way to run a counter-espionage unit, it matched the relaxed traditions of MI5 in the 1930s. Sir Vernon Kell's management style was paternalistic and senior staff tended to share his interests in hunting, shooting and fishing. One former member recalled that her interview involved only two questions – 'where had I been to school, and did I play any games' – while another described the atmosphere as 'like being in a family firm, one felt, secure'.[27]

Actual security, however, was rather less in evidence. The authorised history includes the view of an MI5 official, lodged in the Service's archives:

Security was non-existent. No-one was vetted on joining, in most cases staff were recruited on the basis of knowing someone already employed ... No passes were issued and no-one was on the door to let us in.[28]

Given this amateurish approach, and the meagre finances which encouraged it, MI5's failure to spot warning signs in three seemingly minor cases during 1939 was understandable.

In March a draughtsman working on a secret government project walked out of the Fairey Aviation Company in Hayes, Middlesex. Harry Mayes took with him sketches and blueprints for a new aircraft engine being developed for the Air Ministry; in collaboration with a small rival aircraft and motor design firm, he attempted to cash in on the invention by registering a patent on the engine.[29]

The same month, another draughtsman working in the electrical drawing office of the British Power Boat Company in Hythe was caught removing plans for a secret 70-foot motor boat being developed for the Admiralty. A search of Walter Moore's lodgings revealed that he had already stolen nine similar blueprints including a detailed layout of the engine room machinery and full wiring diagrams.[30]

Neither Mayes nor Moore appears to have had any contact with either foreign spies or domestic pro-Nazis – a fact which persuaded the Director of Public Prosecutions (DPP) to rule out espionage charges; instead their motives were purely financial. Each was convicted on one count of breaking the Official Secrets Act and fined. But the ease with which two British men were able to steal militarily-sensitive information, and their willingness to do so for money, should have rung alarm bells inside Thames House; on the evidence of the two surviving files – both created by the DPP – there is no evidence that MI5 even knew about the cases. It had no such defence in the third.

On July 22, Frederick Donald Ballard, a Master-at-Arms serving on HMS *Coventry*, was drinking in a pub in Portsmouth when he was approached by a man seeking information about his ship. According to the report he gave to Portsmouth City Police: 'A man who was a complete stranger came up to me and said, "I have been trying to meet you for the past three weeks ... When I know you better, we will talk big money, as you are on the *Coventry* which is an experimental ship and it will be worthwhile."'

The man gave his name as Michael O'Riley and told Ballard: 'I am a German Spy, and I hold the rank of Captain in the German Army', and that he had been 'thrown out of Simmonstown Dockyard[31] for being a spy and after that he had gone to Singapore, Bombay, Alexandria, Malta and Germany; after staying in Germany for a short while, he had gone to America where he had worked as an engineer in Ford's Works, Detroit, and that he had returned to England about 18 months ago.'

The two men met again the next evening and Ballard deliberately plied O'Riley with beer. After five pints the self-proclaimed spy talked 'of Germany and his association with it. ... He spoke very freely of Germany, of Hitler, Goering, and Ribbentrop and what wonderful men they were.' He also said that he was employed as a boiler foreman at Portsmouth docks, where he earned £4 10s a week. Ballard then went to the dockyard, but found that there was no one named O'Riley employed there.

A week later the mysterious man approached a second drinker in a different pub. Frederick Cake, a chargeman in the engineering department of HM Dockyard Portsmouth, was enjoying a lunchtime pint when 'O'Riley' struck up a conversation. He said his parents were from Tipperary but that he was from Bonn in Germany and 'I am wholeheartedly German'. He gave his name as 'von Makerjon', and offered Cake £100 for information about submarines at the docks. The conversation was witnessed by Archibalde Hill, a local road sweeper; both he and Cake (who had not previously met, and did not know Ballard) gave statements to the police.[32]

On August 1, the Chief Constable of Portsmouth City Police applied to the Director of Public Prosecutions for permission to charge Michael Riorden – O'Riley's real name – with espionage under Section 1 of the Official Secrets Act. The DPP passed the request on to MI5 where it landed on the desk of Brigadier Oswald Harker, head of B Section and the Service's Deputy Director General.

Harker – a 43-year-old former Deputy Police Commissioner with the Indian police in Bombay – had a reputation within MI5 as 'fearsome ... rank conscious ... [and] good-looking but not clever'.[33] Within 24 hours he sent a brisk note back, dismissing out of hand the Chief Constable's suggestion. Riorden, alias O'Riley, alias von Makerjon, was not charged and thereafter disappears from history.

Given the limited timescale – it would have been impossible for one of the Service's over-taxed staff to travel to the south coast, conduct interviews and report back within less than a day – Harker could not have known whether the man was, as he had claimed, a German spy, or merely a petty criminal willing to chance his arm by seeking military information for personal profit. If MI5 was unable – or unwilling – to trouble itself with relatively simple cases involving self-confessed, if low-grade, spies, the prospects for much more complex investigations into well-connected German agents of influence in Britain were not good. Yet by the spring of 1939 there was abundant evidence that some of the country's most senior aristocrats and military officers had been converted to the Nazi cause.

CHAPTER FOUR

'The Shadow of the German Sword'

'The great work done by Herr Hitler and his associates ... [is]
one of the greatest and most bloodless revolutions in history.'
*Admiral Sir Barry Domvile, former Director
of Naval Intelligence, May 1939*

On Thursday, April 20, 1939 more than 40,000 troops marched through Berlin. Wehrmacht infantry and cavalry regiments, Kriegsmarine naval units and Heinrich Himmler's black-clad SS goose-stepped down the Unter den Linden, followed by armoured cars, mobile artillery and lines of tanks in formation. Overhead, wave after wave of aircraft – 162 bombers and fighter planes from Hermann Goering's Luftwaffe – staged a ceremonial fly-past.

The parade was the largest military display in German history; an emphatic statement of the strength of the Nazi state's armed forces, designed to send a warning to the British and American governments not to stand in the way of Adolf Hitler's plans for European conquest.

Its more immediate and ostensible purpose, however, was to celebrate the Fuehrer's 50th birthday. Two days earlier, the Nazi regime had declared April 20 a national holiday, and on the eve of the great day Hitler drove down the newly-finished East–West central avenue in a parade of 50 vehicles, before watching a choreographed torch-lit procession from the balcony of the monumental new Reich building.

At midnight, Party functionaries presented their leader with lavish tributes of priceless art treasures, rare coins, antique weapons, and a scale model of the triumphal arch that would shortly be erected in his glory at the heart of the capital. For the benefit of the country's citizens – and the watching wider world – the festivities' organiser, propaganda minister Joseph Goebbels, gave a radio address which summoned up the legacy of Ernst Forsthoff's concept of 'The Total State', and made explicit the leadership cult which was driving Germany towards its self-proclaimed destiny.

> The Reich stands in the shadow of the German sword. Trade and industry, and cultural and national life flourish under the guarantee of the military forces. The name of Herr Hitler is our political programme. Imagination and realism are harmoniously combined in the Fuehrer.[1]

Goebbels had invited royalty and politicians from across the world to join the celebrations. On the afternoon itself, 20,000 dignitaries from 23 nations watched and applauded from stands erected along the route as Hitler acknowledged the salutes of his armed forces; but three of the great Western powers – the United States, France and Britain – snubbed the event. In protest at Germany's occupation of Czechoslovakia the previous year, each had withdrawn their ambassadors; America did send a lesser official, chargé d'affaires Raymond H. Geist, but President Franklin D. Roosevelt noticeably declined to send a congratulatory message to the Fuehrer.

In Britain, there had been much soul-searching on how to respond. Relations between London and Berlin were increasingly tense and Whitehall mooted the idea of ignoring the occasion altogether. In the end, the government settled for a compromise by which King George VI followed tradition by sending a birthday telegram while ordering his diplomats and political representatives to stay away.[2]

However, three key pillars of British society – the monarchy, Parliament and the military – were nonetheless informally represented:

Walter John Montagu Douglas Scott, Eighth Duke of Buccleuch, was Lord Steward of the Royal Household, the leading official in the royal court and brother-in-law of the King's younger brother, Prince Henry, Duke of Gloucester; Arthur Ronald Nall-Cain had been Conservative MP for Liverpool Wavertree before inheriting his father's title and taking his seat in the House of Lords as the Second Baron Brocket; while Major General John 'Boney' Fuller was one of the most decorated British Army officers and a celebrated military strategist whose books and lectures on the tactics of armoured warfare had made him a highly visible public figure. All three were fervent British admirers of Hitler and the Reich; all three attended the celebrations as personal guests of the Fuehrer.

Brocket's extreme right-wing opinions, fervid anti-Semitism and enthusiastic support for the German leader – he had enjoyed a personal audience with Hitler during the Munich crisis when German troops prepared to invade Czechoslovakia – had long marked him out a pro-Nazi fanatic;[3] Buccleuch's presence was an embarrassment to the royal family – although since he had travelled to Berlin without troubling to seek the King's approval, Buckingham Palace was able to distance itself from its Lord Steward by issuing him with a stern rebuke and instructions to stay out of sight during the parade.

But it was Fuller's attendance which was most ominous. An unashamed anti-Semite, in 1935 he published a vicious diatribe describing Jews as 'the cancer of Europe',[4] and had lionised Hitler as 'that realistic idealist who has awakened the common sense of the British people by setting out to create a new Germany'. He had also been retained as an unofficial military advisor to the Wehrmacht and was the only foreigner present during the Reich's first armed manoeuvres in 1935. Four years later, after Germany's reinvigorated and fully mechanised armed forces had rumbled past the leader's elevated dais during the birthday parade, Hitler asked: 'I hope you were pleased with your children?' Fuller replied: 'Your Excellency, they have grown up so quickly that I no longer recognise them.'[5]

Despite his unswerving pro-Nazi brand of fascism, Fuller retained a close personal friendship with General William Edmund Ironside, Inspector General of Britain's Overseas Forces – a relationship which gave him privileged access to Britain's army ruling councils.

The presence of Buccleuch, Brocket and Fuller in the VIP enclosure that afternoon in April 1939 was neither coincidental nor an aberration. Rather, it was the culmination of a lengthy and concerted effort by the Nazi state to court influential figures in British society – a strategy which the Fuehrer had spelled out six years earlier.

*

'We need armies', Hitler told the (then) National Socialist politician and author Hermann Rauschning in an interview conducted during the early days of his rise to power:

'But we shall not use them as in 1914. The place of artillery will in future be taken by revolutionary propaganda, to break down the enemy psychologically before the armies begin to function at all. The enemy people must be demoralized and ready to capitulate, before military action can even be thought of ...

'Mental confusion, indecisiveness, panic, these are our weapons. The history of revolutions ... is always the same: the ruling classes capitulate. Why? defeatism: they no longer have the will to conquer.'[6]

It was a succinct and prescient exposition of the third element of Germany's plans for total war. While the Wehrmacht, Luftwaffe and Kriegsmarine built up formidable fighting forces, and the Abwehr established a network of espionage agents, other branches of the regime set about cultivating agents of influence. Two rival ministries were tasked with finding friends and sympathisers in the rarefied strata of Britain's ruling classes who could be induced to support and promote the Nazi cause.

Joachim von Ribbentrop, a decorated veteran of the Kaiser's Imperial Army – he was badly wounded on the Western Front and awarded the Iron Cross – was urbane, well-travelled and ambitious. He joined the National Socialist Party in 1932 and rose through its hierarchy to become Hitler's chief advisor on international affairs a year later. In 1934 he set up the Ribbentrop Bureau, a foreign policy intelligence-gathering unit, politically and financially independent of the Reich's traditional diplomatic corps; within two years it developed contacts in countries across Europe and was well on the way to employing 300 staff in its Berlin headquarters. Like its counterparts in the Abwehr, the Bureau made use of German businessmen living in Britain.

Baron Fritz Thassilo von Nidda arrived in London in November 1927 and formed an international arms dealing company. After Hitler took power, he was appointed head of Auslands (foreign countries) organisation in Britain, the main Nazi Party body for German émigrés, combining this with part-time employment as a paid agent for Ribbentrop. In the summer of 1937, following the discovery and expulsion of another of Ribbentrop's emissaries,[7] Von Nidda was interrogated at New Scotland Yard and admitted 'that he had been writing up political intelligence reports, which had been sent under cover to Berlin, and that he had received a salary of £20 per month for doing so'. There are no details of these reports in the Baron's heavily-weeded MI5 file, but his activities clearly troubled the Security Service: on September 13, 1937 its Director General sent an urgent letter to the Home Secretary demanding Von Nidda's immediate deportation. 'Only today have I received further information regarding this alien's recent suspicious movements', Sir Vernon Kell advised Sir Samuel Hoare, 'and I feel that every additional day he is allowed to remain here may be inimical to the interests of this country'.[8]

A document found in the German Air Ministry building in Berlin after the war included details of British agents of influence Von Nidda had recruited and apparently paid.[9] This included a Metropolitan Police inspector, two army officers – a captain and a colonel – two knights of the realm, one current and one former MP (both on the right wing of the Conservative Party) and Admiral William Reginald 'Blinker' Hall, a former Director of Naval Intelligence at the Admiralty.[10]

Von Nidda left Britain at the beginning of November, but by then his employer had arrived in London. In August 1936 Hitler appointed Ribbentrop as Ambassador to Britain, with orders to court influential figures in politics, the aristocracy and the military. It was a mission which Ribbentrop found most congenial: he held lavish parties at the German Embassy in Carlton House Terrace, at which the cream of society was formally greeted by uniformed SS officers.

Society, in turn, returned the favour, inviting Ribbentrop for weekends in the country at a succession of noble houses. These brought him into close contact with fascist-leaning members of the inner circles of the monarchy. The Duke of Buccleuch was pleased to host the Ambassador at his estate in Scotland; Captain George Drummond, whose personal friendship with the House of Windsor extended to teaching the young Princesses Elizabeth and Margaret to ride, threw a fancy dress party at Pitsford Hall in Northamptonshire at which the guests honoured Ribbentrop by wearing Nazi uniforms; and Dorothy, Dowager Viscountess Downe, goddaughter of King George V and a former Lady in Waiting to Queen Mary, used one of Ribbentrop's visits to concoct with him a plan to send boys from the villages near the Royal Sandringham estate on extended trips to Germany.*[11]

The partying, while fun, had a serious purpose: Ribbentrop's orders were to create a groundswell of influential support for Germany's demands for expansion across Europe and, specifically, to undermine opposition to the Nazi policies within Britain's ruling classes. In this, he was tilling fertile soil.

Fascism, anti-Semitism and admiration for Hitler flourished in the dark valley that was Britain in the 1930s – indeed, it was positively fashionable among the aristocracy and conservative politicians. Lady Alexandra Hardinge, a goddaughter of Queen Alexandra and the widow of a former British Ambassador to Spain, was a vocal and tireless advocate for Nazi Germany.** As late as April 1939 she set out on a speaking tour of the south-west of England to champion the case for the Reich. 'I personally know the Fuehrer', she told an audience in Torquay on April 4. 'He is not a politician. He is a dreamer, and idealist;

---

* There is a singular lack of official documents relating to Ribbentrop's noble conquests. There is no MI5 file on Buccleuch or Drummond in the National Archives, despite their names and suspect loyalty being referred to in the records of other, less elevated fascists. A file on Viscountess Downe does exist, but it has been very heavily weeded to remove almost all of the documents once held within it.

** Given Lady Hardinge's public prominence – national and regional newspapers regularly carried reports of her pro-Nazi speeches – it is strange that there is no trace of an MI5 file on her in the National Archives.

he comes from the people, he has been in prison, he has starved, he has suffered everything a man can suffer. He saw Germany beaten down and he told me that he just had to take over the leadership of the country. I think Hitler has every right to put his country in order.'[12]

The Dowager Viscountess Downe was similarly smitten and had for some years financed 'fascist activities to the tune of £1,250–£1,500 per annum' – the equivalent of more than half a million pounds today;[13] and her equally wealthy and well-connected noble friend, George Lane Pitt-Rivers (one of Ribbentrop's contacts, a cousin by marriage of Winston Churchill and one of the wealthiest men in England), had become so entranced by the Third Reich that he had carried out intelligence work in Eastern Europe on the Fuehrer's behalf. According to a memo in his MI5 file:

> Pitt-Rivers has been known to the Security Service since 1930 as a strong Fascist and associate of those who had similar views. He spent the latter part of 1936 in Europe, visiting Germany, Czechoslovakia and other places. On 8.9.36 he was arrested in Karlsbad by the Czech Police on a charge of espionage. He has since stated that he was in Czechoslovakia working for Hitler.

Nor did Pitt-Rivers – a wounded veteran of the Battle of Ypres – confine his preference for Germany over Britain to the countries in Eastern Europe on which Hitler had set his sights. On his return to London in December 1936 he wrote to the War Office requesting the removal of his name from the regular Army Reserve of Officers on the grounds that he was not prepared 'to serve in any capacity ... a Parliamentary despotism, now styled as His Majesty's Government'. In this lengthy diatribe Pitt-Rivers also gave Whitehall the benefit of his 'extreme political views about international Jewry and kindred topics'.[14]

In Pitt-Rivers and those like him, the Nazi Party saw the potential for deploying Hitler's psychological weapons of 'mental confusion, indecisiveness, panic'; it fanned the flames of this incipient 'defeatism' by inviting a succession of influential and military figures to meet and speak with the regime's leaders. Anthony Ludovici, a leading conservative intellectual and writer, proved a particularly willing visitor.

Ludovici had been wounded on the Somme in 1916 and then recruited by the Secret Intelligence Service; by the end of the First World War he held the rank of Captain and was head of an entire department within MI6. He published widely, promoting his obsessions with the philosophies of Friedrich Nietzsche, the importance of the aristocracy, the futility of democracy and the 'science' of eugenics. These right-wing views, his role as a philosophical *eminence grise* within sections of the Conservative Party and – above all – his role as a serving intelligence officer made him a natural target for recruitment as an agent of influence.

In the spring of 1936 he and the head of a small quasi-fascist organisation, the English Mistery, received an invitation to visit Berlin as official guests of the Nazi Party. Its intentions were, according to Ludovici's posthumously-published autobiography, apparently made explicit. 'The idea was that [we] should meet the leading members of the government and become acquainted with some of the reforms and innovations introduced by the National Socialists since Hitler's advent to power.' True to its word, the Party gave its guests VIP treatment throughout their visit.

> In the course of our stay we were able to hear Hitler speak several times, and were always given such privileged seats at his meetings that we were able to get a close view of him and all his leading colleagues in the government ... Of the whole bunch of men around Hitler ... Goebbels, Himmler, Schirach, Hess, Funk, Ribbentrop, and Goering all struck me as commonplace, if not actually common.
>
> I disliked Hess and Ribbentrop, but little Goebbels, with whom I discussed Nietzsche, seemed to me rather attractive and the most intelligent of the lot.[15]

On a second visit he was treated to further extensive meetings with 'the leaders of the National Socialist Party, including, above all, Hitler himself'; as his hosts intended, these made a powerful and lasting impression, and on his return to England Ludovici published a fulsome endorsement of the Leader in the influential literary magazine *The English Review*.

I witnessed two public appearances of the Fuehrer. I saw him drive into a vast stadium at half-past eight in the morning to address 80,000 children of the Hitler Youth Movement and a few thousand adults; and, an hour or two later, I saw him arrive at the Lustgarten in the centre of Berlin to address a vast assembly of working men and specially invited guests of both sexes. On both occasions something more than ordinary enthusiasm was displayed and no visitor required to understand the language in order to feel the magic of the moment. Long before the actual appearance of the smart black touring car bearing the Leader, the ringing cheers of the populace could be heard in the distance drawing gradually nearer and nearer, until, when the car entered the arena, the whole gathering of thousands took up the cry and, standing with right arms raised, shook the May morning with their greetings.

'Sieg!' (Victory) he cried.

'Heil Hitler!' the throng roared in return.

'Sieg!' he cried again.

'Heil Hitler!' came the response once more.

'Sieg!' he cried for the third and last time.

'Heil Hitler!' was thundered back by 100,000 voices.

One and all displayed the same passionate affection of children in the presence of the Fuehrer, and to watch them was to learn what miracles can still be wrought with the ultra-civilised and often effete populations of modern Europe if only they are given a lofty purpose. This is surely the secret of the perpetual hold religions have on men, and it explains Adolf Hitler's magic influence ... and to have given his nation such a purpose, to have persuaded them that such a purpose can be worthwhile, is the secret of the Fuehrer's magic. To my mind, this constitutes his chief importance to the German nation.[16]

Two years later Ludovici published – under the pseudonym 'Cobbett' – a book endorsing anti-Semitism and calling for a ban on 'mixture with Jews through marriage'. *Jews and The Jews in England* laid out an explicit argument for a British equivalent to the Nazis' Nuremberg race laws.

There can be no doubt that, from the standpoint of a strictly Conservative attitude, the Jew should be precluded from too much control over our institutions and customs, because as they are not an external expression of his type, his intervention as a power over them cannot fail to modify them in an un-English way. Prudence would, therefore, seem to dictate a policy of exclusion both of the Jew and his influence from all those departments of English life in which his influence may so alter the character of the nation as to make it lose all its specific qualities ...

And all bodies of Englishmen who seriously wish to recover English civilization at this stage cannot be regarded as any more than emotional and hysterical flag wavers if they do not see the compelling need of that infinitely difficult task — the task of accompanying any gesture of organized reform by a frontal attack upon the Judaized elements in their kith and kin and their own Judaized values.[17]

Anthony Ludovici was by no means the only right-wing or anti-Semitic political thinker to be seduced by the Nazis' deliberate use of propaganda and spectacle into influencing British public opinion in its favour. But his employment with the Secret Intelligence Service – then belatedly attempting to catch up with the expansion of Abwehr spying stations throughout Europe – made him a particularly valuable recruit.

Since he made little real effort to disguise his willingness to proselytise on behalf of the Fuehrer's new Germany, it is remarkable that he was not dismissed from his job at MI6 until August 1940 – especially since by then his name had featured in covert plans, discovered by MI5, for a violent fascist revolution in Britain.

But of all the British public figures who were invited to enjoy Nazi hospitality in the 1930s, a peppery, short-tempered retired naval chief would prove to give Goebbels' propaganda ministry the best return on its investment. Admiral Sir Barry Domvile joined the Royal Navy in 1892 when he was just fourteen years old. By 1916 he had risen to the rank of Captain and was on his way to a career in the Admiralty, first as Director of Plans, then Chief of Staff in the Mediterranean. In 1927 he was appointed Director of Naval Intelligence – a highly-sensitive office he occupied for the next three years – and he ended his career as President of the Royal Navy War College in Greenwich. By his retirement in 1936 he had added a CB – Companion of the Order of the Bath –

and a CMG – Commander of the Order of St Michael and St George[18] – to his knighthood.

He had also made a good marriage, to Alexandrina von der Heydt, the daughter of a German diplomat and, on her mother's side, the great-granddaughter of the Victorian-era Prime Minister, Sir Robert Peel. The couple lived in the pleasant, leafy environs of Roehampton, and moved in the elevated social circles befitting their rank and status; one of their acquaintances, Lady Mary Royds, was the widow of the Commissioner of the Metropolitan Police. In 1935, a year before he left the Admiralty, she introduced Domvile to Anton Walter de Sager, a Swiss businessman and alleged German spy.

According to Domvile's MI5 file – an extensive record running to five well-filled volumes[19] – the meeting led to a lengthy relationship between the Admiral and the leader of the Third Reich.

This Sager appears to have had useful contacts with Reichsfuehrer Himmler and other prominent Nazis. He invited Admiral Domvile to visit Germany and arranged for him to meet prominent German naval authorities, to visit the concentration camp at Dachau[20] and also to spend three days on a chamois shooting expedition with Himmler.

Admiral Domvile visited Germany again the following year and at the Fuehrer's invitation attended the Party Conference at Nuremberg.[21] In the summer of 1937 he went to Rome, where he witnessed an inspection of young fascists by Mussolini. He then proceeded to Nuremberg where for the second year in succession he attended the Nazi Party Congress at the Fuehrer's invitation.[22]

The massed ranks of marching Nazi troops at Nuremberg evidently impressed the retired Admiral; during the heavily-choreographed rally he had a discussion with one of Ribbentrop's Bureau officials (and 'close personal confidant of Hitler himself'), Walther Hewel; the two men decided that on his return to England Domvile would set up a new society dedicated to improving relations between Germany and Britain.

'The Link', as Domvile called his organisation, rented offices in Southampton Row and quickly found a ready audience for its lobbying on behalf of Berlin. On September 17, 1937 Domvile wrote to

Hewel, thanking him for his 'kindness and attention during the Party meeting which made it an extremely pleasant one for us', and adding that 'Members are coming in fast for the Link'; one month later Hewel received the news that Domvile had signed up 470 registered members.

For their money these subscribers received invitations to public meetings at which Domvile and speakers from the constellation of British fascist parties extolled the virtues of Hitler's Germany, and postal deliveries of pamphlets published (in English) by Goebbels' propaganda department, which highlighted the achievements of the Nazi state. Then, in early 1938, Domvile moved The Link into the offices of another pro-German body, the *Anglo-German Review* (AGR), effectively merging the two organisations and dovetailing their efforts.

The man behind AGR – Cola Ernst Carroll – was the son of a British father of Swiss origin. During the First World War he had served in Royal Artillery and the RFC before turning his hand to journalism. Like Domvile, he was a convert to the Nazi cause and each monthly edition of the *Review* was directly funded by advertisements placed by German firms working to Goebbels' direction.

The formal axis between AGR and The Link was spelled out by Domvile in a letter to his friend and hunting partner, Heinrich Himmler, care of Gestapo headquarters, in March 1938.

Just a line to introduce my friend Mr C.E. Carroll, the editor of the Anglo German Review. As you know he is one of the greatest workers in this country for friendship with Germany, and his paper is most successful in forwarding this object. Incidentally, the Anglo German Review is also the publicity organ of The Link, which is advancing in a very encouraging manner in this country.

Mr Carroll goes to Berlin in the hope of obtaining certain official facilities for his paper, and if you can be of any assistance to him in this direction I shall be very grateful.

I am still hoping to hear that you and your wife are coming over to England; but the message never comes! I expect you are too busy just now, but I hope to see you at no too distant a date – and bring Wolff too.[23]

Reichsfuehrer Himmler was indeed busy. Eight days before Domvile's letter, Germany had mounted the Anschluss which annexed Austria. But other branches of the Nazi regime were available to assist the *Review* and The Link. Goebbels' ministry provided regular shipments of its propaganda newsletter, *News From Germany*, which were promptly sent out to AGR–Link members and subscribers; more importantly, Ribbentrop's Bureau provided substantial funds. In February 1939, MI5 intercepted a letter from Carroll to the Bureau in which he acknowledged the receipt of £180 (equivalent to £8,000 today) but reminded his sponsors that this did not match the £200 *per month* which had been promised.

The complaint evidently produced a response since Domvile's MI5 file notes: 'The Ribbentrop Bureau, therefore, paid Carroll the sum of £750 [£34,000 today] through the German Embassy. This sum was treated by Carroll as a subsidy and was never repaid.'[24]

The Nazi Party organisation in Britain also took what the Security Service described as 'a significant interest in the development of the Link'. Domvile employed the daughter of the German Consul in Glasgow as a secretary in its offices, and MI5 noted with concern that Otto Karlowa, the Landesgruppenleiter (country leader) of the Ausland organisation, responsible for coordinating the activities of 500 Party members living in Britain, ordered its officials in the provinces to go to Link meetings, though they were not – for publicity reasons – to become formal members.

Further evidence of the close relationship between Domvile's organisation and Ausland emerged in a letter Karlowa sent to the five leaders of NSDAP organisations across the country on December 8, 1938, instructing them to attend a Link soirée to be held the following week. 'I have promised Admiral Domvile', Karlowa wrote, 'that we will take part and will see that young ladies attend as dancing partners. We wish to take part in this gathering of the Link, and I request you to take energetic steps to see that this is done.'[25]

Funded by money from Ribbentrop and provided with regular supplies of propaganda by Goebbels, The Link flourished. By the spring of 1939 there were 35 active branches throughout the country, boasting a total of 4,329 members. These held regular meetings and Carroll was pleased to report back to Berlin that he had acquired a professional-standard film and sound projector to show 'German news, instructional and other films to the branches' every month. Nor, he said, was this effort confined to the already committed:

> In addition we may from time to time take a good London cinema by a method which will give the general public an opportunity of seeing German films, none at all of which are being shown in England.

Negotiations were evidently advanced. The manager of Studio One in Oxford Street ('one of the best known London cinemas') had, according to Carroll, agreed in principle to the arrangement.

> The Link would guarantee him half his seating capacity and ... he would fill the rest in his ordinary way. We have found that we can rely on between five hundred and a thousand Link members turning up at all events in London when they are asked to do so.[26]

On May 29, 1939 Carroll wrote again to his contact in the Bureau, this time with news that he was planning to place a series of six articles in a national newspaper. These were to cover 'aspects of Germany, such as social conditions, economic affairs, education and so on, and the whole series will form a complete "statement of the German case". One at least of the articles should be signed by a German of real consequence, whose name is known abroad. Could you arrange that? ... The other articles would be signed by distinguished British people ...'

Domvile, meanwhile, had penned his own panegyric to Hitler's Germany, supplying a foreword to a book by one of The Link's council members, Professor A.P. Laurie. *The Case For Germany* was an unashamed hymn to the Nazi regime and began with a ringing personal dedication to Hitler. 'I thank God that the peace of Europe is in the guardianship of the Fuehrer', Laurie pronounced, 'and therefore, in spite of the frantic efforts of those here and in Europe and in America who want war, secure.'

Since by the time he wrote this, in May 1939, war with Germany was looming, British publishers were unsurprisingly unwilling to touch the book. Instead, the Reich Propaganda Ministry issued it, paying Laurie an advance on sales of £150 (equivalent to £2,200 today). In those circumstances, Domvile's preface was remarkable.

> Professor Laurie writes of the National Socialist Movement with knowledge and with great sympathy. The particular value of the book lies in the fact that it is written by a foreigner who cannot be accused of patriotic excess in his interpretation of the great work done by Herr Hitler and his associates.
>
> I recommend this book with confidence to all people who are genuinely impressed with the desire to understand one of the greatest and most bloodless revolutions in history.

The Security Service and the British government viewed Domvile's activities with increasing concern. On August 3, the Home Secretary denounced The Link in Parliament. 'The professed object of this organisation is to promote understanding between England and Germany', Sir Samuel Hoare told the House of Commons, 'but it does nothing to enable Germans to understand the English view, and devotes itself to expressing the German point of view. The information I have shows that the organisation is being used as an instrument of the German propaganda service and that money has been received from Germany by one of the active organisers.'[27]

Hoare's statement – bitterly, if falsely, denied by Domvile as a 'canard'* – offered a textbook exposition of what Hitler had prophesied six years earlier: Germany had mobilised an army of propagandists inside Britain, whose role was to undermine the country from within. The problem, as the Home Secretary admitted in the same statement, was that he had 'no power to intervene unless an organisation breaks the law' – and English law had failed to keep pace with the new reality.

The freedom of these agents of influence to operate unchecked indicated, to outside friendly observers, a serious problem undermining the nation's readiness for the coming conflict. 'The fear of radicalism

---

* It did not help Domvile's case that he denied Hoare's allegations from Austria, where he and Link members were on a German-sponsored sightseeing tour.

so prevalent among the rich and the ruling classes in England', wrote US Colonel William J. Donovan* in a report on the Fifth Column the following year, 'was used as a potent argument for a more friendly, tolerant feeling toward the Nazi Regime, and as a point of leverage for a policy of appeasement':

> Subtle persuasion, secret pressure, and in all probability, open bribery were all used to break down the loyalty and to secure the cooperation of a few key men in official positions and in the armies.[28]

For the moment Domvile, Carroll, Ludovici, Fuller and their colleagues remained agents of influence rather than of espionage. That would change when, within months, members of The Link and its sister organisations would become involved in clandestine planning for a pro-Nazi fascist revolution. But before then, as the clock ticked down towards September 1939 and the start of hostilities, four unequivocal British spies for Germany were discovered.

---

* William J. ('Wild Bill') Donovan travelled extensively throughout Europe in the inter-war years, collecting intelligence and feeding it back to Washington. In 1941 he was appointed head of the first US government spy agency, the Office of Strategic Services – later to become the CIA.

CHAPTER FIVE

The Last Spies of Peace

'The latest ... anti-aircraft gun has a reputed range of 30,000ft.
The range finder to locate aircraft is 18ft long ... There are
3,000 parts to each gun. Further particulars will follow.'
Coded message sent to German Intelligence, March 1939

On Monday, September 25, 1939 – less than two weeks after Britain declared war on Germany – Mr Justice Oliver prepared himself to address the expensively-tailored prisoner standing before him in the dock of the Old Bailey.

Much of the nine-week trial of Donald Owen Reginald Adams, a 58-year-old racing journalist and occasional tipster, had been held *in camera*. The evidence of those proceedings which took place in public had been extensively splashed across the front pages of the national and regional press: 'Racing Code was Mask For Spy Messages to Germany', reported the *London Evening Standard*;[1] 'Man Named as "Paid Nazi Agent"', the *Daily Mail* informed its readers;[2] while the *News Chronicle*'s banner promised the 'Story of Nazis' Big Offer to London Man to Join Army'[3]. Reports of the verdict and sentence, by contrast, were noticeably low-key and relegated to inside page columns, well below the fold.

The *Daily Mail* was typical, devoting just three paragraphs to the story under the distinctly muted headline, '7 Years Sentence in

Secrets Case'. It did, though, report Mr Justice Oliver's stern rebuke to the convicted prisoner. 'I spent last week trying people for murder', the judge told Adams, 'but I do not know, really, if a man like you is not worse than those murderers, because you took pay for murdering your countrymen.'[4]

There were two important aspects to the espionage trial of Donald Adams, both of which belied the relatively lenient sentence and the downbeat reporting which accompanied it. The first was the evidence heard in secret: this demonstrated not only the lengths to which a British citizen was willing to go to betray his country, but also the ease with which the German Secret Service had recruited its agent. The second – which seems to have been lost in the fog of other war reporting – was that Adams' case marked the fourth discovery inside a year of British spies selling military secrets to the Nazis.

*

In September 1938 Joseph Kelly, a 30-year-old labourer from Bolton, was hired as a bricklayer by contractors building a new Royal Ordnance Factory at Euxton, near Chorley in Lancashire. That he got the job on what would, inevitably, be a militarily-sensitive site was somewhat surprising; he had a string of convictions, dating back to December the previous year, for assaulting a police officer, warehouse breaking, breach of the peace, stealing lead and using false pretences.

In those court appearances he had clocked up fines totalling £20 5s – a substantial sum equivalent to more than a month's wages – which added to his existing debts of £37 14s 7d (around £1,700 today). He had also been sentenced to two years' probation.

Evidently deeply short of money – and with a wife and sickly child to support[5] – Kelly decided that his new place of employment offered the prospect of a quick and easy extra payday. Shortly before Christmas he presented himself at the office of the German Consulate in Liverpool and volunteered his services as a spy. The Consul, Walter Reinhardt, was apparently cautious but took Kelly's name and address and said that this would be passed 'to the right quarter'.[6]

On February 2, 1939, a letter bearing an English postmark arrived at the bricklayer's terraced house in Rigby Street, Bolton. The writer did not give his (or her) name, but said that 'a friend' had provided Kelly's address and referred to 'a previous application'. MI5's files on the case do not contain any further details of the letter's contents, but they evidently gave Kelly enough encouragement to carry out his proposed mission, as well as instructions on how to send the resulting information to German Intelligence. On the night of March 1–2, he broke into the construction offices and stole two blueprints of the site. He hid one in a drawer at home, but posted the second to an address in Sassenheim, north-west Holland.

That house was owned by a young Dutch clerk, employed by the Electricity Supply Corporation in nearby Lisse. Jan Johannes Barendrecht was ambitious and eager to improve his station in life; the previous August he had answered a newspaper advert offering part-time work to 'Correspondents and Trade (Hire-Purchase) investigators'. By the autumn, Barendrecht had been hired, and 'instructed to report on the financial status etc. of a number of local inhabitants' in northern Holland. In addition, his new employers – a German company based in Cologne – told him that he would be expected 'to accept delivery of letters which he might receive from other "commercial correspondents" ... and to forward them to one of four addresses in Germany'. At the beginning of February 1939 he was advised to expect the arrival of letters from England.[7]

Two letters, posted in Bolton, duly arrived and Barendrecht forwarded them on to Cologne. When a third envelope followed, the young clerk evidently became suspicious: he opened it and found a note from Joseph Kelly, enclosing a passport photograph. He sent it on to Germany, but when a fourth letter landed, in which Kelly advised he would travel to Osnabrueck on March 17, Barendrecht decided that he should deliver it by hand. As he subsequently explained to MI5's chief spycatcher, Lt. Col. William Hinchley-Cooke, 'he undertook this journey partly for the purpose of offering his own services as a "travelling commercial agent" in England and partly to demand an explanation as to the reason why his employers in Cologne appeared to have written [to Kelly] in his name'.

In Cologne, these 'employers' told him that it was 'far too dangerous' for them to send him to England; this was evidently enough to convince Barendrecht that he had been duped into working as a post-box for German Intelligence, and on his return to Sassenheim he contacted the British Embassy in The Hague, warning the resident diplomat that 'in a roundabout way and with great difficulty and patience, I have got to know that your own country harbours a traitor who, although himself an Englishman, renders espionage services to Germany'. If the Ambassador would pay his expenses, Barendrecht offered to go to England and investigate.[8]

The Ambassador, however, ignored the letter because (as he later airily explained), 'offers of this type are fairly common and are invariably found to be useless'.[9] It was a missed opportunity – not least because although Barendrecht was forwarding letters from Kelly to German Intelligence in Cologne, it was evident from the correspondence that Cologne was sending its English recruit instructions and expenses via a separate intermediary – or 'cut-out' in espionage parlance.

On March 17 Joseph Kelly took a berth on the SS *Amsterdam*, sailing first to the Hook of Holland before taking an onward train to the German border and then to Osnabrueck. He had told his family and friends that he was going to see a boxing match – an unlikely story which failed to convince his next-door neighbour, who went to Bolton police station to report that 'Kelly had gone to Germany for some illegal purpose'.

A search of the terraced house over the weekend revealed a copy of one of the site plans. When the bricklayer arrived back in Rigby Street he found detectives waiting to arrest him. In short order, he was charged with two offences of espionage under the Official Secrets Act and remanded to Manchester prison.

Joseph Kelly was, unquestionably, an amateurish spy. Aside from his expenses in travelling to Germany, his Abwehr handlers paid him just £30 (£1,800 today) for his efforts. Yet his case highlighted three important problems facing the Security Service.

The first was the role of the German Consul in Liverpool. Walter Reinhardt had clearly acted as a conduit between German Intelligence and a British agent: it was the first direct proof of the involvement of Reich diplomatic staff in facilitating espionage. The Consul was expelled in June 1939, prompting the German government to send British diplomats home from Berlin.[10] The second was evidence – albeit fragmentary – that Kelly's actions had been either aided or prompted by an unidentified English handler. Staff at Manchester prison had sat in on a meeting between Kelly and his father, during which, according to a report by the Governor, 'when asked by his father if there was anybody else [involved] Kelly said that there was an Englishman whose name he didn't know ... and that he had been sent to the German Consul in Liverpool by the unnamed Englishman, and was to say that he had come from Elton'.[11] MI5 was never able to identify this agent.

The third issue – the persistent problem of the inadequacies of the law governing espionage cases – was highlighted by the judge at Kelly's trial before Manchester Assizes in May.[12] After noting that the plans Kelly sold to German Intelligence 'might, in the event of war between this country and Germany, have enabled them to bomb and destroy the factory ... and the lives of men alongside whom you were working', Mr Justice Stable lamented the limited nature of his power to pass a deterrent sentence.

> 'The Act of Parliament enables me to send you to penal servitude for fourteen years ... I observed in *The Times* last week that two men in another country committed an almost identical offence ... [and] they were both executed. We have got in this country what I suppose is a more merciful course.'

He sentenced Kelly to two ten-year terms of penal servitude.[13]

Two other cases that spring bore out Mr Justice Stable's concern, and offered further evidence that the branches of British Intelligence charged with detecting and preventing domestic espionage were not working together. In the same week that Joseph Kelly travelled to Osnabrueck, a shabbily-dressed former army private arrived at the port of Grimsby with a ticket to travel to Hamburg.

William Wishart was 24 years old and, like Kelly, married with a young child. He had joined the Royal Scots Regiment in 1933, serving briefly and without distinction: he deserted the following year, was court-martialled in 1936 and eventually discharged two years later as 'physically unfit for any form of army service'. He spent the next six months unemployed and living with – or off – his wife in a bungalow near Catterick Army Camp in Yorkshire; yet despite his severe shortage of money he was able to make occasional – and unexplained – trips to London where he stayed variously at an ex-servicemen's club and a small hotel off Russell Square.[14]

When he arrived at Grimsby docks on March 11, 1939 Wishart's appearance and behaviour attracted the attention of the Special Branch. According to a report filed the same day, the officer monitoring departures and arrivals, a Sergeant Daniel, was suspicious because Wishart 'appeared to be rather slovenly dressed for a saloon passenger and ... seemed nervous'. Since Wishart's passport had been issued just three days earlier, the sergeant questioned him about the reasons for his trip to Germany.

> He stated that about 4 years ago he met a German in Leith and became friendly with him. Three weeks ago he met this person in England and made arrangements to visit him in Germany with the idea of him (Wishart) getting a job there. He stated that this 'pal' (whose name he could not remember) would meet him on arrival in Hamburg.[15]

Wishart also told Sergeant Daniel that he was an 'unemployed motor mechanic', and went on to give a succession of contradictory answers about his plans for returning to England; at first he said that he would come back from Hamburg direct, then that he might go on to Denmark. When Daniel pressed him, Wishart became flustered, insisting that 'he could please himself how long he stayed away'.

The entire story seemed implausible and, his suspicions thoroughly aroused, Daniel sent a message back to Special Branch headquarters asking for guidance; but when the local intelligence officer reported that there was no trace of William Wishart on the crime index, Daniel let him board the steamer.[16] For the next six months the Security Services lost track of Wishart. It would not be until September 6, three days after the outbreak of war, that he was arrested – probably because his wife and eleven-month-old son turned up at Catterick Camp welfare offices complaining that they had been deserted and left destitute. Only then was MI5 able to piece together the story of Wishart's involvement with German Intelligence.

He had been recruited in the summer of 1938 by an attractive young German woman he met at the Military Tattoo in Roundhay Park, Leeds. According to Wishart's own statement, she said her name was 'Dora or Dinah Hookem' and that she was employed as a nurse by a local English family. They exchanged addresses and shortly afterwards 'Dora/Dinah' sent Wishart a letter holding out the prospect of work as a motor mechanic in Germany.

'She wrote to me ... and offered me if I wanted a job I could write to this address, or go to this address, and they would see about giving me a job.' After two further letters – both of which Wishart burned – he set off for the address she had given him: the Seaman's Institute in Hamburg. This address had featured in the Jessie Jordan case as a base for Abwehr operations, and the following day Wishart was contacted there by a German Intelligence handler.

'I do not know his name', Wishart said in a statement on September 26. 'He only said he comes from Dinah and his name was Fritz, a cousin or something or other, and I was to go with him, so he took me to a hotel and he paid the bill for [me] to stay there. He said all expenses would be paid if I went on.'

Wishart was happy to 'go on' and spent the next ten days being questioned and briefed by 'Fritz' in houses across the city. Nor was there any doubt about what the Abwehr agent wanted: details of British military vehicles and the technical specifications of large artillery pieces. Wishart agreed to send the information to an address 'Fritz' provided; just as in the Jessie Jordan case two years earlier, this was a post office box in Hamburg.

He returned to England with £10 as payment for his recruitment. He then went to Catterick Camp, after which he posted some of the intelligence 'Fritz' had requested. And the Abwehr was evidently pleased by what he sent: in August a letter, posted in Hull and addressed to Wishart, arrived at the ex-servicemen's club in London. It contained a cryptic message from someone signing herself 'Mother Vera', as well as three Bank of England £5 notes.

Dear Boy. I was glad to get your letter. So you are tired of wandering and want some cash. I have taken it of my savings but do not spill it.

Do not change at banks. Hope to get good news from you. Are you coming home soon?

Wishart never admitted exactly what information he gave the Abwehr, nor could he offer an explanation for the payment from 'Mother Vera'. By the time MI5 was brought in, the trail of his contacts had gone cold – though, as it noted on his file, 'it seems improbable that £15 would have been sent unless Wishart had done something since his return from Hamburg'. Under the circumstances, the best the Security Service could do was to seek Wishart's internment under the new Defence Regulations.

'This man has been voluntarily to Germany in order to arrange to do German Secret Service work against his own country', an officer in Oswald Harker's B Branch argued on September 22. 'There is insufficient evidence to justify a trial, and I therefore strongly recommend that he should be interned for the duration of the war.'[17]

If Wishart's case – and the evident failures of joined-up intelligence work it revealed – had been an isolated example, there might have been less cause for concern. But at the same time as he was sending information to Hamburg, the Abwehr recruited another British agent.

Edwin Heath was 55 years old, a con-man, a bigamist and a thief. The version of his life recorded in Metropolitan Police criminal record file No. 6437/22 showed him to have been made bankrupt in 1922 and from then until 1937 to have amassed a lengthy criminal history under his own name and an impressive number of aliases: Major Henderson, Major Percy Gordon Lennox and plain Mr E. Edwards were just a few of the identities he had been known to adopt in pursuit of easy money.

His docket included convictions for selling razor blades with forged trademarks (Marlborough Street Police Court, fined £10 with £36 10s costs); forgery and obtaining property by deception (Old Bailey, four years' penal servitude); stealing a car and obtaining money by false pretences (Old Bailey, eighteen months' hard labour); bigamy (Old Bailey, fifteen months' hard labour with seven other offences taken into consideration); and multiple counts of fraud (Liverpool Assizes, twelve months' imprisonment).

He had not confined this career in crime to the United Kingdom. In 1924 he stole a chequebook and obtained 'considerable sums in France and on the Continent' by forging its owner's signature. The following year he was arrested in Madeira for cheque frauds carried out from San Remo in Italy to San Sebastián in Spain, but quickly escaped from prison by feigning illness.

He also developed a profitable sideline in parting unsuspecting wealthy women from their money and valuables. In January 1933 he proposed marriage to a 'lady of independent means' whom he met at a seaside hotel in Falmouth, and subsequently stole jewellery worth £332 from her. He was arrested and admitted the theft, but his embarrassed victim declined to prosecute.[18] In summary, as a lengthy Special Branch report on his life noted:

> Heath is a scoundrel of the first water. He has a fairly extensive know-ledge of electrical and mechanical engineering and is an adept in financial affairs. These assets, combined with a plausible tongue, have been used by him to defraud the credulous and to prey on wealthy women.[19]

Against this background it was, perhaps, unsurprising that when, on April 30, 1939, he walked into New Scotland Yard to volunteer information about a suspicious letter he had been sent from Germany, the Metropolitan Police was somewhat sceptical. The story he told an Inspector Newton from Special Branch was that two weeks earlier he had received – allegedly unsolicited and out of the blue – a letter, posted in England but sent by a man called 'Barlen' in Duisberg in north-west Germany; the letter – which Heath said he had destroyed – contained a Bank of England £10 note. According to the police account of Heath's interview:

> The writer said he was sending this money to Heath as he had heard he was in financial difficulties, also that his firm was willing to offer Heath a commission agency. Heath said he kept the money, then wrote expressing surprise at its receipt as he had never previously heard of Barlen or his firm, and his willingness to accept the commission agency for Barlen's firm.

On April 27, 1939, Heath received a reply to his letter from 'Barlen'. Evidently he did not destroy this because he showed it to Inspector Newton. In it 'Barlen' asked Heath to meet him on May 3 at the 'German air station Essen-Mulheim', and helpfully provided the time of the plane he should take; the note also assured Heath that all his expenses would be met by 'Barlen's' firm. Two days later, Heath told the detective, he received a phone call at his wife's north London hairdressing salon; the caller would not give his name but said: 'Regarding your proposed trip: franking necessary: see Major Feldman's secretary at Carlton Terrace and things will be all right.'

Heath's ostensible purpose in reporting this to the police was to seek advice on the propriety of keeping the proposed appointment with 'Barlen'. Inspector Newton was apparently non-committal, and in the event, Heath was unable to get a passport in time; the rendezvous was postponed.

On June 1, Heath phoned Newton saying he had 'received several more letters from Barlen, asking Heath to meet him on the Continent and that some of them enclosed money'.[20] Once again he asked for police guidance; once again, none was forthcoming.

Had the Metropolitan Police Special Branch bothered to consult MI5, it would have discovered that the Security Service held a file on Edwin Heath – one which, since it explicitly highlighted his previous involvement with German Intelligence, should have rung alarm bells.

In February 1937 Heath approached Major Kitschmann, then Assistant Military Attaché at the German Embassy in London, explaining that his mother was German and offering to give information about armaments. A meeting was arranged but there was a muddle as to the rendezvous and it never took place ...

In February 1939 Heath got in touch with Major Soltmann, Kitschmann's successor at the German Embassy and arranged to call on him. Whether they met, and what passed between them if they did, is not known, but on the whole facts of this case there is an overwhelming probability that it was as a result of this démarche [stratagem] that Heath got in touch with the German Secret Service.[21]

In the absence of any advice to the contrary, Heath went to meet his contact in Brussels on June 2. Over a three-hour lunch at the Plaza Hotel, 'Barlen' asked for Heath's date and place of birth, his parents' racial lineage, his army history and whether he 'still associated with army officers in England; was he able to find out details regarding munitions and their supply; could he furnish a list of all civil and military aerodromes in England, together with maps showing their position; was he willing to act as an agent for Germany?' If so, he would be sent instructions to contact a man at the Vickers armaments works in Trafford Park, Manchester and two petrol stations in southern England. Before they parted 'Barlen' gave Heath £20 on account (£900 today) 'and assured him he would be amply repaid for any information given'.[22]

On his return, Heath went back to Special Branch and reported what had transpired. He assured Newton that he hadn't given 'a definite assurance' that he would provide 'Barlen' with the information requested, but told the detective that he was willing to work as a double agent to expose the activities of what he now knew to be a German espionage network. When, by June 19, there was still no response from Special Branch, Heath posted a letter to 'The Commissioner of Police, New Scotland Yard':

> I want to help my country if possible but it appears in the face of things that the powers that be are not interested. As far as I am concerned I feel that I could be of some assistance if I could get to know what I am to do under the circumstances as I am satisfied there is more behind this than meets the eye.
>
> Will you please let me know if I am to drop the whole thing and not communicate with my correspondent, or am I to 'lead him up the garden' & get some useful information out of him eventually for the benefit of my country.[23]

The Commissioner did not trouble to reply to this appeal, and the events of the next two months bordered on farce. Heath repeatedly telephoned and visited New Scotland Yard and sent a second letter to the Commissioner, asking for 'an assurance from the authorities that he will be in order to "run with the hare and hunt with the hounds"'.[24] Other than sending a cursory acknowledgement and saying that it had 'referred the matter to the appropriate department', the Metropolitan Police did nothing with the information Heath had provided until August 10, when Inspector Newton declined his offer of assistance and warned him not to have any future contact with the German espionage organisation.

By then it was too late. Heath had already exchanged a series of letters with his contacts and had agreed to provide intelligence – both sides used the code word 'stamps' to disguise the exact nature of the information – for which he was to be paid £200 (more than £9,000 today); he had also travelled to Amsterdam for a new meeting with his handler, during which 'Barlen' introduced him to his own 'chief' and rewarded him with an interim payment of £20.

It took until September 6 for the Metropolitan Police and MI5 to arrest Edwin Heath. When they searched his home in Hendon they discovered proof that he had been spying; he had researched the location of RAF establishments, recording the numbers of pilots and observers based at them, as well as details of the Thames ammunition works. He had also photographed barrage balloons and gasometers, and noted in his diary the addresses of two explosives companies; one, according to MI5's records, was controlled by 'one of the leading Nazi agents in this country' while the second shared the offices of Otto Karlowa, 'the acknowledged leader of the Nazi Party in London'.[25]

It was clear from the outset that, despite the clear evidence against him, it would be impossible to charge Heath with spying; he had repeatedly reported his contacts with German Intelligence to the Metropolitan Police and even sought official sanction to engage in espionage. Instead he joined the growing number of men and women interned, without trial, under the new Defence Regulations[26] – a tactic which would, very soon, cause as many problems as it appeared to solve.

At the same time that the government's Law Officers reluctantly ruled out a prosecution of Heath and William Wishart, MI5 was preparing for a trial which showed its ability to protect the country in a rather better light.

The Security Service had been watching Donald Adams since he contacted the War Office in 1936, volunteering his services as 'a secret agent in Palestine'. He was then 54 years old and, on the face of it, reasonably well qualified for the role. During the First World War he had joined the Army Service Corps in Egypt, rising to the rank of Lieutenant; when he moved from active duties to the Army reserve list in 1921, his record listed his service as 'satisfactory'.[27]

But his post-war activities in Cairo were rather less impressive. Without any regular employment, he supported himself by becoming the ponce for a succession of local prostitutes. By 1924, the authorities had had enough of the troublesome ex-soldier: in May, the British Consul wrote to the Foreign Office to advise them that Adams would be repatriated – effectively expelled – from the country with a firm recommendation that he should not be allowed back.

> I would request that instructions be given to the Passport Office to refuse Mr Adams facilities to return to Egypt, observing that he is an exceedingly undesirable character, not only on account of his habitual drunkenness, but because he has victimised more than one woman in Cairo, having lived on their earnings and then abandoned them and their illegitimate children.[28]

This chequered past led the War Office to decline Adams' offer to act as a spy on its behalf. Rebuffed by his own country, the following year he volunteered his services to German Intelligence; it was pleased to recruit the former soldier and he began sending regular reports to its cut-out agents in Holland and Belgium.

MI5 had been monitoring mail sent to several of these addresses since the discovery of Jessie Jordan's spy network. In November 1938 it intercepted a letter from Adams in which he acknowledged receipt of £10 sent to him by Kol & Company, private bankers based in Amsterdam. It was a familiar name to the Security Service; the bankers were known to be one of the Abwehr's chosen means of paying 'agents of the German Secret Service operating in Britain'. Further enquiries, in the spring and summer of 1939, revealed that 'the agents with whom Adams has been in contact are in fact identical with "Sanders" of the Jessie Jordan case and "Col" who featured in the recent Kelly case at Manchester Assizes'.[29] Hinchley-Cooke began to take a closer look at Donald Adams and his activities.

He was, in theory, a freelance racing journalist and occasional horse tipster. There are no details of his employers in his voluminous case file, but Adams' passport showed that he had sufficient funds to travel frequently to Dresden, Hannover and Hamburg, and was able to afford a flat in pleasant tree-lined road in Richmond. A Home Office warrant to monitor the mail arriving and being sent from there showed that 'he sent a certain amount of information to a number of cover addresses, and in return received irregular payments varying from £5 to £10 at a time'.

> From the correspondence which was seen it was quite clear that he was anxious to please his German masters to the best of his ability, and that he was all out to get as much money as possible from them in return.[30]

He was also evidently aware of the risks he was taking. An entry in his file in June 1939 noted: 'Recent experience shows that Adams frequently rings the changes on addresses to which he sends reports intended for the German espionage organisation. Luckily he addresses the envelopes in his own handwriting which is very distinctive.'[31]

By then, Hinchley-Cooke had amassed a slew of evidence that Adams was spying for Germany. Correspondence intercepted between February and March had revealed exchanges in which he was asked for – and had sent – secret military information, disguised in a straight-forward alphanumeric code. Two letters, in particular, were damning.

On February 1, Adams received a coded message from his handlers headed 'tips for next race'. Its contents, however, had nothing to do with horses; once deciphered it read: 'Get manual for anti-air gun for po[i]nt five [i]nch manuals and instructions of signal troops for telegraphy radio telephone set.'[32] In March, Adams supplied the information requested.

> The latest 4 dec. 5 [4.5 inch] anti-aircraft gun has a reputed range of 30,000ft. The range finder to locate aircraft is 18ft long. The shell is loaded and the gun is fired in a pit. There are 3,000 parts to each gun. Further particulars will follow.[33]

That same month Adams' handlers sent him new instructions: 'Join territorials or any army job. Thers [*sic*] big money for you.'[34] Then, in June, Adams sent a detailed report on the barrage balloon network which was being erected over London as defence against expected German bombing raids.

> These balloons are made of Egyptian Cotton (not silk), and when inflated, each balloon holds 20,000 cubic feet of hydrogen. Each balloon is attached to a motor lorry by one steel cable, which is run off a winch on the lorry, which has a crew of ten men.
>
> There are fifty of these captive balloons allocated to each squadron (in fifty vehicles, with ten men each). These balloons have a limited range according to the length of cable, and might go up to 10,000 feet. There are ten squadrons around London, and the three principal depots are in Kent, Surrey and Middlesex; situated at Kidbrook[e], Hook and at Stanmore.
>
> This gives 500 Balloons to form a chain round London, but under the revised conditions owing to the great recruiting boom, I understand squadrons are being formed around various large towns.
>
> There are eleven officers with 500 men for each complete squadron. These include one regular officer of the RAF and 50 regulars from the Royal Air Force ... all men accepted for service under 38 years must be unfit for any other service in the Forces. Many ex-service men over military age have joined ... but the present strength is far below the original authorised establishment of 60,000 men.[35]

It was the final piece of evidence MI5 needed. At 8.00am on June 30, Hinchley-Cooke and a Special Branch inspector knocked on the door of 11 Friars Stile Road in Richmond, armed with a warrant for Adams' arrest. A search of his top-floor rooms uncovered 'a large quantity of correspondence and data relating to military and air defence matters' as well as pamphlets sent to him by Goebbels' propaganda ministry. When they arrested and cautioned him, Adams was remarkably laconic, saying only, 'I see, right ho'.[36] Later that day he was charged with eighteen separate offences under the Official Secrets Act – one for each documented instance of 'obtaining, recording and communicating information calculated to be useful to an enemy'.

Throughout his time on remand, Adams maintained his innocence, claiming that while he had sent information to his contacts in Germany, he had done so as part of his job as a journalist, and that most of the material was already in the public domain; then, on the eve of his trial at the Old Bailey, he changed tack, pleading guilty to all charges. The tactic, suggested by his barrister, did not spare him the judge's wrath. 'You have pleaded guilty to one of the most shocking charges at a time like this when we are at war', Mr Justice Oliver told Adams. He then sentenced him to seven years' penal servitude.[37]

The prosecution of Donald Adams showed that, given sufficient time and resources, MI5 was able to uncover British agents working for German Intelligence, and successfully take their case to court. Unfortunately, on the outbreak of war the Security Service was short of money and manpower – and was about to become entangled in the political controversy and bureaucratic chaos caused by the government's policy of internment without trial.

CHAPTER SIX

Phoney War

'I desire to place my services and my life at the disposal of the
Reich ... Please consider me as being in your service, for any
task under any circumstances and at any time. Heil Hitler'

Letter from William Craven, British fascist,
to German Intelligence, May 1938

On Monday, October 23, 1939, Sir Vernon Kell, Director of the
Security Service (DSS), walked through the main doors of
the Foreign and Commonwealth Office building on King Charles
Street. His business that morning was not with the government's diplomatic corps, but rather with the mandarins of the Home Office, who
enjoyed the comforts of a separate section within the splendidly ornate
Whitehall address. He did not like what he found.

'D.S.S. is staggered by the atmosphere of the Home Office', Captain
Guy Liddell, Deputy Director of MI5's B Branch, noted in his diary. 'He
says they do not seem to realise that there is a war going on. He arrived
there at 9.30 ... and was unable to see anybody in authority. He could
find nobody for an hour and a half except the charwomen.'[1]

Liddell was a decorated veteran of the First World War who had
worked for the Metropolitan Police Special Branch, countering Soviet
espionage. He was transferred to MI5 in 1931, as part of one of the

periodic settlements of the turf wars between the two services, and would rise steadily through its ranks. He was also an assiduous diarist: from August 1939 to the end of the war he dictated a daily journal to his secretary – a volume which was given the codename 'Wallflower' and deemed so sensitive that until its declassification in 2002 it was kept under lock and key in the safes of successive Directors General of MI5.

Liddell's diaries offer a revealing first-hand account of the Security Service's triumphs and failures throughout the six years of the Second World War, providing both an index to otherwise secret cases and an often acerbic commentary on the succession of internal battles fought between MI5 and its political masters in Whitehall. And they make clear that, at the very moment Prime Minister Neville Chamberlain advised Hitler that Britain was at war with Germany, neither the Security Service nor the Home Office was fit for the road ahead.

*

On September 3, 1939, the Home Office was placed under the management of a new Home Secretary. Sir John Anderson was a clever and dedicated public servant but, as *The Times* delicately noted the following day, 'not in his first youth'. He was 57 years old and had spent almost all his working life as an administrator, first with the Colonial Office, then the Ministry of Shipping.

He was also a Home Office veteran, having served as Permanent Under-Secretary of State (PUS, the most senior civil servant in the department) throughout the turbulent years of the early 1920s, and had been in charge of enacting the government's policy during the 1926 General Strike. After a five-year posting to India, in 1938 he belatedly entered electoral politics, winning a seat in the House of Commons representing the Scottish Universities.[2]

But at heart, Anderson was a bureaucrat. An aloof and rigidly proper public servant – he habitually wore the Whitehall 'uniform' of wing collar, cravat, striped trousers and gold watch chain – as PUS he reportedly once rebuked an overly-friendly incoming Home Secretary, saying: 'I have been brought up in a profession which has taught me that it is wrong to give expression to emotions, either of pleasure or sorrow.'[3] His working day was similarly traditional; he arrived at his desk at 10.15am and worked until 6.15pm, with an invariable one-hour lunch break in the early afternoon. He was, in short, the quintessential mandarin.

His own PUS was cut from similar cloth. Alexander Maxwell had been a civil servant for 35 years and was deeply wedded to the belief that the Home Office was the guardian of liberal ideals, standing firm against the demands of the state to erode individual liberties.

The Security Service was, to a degree, the embodiment of those dangers. But at the beginning of the war this was rather more theoretical than real, since MI5 was in very poor shape. Kell was then 65 and in declining health, and had planned to retire the previous year: instead, he was retained on an informal rolling twelve-month contract. By September 1939 he was, according to the Service's own authorised history, out of his depth, and had failed to plan for the demands of war. Although the budget for new staff increased, enabling the total number of officers to rise to almost 100,[4] an internal review by his successor noted that their recruitment was somewhat random:

> When the war broke out, each officer 'tore round' to rope in likely people; when they knew of none themselves, they asked their acquaintances. Occasionally recruits were brought in who knew other 'possibles' ... If I am correctly informed, there have been cases in which recruits have been taken on by divisions (or sections) without so much as informing Administration.[5]

This haphazard process was not entirely unprofitable: among an array of talented lawyers and academics brought in to the Service, Guy Liddell recruited Victor Rothschild, a gifted polymath who founded MI5's first counter-sabotage branch and who would, in time, run one of its most important undercover agents. But it added to the existing chaos caused by an enforced change of address.

At the end of August 1939 the Security Service moved out of Thames House and into the cells of Wormwood Scrubs prison in west London. The move was needed to accommodate the Service's increased workload, but it was so sudden and ill-planned that the arriving occupants found unemptied chamber pots in their new 'offices' – none of which had handles or locks on the inside of the doors, thus ensuring 'a good chance of being locked in by unwary visitors turning the outside door handle on leaving'.[6] A rather more fundamental problem was where to locate the Registry files on those individuals suspected of spying or treachery: the solution – a section of the prison cleared of its previous inmates – would, within a year, prove disastrous, when it took a direct hit during a bombing raid.

By the time Anderson took the reins, the Home Office and the Security Service were at loggerheads over how to handle the threat – perceived or real – of potential Fifth Columnists across the country. Initially, the Home Office had planned to adopt the First World War policy of interning all enemy aliens; by contrast, MI5 argued that this was 'unnecessary on security grounds and inflicts great hardship on innocent people'.[7]

But as war drew closer, the Home Office reversed its policy. In January 1939 it noted in a memorandum that while there would be no blanket policy of mass internment, once the conflict began it was 'almost certain that this course would very soon be forced on the Government by public opinion, especially in the event of serious air raids'.[8] By the end of August it had set up plans for 120 tribunals across the country which were to sort the 'aliens' into three groups. Category A covered the 569 German nationals – all men: women were specifically excluded – who posed such a threat that they were to be interned immediately. Category B was for those deemed a lesser threat; the 6,800 aliens in it would be subject only to restrictions on their movement and employment. Those placed in the final classification – the vast majority of those who had fled the Reich for sanctuary in Britain – were to be left completely at liberty. On August 28, Maxwell informed Kell that MI5 was expected to service the tribunals, providing evidence on approximately 70,000 men and women.

It was a recipe for disaster. In September, MI5 was required to process an average of 6,800 vetting enquiries *per week*.[9] Jack Curry, a B Branch officer who had been investigating domestic fascists since 1934, complained about 'the impossible task of obtaining concrete evidence against individual enemy aliens' – a burden which overwhelmed the Security Service 'in a mass of detailed enquiries'.[10] His colleague

Guy Liddell estimated that 'four-fifths' of MI5's already over-stretched time was devoted to working for the Aliens' Tribunals, and that even the evidence it managed to collect was frequently ignored.

> The proceedings were laughable ... Our records were not consulted, except to a small extent in the metropolitan area; the chairmen had no standards and no knowledge of the political background of those who came before them; no record of the proceedings were kept.[11]

The demands of servicing the Aliens' Tribunals left MI5 short of time, money and manpower to focus on catching German spies still at large. That there were still Abwehr agents operating in Britain – despite a substantial evacuation of Nazi Party officials and Embassy staff on the outbreak of war – is clear from an entry in Guy Liddell's diary on September 6:

> Hinchley-Cooke, on the basis of a suspect telegram, interrogated a German at the London Hotel and took certain of his correspondence including a letter in code to somebody up north. The code had the appearance of being a perfectly ordinary business one, but the man at the London Hotel was obviously so alarmed that enquiries were made. It now turns out that the individual in the north, Raydt,[12] has confessed that he was a German spy.[13]

Just as pressing, however, was the requirement for Kell's officers to investigate the threat posed by pro-Nazi British citizens. And, in a carbon copy of the problems posed by the Aliens' Tribunals, MI5's position was worsened by the Home Office policy on interning British citizens.

From September 1, Regulation 18B of the Emergency Powers Act 1939 gave the Home Secretary the right to sign an order for the detention without trial of anyone he suspected with 'reasonable cause to be of hostile origin or associations or to have been recently concerned in acts prejudicial to the public safety or the defence of the realm'. Because this represented a direct contradiction of centuries of English law, the Home Office created two key safeguards: anyone arrested and interned under the regulation was entitled to be given a statement of the case against him (or her) and to have the right to challenge this in person.

Anderson's predecessor, Sir Samuel Hoare, had intended that such challenges would be heard by a sitting judge – effectively ensuring that the resulting decision had the force of law. Under Anderson and Maxwell's direction, the Home Office rowed back on this limitation to executive powers: instead, they established an Advisory Committee, composed of the great and good, who would hear appeals but – crucially – whose recommendations would not be binding on the Home Secretary. It was a classic Whitehall fudge and one which would backfire almost immediately.

William Craven, a 25-year-old unemployed Liverpool clerk, was arrested on September 1, 1939 – one of the very first British citizens to be detained under Regulation 18B.[14] Craven was a card-carrying fascist and – in his own words – 'a strong admirer of the Germans and Adolf Hitler'.[15]

In 1936 he had joined Oswald Mosley's British Union of Fascists, and for two years was one of its most prominent public speakers in the north-west. In March 1938 he resigned his membership, disillusioned by the movement's failure to win wider public support. 'As a Fascist', he subsequently explained, 'it was pretty hopeless to try and get people to see what I call their responsibilities.'[16] Six months later, however, he was back in the fold: the local BUF membership officer bent the party's rules (which required a longer period between resignation and rejoining), telling Craven that 'you are a true and sincere Fascist'.

In the intervening period, Craven had applied to the Liverpool branch of the Deutsche Arbeitsfront – the Nazi Party-controlled German organisation which replaced independent trade unions – volunteering his services as a clerk. But it was a letter he had written a year earlier which had brought him to the attentions of MI5.

On May 5, 1938, the General Post Office (GPO) sent Hinchley-Cooke a photostat of a message it had just intercepted. The envelope, postmarked May 3, was addressed to 'The German War Ministry, Berlin' and sent care of Walther Reinhardt, the German Consul in Liverpool who was to feature in the Joseph Kelly case. In the letter, sent from his lodgings in Toxteth, Craven declared his loyalty to the Third Reich and volunteered to work on its behalf.

As a Nordic Aryan I believe the future of white civilization is in the hands of Germany, united under Adolf Hitler, and because of my beliefs I have severed my connection with the British Union of Fascists. I desire to place my services and my life at the disposal of the Reich and eventually to take the honour of becoming a German citizen, to which end I am prepared to formally renounce my British nationality[,] an act which in spirit I have relinquished.

I am 24 years of age, single and of an athletic disposition ... at the moment I am studying the German language. Please consider me as being in your service, for any task under any circumstances and at any time. Heil Hitler.[17]

William Craven was precisely the sort of domestic, pro-Nazi fascist at whom Defence Regulation 18B was aimed. Hinchley-Cooke placed Craven's name on the Suspect List, and within hours of the internment powers coming into force, Liverpool Police arrested him. What followed was farcical.

On Monday, September 25, the Home Office Advisory Committee convened in the convivial surroundings of Burlington House, a Palladian mansion opposite Fortnum & Mason on Piccadilly. The chairman was Sir Walter Monckton, a first-class amateur cricketer for Eton and Oxford and advisor to King Edward VIII during the 1936 abdication crisis.

Although he was a lawyer, Monckton had never tried a case, much less sat as a judge. Nor were the three other Committee members any better fitted for the task. Sir Arthur Hazlerigg was the 13th Baronet of Noseley Hall in Leicestershire. Like Monckton he had played first-class cricket, captaining the county side for three years. Other than appointments as High Sheriff and then Lord Lieutenant of Leicestershire, he had no professional qualifications which would have prepared him to hear appeals. The other two members, William Collison and J.J. Mallon, were both academics.

The transcript of that morning's proceedings revealed the futility of handing vital decisions on national security to untrained aristocrats and pillars of the educational establishment: the Committee's questions were vague and prolix, allowing Craven to dissemble, justify his actions or – when the occasion demanded – lie outright.

He admitted volunteering his loyalty and services to German Intelligence – sentiments he said were 'quite genuine' but written during 'what I might call a period of disillusionment ... I did believe, apart from the Government of Germany, or the present war, that the future of western civilization had gone.' Similarly, his offer to assist the Deutsche Arbeitsfront was entirely innocent: although he told Monckton that he knew that this was a Nazi Party organisation, 'I did not intend to be a spy; I wanted to assist them in any way I could in a clerical capacity ... as far as I know, the Labour Front had nothing to do with espionage services.'[18]

The Security Service knew that all organs of the Nazi Party in Britain had been directed to develop intelligence and cultivate agents. But since the design of the Appeals Committee hearings did not allow for MI5 to be represented during an appellant's testimony, there was no opportunity for MI5 to challenge Craven's claims; nor did the Committee members do so.

Instead, they sent a report to the Home Secretary recommending that Craven should be released; on October 26 Maxwell signed an order ending his detention. It would not be the last that the Home Office, the Advisory Committee and MI5 heard of William Craven, but the case set the tone for all that was to follow between them: from October onwards, all three departments would become locked in an increasingly bitter feud at the very time a unified effort to combat the threat of pro-Nazi British citizens was needed.

The war in Europe had not, at that stage, developed into the major conflict it would shortly become. Although German U-boats had sunk two British battleships – HMS *Courageous* and HMS *Royal Oak*, with the loss of 1,346 men – there were no land battles on the Western Front. Winston Churchill, then First Sea Lord, described this as a 'twilight' period, while newspapers referred to 'the Bore War' or 'the Phoney War', and complained that Britain's main military objective appeared to be the dropping of millions of propaganda leaflets over Germany. But on the Home Front, MI5 was waging a very real war against domestic traitors.

On September 4, Arthur Graham Owens – a short, chain-smoking Welsh electrical engineer of dubious honesty and looser morality

– contacted the Metropolitan Police Special Branch to volunteer his services as an agent. It was a remarkable and brazen move: Owens had been previously – if briefly – employed by MI6 during the summer of 1936, providing it with intelligence gathered during his business trips to German naval bases in Kiel. Two years later, however, he was recruited by Dr Nikolaus Ritter, the Abwehr spy-handler who had run agents in Britain. In return for regular payments and the provision of attractive women as sexual partners, Owens signed up with German Intelligence. It recorded him as agent A3504, assigning him the code-name Johnny.[19]

In September 1938 he made contact with MI5, ostensibly after a change of heart, and agreed to work as its informant. Early in 1939 he handed over a shortwave radio transmitter he had been given by his German paymasters: keen to keep the nascent double-cross scheme going, Major T.A. ('Tar') Robertson had the set returned to Owens. The following August he used it to provide genuine intelligence to Ritter – a betrayal which led to his arrest on September 1939.

Robertson would go on – with varying degrees of success – to turn Owens into a double, possibly triple agent, adding the British codename 'Snow' to his existing German cryptonym. As such, his case would be largely removed from MI5's B Branch, tasked with uncovering traitors on the Home Front.[20] However, it did throw up evidence of another British-based agent employed by Dr Ritter.

MI5 knew that Owens had been receiving regular cash payments from his Abwehr controller, sent through the mail from a cut-out in England. Agent 'Snow/Johnny' did not know the identity of his pay-master and by the autumn of 1939, the Security Service had been unable to trace him or her. Then, in November, it had a stroke of luck.

In the most recent remittance, three of the four Bank of England £5 notes had been stamped on the back with the words 'S & Co. Ltd' – an identification mark used by the West End department store Selfridge's. In common with other large London emporia at the time, Selfridge's provided a cashier service which enabled its customers to cash cheques and change currency. On November 17, armed with the notes' serial numbers, Robertson's deputy, J. Richman Stopford, interviewed the cashiers: one recalled handing them to a distinctive customer.

She told me that a tall elderly lady with grey hair, probably wearing glasses, dressed in black or a dark costume with black furs and carrying a dark, rather large attaché case, had taken five £1 notes out of an envelope in her handbag and asked if the assistant could get her a £5 note in exchange as she wished to send it away. The assistant said that the lady was particularly charming and well-spoken.[21]

Unfortunately, neither the cashier nor her assistant had checked the woman's identity. But Stopford, a former banker, saw that her particular method of operation might provide a trail which could be followed.

Her technique appears to be to draw £1 notes from her bank or somewhere else, and turn them into £5 notes at any suitable place such as a store, thinking that in this way she cannot be traced by obtaining £5 notes from a bank. She is probably a person of means and probably lives in the country, having come up to London to shop. She may live in the district not far from Bournemouth and Southampton, as two previous remittances [to Owens] were posted at those towns.

It may be that this new technique of making payments has been communicated to other German paying agents. If any notes that are found have a stamp on them, and the date of posting can be ascertained, it should not be difficult to trace the circumstances of the note being obtained in the same way as I have done at Selfridge's. It is important that it should be done quickly, so that whoever hands out the note has not forgotten the description of the person to whom it was given.

Stopford's memo evidently rang some bells in a different branch of MI5. For more than a year Robert Wiggins, a retired soldier from Parkstone, near Bournemouth, had been sending complaints to the War Office about a neighbour he believed to be an active German sympathiser. Mathilde Krafft was the 64-year-old widow of a German national who had taken British citizenship; she had been overlooked as a candidate for the internment of aliens both because she was British by marriage (although she retained a German passport) and because women were specifically excluded from Category A, the classification which led to automatic detention. She lived in an isolated house overlooking the harbour and, according to Wiggins, made no secret of her pro-Nazi views; his warnings, however, had apparently not been heeded and when Stopford and Robertson went to interview him in early December he 'expressed extreme indignation that none of his letters should have been answered until after a very long delay when a form was sent to him asking what his letters said'.[22]

Checks with the local police revealed that it, too, had raised suspicions about Mrs Krafft – not least because, from 1937 onwards, she made repeated journeys to Hamburg. More tellingly, the manager of the Midland Bank branch where she kept an account provided evidence of a series of suspicious transactions; each followed her German trips and largely coincided with the subsequent payments to Owens.

> The examination of Mrs Krafft's account showed that she had drawn out on many occasions the sum of £25[23] all in £1 treasury notes. The three particular dates of October 23rd, November 1st and November 13th, 1939 [the dates of payments to Owens] all had entries to show the drawing of £25 in cash.[24]

Given its location, MI5 ruled out setting up observation of Mrs Krafft's house. But in late November a Home Office warrant to intercept incoming and outgoing mail yielded a letter showing that she planned to take the train to London on December 7, for a meeting with W.M. Muller & Co., her regular travel agency. Stopford arranged for the Selfridge's cashier and her assistant to meet him at Waterloo station that morning: together they watched passengers disembarking from the two lunchtime Bournemouth trains, but neither woman was able to spot Mrs Krafft. Undeterred, Stopford hailed a taxi and headed over to the travel agency.

> I took the two girls to Moorgate and kept observation on Muller's office from about 2.10pm till 3.[0]5pm. There was an elderly lady standing in the office talking to two men and Mrs Longstaff and Miss Beedell [the cashier and her assistant] walked by the window and identified her as the woman to whom they had given the £5 notes

in Selfridge's ... Neither Mrs Longstaff nor Miss Beedell had any doubt about Mrs Krafft being identical with the woman they had described to me.[25]

On the surface the operation had been a success: the identification, the evidence of the notes sent to Owens as well as her suspicious travel and banking transactions were more than enough to justify arresting Mathilde Krafft. But, in the hope of tracing other Abwehr agents in Britain for whom she was the paymaster, MI5 decided to wait and to keep her under observation. This, too, was good practice, but what followed would highlight the problems which continued to undermine the Security Service's best efforts.

The Home Office warrant produced further intercepted letters: these showed that Mrs Krafft was in regular correspondence with a Miss Editha Dargel in Copenhagen. Denmark was then a neutral country, but its pro-British government was under increasing pressure from domestic fascists, and its capital was known to be a forward operating base for the Abwehr.

MI5 asked MI6 to undertake discreet enquiries about Miss Dargel; it, in turn, passed the request to Danish police who, in January 1940, interrogated her vigorously, in the process revealing the involvement of British Intelligence. The move – 'a bad slip-up', as Guy Liddell noted in his diary – produced a disastrous outcome.

> The Danish Police blundered in and asked her whether she knew a Mrs Krafft, hence a letter from Editha Dargel to Mrs Krafft telling her not to correspond in future and a wireless communication to 'Snow' that his friends are closing down for the time being.[26]

With their target alerted, and the trail now cold, the Security Service cut its losses and some weeks later Mathilde Krafft joined the small group of women interned under Regulation 18B in Holloway prison. What made the debacle even worse was that the clumsy approach to Editha Dargel had been entirely unnecessary: among the thousands of files crammed into the Registry's temporary home in Wormwood Scrubs prison was a dossier on her dating back to the spring of 1938.

This showed that MI5 had been aware of her connection with Mrs Krafft – she was even listed as her adopted daughter; more importantly, the file recorded that she had been expelled from Britain in spring 1939 due to her work on behalf of the Deutsche Arbeitsfront and German Intelligence – activities which were, on the Security Service's own recommendations, deemed dangerous to Britain's national interest.[27]

The Krafft and Dargel failures suggested that too many demands were being placed on a Security Service that was both still amateurish and over-stretched. Two other cases – both revealed only in brief and fragmentary ancillary documents – strengthened that impression.

In December 1939 the Metropolitan Police Special Branch received a tip-off from a source inside Oswald Mosley's British Union. Guy Liddell recorded the incident in his daily journal.

> A man called Millbank, a member of the British Union of Fascists, has reported to Special Branch that a Miss Dorrie Knowles has asked him to communicate certain information to Germany relating to explosives being manufactured by the firm in which she works. Both the girl and Millbank have been interviewed and we are suggesting to Special Branch that her house should be searched. She is only seventeen, but nonetheless a sophisticated and a confirmed liar. Her mother, who is of German origin, is in a mental home.[28]

The young would-be spy was evidently unshaken by her interrogation and determined to carry out her mission. Four days later, on December 7, Liddell wrote again:

> Dorrie Knowles, the 17-year-old girl with a German mother, is being very difficult. She still intends to engage in espionage ... on behalf of Germany if she is given a chance. It seems likely that we shall have to intern her under 18b. D.S.S. [Sir Vernon Kell] is discussing the case with Maxwell.[29]

Despite this intransigence – and despite previous trials of would-be German spies – Dorrie Knowles was never prosecuted. There is no trace of an MI5 file on her in the National Archives, nor is there any indication that the Home Office agreed to intern her under Defence Regulation 18B, and even if it did, whether the Advisory Committee subsequently recommended her release. Dorrie Knowles simply disappears from the official history of British citizens eager to betray their country during wartime.

Records of the second case are even more inadequate. Olive Hamilton-Roe was a young society woman who belonged to what seemed a faintly bohemian set of equally privileged friends, centred on the Russian Tea Rooms in South Kensington. She was also serving in the Women's Auxiliary Air Force, working at a military base somewhere in the south-east, where WAAF members handled ciphers, codes, and reconnaissance information, as well as crewing the radar station and the barrage balloon unit.

In October 1939 Hamilton-Roe was charged, under the Official Secrets Act, with possession of 'confidential documents which were likely to be of assistance to an invader': the documents had been stolen from the WAAF base. She was fined £20 – equivalent to almost £1,000 today.

As with Dorrie Knowles, there is no MI5 file on Olive Hamilton-Roe in the National Archives. The only reference to her – and to her crime – is a fleeting note in the file on one of her fashionable set of friends.[30] Yet that group would, within six months, be at the centre of one of the biggest spy scandals of the war – and one which would reveal the extent of the threat posed by pro-Nazi British fascists.

CHAPTER SEVEN

'Perish Judah!'

'All really true friends of Germany should be prepared to work
against this war, even to the extent of espionage or sabotage'
T. Victor-Rowe, organiser, The Nordic League, September 1939

In July 1939, Herbert von Dirksen, the Third Reich's Ambassador to
the Court of St James, sat down at his desk in the German Embassy
in Carlton House Terrace to compose a dispatch to his masters in Berlin
about public opinion in London towards the looming war.

The signs were not hopeful: a year earlier, as the Munich crisis
smouldered, he warned Hitler about the 'psychotic' attitudes of the
British people, bluntly advising that 'They are ready to fight should their
government show them that this is necessary in order to put an end
to the subjectively experienced threats and uncertainty'.[1] One trend,
however, offered crumbs of comfort.

> Anti-Semitic attitudes are revealed more clearly by conversations with
> the man in the street than by press sources.
>
> Here, except in Left-ish circles, one can speak of a widespread
> resentment against the Jews which, in some instances, has already
> assumed the form of hate. The view that the Jews want to drive Britain
> into war with Germany finds widespread belief.[2]

A month later, Dirksen – himself an anti-Semite who later boasted of being 'proud of my purely Germanic blood'[3] – was relieved of his post and the German Embassy shuttered when Britain declared war. He had, though, been largely correct in his assessment of the public mood: a report by the Mass-Observation social research organisation* in November 1939 found that 17 per cent of those whose opinions were sampled (or overheard) 'gave a cynical reason for Britain's war aims, including many statements that it was "for the Jews"'.[4]

Anti-Semitism had been endemic in Britain for more than a thousand years, but in the 1920s and 1930s, the widespread dissemination of *The Protocols of the Elders of Zion* – a bogus document which purported to show the existence of an (entirely fictional) international Jewish conspiracy – helped it move beyond its heartland in the aristocratic elite. During the years of the Depression it gained a foothold in the middle and working classes – both affected by mass unemployment and Britain's financial crises.

By the 1930s it became overt: a prejudice that dared not only to say its name, but which provided a platform for those seeking – and many of those occupying – public office. In March 1933, Edward Doran, Conservative MP for Tottenham, took to his feet in the House of Commons to denounce the threat posed by the arrival of Jewish refugees in Britain, demanding that the Home Secretary 'take steps to prevent any alien Jews from entering this country from Germany'.[5] Six years later, after Hitler's anti-Semitic laws had forced thousands into exile and incarcerated many more in concentration camps, the Reverend James Black, Moderator Elect of the Church of Scotland, felt able to give a speech in Greenock entitled 'The Enigma of the Jew'. According to an account in the *Glasgow Herald*:

> Dr Black said that politically the Jewish question presented the greatest problem in Europe today. There were only two ways to convert the Jews, and these were to fight them or to convert them ...

---

* Mass-Observation was a private organisation founded by anthropologist Tom Harrison in 1937, with a mission to record everyday life in Britain by means of 'listening in' on conversations and the collation of diaries by volunteers. During the Second World War it also undertook surveys on behalf of the British government.

Herr Hitler today was only imitating others, and his methods had done no good. The problem which the Jews presented was that they had the presence among other nationalities of a race of people with no land of their own who still wished to preserve their racial identity and remain unassimilated with the people among whom they dwelt.[6]

Evidently, the Reverend Black's views raised no eyebrows in clerical circles. Within months his position as temporary Moderator – essentially its leading cleric and public face – was confirmed by the Church's General Assembly. Nor was he an isolated example. In England, the Reverend Henry Dymock, Vicar of St Bede's church in Bristol, regularly pronounced his views that Jews were guilty of 'vile usury', and that they sought to engulf the world 'in a bath of blood' through their control of the national press.[7] The Church of England took no action against him, or those of his fellow clerics who preached anti-Semitism. Little wonder, then, that in 1936 a leading fascist newspaper was able to assure its readers that 'there is nothing whatever inconsistent [in their political beliefs] with Christian teaching; rather between Christianity and Fascism there is a harmony of ideals'.[8]

Anti-Semitism was not, of course, the root cause of British fascism; rather, it provided a fertile loam for the seed to germinate and grow; then, as it flourished, the plant and the soil became so tightly bound as to be indistinguishable.

The premier political 'brand' was Oswald Mosley's British Union of Fascists and National Socialists (later shortened to the less provocative 'British Union').* Within two years of its formation in 1932 it had attracted 40,000 members,[9] and its weekly newspapers, *Action* and *Blackshirt*, boasted circulations of 26,000 and 33,000 respectively.

In November 1933 the Home Office instructed MI5 to monitor Mosley's growing movement – though unaccountably this was not to begin until the spring of the following year.[10] It was concerned by

---

* Sir Oswald Mosley, a former MP – first for the Conservative Party, then for Labour – formed the British Union of Fascists in 1932. Its policies combined Keynesian-style economics with protectionism and, from 1936 onwards, became increasingly anti-Semitic. Its members adopted black uniforms, modelled on those worn in Nazi Germany.

the potential threat to public order posed by thousands of violent uniformed BUF members bent on confrontation with Jewish communities, rather than by the question of whether the party was – or could be – a danger to national security. In part this was the result of advice from Maxwell Knight who, by dint of his previous infiltration of the British Fascisti, had become one of the Security Service's few 'experts' on the movement. Reporting on information gleaned from his contacts within Mosley's organisation, Knight consistently downplayed the potential for trouble, insisting that the BUF was motivated by 'a genuine, if wrongheaded patriotism'.[11]

By April 1934 Knight was forced to backtrack. MI5 discovered that to keep his party afloat, Mosley had sought – and was receiving – regular large donations from Mussolini: in one year alone £60,000 – equivalent to £3 million today – was paid into a secret account held at the Charing Cross branch of the Westminster Bank.[12] This clear evidence of a foreign fascist state funding the leading British fascist party should have caused the Security Service real concern.

Yet, although it prompted Sir Vernon Kell to seek information on the movement from chief constables across the country, he subsequently felt able to advise the Home Office that the prospect of a fascist coup was 'still far away'.[13]

For a time – at least as far as the BUF was concerned – Kell's assessment seemed realistic. The violence at Mosley's Olympia rally in June 1934, when stewards ejected anti-fascist disrupters, led the *Daily Mail* – hitherto the party's most influential supporter in Fleet Street – to withdraw its backing, and by October 1935 membership had fallen to just 5,000.[14]

But the British Union was only the most publicly visible vanguard of the wider fascist movement; in its shadow a handful of smaller – often rivalrous – groups sprouted. None ever achieved more than a few thousand members, many of whom were promiscuous in their loyalties, belonging to several organisations at the same time. But these tended to be much more militantly anti-Semitic and pro-Nazi than Mosley's party, and each would produce leaders who, in the early days of the war, would embark on the road towards a violent fascist coup d'état.

The first group, the Imperial Fascist League (IFL), had been formed in 1928 by Arnold Leese, a retired veterinary surgeon from Stamford, Lincolnshire, who moved to Guildford in Surrey the better to promote his cause to the middle classes resident in the home counties.

Overtly anti-Semitic and pro-Nazi, IFL members wore a uniform of black shirt, khaki breeches, puttees over black boots, together with an armband depicting the Union flag with a swastika imposed on the top. It also published its own newspaper, *The Fascist*, and pumped out a stream of rabid pamphlets on the subject of racial nationalism and the danger posed by 'the Jew'.

Leese successfully courted notoriety through a series of leaflets in which he accused Jews of conducting ritual murder against Christians (a resurrection of the old blood libel which had been one of the central planks of anti-Semitism across Europe for several centuries). Finally, in September 1936 he and his printer were charged with seditious libel and conspiring to cause a public mischief. They were acquitted on the first count but jailed for six months on the second.[15]

By any definition, Leese was a menace. But, strapped for funds and resources, the Security Service did little to monitor him or his organisation. Instead it was left to the Board of Deputies of British Jews to infiltrate an undercover agent into IFL meetings. In April 1937, the Board's spy gained access to a lecture, given by IFL vice-president Henry Hamilton Beamish and Leese, to the weekly 'Graduate Association' (leading members) meeting. According to his report:

> Beamish told the audience that 'Germany was a great country because Hitler had named the enemy' and that 'the IFL knew of three remedies to the Jewish question: to kill them, to sterilize them or segregate them' ...
>
> After the applause had subsided Leese then spoke to the effect that national socialism had been vilified in this country and that Germany was supposed to have nudist camps of unclean practices, which was untrue, but the IFL's photographers had penetrated into nudist camps in this country, which were perfectly foul and run by Jews.[16]

If Leese's remarks appeared bizarre and clownish, those by Beamish – the son of an admiral who had been aide de camp to Queen Victoria, and the brother of a Conservative MP – openly supported the pogroms and persecution of Nazi Germany. Nor was there much doubt about the loyalties of the IFL's 'Graduate Association': the meeting ended with all its members rising to their feet, giving the Nazi salute and shouting 'Heil Hitler'.

There is no reliable figure for the size of the IFL. Leese claimed a membership running into the thousands, but the reports of the Board of Deputies' undercover informants suggested that number was grossly inflated. Yet it, and most of the other 'fringe' fascist parties, were so vehemently anti-Semitic and unswervingly loyal to Germany that they represented a genuine threat.

The National Socialist League (NSL) was a case in point. It was formed in March 1937 by two former BUF officials, William Joyce and John Beckett; both had been expelled by Mosley in one of the fascist movement's frequent schisms and resultant financial crises.

The NSL was generously funded by Alex Scrimgeour, a wealthy stockbroker, and unequivocally rooted in an admiration for Hitler and the 'achievements' of the Third Reich. It was also explicitly 'revolutionary'.

Joyce set out the party's ideology in a pamphlet entitled *National Socialism Now*, which called for a specifically British version of German Nazism. This, argued Joyce, was a philosophy which represented 'the revolutionary yearning of the people to cast off gross, sordid, democratic materialism without having to put on the shackles of Marxian [*sic*] materialism'.[17] By the time this manifesto was published in 1937, both Joyce and Beckett had realised that war would come, sooner or later. When it did, they pronounced, the proper role of Britons in a European conflict was to be Hitler's helpmates. 'If Germany needs help in hurling Orientals back to the Orient, she is entitled to receive it from those who prefer white manhood and government to any other.'[18]

The National Socialist League did not last long.[19] Beckett, a former MP for the Independent Labour Party, quit in late 1938 to form the British Council for Christian Settlement in Europe and then the British People's Party. Both would soon become involved in plotting a fascist coup.

Joyce meanwhile fled to Berlin in August 1939 to avoid arrest under the forthcoming Regulation 18B. Here he began making propaganda broadcasts on behalf of the Nazis, which were beamed back to Britain on shortwave radio: because of his sneering, quasi-upper-class delivery, he was quickly dubbed 'Lord Haw-Haw'.

The real importance of the NSL, however, was not its limited life-span or meagre membership, but its apparently deliberate policy of forming covert alliances with other equally shadowy groups. One of these in particular would play a major role in fascist plots to betray Britain to Germany during the months of the 'Phoney War'.

In 1935 two German agents employed by the Nordische Gesellschaft (Nordic Association) – ostensibly an organisation dedicated to strength-ening political and cultural ties in the German–Nordic diaspora, but in reality an arm of German Intelligence – arrived in England.[20] Their mission was to establish a pro-Nazi beachhead inside middle- and upper-class British society.

The Nordic League – as the new organisation styled itself – purported to be 'an association, rather than an organisation, of race-conscious Britons', dedicated to supporting 'those patriotic bodies known to be engaged in exposing and frustrating the Jewish stranglehold on our Nordic realm'.[21] Rather more accurately, it was the semi-public face of a clandestine and avowedly violent group of anti-Semites, The White Knights of Britain, also known as 'The Hooded Men'.

This 'secret society' based itself on the Ku Klux Klan in America, and had a self-proclaimed mission 'to rid the world of the merciless Jewish reign of terror'.[22] The Knights shared their London headquarters with the Nordic League – rooms above a pub in Lamb's Conduit Street, off Theobalds Road – and met in halls draped with swastikas. Members were required to swear a blood-oath of loyalty to the organisation's patron saint, King Edward I, who, by a royal edict in July 1290, had expelled all Jews from England. The penalty for disclosing any of the secrets of the order was death.

The Knights' leader – he was called 'Chancellor' in homage to Hitler's original title – was a virulently anti-Semitic and fervently pro-Nazi former Royal Naval officer, Commander E.H. Cole; when the

Knights officially merged with the Nordic League in 1937, Cole took over the reins of the new organisation.

For four years the Nordic League held public meetings at which speakers from the Imperial Fascist League, the National Socialist League and Admiral Barry Domvile's The Link called for the shooting of Jews and praised Hitler; its motto was 'Perish Judah'.[23] The Board of Deputies of British Jews sent undercover agents to infiltrate several Nordic League meetings. One of these spies in particular – a former Special Branch inspector named Pavey (no first name is given in his reports) – provided a revealing picture of the League and its supporters.

The meetings he attended attracted between 60 and 200 members and included 'a fair sprinkling of women, obviously of the upper classes'. At one talk on March 27, 1939 Major General John 'Boney' Fuller – the well-connected military leader who had been a personal guest of the Fuehrer at his 50th birthday celebrations – regaled his audience with his thoughts on 'The Hebrew Mysteries'; Pavey noted the presence in the crowd of 'expensively dressed society ladies' and men 'who bore the unmistakeable stamp of the army officer in mufti'.[24]

The League was primarily an upper-middle-class body (as opposed to Mosley's more determinedly populist BUF), but there was crossover between it and the working-class fascist movement. On May 15, 1939, Richard 'Jock' Houston, formerly one of the BUF's most fiery rabble-rousers, was invited to speak at a League meeting. Cole introduced him as 'a house painter', before warning the upper-crust audience that there was no room for snobbish attitudes in the fascist movement.

According to Pavey's report, Cole then denounced the recently reintroduced limited conscription of men to the armed forces – a somewhat belated preparation for war with Germany grudgingly agreed by Prime Minister Neville Chamberlain on April 27 – as the result of underhand machinations by 'International Jew Money Power'. He then demanded that Houston should go back and 'tell your people' to join the army willingly, receive military training and then, 'By God! Tell them to shoot the Jews'.[25]

For good measure, Cole called Hitler 'that Man of God across the sea, that Great Crusader ... for whom one would be proud to die'[26] and pronounced that 'extermination is the only solution to the Jew problem in Palestine'.[27] Nor could Cole be dismissed as a bigoted but otherwise harmless loudmouth: Home Office files on the Nordic League show that after at least one meeting he 'drove to the German Embassy, arriving at about 11.30pm and remaining until 12.45am'.[28]

Cole's contacts with officials of increasingly hostile governments were not an isolated concern. At least two other leading Nordic League officials were communicating with the intelligence services of Germany and its close ally, Japan.*

Serocold Skeels was a sometime journalist and private tutor (he had a habit of styling himself 'Professor' although he had never taught in anything other than secondary schools). Born in 1874, educated at Malvern College and Wadham College, Oxford, he had been a missionary in South Africa before serving in the Boer War as a trooper in a British infantry regiment. On the outbreak of the First World War he returned to England and obtained a commission. He did not, however, see action, getting no closer to the front line than a recruiting office in northern England.

By 1933 he had become rabidly anti-Semitic and, in the words of a subsequent MI5 report, 'identified himself with the Fascist movement'. He joined the Imperial Fascist League and in September travelled to Berlin to meet Nazi Party leaders. Evidently the trip went well: Julius Streicher, Gauleiter of Franconia[29] and publisher of Hitler's favourite Jew-baiting newspaper, *Der Stürmer*, was sufficiently impressed to recognise him as the official representative of the IFL and invited him to address a mass meeting in Nuremberg. Skeels' speech gave a clear indication of his admiration for – and loyalty to – the Third Reich.

> We know that the question before you tomorrow is 'are you for the Nordic race or are you for the Jewish race?' ... We desire friendship between Germany and England. We are your Nordic brothers and never again shall there be war between our peoples. On my return

---

* Although the Tripartite Act, formally cementing an alliance between the Axis powers of Germany, Japan and Italy, was not signed until September 1940, Berlin and Tokyo had committed themselves to the Anti-Comintern Pact against the USSR in 1936. After the signing, Nazi Germany's government included the Japanese people in their concept of 'honorary Aryans'.

to England I shall tell the truth for Germany. In England today the gateways to truth are shut and the Jews have all the keys, but we shall force them open with truth. You have won in spite of everything. Our fight is beginning. Sieg Heil! Heil Hitler![30]

Skeels was true to his word. In January 1934 he stood (unsuccessfully) as Parliamentary candidate in Cambridge for the United British Party (UBP), a short-lived and vehemently anti-Semitic fringe group, and used his platform to accuse Mosley of being 'a charlatan who was being paid by the Jews'.[31] The IFL expelled him when it discovered his involvement with the UBP, and he quickly moved on to the Nordic League; within its warm embrace he became, according to MI5's reports, 'one of the more extreme and more unbalanced' speakers at its meetings.[32]

Because the Nordic League operated largely in secret, there are no newspaper reports of Skeels' speeches. But a contemporary Home Office file entitled 'Jew Baiting by Fascists, 1936–1937' gives an indication of their contents. In March 1939 Skeels had, it recorded, denounced preparations for the coming conflict with Germany, declaring that 'it was a Jews' war ... that we should be asked to fight. Hitler had sworn to destroy the world's Number One Enemy. He was succeeding beyond measure. The Jews and their rotten masonic institutions were disappearing under the Crusader's hammer blows – and we should be asked to stop them. It was unthinkable.'[33]

But Serocold Skeels was not content merely to address meetings and fulminate against the international Jewish conspiracy (as he saw it). On May 18, 1939 he wrote to a contact he had made in the German Embassy in Carlton House Terrace.

For many years I have been constantly and strenuously engaged in the struggle against the Judao-Masonic conspiracy for world domination. It therefore occurs to me that at the present crisis my knowledge gained over 30 years research and actual experience, my energy both with pen and voice, and my thorough understanding of the peculiar psychology of my fellow-countrymen might usefully be employed in helping to prevent the consummation of the incalculable catastrophe of a criminal, insane, fratricidal suicidal civil war and to bring about reconciliation, friendship and alliance between the two great branches of the Nordic or Aryan Race.

The Nordic League, upon whose Council I am, exists to unite in a National Front the various patriotic societies in England who realise and are resisting the stranglehold of the International Jew upon Britain and the British Empire, to make common cause with our kinsmen across the North Sea, and if possible to win over the Nordic countries of the Baltic by an appeal to their Blood and Race, to join the Anti-Komintern Front, acting as a link to reconcile the German and English peoples.

I propose to place myself unreservedly in the hands, and at the direction of, the Propaganda Ministerium with regard to the dissemination of truth by the production of pamphlets, the giving of lectures or speeches, and if considered advisable, broadcasting to bring about mutual understanding between our people.

Reminding the Embassy that he had been a welcome guest in Germany in 1933 and that he had 'made the acquaintance of that doughty fighter, Herr Julius Streicher', Skeels signed off with a heartfelt plea. 'I shall count it as a great privilege if I am accepted and welcomed in Germany as a loyal comrade in the Great Cause.'[34]

There is no recorded response from the Embassy in official files. But by the time he wrote his pledge of loyalty Skeels had already embarked on a role that would – by modern understanding – qualify him as a recruiter for 'the Great Cause': from September the previous year he had been grooming a young and vulnerable boy, placed in his care, to join German Intelligence. It was a scheme which would, in time, land them both in the dock at the Old Bailey.

MI5, then still understaffed and struggling to make up the lost years in which too little attention had been paid to British fascists, had little hard information of its own on the largely clandestine activities of Skeels and his colleagues. As a memo from Maxwell Knight's B Branch noted on June 8: 'The Nordic League is itself a nebulous body and does most of its work through the medium of other organisations – ie: BUF, Imperial Fascist League, Militant Christian patriots, English Mistery,

National Socialist League etc.'[35] It had, though, picked up worrying indications that some of the League's leading members were involved with foreign intelligence agents.

Oliver Conway Gilbert was a radio and electrical engineer who operated from retail premises off the Edgware Road, just north of Marble Arch. In the summer of 1938 he was 35 years old, divorced and – according to the tax accounts filed for Gilbert's Electrical Ltd – short of money. He had a lengthy history of extreme right-wing activism: at various times he had been a member of the Imperial Fascist League, the White Knights and the BUF, for whom he had worked as a propaganda officer. He was also a founding member of the Nordic League and sat on its fourteen-man ruling council.

Despite this, the Security Service had no substantial information about him until September 1938 when officers from its specialist 'watchers' branch reported on the movements of a suspected German spy. Ernst Wilhelm Kruse was a former First World War U-boat captain who had joined the ranks of Abwehr agents sent 'to obtain information regarding British armaments and preparations during the [Munich] crisis'.[36] On September 21 he called at Gilbert's shop in Shouldham Street, staying for around five minutes.

Although Kruse was under sufficient surveillance to warrant his own file being opened in MI5's Registry – its reference number was PF 68038 – there is no trace of this in the National Archives and from September 1938 the enigmatic submariner-turned-spy disappears from the official record. However, he was not the only foreign agent to call at Gilbert's Electrical Ltd.

Takuidi Egushi – sometimes spelled 'Eguchi' in MI5 reports – was London correspondent of the *Tokyo Shimbun* newspaper. He had lived and worked in Britain since 1914 and was married to an English woman. Since 1927, however, the Security Service had marked him out as an agent of the Imperial Japanese Military Intelligence Service, and ten years later he was a regular attendee of Nordic League meetings. Between October 1938 and the beginning of September 1939, MI5 surveillance showed Egushi making repeated visits to Shouldham Street, taking away packages of documents. The watchers could not get close enough to discover what these were, but when Gilbert was arrested under Regulation 18B on September 23, the mystery was solved. According to a report documenting his interrogation:

> Gilbert admitted that he had acted as agent or political informer for Eguchi and said that he had worked for Eguchi in inquiring into anti-Japanese activities in this country on the part of the Communists.[37]

It would not be the last time that Egushi's name was associated with a shadowy cabal of British fascists.

Gilbert was the second Nordic League official arrested that month: his colleague, T. Victor-Rowe – a former Dragoons and Naval veteran who, like Gilbert, had been a leading light in the BUF before throwing in his lot with the League – ran an import company specialising in German goods and, according to the information MI5 collected, had substantial wealth which bore no apparent connection to his legitimate business. He was given to boasting about his ability to travel to Germany through Croydon airport without passing through airport control, and his flat was festooned with Nazi regalia. All of which made him a suitable subject for the Security Service's close attention.

Yet although it did maintain a file on him – PF 47849 in the Registry – there is no trace of it in the National Archives today. Only fragments of the evidence contained within emerge from the dossier kept on other British fascists – but those fragments suggest that Rowe was, as MI5 put it, 'a dangerous man in time of war if he should fall into hands which were capable of using him'.[38]

The basis for that assertion was a report, from one of Maxwell Knight's undercover informants inside the fascist movement, of a conversation with Rowe. According to the account, dated September 7, 1939:

> Victor Rowe said that all really true friends of Germany should be prepared to work against this war even to the extent of espionage or sabotage, and he said quite definitely (for what Rowe's statements are worth) that the person who was in charge of the Nordic league sabotage arrangements was Conway Gilbert ...[39]

It is impossible to tell whether Rowe's claims about Gilbert were true: there are no accounts in his heavily-weeded Security Service file of him actually carrying out sabotage – though the discovery in his flat of a loaded .32 Browning automatic pistol, and 109 rounds of ammunition for it, suggested a man prepared for violence.[40] But in any event MI5's chief concern about the Nordic League was not Gilbert or even Rowe; instead, it was an impeccably-attired aristocrat with an equally important – and disturbing – address. As a memo dated June 8, 1939 reported:

> The man who might be termed the most outward and visible signs [*sic*] of the Nordic League is Capt. Maule Ramsay MP. All our observers agree that this man is either a completely honest fanatic or a most dangerous mixture of fanatic and crook ... it is certain that if any member of the Communist Party made speeches like many of the speeches recently made by Capt. Ramsay he would certainly lay himself open to a charge of incitement to violence.[41]

Archibald Henry Maule Ramsay – known to his close friends and associates as 'Jock' – had been a captain in the Coldstream Guards during the First World War; badly wounded in France in 1916 – a German bullet cut through his heart muscles and one of his kidneys – he was invalided out of the Army and turned to right-wing politics. In 1931, at the age of 37, he was elected as Conservative MP for the Scottish borders constituency of South Midlothian and Peebles.

He had, by then, made a very good marriage to the Honourable Ismay Lucretia, daughter of Viscount Gormanston and the widow of Lord Ninian Crichton-Stuart. They enjoyed the luxury of a Scottish estate – the fairytale-gothic Kellie Castle in Arbroath – and a fashionable London address in Onslow Square, South Kensington. Both Ramsays were ardent and passionate anti-Semites: 'Jock' had swallowed (by his own account) the global Jewish plot detailed in the bogus *Protocols of the Elders of Zion* – despite the fact that this had been exposed as a fraud in the entirely respectable pages of *The Times*.

By 1939 he was a frequent and popular speaker at Nordic League meetings; on February 13, in what he took to be the security of

like-minded fascists gathered at the League's headquarters, he praised
Hitler as 'that splendid fellow', expounded on the 'Jewish conspiracy'
and hinted that he would be prepared to use violence to solve 'the
Jewish problem'. Unknown to him, retired Special Branch Inspector
Pavey had infiltrated the event and provided MI5 with an account of
Ramsay's speech.

> Ramsay said he had 'come along to address the Nordic League on the
> subject of the common enemy – not the Germans or the Italians or
> the Japanese, but World Jewry ... It may be a revelation to some of you,
> he went on to say, but it is a proven fact that the Irish Republican Army
> is a Moscow controlled body, financed by Jewish gold ...
>
> Having lost Germany, Italy, Hungary, Czechoslovakia and now
> Spain, the Jewish High Command were concentrating on Britain and
> France. A world war, and that very soon, was the only way to the fulfil-
> ment of Zionist ambitions ...

Ramsay then related a story told to him by 'the Arab Mayor of
Bethlehem', with whom he was very well acquainted.

> Three Jews entered the Church of the Nativity. Standing before the
> Manger in which Christ was laid, they made unseemly and blasphe-
> mous remarks. They were kicked out and later the mayor placed in the
> right hand of each of his three sons a revolver and commanded that
> they should shoot every Jew they saw in Bethlehem.
>
> Turning dramatically to his son, who occupied a seat on the
> platform, Captain Ramsay said 'I may have to do this with you
> before long'. His observation was greeted with loud and long
> applause.[42]

Ramsay's anti-Semitism was obsessive and overwhelming. He was so
convinced of the need to fight Jewish influence that he was happy to
expound on it to MI5's Deputy Director General, Oswald Harker. Over
drinks at the Carlton Club in the summer of 1939 (Ramsay suggested
dinner, but Harker demurred), he described 'a gigantic conspiracy ...
being engineered against Gentiles throughout the world'.

He is a pleasant spoken man, apparently quite sincere and equally quite incapable of taking an objective view ... He referred briefly to the Protocol of Zion [*sic*] and elaborated the theory that the Russian revolution, the Revolution in Spain and all the other ills throughout the world are directed and controlled by some mysterious body whose object is the elimination of the Gentiles ...

The tragic thing about it all to my mind is that Ramsay is really quite sincere and honest in his beliefs ... I did not think it a suitable moment to try and draw him on the subject of the Nordic League, as ... had I done so it would not be a question of dining but of spending the rest of the night with him.[43]

Other Security Service officers were, thankfully, a little more assiduous than Harker in trying to discover what Ramsay was doing in the Nordic League. A memo by Maxwell Knight, filed on the same day as the Deputy Director General's note, recorded information gleaned from one of B Branch's informants; it described a conversation, at a League meeting, with Takuidi Egushi, and seemed to indicate that Ramsay was viewed as an important asset by the Nazi regime.

This Japanese man [Egushi] is worthy of some notice. He has recently been in Munich where he had a long talk with Hoffman [a senior propaganda ministry official] on the subject of the Nordic League ...

The Jap claims that Hoffmann reprimanded him severely because in a report which the Jap sent to Tokyo he had mentioned Captain Maule Ramsay's name. Hoffman was very frightened that somehow the news of Ramsay's activities might reach the British Ambassador in Tokyo who might report it back to the Foreign Office in London, with the result that 'Capt. Ramsay's valuable work for Germany would be entirely undone'. The Jap claims he acted quickly and prevented R's name being mentioned.[44]

Ostensibly, Ramsay's activities were limited to commissioning the printing of thousands of 'sticky-backs' – self-adhesive labels to be fixed to 'lamp posts, Church boards, bus stops [and] phone kiosks'[45] – which denounced the coming conflict as 'a Jew's War!'.

Behind the scenes, however, he had begun formulating plans for a new and highly secret organisation to replace the Nordic League. It was to be called 'The Right Club'; members were divided (by Ramsay, according to his perceptions of their descending levels of ability) into Wardens, Stewards, Yeomen, Keepers and Freemen. Membership costs ran from a £25 joining fee, with a further £10 and 10 shillings annual subscription,[46] for the most senior class (Wardens), to 2 shillings and sixpence for the lowest (Freemen).

Suitable candidates were encouraged to send applications to Ramsay, care of his office in the House of Commons. Once accepted, each was sworn to secrecy and issued with a specially-manufactured badge: an eagle killing a snake and bearing the initials 'P.J.' – by then universal fascist shorthand for 'Perish Judah'. According to a letter sent on Ramsay's behalf by his son:

> The aim of the Club is to co-ordinate the activities of all the patriotic bodies which are striving to free this country from the Jewish domination in the financial, political, philosophical and cultural sphere.
>
> The organisations in question are such as the following: British Union, Nordic League, National Socialist League, Imperial Fascists, The Link, Liberty Restoration League and a few others.[47]

However, even this ambitious scheme – no leader, however charismatic, had ever managed to weld the endlessly-feuding web of British fascist organisations into a united front – was not the true purpose of the newly-minted organisation. This, according to undercover agents who infiltrated the Right Club's 'Inner Circle' on behalf of MI5 and Special Branch, was to prepare for an imminent fascist revolution, to be brought about by a military coup d'état.

Meanwhile, the self-declared organiser of this secret – and unquestionably traitorous – plot availed himself of the privileges and salary (£600 per annum – equivalent to £27,000 today) accorded to an MP. On September 4 – one day after war was declared – Captain Archibald Maule Ramsay sat down in the House of Commons library and penned a laborious parody of 'Land of Hope and Glory' to entertain Right Club members.

Land of dope and Jewry
Land that once was free
All the Jew boys praise thee
Whilst they plunder thee.

There was much more in this vein – and much more to Ramsay and the Right Club than bad, anti-Semitic doggerel. Within six months they would penetrate sensitive government ministries, the armed forces, the police and even MI5 itself; their activities on behalf of Nazi Germany would cause a serious diplomatic problem for Britain and the United States, and lead to a highly damaging trial. But before then, the Security Service would uncover espionage and treachery within the highest reaches of the country's traditional ruling class.

CHAPTER EIGHT

Lords Traitorous

'In the event of the Duke falling into the hands of the
enemy he would be likely to be set up as a gauleiter
or the head of a puppet British Government.'
Summary of case against the 12th Duke of Bedford,
December 1941

William Francis Forbes-Sempill could trace his noble lineage
back to 1489. His ancestors had fought at the Battle of Flodden,
served the Court of James VI of Scotland and sat on the comfortable
leather benches in the House of Lords for more than two centuries. As
a young man he enjoyed the courtesy title of Master of Sempill before,
in 1934 and at the age of 41, succeeding his father (an aide de camp to
King George V) to don the ermine as the 19th Lord Sempill.

By then he had earned a reputation as both a decorated pilot during the First World War and a pioneering civil aviator – between 1930
and 1936 he made record-breaking non-stop flights from London to
Stockholm and Berlin – whose knowledge of the mechanics of flying
brought international acclaim and consultancies with governments
across the globe.

In February 1940 he was employed in the Department of Air
Matériel, a procurement and logistical section of the Ministry of

Aviation. It was a role for which he was – on paper – well qualified by training and experience.

It was also, however, a job which gave him access to highly classified military information in some of the most sensitive areas of the war; a fact which was surprising, given the noble lord's history. Because William Forbes-Sempill was a spy who, for more than fifteen years, had been selling British military secrets to a foreign power.

*

That there were fascists – or at least fascist fellow-travellers – sitting in Parliament's Upper Chamber was no great secret. In addition to Lord Brocket and the Duke of Buccleuch – both enthusiastic celebrants of Hitler's 50th birthday – there was a clique of reactionary aristocrats whose anti-Semitic obsession led them to adopt the ancient proverb 'the enemy of my enemy must be my friend'.

Hugh Richard Arthur Grosvenor, known to his friends as 'Bendor' and to his Peers as the 2nd Duke of Westminster, was a firm believer in conspiracy theories about the Jews, and blamed them (with their alleged allies in communism) for stirring up trouble between Britain and Germany. He spent the first months of the war demanding that peace be made with the Reich. Lionel Walter Erskine-Young, 29th Earl of Mar, was a member of both The Link and the Right Club, and gave financial support to the BUF. His colleague, David Bertram Ogilvy Freeman-Mitford – the 2nd Baron Redesdale – not only donated funds, but gave two of his seven daughters to the cause.*

Redesdale, Arthur Wellesley, 5th Duke of Wellington, Charles Alexander Bannerman Carnegie, 11th Earl of Southesk, and Randolph Algernon Ronald Stewart, 12th Earl of Galloway had all paid the £25 fees to be made Wardens of the Right Club (which also boasted a dozen members in the House of Commons). Their noble colleague, Gerard Wallop, 9th Earl of Portsmouth, who bore the title Lord Lymington, wrote a succession of articles in late 1939 in his own monthly journal,

---

* Diana Mitford married Oswald Mosley and was interned under Regulation 18B between 1940 and 1943. Her sister, Unity, became a close friend of Hitler and shot herself in the head on the outbreak of war; badly injured, she lived on until 1948.

The New Pioneer, in which he complained about the mass evacuation of working-class people from inner London to the rural idyll of his Hampshire villages, and denounced Britain's Jewish refugees, among whose number, he argued, 'some will doubtless spy for the highest bidder'. He also used his privileged position to urge the government for a suspension of the war in favour of a negotiated peace with Germany.[1] By February 1940, although he had stopped making ringing endorsements of Hitler, he was one of a group of aristocrats who began attending secret meetings of pro-Nazi politicians, convened by Admiral Barry Domvile.

He was not alone in these efforts: several weeks after the war began, the Duke of Buccleuch used his position to lecture the Under-Secretary of State for Foreign Affairs, R.A. 'Rab' Butler, on the need to negotiate peace with Germany, while pointing the finger at Churchill as the main obstacle to his plans.* 'I suppose Winston can successfully veto any move towards peace', he grumbled at Butler.[2]

If, in reality, he had no such veto, Churchill, then First Lord of the Admiralty and deeply worried by the lingering air of appeasement still clinging to Chamberlain's government, appears to have taken it on himself to advise the aristocratic 'peace at almost any cost' faction within Parliament of the risks they were running. He warned the Duke of Westminster that 'very hard experiences lie before those who preach defeatism and set themselves against the will of the nation'.[3]

That Churchill had good reason to be suspicious of the government's willingness to consider aristocratic pleading for peace with Hitler is borne out by a letter published in *The Times* on October 6, 1939. Douglas Douglas-Hamilton MP, the Marquess of Clydesdale – he would become the Duke of Hamilton in May 1940 – had, in the mid-1930s, travelled to Berlin as the guest of senior Nazi officials and firmly believed that Britain should be fighting the Soviet Union, not Germany. His letter was careful to avoid explicitly endorsing the Fuehrer – 'Britain had no choice but to accept the challenge of Hitler's aggression' – but argued

---

* Buccleuch lobbied both the government and the royal family until, in the early summer of 1940, the King relieved him of his duties and sent him into a de-facto exile on his Scottish estates.

that 'we do not grudge Germany Lebensraum, provided Lebensraum is not made the grave of other nations. We should be ready to search for and find a just colonial settlement.' Since Lebensraum ('living space') inevitably required Germany to invade and subsume neighbouring countries – and was a fundamental plank both of the Third Reich's raison d'être and Hitler's personal popularity at home – Clydesdale's plea was absurdly naive.

It appeared, however, to be at least tacitly supported by senior figures within the government. The Marquess cleared his letter for publication with the Prime Minister and the Foreign Secretary, Lord Halifax.[4] It would not be the last occasion on which Halifax's name would be associated with pleas to accommodate Hitler and his plans for European domination.

However, for all their pro-German or anti-Semitic sentiments, none of this aristocratic cabal of appeasers indulged in outright treachery. That was left to two other members of the House of Lords: Lord Tavistock, later Duke of Bedford, and Lord Sempill.

William Forbes-Sempill joined the Royal Flying Corps in 1914; within a year he was promoted to Flight Commander, before switching to the Royal Naval Air Service where he became a Squadron Commander; by the end of the First World War he held the rank of Colonel. He was, unquestionably, a highly talented flyer and an expert on military aviation – qualities which, as a civilian consultant, made him very attractive indeed to a number of nations in the 1920s. One, in particular, sought out his services.

Japan was then setting out on a nationalist and expansionist road and wanted to build up its military muscle: Sempill was just the man they needed. Between 1920 and 1923 he headed a civilian mission to Tokyo, helping the Imperial Navy to establish an aircraft carrier fleet and training its pilots.

For his efforts Sempill received the gratitude of Japanese Prime Minister Tomosaburo Kato, who sent him a personal letter thanking him for his work which was 'almost epoch-making'; more practically, he was also taken on as a paid agent of Japanese Intelligence.

The Security Service began watching the dashing young aristocrat on his return to England, monitoring both his correspondence and that of the Japanese Naval Attaché in London: these showed, according to a note in Sempill's (very heavily censored) MI5 file, that: 'It is quite clear that not only is Sempill admittedly furnishing the Japanese with aviation intelligence, but that he is being paid for doing so.'[5]

Among the secrets Sempill provided to his handler, Captain Teijiro Toyoda, were the blueprints of 'large bombs', aircraft sound detectors for use in the air, and 'the latest RAF aero cameras'.[6] But it was his attempts to obtain details of a top-secret new reconnaissance aircraft, the Blackburn Iris flying boat, then being developed for the British Air Ministry, which proved the final straw. In May 1926 he was summoned to Whitehall to be confronted about his espionage.

He was not, however, to be prosecuted. Despite the very clear evidence of spying, the Attorney General had advised against mounting an Official Secrets Act trial. Instead, Sempill was 'talked to in a friendly manner with a view to letting him know that his activities were not unknown to the Authorities concerned and that he had better be more careful in future what information he disclosed to Foreign Powers', and advised of 'his good fortune in not being prosecuted, winding up with a warning regarding the Official Secrets Act and his duties thereunder in the future'.[7]

Ostensibly this remarkable decision was made to prevent disclosure of MI5's use of Home Office warrants to intercept suspicious correspondence. But this seems to have been a fig-leaf to disguise the more likely explanation: a desire not to expose a man of his rank and privilege as a traitor. Certainly, in the letter he sent to the Air Ministry on May 7 (the day after he received a formal dressing down), Sempill said that he had known 'for considerably over a year that my correspondence and telephonic communications were watched'.[8]

The Security Service was clearly unimpressed, but in the face of the government Law Officers' determination, it had to settle for a demand that Sempill be kept away from military facilities in future.

'I think we are entitled to suggest formally in writing to the Air Ministry', Deputy Director General Oswald Harker noted in the growing Registry file, 'that, in these circumstances, it seems urgently necessary from a defence security standpoint that steps should be taken to place Sempill on the Blacklist as regards the receipt of information from, and visits to, the Air Ministry or any establishment engaged in the design or manufacture of modern aircraft on behalf of the Air Ministry.'[9]

If the government and MI5 hoped that a gentlemanly, if firm, warning would deter Sempill from further contact with the intelligence services of foreign powers, they were sorely deluded. Between 1936 and 1938, monitoring of mail to and from his London address suggested that he was continuing his efforts to gain sensitive military information. Much of his file relating to this period appears to have been damaged by fire – most likely during the raid which hit the Registry offices in 1940 – and what survived has been stripped of many of its original documents. But a few remaining fragments hint at concerns that Sempill was obtaining information on a secret underground fuel storage scheme under consideration as part of pre-war planning near the important naval base at Falmouth. A note on the Minute Sheet in August 1937 warned: 'It is most likely that any information about this scheme ... may have come to the ears of Lord Sempill ... before it reached the First Lord [of the Admiralty] or CID [Committee on Imperial Defence].'[10]

Sempill had, by then, taken his seat in the House of Lords and was a council member of Admiral Domvile's pro-Nazi propaganda organisation, The Link. Two years later he was registered as a Warden in Ramsay's Right Club. Despite this, and his record as a foreign spy, on the outbreak of war he persuaded the Air Ministry to give him a job in the Department of Air Matériel – a post which carried the rank of Commander in the Royal Naval Volunteer Reserve and gave him access to sensitive information about military aircraft. Harker's request for the noble lord to be blacklisted had, apparently, been forgotten: the result was predictable.

In February 1940, MI5 intercepted correspondence between the London offices of the Mitsubishi Company, its head office in Tokyo and the Imperial Naval Air Force: it showed that for more than fifteen years Sempill had been – and continued to be – in the pay of Japanese Intelligence.

The first letter, sent from Mitsubishi Heavy Industries in Tokyo to the manager of its London branch on February 27, was headed: 'Fee as Advisor paid to Lord Sempill':

I have to acknowledge your confidential letter of September 11th 1939, on this subject in which you refer to the use both direct and indirect of Lord Sempill by our Military and Naval Attachés in London and recommend postponement for one year of the said fee ...

I subsequently received a communication from our Naval Attaché in London, through headquarters, asking that the fee might be continued if it had not been reduced in amount.[11]

Two days later, in a letter to the Japanese Naval Air Force headquarters, the Mitsubishi manager expanded on the 'Honorarium paid to Lord Sempill' and the request of the London Naval Attaché to continue paying this:

Our company, ever since the year 1925 ... has annually paid an honorarium of £300. As however we have lately made scarcely any direct use of this gentleman we have it in mind to reduce the amount to half. But after careful consideration we have decided to pay £300 as usual this year and afterwards for the time being £200 a year and preserve our connection with him, making a sacrifice from the national standpoint at the present time. We shall be glad if you will take note of this and make as full use as possible of this connection in the future.[12]

The importance of this correspondence was not lost on MI5. It noted that Mitsubishi was not simply a private company, but an arm of the Japanese military.

It is well known to those who have a knowledge of Japanese affairs that, generally speaking, every Japanese is expected to work for the national interest, and that this applies to Japanese firms who are equally expected to place themselves at the disposal of the Japanese authorities. Among the firms who work for the Japanese Intelligence, it is believed that Mitsubishi play a prominent part.[13]

More pertinently, the clear implication was that Sempill was a long-standing paid agent of the London-based Naval Attaché, who had made either direct or indirect use of his services since 1925 – despite Sempill's promise not to have any further dealings with the Japanese military.*

There is no rational explanation for what followed. Sempill was summoned to the Air Ministry and asked for an 'assurance' that he would cease providing intelligence to Japan. He duly gave a 'solemn undertaking that so long as I am employed in Naval Service I will in matters connected therewith ... make no communication with the Japanese subjects in relation thereto, or to British subjects, or the subjects of other countries in their employment'.[14]

This proved as worthless as his previous promise. Within a year, and using his influence as a sitting member of the House of Lords, he pressured the Home Office to release a Mitsubishi manager in London who had been arrested under Regulation 18B; the intervention proved effective and the man spent no more than 48 hours in custody. Sempill promptly telegraphed Mitsubishi's head office in Tokyo: 'Delighted results. Proud to help. Working hard cause.'[15]

An MI5 search of Sempill's offices also produced clear evidence that he remained on the Japanese payroll and that he had used his position at the Air Ministry to collect 'information on aircraft – both German and British', 'tanks', 'aerodromes across Britain', 'searchlights on fighters', 'bombsights', 'armour piercing guns', 'gyro sights' (which were 'a highly important most secret development') and 'numerous secret Air Ministry documents relating to recent air accident investigations'.[16]

Sempill's Security Service file shows that Churchill ordered his dismissal from the Department of Air Matériel[17] and that MI5 planned to have him arrested under Regulation 18B.[18] Inexplicably, neither happened. He was, instead, left free to enjoy all the privileges of his rank and status throughout the war.

The best that could be said on behalf of Lord William Forbes-Sempill was that the country he spied for was then not officially a hostile power – although, as Churchill growled in his letter on the case in September 1941, that was certain to change:

---

* According to Richard Aldrich, Professor of International Security at the University of Warwick, the information and expertise Sempill provided to Japan enabled it to launch the attack on the US fleet at Pearl Harbor in December 1941. 'The Traitor of Pearl Harbor', *New York Times*, May 27, 2012.

At any moment we may be at war with Japan, and here are all these Englishmen, ... moving around collecting information and sending it to the Japanese Embassy. I cannot believe that the Master of Sempill ... [has] any idea what [his] position would be on the morrow of a Japanese declaration of war. Immediate internment would be the least of [his] troubles ...[19]

For the other Lords Traitorous, however, there was no such excuse.

In February 1940, Hastings William Sackville Russell was 52 years old and the fourth-richest man in Britain. While waiting to come into his inheritance as the 12th Duke of Bedford, he enjoyed the courtesy title Lord Tavistock, and the considerable privileges which his social status conferred.

He had graduated from Balliol College, Oxford before the First World War and had obtained a commission in the 10th Battalion, Middlesex Regiment. However, he never saw action of any description: official accounts of his life tend to imply that he was prevented from doing so by illness, although a caustic note, dated December 1941, in his once-voluminous MI5 files recounted an allegation that 'he deserted and was found in hiding at Dover'.

It is said that the late Duke [Tavistock's father, Herbert Russell, 11th Duke of Bedford], as a result of this, asked in the House of Lords whether he could break the entail and disinherit the present Duke. There is no confirmation of these stories, which come from a reliable source and enquiries at the War Office confirm that the War Office papers relating to this man were destroyed by fire last year.

Whatever the truth of the story the Duke was an active pacifist during the last war ... This may be accounted for to some extent by the fact (if such it be) that his governess, Miss Green, who had been governess in the Kaiser's family, inculcated in him a love of Germany. She used, it is said, to visit him every week when he was at Eton and Balliol.

During the last war the Duke fell into the hands of every kind of crank and eccentric. His activities and opinion resulted in an estrangement between him and his father... The Duke has been described by one who was in close touch with him for a number of years as a sexual pervert, physical coward and a rebel against all authority.[20]

The author of this report was Edward Blanshard Stamp, one of a group of young barristers brought into the Security Service to handle its difficult relationship with the Home Office.[21] He wrote the memo two days after Lord Tavistock took his seat in the House of Lords; but its acerbic tone was due to events which took place nineteen months earlier during the last weeks of the Phoney War.

Tavistock had been active in politics for much of the 1930s, flirting first with socialism and communism before becoming enamoured of the fascist regimes in Italy and Germany. He had also developed a near-obsession with the need to reform international finance: this, according to Stamp's memo, 'explains to some extent his sympathy for Hitler who he believes has abolished the capitalist system and imposed something in its place which at least resembles the Duke's own ideal of how our monetary system ought to be worked'.[22]

This sympathy for Germany and its Fuehrer led Tavistock to support the Austrian Anschluss in 1938 and thereafter to throw in his lot with the group of pro-Nazi fascists coalescing around John Beckett. The noble lord's money funded Beckett's British Council for Christian Settlement in Europe (BCCSE) and its successor, the British People's Party – both of which would trouble MI5 during the darkest days of the war.

These associations led MI5 to seek a Home Office warrant to intercept Tavistock's mail. In October 1939 this yielded a letter to one of his fellow-travelling fascists in which he made clear his admiration for Hitler and blamed the British government for its failure to meet the Fuehrer's demands.

When [Hitler] offered disarmament on equal terms down to a force of 200,000 men they ignored the offer; when he was willing to do away with the bombing aeroplane, they were not willing; and when last spring he made quite reasonable proposals to Poland, these proposals were rejected.

You cannot trifle in this way with a man of Hitler's temperament and not expect trouble. All the so-called offers to help to Germany have been obvious bribes ... when a promising start seems to have been made at Munich, everything was sacrificed directly Chamberlain returned by his advocacy of a continuation of rearmament at the precise moment when he should have suggested a conference to consider disarmament.[23]

Nor did Tavistock confine himself to private letters. Throughout the first months of the war he wrote regular articles for *The Word* – a monthly journal published by a leading anarchist[24] – as well as the BUF newspaper *Action*. For the latter's January 1940 issue he pronounced it high time that the British people should wake up to 'the truth about this war and the men who made it' – a barely-disguised rehash of the fascist slogan that this was a 'Jews' War'.

Despite the very wide powers of suppression conferred by the 1939 Defence Regulations, the expression of dissenting opinions about the war was not, in itself, an offence. Communicating or consorting with the enemy, however, was unquestionably unlawful. Regulation 18B authorised the Home Secretary to order the arrest of anyone whom he had 'reasonable cause to believe' had 'hostile associations' or was a member of an organisation which had 'associations with persons concerned in the government of, or sympathies with the system of government of, any Power with which His Majesty is at war'.

In February, Tavistock decided to ignore these prohibitions, and made arrangements to travel to Dublin for a meeting with officials of the German Legation. His aim was to negotiate peace terms between Britain and the Third Reich – a draft agreement of which he and Beckett planned to publish in the pages of the *Daily Express* as a means to 'bounce' the British government into accepting Hitler's terms.[25]

MI5 got wind of the scheme through informants Maxwell Knight had inserted inside the British Council for Christian Settlement. It was in no doubt about the illegality of what both men planned. An (undated) memo by Harker noted:

Beckett is fully aware that these negotiations have rendered himself ... and the Marquis [*sic*] of Tavistock liable to proceedings for treasonable activities, and Beckett is most anxious that if there is to be a martyr, the martyr should be the Marquis of Tavistock and not himself, in fact he has already prepared for a big press campaign over 'Tavistock's martyrdom'.[26]

However, the Security Service appears – at that point – to have been kept somewhat in the dark by its masters in Whitehall; it did not know that Tavistock's mission had been given semi-official sanction, nor that some of the most senior figures in government were turning a blind eye to treason.

Since the outbreak of war, anyone – aristocrat or commoner – seeking to travel outside Britain's borders needed an official exit permit, stamped by the Foreign Office and which stated the purpose of the journey. There is no indication in Tavistock's suspiciously heavily-weeded files that he applied for, or was granted, any such authorisation; however, a subsequent memo by Stamp suggests that the Foreign Secretary was aware of the Dublin trip before it happened.

> Through some means, which has not been ascertained, he [Tavistock] obtained from some German source, almost certainly through the German Embassy in Dublin, what he conceived to be the peace terms which Hitler was prepared to accept ...
>
> Lord Halifax refused to give any assurance that the matter would be followed up; and the Duke, after some correspondence, asked if there would be any objection to his going to Dublin to visit the German Legation and to ask for such proofs of authenticity as Lord Halifax might consider necessary to establish the position.
>
> Lord Halifax informed the Duke that he could not prevent him going to Dublin if he wished to do so but that there could be no question of him being entrusted with any mission. On receipt of this information the Duke proceeded to Dublin.[27]

Halifax's claim that he was powerless to prevent Tavistock going to meet and negotiate with officials of a country with which Britain was at war was nonsense. Not only did the Foreign Secretary have complete authority to block the exit visa, but even attempting to make contact with Nazi officials in Eire was a serious criminal offence: the following year, two Dundee youths would be jailed for three months each for trying – unsuccessfully – to telephone the German Legation in Dublin as a prank.*

There is no official record of the German terms which Tavistock brought back from Dublin. The copy originally included in his own file is missing, and the Reich's diplomats subsequently disowned them; a report by one of Knight's agents inside BCCSE, however, gives a clear idea of what was proposed.

> John Beckett came into his office [on] 26.2.40 in a great state of excitement ... Beckett definitely stated that the peace terms had been confirmed ... They then included the restoration of Bohemia, Czecho-Slovakia, and Poland, the settlement of Austria, the withdrawal of Hitler to a nominal post in the government of the Third Reich, and an admission of the mistakes made by the Nazi Government in their treatment of the Semitic problem and of the Polish and Czecho-Slovakian questions.
>
> The process by which they reached the Marquis [sic] of Tavistock seems to be roughly as follows: they were given to a member of the Dail in Eire who passed them on to a man; this man memorized them and gave them to Tavistock ... The document is about 20 pages long and has been typed, presumably by Tavistock's secretary.[28]

Tavistock's adventure was raised in the House of Commons on March 4. Two senior backbench MPs – one Conservative, one Labour – demanded an assurance from the Home Secretary that the government would prevent any future private peace missions by well-connected Nazi fellow-travellers.

---

* On June 24, 1941, Robert Webster Ireland and Gordon Archer (21 and 17 years old respectively) pleaded guilty to 'attempting to communicate with persons at the German legation in Dublin'. Perth Sheriff's Court heard that they made the single unsuccessful attempt 'as a prank'; nonetheless, Sheriff Valentine jailed both young men and pronounced that 'an attempt by any persons to put themselves in communications with the enemies of this country must be sternly repressed'. *Perthshire Advertiser*, June 25, 1941.

Brigadier General Edward Spears – a retired army officer and long-time opponent of Chamberlain's appeasement policies[29] – asked Sir John Anderson to 'take steps to put a stop to the activities of highly-placed persons and others putting forward German propaganda in the form of peace proposals supplied by German agents'; while George Strauss,[30] his colleague on the Labour benches, pointedly requested that the Home Secretary should 'use his powers to prevent British nationals from communicating with the enemy by personal visits to German Embassies or Legations in neutral countries'.

Anderson was in a difficult position. While Tavistock's actions were unquestionably illegal, his status rendered him effectively immune from prosecution. 'While there is general agreement that activities of the kind to which the Questions refer are to be deplored', the Home Secretary told the House, 'I do not think the incident can properly be regarded as affording sufficient grounds for the imposition of additional penal restrictions.'

Strauss, however, was not ready to let the matter rest so easily, rising to his feet to ask: 'Does the Right Hon. Gentleman mean that he has no powers now to deal with an English national who communicates with the enemy through Legations in Ireland or any foreign country?'

Once again, Anderson dissembled. 'I did not mean to convey that I have no powers, but that I do not think any additional powers are required' – a response which prompted Spears to take the unusual step of naming names.

Is the Right Honourable Gentleman aware that a number of persons in the 'Christian Settlement Group' under the chairmanship of Lord Tavistock were previously connected with the 'Link', and are the activities of this group and its connections and communications with enemy agents being closely watched?

The best the Home Secretary could muster in response to this pincer attack from right and left was a somewhat tepid assurance that, 'I think we are fully aware of what is going on'.[31]

Tavistock himself was unrepentant. Five days after being named and shamed in the Commons, he wrote to Spears to justify his actions and, for good measure, to defend both Hitler and Germany's 'exceedingly reasonable' demands for territory in Poland.

> I judge from your recent question in the House that you consider contrary to the national interests my recent attempt to obtain, through the German Legation in Dublin, a statement of terms on which the German Government would be prepared to conclude peace.
>
> I took this step owing to the persistent failure of the British Government to put forward any constructive proposals of its own or to display the slightest intelligence in their handling of the diplomatic situation when, in the past, such proposals have been put forward from the German side or by neutrals.
>
> Even if Hitler were all that you believe him to be, by reason of lack of imagination, when Hitler has made speeches both before and after the war, chance after chance has been missed of putting him in a most awkward position and turning not only neutral opinion but the opinion of the moderate section of the German people strongly against him.
>
> I do not know precisely on what grounds you consider this war to be justified. Although the exaction of vengeance on behalf of the Jews is not yet one of our acknowledged war aims, it may be that you think that war is justified by reason of the atrocities which, it is claimed, have been committed inside Germany. If this should be your point of view, I should recommend you to make yourself better acquainted with the atrocities which we have been committing in Palestine.[32]

Other, lesser mortals had been interned under Regulation 18B for expressing such naked pro-German sympathies, but Tavistock's lineage and privilege appear to have been crucial in insulating him from detention. In the months to come, the Home Office would display a remarkable eagerness to prevent his name from being discussed in other cases heard by the Appeals Committee on internment, and the best the Security Service could achieve was his name being placed on the secret list of those to be detained if, or when, Germany invaded Britain. It gave a stark explanation for this:

In the event of the Duke falling into the hands of the enemy he would be likely to be set up as a gauleiter or the head of a puppet British Government.[33]

But there was an additional impediment to taking action over Tavistock's trip to Dublin: his was not the only informal peace mission to which the Foreign Office turned a blind eye.

James Lonsdale Bryans was a 46-year-old self-described author (though he had no British publishing history to support the claim). He was, however, impeccably upper-class: he counted Eton and Balliol as his alma maters and cited Brooks – the haunt of aristocratic politicians for more than a century – as his London club. He was a vehemently anti-Semitic and pro-Nazi fascist, and believed that it was Germany's right to rule Europe, leaving Britain free rein throughout the rest of the world.

Between September 1939 and the end of February 1940, Bryans embarked on two attempts to communicate directly with the Fuehrer and to bring back to London peace terms acceptable to the Third Reich; both were backed financially by two familiar names from aristocratic fascist circles – Lord Brocket and the Duke of Buccleuch.

On both occasions – despite a growing file inside MI5's Registry which showed him to be known for 'views sympathetic to Hitler' – he secured exit permits allowing him to travel to Mussolini's Italy. The second trip, in particular, was specifically authorised at the highest levels of the Foreign Office. According to a Security Service report, written by Stamp:

A second exit permit was granted to him on the 8th January for the purpose of proceeding to Rome, ostensibly to visit Messrs. Mondalori & Co, publishers. This permit was granted at the request of Mr. C.G.S. Stevenson, Private Secretary to Lord Halifax, who requested that all possible facilities should be granted to Bryans.

When Bryans visited the Passport Office he informed [the officials] that it might be assumed he was undertaking some special work for the Foreign Office.[34]

In reality, Bryans' travels had a rather different purpose: he was – according to a letter he had sent to a German publishing company

– attempting to gain 'an audience with the Fuehrer', who, he said, was 'a man ... of faith and genius'.[35]

His contact and go-between was a Danish Abwehr agent, Ole Erik Andersen; according to a report of MI5's subsequent interrogation of Andersen:[36]

> Bryans told him about his contacts with Lord Halifax, and he impressed upon him that actually all his travels were at the request of this gentleman ... The interrogation boils down to the following: A person, now at large, can impress upon neutrals, who apparently believe him, that, with the help of wealthy friends and on commission for the Foreign Secretary of State, he is going to propose to Hitler that England should between them divide Europe.[37]

Bryans was, as MI5 noted, very clearly guilty of a serious offence – and one which had sent other, less privileged men to prison. But the Foreign Secretary's support evidently saved his skin. Stamp noted in Bryans' now-bulging file:

> I should very much like to see Mr Lonsdale Bryans detained but the position is very delicate and it is I think certain that if he were detained he would peach on the Foreign Office and his story would be all over the country.[38]

James Lonsdale Bryans, like his sponsors, Lord Brocket and the Duke of Buccleuch – and the equally traitorous Lords Sempill and Tavistock – never spent a single day in custody. Although MI5 argued for internment of aristocratic traitors, their wealth, status and connections in government protected them from the laws applied to less fortunate British fascists.

But the Phoney War was drawing to a close. Hitler – that man of 'faith and genius' – was now ready to pursue the Reich's ambitions for total control of Western Europe.

CHAPTER NINE

Two Weeks in May

'We cannot be sure that, when the real emergency
comes, the traitors within our gates, directed by some
organization which we may so far have been unable
to detect, may not deal us a crippling blow.'
Sir Maurice Hankey, Report to War Cabinet,
May 11, 1940

A t 5.15am on Tuesday, April 9, 1940, German troops invaded
Denmark and Norway. Hitler and his military High Command
had been planning Operation Weseruebung for almost four months,
but in the event Danish forces surrendered within six hours of the first
landings. Norway would prove a harder nut to crack; the campaign
there would drag on for several weeks but the Nazis' ultimate occupation was greatly assisted by an internal coup d'état, launched by the
local fascist leader, Vidkun Quisling.

What Germany had dismissively referred to as *der Sitzkrieg* ['sitting
war'] and France had been pleased to term *la drôle de guerre* ['joke war']
was over: from early April there would be nothing sedentary about the
Wehrmacht's tactics – and precious little for those in its path to laugh
about.

On May 9, Aufmarschanweisung No. 4, Fall Gelb ('Deployment
Instruction No. 4, Case Yellow') was put into operation. Within

24 hours, German troops occupied Luxembourg, marched into Holland, and prepared for an assault on Allied forces in Belgium: neither of the two 'Low Countries' would last long against the might of Hitler's Blitzkrieg, and, with France plainly next in his sights, Britain finally confronted the very real prospect of invasion. It was not remotely prepared.

Neville Chamberlain, the architect of appeasement, was in deep trouble. On May 8, amid reports of British losses in Norway, the House of Commons voted on a motion of no confidence; although the government survived, winning by a majority of 81, 33 members of Chamberlain's own Conservative Party voted against him and a further 60 abstained. The writing was on the wall and clear. The following day, Chamberlain resigned, to be replaced (despite an ill-advised, last-minute attempt to install Lord Halifax atop the government) by the First Lord of the Admiralty, Winston Churchill.

Churchill inherited a mess: militarily,[1] politically and – especially – on the Home Front. As he entered 10 Downing Street, the Home Office and MI5 were effectively engaged in a war with each other over the threat posed by pro-Nazi British fascists, and how many of these should be interned under Regulation 18B.

A diary entry by Guy Liddell in January, recording a visit to the Security Service by the Home Office mandarin, Frank Newsam,[2] offered a revealing insight into the problem.

Newsam called in today. He has just returned to H.O. [Home Office] from one of the Regional Commissioners offices. He was very full of himself and at present he is going to take over all matters of H.O. policy which affect MI5. He seems to have some idea that we were not altogether satisfied with what the H.O. were doing, and he probably came down to find out what the trouble was. We left him in no doubt that the present policy or lack of it was seriously hampering our work. He tried to defend the Home Secretary by saying that as long as the war was in its present state he had to be answerable in the House in the ordinary peace-time manner. It was not therefore possible for him to take action in many cases where we might think it desirable.

I pointed out as politely as I could that we were after all in the middle of an extremely serious war and that it was surely up to the Home Secretary to give the public a lead in these matters and to explain to them that certain precautions had to be taken in the national interest although this might be unpleasant for those concerned ... I feel that Master Newsam will need enlightening ... if he is to be of any use to us.[3]

Within ten days of Liddell's journal entry, the prosecution of two foot-soldiers of British fascism confirmed MI5's fears about domestic German sympathisers. William Alexander Crowle was employed in the Royal Navy dockyard at Devonport; he was also a member of the town's BUF branch, where he met a local farmer, Claude Félix Pierre Duvivier – a former Belgian national who had acquired British citizenship and who also belonged to The Link.

Both men were, from evidence seized in a search of Duvivier's house, unquestionably pro-German. In correspondence between them after the first naval encounter of the war – the Battle of the River Plate in the South Atlantic – Duvivier mourned the sinking of the Kriegsmarine pocket battleship, *Admiral Graf Spee*.

It was a three to one battle and I should have liked to have seen matters reversed ... My heart goes out to those men on the *Graf Spee* – heroes fighting for the cause, every one of them ...

But it was their actions, not their sympathies, which led them to the dock of Exmouth Court on January 30: both pleaded guilty to 'recording information which would be directly or indirectly useful to an enemy'.[4]

Much of the evidence was heard *in camera* and there is, surprisingly, no Security Service file on Duvivier and Crowle in the National Archives. But press reports of the public sections of their trial showed that three weeks after war was declared, Duvivier asked Crowle to send him news of ships berthed at Devonport; a month later, on October 23, Crowle obliged – providing the militarily-sensitive news that HMS *Repulse* was anchored in the dockyard, and including details of the damage inflicted on other warships.

This was not mere idle chatter among pro-Nazi fascists: Duvivier had agreed with the editor of the BUF newspaper, *Action*, that it should publish the information he gleaned from Crowle, and had a typed-up letter containing the details ready to post when police arrested him. He and Crowle were each sentenced to six months' hard labour.

MI5 was plainly worried by the implications of the case, and had a remarkably frank interview with Sir Oswald Mosley about his personal admiration for some aspects of the Nazi regime and the potential threat posed by similarly-minded BUF members. On January 30, Liddell recorded this in his diary.

Among other things Mosley said he thought Germany could withstand a blockade for at least seven years, and that there was no possibility of internal upheaval since the Gestapo was the finest secret police the world had ever seen.

He did not think Hitler wanted to smash the British Empire. He had had personal contact with him on two occasions and both he and his wife were convinced that Hitler did not want to harm England in any way.

The Duvivier file was then produced and contained ... correspondence which made it clear that certain members of the BUF had an almost unbalanced admiration for everything German. The leader was asked whether he approved of this. He said he quite realised it and it was a great worry to him ... He admitted that an enemy agent would find a pro-Nazi member of the BUF a good cover for his activities.[5]

On that, at least, MI5 agreed. It wanted the government to proscribe the BUF, ban its newspapers and authorise the detention of its leading officials. Sir John Anderson, his PUS Sir Alexander Maxwell and Assistant Under-Secretary of State Frank Newsam, however, all demurred: an entry in Liddell's journal recorded the Home Office's intransigent opposition to such drastic action.

D.S.S. [Sir Vernon Kell] tells me that Maxwell has refused to consider our representations about the internment of 500 members of the BUF. Later I had a long conversation with Newsam. I told him that I was very concerned about our suggestion having been turned down ... It was quite obvious from the general make-up of the Party, from its publications etc., that it was actively assisting the enemy ...

Newsam seemed to doubt whether any members of the BUF would assist the enemy if they were able to land in this country. I said that I had not the slightest doubt that they would ... I told Newsam that there were after all some quite intelligent people in this office who had given careful study to the matter and that that was their considered view.[6]

Whether MI5 was equipped to handle the ramifications of what it was asking for was, to say the least, doubtful. By the spring of 1940, the Security Service was, according to its official historian, 'close to collapse'. Demands on it for vetting – both of foreign nationals and Britons seeking official exit permits – had steadily risen and were averaging 8,200 per week. Some of these requests were 'almost Gilbertian in their bureaucratic absurdity – such as the attempt to insist that it vet individually all enemy aliens (even in Category C) who were permitted to post parcels abroad'.[7]

The simmering tensions emerged into open warfare in the course of an enquiry into the entire British Intelligence establishment's fitness for purpose. This had been ordered the previous December by Chamberlain and Halifax and was headed by Sir Maurice Hankey (then recently ennobled as 1st Baron Hankey), an eminent Whitehall mandarin who had previously occupied the posts of Cabinet Secretary, Secretary of the Imperial War Cabinet during the First World War and, ultimately, Clerk to the Privy Council.

Throughout March and April he took evidence from the Home Office, the Security Service, Special Branch, the Director of Public Prosecutions and Norman Birkett KC, the barrister who headed the Aliens' Tribunal set up to hear challenges by German nationals interned on the outbreak of war.

Hankey noted that the question of which department MI5 reported to was 'rather anomalous' and that 'at the present the Department is somewhat isolated; rather a lost child – a position which is not improved by its present location in Wormwood Scrubs'. One of the witnesses from the Security Service – Hankey did not name him – complained that as a result of this (and the lack of any government ministry to which it could appeal in the case of frequent disputes over policy with the Home Office) MI5 was 'too much in Purdah'.[8]

But it was the vexed question of what to do about the vast number of enemy aliens which exposed the real tensions. The government's policies, Hankey reported, had caused severe problems:

> The work of the Aliens' Tribunals set up by the Home Secretary, which have examined the cases of 73,353 German or Austrian aliens, has added enormously to the work and has involved a very large expansion of the Security Service.
>
> The Registry, for example, where the card indexes and files are kept has had to expand nearly four-fold since the outbreak of war, and will certainly have to expand further as the war goes on. In these circumstances it is perhaps not surprising that the representatives of some of the Government Departments, when pressed on the point, stated that the Security Service is sometimes rather slow in answering queries.[9]

Remarkably, given its limited manpower and budget – just £93,000 for the year 1939–40 (equivalent to just over £4 million today) – MI5 had conducted a substantial number of detailed interviews with those interned: '250 enemy aliens have been interrogated at length', Hankey recorded approvingly, 'and full reports have been sent ... on over 600 cases.'

Quantity and quality were, however, different matters. While 'on the whole the Government Departments were fairly well satisfied ... there was a rather general belief that the officials of the Security Service, from the very nature of their work, tend to become unduly suspicious'.[10]

MI5's chief accuser appears to have been Birkett. A former Methodist preacher who had been declared medically unfit for service during the First World War, he had devoted himself instead to the criminal defence Bar; described by those who admire him as 'one of the most prominent Liberal barristers in the first half of the 20th century' and with a reputation for successfully defending clients even when there appeared a watertight case against them,[11] Birkett laid into the evidence which MI5 provided to his Tribunals.

Mr Norman Birkett had not come into direct personal contact with the Security Service but only with the barristers who had been retained by the Department to present their case to the Tribunal. To these [lawyers] he paid a warm tribute.

He mentioned, however, some 'gross mistakes and stupidities' that had been committed at the outset of the war in the internment of particular enemy aliens on the advice of the Security Service. He did not suggest that their advice was consistently wrong, but he said it had been 'frightfully wrong' in some particular cases. Some individuals were kept interned for months against whom the evidence proved on enquiry to be nil.

In some instances grave hardship was inflicted on perfectly innocent people, affecting their relations, dependants, fortunes, business and prospects, for no better reason than that under pressure they have been found to have joined the *Nazional Socialistiche Deutsche Arbeiterpartei* or the *Deutsche Arbeitsfront.*

Mr Birkett did not dissent from the view that in the circumstances of the outbreak of war, when no man could foresee the result of the expected whirlwind attack on this country, the policy of interning these people may have been a wise one. Neither did he dissent from the opinion that, bearing in mind what has recently happened in Norway, membership of the NSDAP or DAF was a factor to which the Security Service may have been right to give weight, though he pointed out that such persons, being marked men, were not likely to become spies or saboteurs. But he made the point that, if the Security Service had been able to interrogate these people earlier, they would have been released much sooner and the infliction of much real hardship would have been avoided.[12]

There was an element of truth in Birkett's charges. MI5 reports to the Tribunals were sometimes vague and occasionally ill-sourced – inevitable, since as Hankey observed, 'the Security Service was terribly overburdened in the early days of the war. The waves of refugees which had poured in recent years into this country in succession from Germany, Austria, Czechoslovakia and Poland had created an almost unmanageable problem at the outset of war, until the staff of the Department had been expanded sufficiently to cope with the additional work'.[13] Equally, however, there was good evidence that some enemy aliens – a small but potentially important minority – posed a genuine threat: Mitzi Smythe was a case in point.

She had been born in the north Rhineland province of Westphalia in 1901 but at the age of 22 had married Thomas Round, a British soldier serving with the military police in Germany, and thus acquired UK citizenship. In 1924 the couple came to Britain and, after brief spells in Bedford and Aldershot, eventually opened a tea rooms business in Dover. Round deserted her in 1931 and appears to have subsequently 'married' someone else, leading to a charge of bigamy and a nine-month sentence in Wormwood Scrubs.

Mitzi Round, as she then still was, moved further up the Kent coast and opened a boarding house in Ramsgate. She began a relationship with one of her guests, a mining engineer called William Smythe, and began using his surname instead of her own.

By the start of 1938 she had joined the Sandwich branch of the BUF (then run by an enthusiastic upper-class fascist, Lady Grace Pearson*) and was hawking *The Blackshirt* newspaper on the streets. More disturbingly, she was also gaining a reputation for trying to obtain information from military personnel stationed nearby. As her MI5 file noted:

> Since about 1936 Mrs Smythe has repeatedly come to the notice of the police and the military authorities in the neighbourhood of Ramsgate by reason primarily of the fact that she had deliberately sought the acquaintance of officers and men of the fighting forces, in particular the RAF.[14]

Ronald Dines was one of those whom Smythe pumped for information. An 'airman' (there are no details of his actual rank in MI5's files), in April 1938 he was posted to RAF Manston and needed local lodgings; he rented furnished rooms at Smythe's guest house, 'This'll Do',

---

* Lady Grace Pearson was the sister of Henry Page Croft, Conservative MP and Under-Secretary of State for War. She stood for election as BUF candidate in Canterbury in 1936 and was a close friend of Mosley. There is no MI5 file on her in the National Archives.

on Royal Road in Ramsgate. According to a signed statement he made on May 14:

> Soon after I went there she told me that she was from Austria ... She also told me that her father was an officer in the German Army and that her brothers were officers in the German Air Force. She also spoke to me about Manston Camp and asked if I had ever seen the underground hangars ...
>
> She asked me if the 'big silver machines' were the only type of plane at Manston, but I told her I did not know ... About the third week we were at the house, Mrs Smythe brought some post in and opened it. I saw that the letters were from a newspaper in Germany and they contained literature of a Nazi nature. She showed me this and also pictorial books relating to Hitler. She has often had conversations with me respecting Hitler and the Nazi regime in Germany and said that it would be a good thing if it was everywhere.
>
> On one occasion she asked me if revolvers were very expensive in England and said that she could get any amount of them in Germany at three marks each, and could bring them back to England with her as she was not searched at the Customs. She has told us that she goes to Germany several times each year.[15]

When Smythe gave Dines German propaganda, asking him to distribute this in the dining hall at Manston, he reported the request to the base police and handed over the pamphlets. There appears, however, to have been no follow-up either by the RAF or by Kent Constabulary – a failure which, according to the Security Service account of her case, allowed her to move from fascist proselytising to espionage.

At the end of April 1939 she was arrested after making an unauthorised visit to a local refugee camp. The incident was bizarre but offered further evidence that she was trying to send information to Germany.

> On the 30th April the Sandwich Police reported that they had received a complaint that Mrs Smythe had called at the Refugee Camp at Richborough at 2pm on 28th April 1939. Having been refused

admission, she staged a fainting attack and was taken into an office near the camp entrance.

She left the office and got into conversation with a young German named Gert-Horst Spiers whose parents reside in Cologne. She is said to have persuaded this young man to write a letter to his parents and give it to her to give to a young woman named Dennehy who was shortly going to Germany and whose passport Mrs Smythe showed to the young man.

Mail to and from inmates was strictly controlled and the letter was intercepted at the gate: it appeared to contain a coded message. Addressed to 'Dear Parents', it read:

> This afternoon Major Dennehy and his daughter came from London and called on me. You will remember that it is the family with which you lived when you were in London. You would not recognise Miss Billy at present, for she has grown up in the meantime. Billy will be there on Monday morning. If there are any small things you want to give her for me, you may do so.

Spiers was interviewed by the police. He said he didn't know anyone called Dennehy and that no one of that name had been to see him in the camp. As MI5 subsequently noted:

> It appears that Mrs Smythe desired to obtain the address of Spiers' parents for some reason. The Commandant of the Camp also told the Police that Mrs Smythe had spoken to two refugees in Woolworth's Stores in Ramsgate, about a week before, and had obtained from one of them the address of his wife in Germany.[16]

Despite her arrest, no further action was taken against Mitzi Smythe: she remained, undisturbed, in 'This'll Do' – a freedom she used, according to her MI5 file, to redouble her efforts on behalf of Germany.

> Shortly after the outbreak of war the Ramsgate Police received information that Mrs Smythe had stated she got a naval officer[17] very drunk

one night, and obtained information from him. The information included the route of a ship which was subsequently sunk. It was also stated that Mrs Smythe had endeavoured to get a message to a Dutch ship lying in Ramsgate harbour in order that such message should be conveyed to Germany.[18]

Ramsgate Police intercepted the message and sent it to the Admiralty for its advice. Since there was 'no doubt that it contains references to the sinking of, and damage to, British warships ... the naval authorities took a serious view of this piece of paper'.[19]

Mitzi Smythe exemplified the problems facing MI5. She was, as her file recorded, 'of hostile origin' and might have come under closer scrutiny as a former German national had it not been for the fact that she had acquired British citizenship by marriage – a confusion which was confirmed when she was unlawfully arrested, on May 22, 1940, under Regulation 18D, used for enemy aliens, rather than the correct 18B. She had also slipped between the cracks of Britain's still unco-ordinated counter-intelligence efforts: her eventual arrest was made on the orders of Sir Arthur Jelf, the regional Security Control Officer at Folkestone, on the basis of police evidence, since the Security Service had apparently not been informed of her activities.[20] By the time it got hold of her she had spent several months in detention and refused to answer any questions; as her interrogators ruefully noted, unless MI5 resorted to torture, there was no prospect of discovering the names of her contacts.

We both came to the conclusion that Smythe was a liar; when awkward questions were asked she either remained silent or pleaded lack of memory. A stronger interrogation which you may think still advisable might produce different results, but [Major 'Jock'] Whyte was definitely of the opinion that no useful purpose would be served by pursuing the matter, and accordingly I let it drop.[21]

Smythe remained in detention for the rest of the war. But even as she began her internment, events in Europe had overtaken and overshadowed individual cases of suspected espionage.

On May 14, Hitler's troops took complete control of the Netherlands and swept on into Belgium. The extraordinary speed of the German advance would cause a dramatic *volte-face* in the government's approach to domestic subversion; at the heart of this change were fears about Nazi Fifth Columnists waiting to welcome – and assist – the Wehrmacht when it landed in Britain.

The day after the Dutch army surrendered, Churchill's War Cabinet received a report from Sir Nevile Bland, Britain's most senior diplomat in Holland. Bland had crossed the North Sea on a Royal Navy warship, narrowly escaping several attacks by the Luftwaffe. In the comfort of the International Sportsman's Club on Mayfair's Upper Grosvenor Street, he hand-wrote a 1,000-word account of how the Netherlands had been taken: he headed this, unequivocally, 'Fifth Column Menace'.

The German parachute troops who attacked and captured Rotterdam and The Hague were, Bland asserted, 'boys of 16 to 18, completely sodden with Hitler's ideas, and with nothing else in their minds but to cause as much death and destruction as they could before being killed themselves'. The explanation for the astonishing success of such youthful forces was that they were aided by local pro-Nazi sympathisers and sleeper agents, who had given the invaders information about the disposition of the Royal Dutch Army as well as a list of key officials who were 'to be shot on sight'.

Some members of this Fifth Column were German (or German-origin) domestic staff, working in the houses of Dutch government ministers – and, Bland claimed, Britain faced exactly the same problem:

> Every German or Austrian servant, however superficially charming and devoted, is a real and grave menace ... I have not the least doubt that when the signal is given, as it will scarcely fail to be when Hitler so decides, there will be satellites of the monster all over the country who will at once embark on widespread sabotage and attacks on civilians and the military indiscriminately. We cannot afford to take this risk. All Germans and Austrians, at least, ought to be interned immediately.[22]

Bland's report has been widely mocked in recent years – dismissed by academic critics of Britain's wartime internment policy as the paranoia of an Old Etonian who 'like many who employ domestic servants, nourished a deep fear of their treachery'.[23] The truth is a little more complicated and nuanced.

Some of Bland's claims were, unquestionably, wrong: the role of German parachute forces in defeating Holland was much less crucial than he reported, and his warnings about the threat posed by 'the paltriest kitchen maid' were, to say the least, overstated. They were not, however, without foundation in fact: the case of My Eriksson was proof that the Abwehr had deliberately placed agents inside some of Britain's most powerful homes, and MI5 was then deeply concerned about one particular employment agency specialising in providing German domestic servants to British employers.

The business – the International Employment Agency (IEA) – had been operated since 1936 by an ostensibly British woman, Margaret Elizabeth Newitt. She was, in fact, German, having been born Margaret Winter in Berlin in 1891. She had married a British soldier serving in the Army of Occupation on the Rhine and come to Britain in 1935, some four years after her husband's death.

On the orders of the German Embassy and the leader of the Nazi Party organisation in England, she established the IEA to import domestic servants from Germany to Britain – a task which the Embassy told her 'would be doing the German Government a great service'.

MI5, which learned about the scheme in 1936, was certain that the maids and cooks for whom Newitt secured positions were working for Berlin: its Statement of Case against her noted that in September that year the British head of the Deutsche Arbeitsfront – the official Nazi trade union organisation – advised his head office 'that for well known reasons the placing of maids in English households could not be done by the DAF, but that arrangements had been made for such requests to be dealt with by Mrs Newitt'.

From this time onwards there is abundant evidence that Mrs Newitt was in the closest touch with important officials of the Nazi Party and the DAF in all matters concerning the placing of German domestic servants in this country ... It is quite clear from documents in our possession that requests made to the German Embassy or to the headquarters of the NSDAP either by domestics seeking situations or by families who wished to engage German domestics, were invariably referred to the International Employment Agency. In replying to German employers Mrs Newitt almost invariably concluded her letters with the words 'Heil Hitler'.[24]

Exactly which servants Margaret Newitt placed in whose households has, unfortunately, been removed from her extremely heavily-weeded file. The reason for this substantial redaction, attested to by fragments of information in the surviving documents, is that MI5 took over the International Employment Agency and ran it as a 'sting' operation. Sadly, the details of what intelligence – if any – this subterfuge yielded have been removed.[25] Nonetheless, her case, and that of My Eriksson, showed that warnings about the potential threat from German nationals working as domestic servants were not merely a melodramatic expression of upper-class paranoia.

Sir Nevile Bland's report was presented to the War Cabinet on May 15. Churchill reacted by demanding that 'there should be a very large round-up of enemy aliens and suspect persons in this country' and sent his most senior ministers away to come up with suitably draconian proposals[26] – a comment which, by some accounts, fired the starting gun for mass internment of German (and later Italian) nationals resident in Britain. In reality, the government had begun tightening its grip on enemy aliens some weeks earlier, prompted by stirrings of public unease. Inevitably, given the fractured nature of relations between the Security Service and the Home Office, this had fuelled the growing internal warfare. Guy Liddell noted the tension in a typically frank diary entry.

There is a growing storm in the press about enemy aliens. 70 MPs are threatening to raise the question in the House. Norman Birkett has made a most improper broadcast on the subject of enemy aliens under his pseudonym of 'Onlooker' which is known to almost everybody. It looks as if he made this broadcast under H.O. inspiration.[27]

By the end of May an additional 8,000 Germans and Austrians were interned; when Italy declared war on June 10, 4,000 Italian men joined them. If understandable, the move would prove catastrophic on three counts. Because insufficient attention had been paid to where to house the rapidly-growing numbers of those interned, more than 7,500 were put on transport ships and sent to Britain's colonies in Canada and Australia. On July 2, one of these vessels, the *Arandora Star*, was attacked and sunk by a U-boat; more than half of the 712 Italians, 438 Germans, and 374 British seamen on board lost their lives.

Before then, however, the round-up led to a press-inspired panic over the threat of 'enemies within'. The *Daily Mail* led the charge, demanding that all aliens – men and women – be rounded up urgently and held in 'a remote part of the country'.[28] Bland, too, fed the flames: in a BBC radio broadcast on May 30 he gave the public a taste of what he had told the War Cabinet.

> 'It is not the German or Austrian who is found out who is the danger. It is the one, whether man or woman, who is too clever to be found out. That was apparent in Holland where ... many of the obvious fifth columnists were interned at the outbreak of war – but where there still remained a dreadful number at large to carry out the instructions they had from Germany.
>
> 'I have had German friends in the past, and I hope that I may live to have a German friend or two again one day; and I hate to have to say this to you, but I find it my duty to say it, and say it I will. Be careful at this moment how you put complete trust in any person of German or Austrian connections. If you know people of this kind who are still at large, keep your eye on them; they may be perfectly all right, but they may not – and today we can't afford to take risks.'[29]

The third problematic outcome of the aliens round-up was less immediately visible: by stigmatising foreigners – the majority of whom posed no threat, and who were, in reality, refugees from Hitler's persecution across Europe – it disguised the far more serious danger from domestic fascists and Nazi sympathisers.

At the start of the crisis, on May 11, MI5 had sought approval for the arrest and detention of 500 leading BUF officials; the Home Office refused even to consider such a large-scale abrogation of traditional British liberties. On May 21 the dispute came to a head at a summit between the warring parties: from Liddell's unusually long diary account, it did not go well.

At 7pm today I attended a meeting at the Home Office which lasted until 8.45. The Home Secretary Sir John Anderson, the Director-General, Sir Alexander Maxwell, Charles Peake,[30] Sir Alan Brooke,[31] myself and Max Knight were present.

Anderson had our original memo which was turned down about ten days ago and wanted to have detailed information in support of the various statements made. M [Maxwell Knight] was extremely good and made all his points very quietly and forcibly. I did not interfere at all except on one or two occasions.

Anderson began by saying that he found it difficult to believe that members of the British Union of Fascists would assist the enemy. He had been studying the recent number of *Action* where Mosley appealed to the patriotism of its members.

Max explained that this was merely an example of how insincere Sir Oswald Mosley really was and how many of his supporters simply regarded utterances of that kind as a figure of speech ...

Sir John Anderson said that he needed to be reasonably convinced that the BUF might assist the enemy and that unless he could get such evidence he thought it would be a mistake to imprison Mosley and his supporters, who would be extremely bitter after the war when democracy would be going through its severest trials. I longed to say that if somebody did not get a move on there would be no democracy, no England and no Empire, and that this was almost a matter of days.

I did strongly stress the urgency of the matter and said that surely, rather than argue the fine points of these various cases, wasn't it possible to make up our minds whether the BUF was assisting the enemy and if we came to the conclusion that it was, wasn't it possible to find some means of dealing with it as an organisation.

Anderson rather skated over this but he seemed to have a great aversion to locking up a British subject unless he had a very cast-iron case against him. He was, however, I think considerably shaken by the end of the meeting and he asked us for further evidence on certain points which he required for the cabinet meeting which was to take place tomorrow evening.

Either he is an extremely calm and cool-headed person or he has not the least idea of the present situation. The possibility of a serious invasion of this country would seem to be no more than a vague suggestion in Anderson's mind.

The following day, Anderson reported to the War Cabinet, telling the assembled politicians and civil servants that MI5 believed more than a quarter of BUF members would be 'willing if ordered to go to any lengths on behalf of Germany' (although he could not resist the caveat that the Security Service 'had no concrete evidence' to back up this claim).[32]

The Cabinet settled for what amounted to a compromise. Regulation 18B was strengthened to allow the internment of anyone 'showing sympathy to enemy powers', and orders were signed for the detention of Mosley and 32 of his highest-ranking supporters. For the remainder, however, Anderson's intransigence prevailed – much to the disgust of Guy Liddell.

In my view the reluctance of the H.O. to act came from old-fashioned liberalism which seemed to prevail in all sections. The liberty of the subject, freedom of speech etc. were all very well in peace time but were no use in fighting the Nazis.

There seemed to be a complete failure to realize the power of the totalitarian state and the energy with which the Germans were fighting a total war.[33]

Liddell's comments threw into stark relief the fundamental dilemmas underlying the war on the Home Front: to what extent could the ends justify the means, and if they did, whether (in the words of American founding father Benjamin Franklin) 'those who would give up essential

Liberty, to purchase a little temporary Safety, deserve neither Liberty nor Safety'?[34]

The Security Service, the chiefs of the armed services and – for the time being – the Prime Minister stood on the side of practicality over ethics; Anderson, Newsam and the traditional bastions of liberal values in the Home Office argued for the opposite. They continued to do so despite a very clear warning at the end of Sir Maurice Hankey's report into MI5, delivered to the War Cabinet on May 29:

> We cannot be sure that, when the real emergency comes, the traitors within our gates, directed by some organisation which we may so far have been unable to detect, may not deal us a crippling blow. For this reason I trust that all concerned will give the fullest possible weight to any precautions which the Security Service may see fit to recommend.
>
> We simply cannot afford to take any risks, and such injustice to which such precautions may give rise are of minor importance compared with the safety of the State.[35]

Grudgingly, the Home Office accepted Hankey's advice: on May 30, the BUF was banned, although there was not to be any attempt to round up the bulk of its members. But Mosley's party was only the most visible of the myriad fascist – and often pro-Nazi – organisations lurking in its shadow. As the summer of 1940 progressed, and invasion by Hitler's troops turned from a possibility to a probability, the evidence of a threat from home-grown traitors and Fifth Columnists grew. The underlying challenge of what to do about them remained, however, largely unresolved.

CHAPTER TEN

Assisting the Enemy

'When the country is invaded by Germany they would set up a
Government of the BUF which would be under German control'
Statement of witness in R. v Swift and Ingram, July 1940

Wanda Penlington was scared.

It was approaching 11.00pm on Thursday, May 23, 1940;
she and her lover, William Gutheridge, were in an insalubrious area
of Harlesden, west London, when they spotted a policeman watching
them from a nearby corner.

Neither Penlington nor Gutheridge were strangers to the law: both
had histories which would, at the very least, make their presence on
the darkened streets difficult to explain. But what truly worried the
21-year-old tailoring machinist was the contents of her handbag; she
and Gutheridge had just carried out nine acts of deliberate sabotage
– all aimed at impeding the wartime emergency services – and the
evidence of their crimes was stuffed in the bag swinging at her hip.

Their actions – prompted by news of Mosley's arrest earlier that day
– would shortly land them in the dock at the Old Bailey. Their case did
not generate much press interest – the Home Office and government
Law Officers had decided the previous autumn that 'no reference is
to be made in the Press to arrests or sabotage cases or to cases held in

camera'[1] – and the *Daily Mirror* consigned the news to the bottom of page eleven on July 25. But their small and rather sad stories were an early sign that MI5's warnings to the Home Secretary were justified: a significant section of the rank and file membership of the British Union of Fascists was actively seeking to help Germany win the war.

That summer, as the British Army struggled back from Dunkirk and the country faced the very real prospect of a German invasion, there would be many more cases like those of Wanda Penlington and William Gutheridge – and the public's fears of a Fifth Column waiting to greet them grew.

*

Although large portions of trials were held in secret, and newspapers were either discouraged or forbidden from publishing too many details of prosecutions under the Official Secrets Act and Defence Regulations, the press campaign for more to be done about the 'Fifth Column menace' had not abated. An editorial in the *Sunday Times* captured the prevailing mood.

When the nation is at last bracing itself to meet the requirements of total war, it is entitled to insist that no measure for its security shall be omitted by the government. In particular, it requires the most effective protection against Fifth Column activities.

This is not an unrelated problem, because one of the chief purposes for which Fifth Columns exist is sabotage in all its forms. Espionage also is particularly important where the making of war material is concerned.

The antidote is a public preventative service whose energy and thoroughness are questioned by nobody. Public opinion is restive – and reasonably so – against the apparent apathy of the Home Office in this matter.

The lessons of Norway and Holland stand written in letters of blood for all to read. There is no sign that Sir John Anderson's officials have read them. They have done far too little, and done it with a strange air of reluctance. Everywhere there is an uneasy feeling that people are at large who ought to be interned. ... Defence against the

Fifth Column is, in the first instance, a Home Office problem. Let that department see to it in time. There will be no mercy for it if it lets us down.[2]

Whether the press was responding to genuine and widespread anxiety, or whether it actually created it, there was a surge in reporting of suspicious activities by the public. Some of these were, as the official history of MI5 suggested, 'deluded':

Marks on telegraph poles were frequently interpreted as codes designed to guide a German invasion ... Pigeons were widely suspected of secret intercourse with the enemy ... [and] one new recruit spent his first day in the Security Service in June 1940 dealing with a series of time wasting reports pointing to the danger of sentries being poisoned by ice-creams sold by aliens.[3]

Absurd or not, each report had to be followed up. A diary entry by Guy Liddell on July 3, 1940 summed up the problem.

Another mare's nest was investigated today. A female had communicated with a male at a certain London telephone number. The male voice said 'Go to the road which is called after the name of a river, proceed along it until you see a red flower pot. Knock four times on the door and give the password'. Enquiries showed that the message was from a Scout Master to a Boy Scout who is being trained in the powers of observation.[4]

Little wonder, then, that Liddell concluded: '5th Column neurosis ... is perhaps one of the greatest dangers with which we have to contend.'[5]

But away from what a Home Intelligence report to the Ministry of Information termed 'Fifth Column hysteria',[6] there was very real evidence that pro-Nazi British fascists were engaging in sabotage, espionage and preparation for an armed uprising. Between June and September 1940 a succession of men and women were sentenced to lengthy terms in prison for offences under the Official Secrets Act or Defence Regulations. Each was a member of the British Union – often also belonging to other fascist organisations such as The Link; and each committed their crimes with the express intent of assisting the enemy forces now gathering on the other side of the Channel.

William Gutheridge was 27 and – notionally, at least – an electrical welder. According to his criminal record, however, he was more regularly 'employed' as a ponce who lived off the immoral earnings of his girlfriend and part-time prostitute, Wanda Penlington. She was the child of Polish immigrants who, by the age of 21, had given birth to two children by different fathers and abandoned them both. By the start of the war the couple were living together in a shabby bedsit in Harlesden, where Gutheridge was an active member of the BUF. According to Penlington's police statement, this activity went beyond attending branch meetings.

> He would do anything to help the Germans. He can speak a bit of German and Italian. He hates English people like poison ... He had a map with all the ammunition factories, aircraft factories and aerodromes and some factories in Park Royal ... marked on the maps ... He said he'd like to do something with the railway lines at the Tube stations ...
>
> He often said he wished he had a pair of wire cutters to cut the telephone wires down. He said he wanted to climb up the poles and cut the wires down so as to disconnect all the wires and disarrange the telephone system.[7]

On May 23, Gutheridge stopped talking about sabotage and acted:

> When he heard the news about Mosley being arrested he said 'Now the fun starts. I'm going out when it's dark to do some damage' ... He mentioned ... that he was going to damage the public phone boxes so as to stop them communicating with the wardens if there was an air raid. I didn't want to be left on my own in case he got pinched or something, so I went with him ...
>
> He took a pair of scissors, my scissors, out of the drawer, and set off about half past ten. There was only us two. The first one was in Acton Lane, there was four in Park Royal and four in Harlesden.

He told me to stand outside when he did the first one and I saw him do it – cut the wire and cut the mouthpiece and combined part away and put it in his pocket. As he came out of the box he threw it away and he did the same with five of them but just cut out the wires with the other 4 – the last 4 – and left the mouthpieces in the boxes.[8]

On his arrest Gutheridge made only a brief statement in which he admitted the sabotage. 'I did the damage to the telephones as a protest to what I thought was the unjustifiable arrest of Mosley which had been announced on the wireless that day', he told police in Portsmouth on June 17. 'I did not intend to harm the country in any way, but it was only as a protest as I have said.'[9]

Penlington, however, told a different story, and one which explained why her lover was on the south coast when he was caught.

He got fixed up for a job with a Portsmouth firm ... he said he wanted to be near the shore or the docks – he hoped he'd be able to get some explosives to do as much damage as possible ...[10]

At their Old Bailey trial on July 24, Gutheridge was sent to prison for seven years; Wanda Penlington escaped a custodial sentence and was bound over for two years.

If their act of sabotage seemed petty, their convictions were the first hard evidence to support MI5's contention that there were a number of Nazi sympathisers still at large, willing and able to assist Germany.

Reginald Smith, a nineteen-year-old clerk in the Admiralty Charts Depot at Grimsby, was arrested in June 1940 in possession of a document showing the location of aerodromes throughout England, flying charts, a German army cap and a Webley revolver (for which he had no firearms licence). He was jailed for three months.[11] The same month, Thomas Hubert Beckett, a 35-year-old draughtsman in the Air Ministry at York, was found in possession of a map of local air bases as well as a detailed and up-to-date list of more than 600 RAF stations throughout the British Empire. Both documents were, according to East Riding Constabulary, 'highly secret, and very important and without doubt could be of great value to the enemy'; more troublingly, Beckett appeared to have gone out of his way to obtain the information within them, since it 'was not prepared in the normal course of his duty, and could only be compiled from highly secret RAF documents and correspondence'.[12]

Beckett was a long-time BUF activist. He had joined the party in 1937 and according to both his wife and the landlady of their rooms in Streatham, south London, he regularly went to its meetings dressed in full fascist regalia – 'a high neck black blouse, black breeches and black cavalry boots ... a belt with the buckle consisting of the circle and flash, the fascist emblem'.[13] He had also been in contact with the German propaganda ministry which, at his request, had supplied him with news sheets: Beckett handed these out at the Air Ministry offices in York.

He was arrested on June 9 and charged with two counts of espionage under Section 1 of the Official Secrets Act. Five months later he was convicted, at an *in camera* trial before York Assizes, on both charges; sentencing him to three years' penal servitude, Mr Justice Cassels was moved to question how a known and active fascist was able to work in such a militarily-sensitive government department:

'How it came about that you should have continued to have employment in the Air Ministry when your interests, not to say your
sympathies, were with such an organisation as the British Union of
Fascists is a little difficult to understand.'[14]

The judge's comments were relayed to the Home Office which, in turn, passed the same question on to MI5. It, unfortunately, knew nothing about either Beckett or the prosecution: neither East Riding Constabulary nor the government Law Officers had seen fit to inform the Security Service prior to his conviction – an oversight which made it impossible to discover whether Beckett was an active agent of German Intelligence or to whom, if anyone, he had given the secret documents. It was another indication that, a year after the war began, Britain's counter-espionage efforts were still depressingly fractured: that summer another case made the point even more clearly.

Frederick Roesch, a 27-year-old lathe operator, was arrested in June and subsequently jailed for ten years at the Old Bailey. He had been caught with a sketch showing the location of munitions factories near Kingston upon Thames, together with a diary containing 'notes on rifle instruction, military surveys, order of companies of soldiers etc., sketches of various rifle sights, sketches of positions of troops, guns, trenches etc [for] when a company is ready to go into battle'; he also possessed a German pistol and fourteen tear gas cartridges.[15]

The case was particularly disturbing for the Security Service – and not just because, as with Thomas Beckett, neither the police who arrested him nor the government Law Officers who sanctioned his prosecution under the Official Secrets Act had told MI5 about Roesch.

What made this all the more surprising was the Roesch family background. Although born in Britain, Frederick's parents were both German – his father was interned during the First World War and died in British captivity – and he and his three siblings had spent much of their childhood in Germany.

He had arrived back in England in 1935 after a year's training at a school run by the Sturmabteilung, or SA – the original paramilitary wing of the Nazi Party – and had been taken on by Siemens Schuckert. After his conviction, MI5 began hurried investigations into his family and contacts: they strongly suggested that Frederick Roesch was a spy. A note in his file by B Branch's Dick White[16] recorded:

> From a study of his papers, I should say that Roesch certainly worked for the Germans after his arrival here in 1935. It is possible that he made his reports either to the head of the D.A.F. section in Siemens Schuckert or to someone in the German Railways Information Bureau. It is further possible that one or other of the foreign addresses [found in his diary], particularly the one in Holland, may have been used by him for sending information out of the country. The possession of the revolver bought in Germany suggests that he may have been sent here by the Germans to work against us.[17]

Thomas Beckett and Frederick Roesch were not the only instances of the various arms of law enforcement, government and the intelligence service acting independently and without consulting their colleagues in the war on the Home Front. The trial of two British fascists at the Old Bailey in early July 1940 illustrated the seriousness of the problem.

Marie Louisa Augusta Ingram was 42 and a domestic help in the home of a Royal Navy officer who worked at the top-secret Mine Development Department at Southsea on the Hampshire coast. She was an attractive and vivacious woman who supplemented her wages with shifts at the local Auxiliary Fire Service. Much of Mrs Ingram's (eventual) MI5 file was destroyed in the bombing raid which hit the Registry in September 1940, but the surviving pages make clear that she had been born in Germany, had married a British Army sergeant in Cologne in 1922 and then emigrated to England one year later. Because her marriage gave her British citizenship, she had not been included in the lists of enemy aliens compiled before the war: as a result the Security Service had not been asked to vet her and had no idea that she even existed – much less that she was an active fascist and engaged in intelligence-gathering.

In May 1940 she struck up a friendship with Cecil Rashleigh, a retired painter and decorator who was working part-time as an auxiliary fireman. Evidently the two got on well enough for Mrs Ingram to reveal herself as a pro-Nazi recruiter on behalf of the British Union of Fascists. According to Rashleigh's subsequent statement to Portsmouth Police: 'During these conversations she usually became very vehement and openly displayed her hatred of England.'[18]

Either on his own initiative or – more probably – encouraged by a Portsmouth Special Branch officer, Rashleigh spent the next few weeks as a de-facto undercover informant.

'With a view to finding out the depth of her antipathy to this country I pretended that I [agreed] with her views ... On one occasion she asked me if I had ever thought of being a member of the BUF.'[19]

On May 13 Rashleigh had a second and longer conversation with Mrs Ingram at her flat near the seafront.

'She spoke to me about Germany and the Nazi regime. She mentioned that she had a brother in law who was a staff officer in the German

High Command and during the conversation I suggested that it was rather difficult now to correspond with him, but she informed me that it was no trouble at all and that she could get anything through to Germany.'

Cecil Rashleigh was, however, more than a mere informant. At the end of their discussion he told Mrs Ingram that he was friendly with a man in the Royal Tank Corps who was disgruntled, and hinted that his friend might, potentially, be usefully disloyal; in doing so, Rashleigh stepped across a legal threshold to become, essentially, an *agent provocateur*. He seems to have been convincing, because Mrs Ingram quickly sent him to see a contact of hers – 'a man of action' as she described him.

The contact turned out to be William Swift, a 57-year-old former RAF sergeant working as a storekeeper in Portsmouth dockyard and who was also a local BUF organiser. On the night of May 14, Rashleigh went to his home together with a Corporal Baron,[20] his 'friend' from the Tank Corps. He explained that he had been sent by Marie Ingram and told to ask for 'instructions'. The conversation quickly turned to the expected arrival of Hitler's forces in Britain.

'Swift told me that when the country is invaded by Germany they would set up a Government of the BUF which would be under German control. He talked at length ... and spoke in admiration of the Nazi regime.

'He then went on to speak of the formation of the local Defence Corps and stated that the Government were playing into the hands of the Fascist party, as it was an easy way for them to obtain arms and ammunition. He informed me that I should enrol in the Local Defence Corps as soon as possible.

'Before leaving Swift told me that I should burn all correspondence I received and that I should put my membership card in the back of a picture frame or secrete it somewhere where it could not be found in the event of a raid.'[21]

The following day Rashleigh and Baron went to see Mrs Ingram: she asked them if they could get designs of new tanks being constructed and when Baron said he could get blueprints, 'Mrs Ingram said "get as much as you can and it will be passed on to Germany"'.[22]

Before the end of the month, Swift and Mrs Ingram were arrested and charged with conspiring 'with intent to do acts likely to assist an enemy or to prejudice the public safety'. At their Old Bailey trial, both pleaded not guilty, but after Cecil Rashleigh gave evidence – the court was closed to press and public throughout the three days of the hearing – both were convicted; Marie Ingram was jailed for ten years, Swift for fourteen. 'It is a dangerous conspiracy that has been brought to light by this case', prosecution counsel Mr Anthony Hawke solemnly pronounced.

That summer, fears of such 'traitorous' conspiracies were stoked by new cases revealing a disturbing combination of the theft of militarily-sensitive information with the stockpiling of illicit weapons by British pro-Nazi sympathisers. On June 9, Guy Liddell dictated an entry in his journal, recording the detention of a 32-year-old examiner with the Air Ministry.

> We have now arrested one William Gaskell Downing ... and his German mistress Lucy Sara Strauss. When Downing's room was searched eight Winchester repeater rifles were found, with telescopic sites [*sic*] and 2,000 rounds of ammunition. No adequate explanation was forthcoming as to why he was in possession of them. He also had photographic representations of ... an Air Ministry pass.[23]

Gaskell was charged with offences under the Official Secrets Act and tried in Manchester on July 16. All the evidence was heard *in camera* and there is no press record of his conviction and six-year prison sentence. His case was, however, raised in the House of Commons in the context of a belated and hurriedly enacted new law. On July 24, Edmund Radford, Conservative MP for Manchester Rusholme, rose to ask the Attorney General:

> 'Why he did not order the prosecution under the Treachery Act of the Air Ministry inspector, William Gaskell Downing, who was sentenced at Manchester, on 16th instant, to six years' imprisonment for making

photographs of an aeronautical inspection badge, an Air Ministry pass and a permit to enter certain premises?'[24]

Until May 23, 1940, Britain did not have a law covering treachery. This omission – making it almost impossible to prosecute either German spies or British citizens working on their behalf for the worst acts of treason – had been spotted, according to an entry in Guy Liddell's journal, less than a week after the war began.

It has now been discovered that in the mass of regulations under which we are working it would be extremely difficult to impose the death penalty on a spy, if we happen to catch one. We could only proceed under the Treason Act and the Director of Public Prosecutions thinks that we should meet with a good deal of difficulty in proving our case.[25]

The problem, as he noted a month later, had been missed by the Home Office during the lengthy pre-war years of bickering over policy.

The matter appears to have been overlooked in our Defence Regulations. The Director of Public Prosecutions says that procedure by trial for high treason would be far too cumbersome and in a number of cases ineffective. For instance, if a German arrived at one of our ports and was arrested before he had time to do anything, there would be no very good grounds in the absence of special information regarding his mission for preferring a charge of high treason. He could moreover say that he owed no allegiance to the King and therefore could not commit an act of high treason.

It was agreed by all the high legal pundits who discussed this matter that it could not be left to the judge to decide whether a spy should be shot or sent to penal servitude for life. A law should be framed so that if the man was convicted of espionage the judge had no alternative but to sentence him to death on the same lines that he would sentence a murderer.

It was of course always open to the King to whittle the sentence down to three weeks if he so desired.[26]

Evidently, the Home Office was not sufficiently concerned by this omission to draft new legislation in timely fashion. Two months later Liddell noted acidly, 'We are still without a death penalty. The Home Office is now trying to get all cases dealt with by a Jury',[27] and a further three months passed without resolution. On March 18, 1940 Liddell wearily observed:

> There has ... been another hitch ... The previous difficulty was that the Army Council said that they did not wish to carry out the execution of a man unless he had been tried under Court Martial. It has now been decided that enemy aliens and army officers can be tried by Court Martial. Neutrals and other British subjects should be tried by a civil court.
>
> The Bill was presented to the Home Office, but the Home Secretary took the view that 'assistance to the enemy' was too wide and that a Bill would never get through the House. It was argued that if it could be shown that a man had sold a pair of socks to the enemy the Judge would have no option but to sentence him to death ...
>
> We have been asked to submit another draft, defining espionage more precisely.[28]

It took the fall of Norway, Holland and Belgium for Whitehall's bureaucrats to agree on the text of a new law. On May 22, the House of Commons passed the Treachery Act in record time; the following day the House of Lords followed suit and the King gave royal assent. The key clause of the Act was broadly-drawn and unequivocal.

> If, with intent to help the enemy, any person does, or attempts or conspires with any other person to do any act which is designed or likely to give assistance to the naval, military or air operations of the enemy, to impede such operations of His Majesty's forces, or to endanger life, he shall be guilty of felony and shall on conviction suffer death.[29]

There remained, however, lingering suspicions about the willingness of the Home Office and the government Law Officers to use the new law – concerns which prompted Edmund Radford's demand to the Attorney General for an answer in the House.

Sir Donald Somervell had been Attorney General for three years, and Solicitor General for three years before that; he drew on his reputation for lengthy and honourable public service to reassure MPs that justice would be applied impartially – Downing's offences did not, he insisted, meet the standard of treachery – and without any improper interference.

> 'Each case has to be considered on its own merits, in the light of the code contained in the Treachery Act, the Official Secrets Act and the Defence Regulations. Different and graver facts have to be established to justify proceedings under the Treachery Act than under the other provisions.
>
> 'If my Honourable Friend has a suspicion which he appears to have, that there is any reluctance to invoke the Treachery Act in a proper case, he will be glad to be assured that his suspicions are quite unfounded.'[30]

This emollient answer did not – quite – satisfy the Labour MP Sydney Silverman, a forceful advocate for the victims of Hitler's anti-Semitic pogroms and a vocal opponent of capital punishment. 'Will the Right Honourable and learned Gentleman take care', he asked Somervell, 'that, in exercising his functions under this Act, he will not allow himself to be influenced by political pressure of any kind?' To which the Attorney General insisted: 'There is no question of politics at all.'[31]

It was a noble promise, but one which, in the context of government policy towards British fascists working on behalf of Germany, would soon prove somewhat hollow.

For some months Maxwell Knight's informants inside the BUF had been reporting that some of its officials were preparing for a violent coup d'état: Mosley had told followers 'our time is approaching', and senior officials had been told to be on standby for 'the showdown' to begin.[32]

The Security Service also had information that in at least two separate strongholds of the Party – Yorkshire and London – diehard British pro-Nazis had been stockpiling weapons in expectation of the great day. What transpired, in the weeks following Mosley's internment, both strengthened this evidence and painted a depressing picture of the ease with which well-connected fascists could escape the consequences of their actions.

Charles Stephen Geary was 48. A veteran of the Royal Engineers during the First World War, and of the notorious 'Black and Tans' paramilitary unit which carried out a brutal counter-insurgency campaign on behalf of the British government during the Irish War of Independence, he had been a minor official in the old British Fascisti party from 1925–29 before throwing in his lot with the BUF in west London.

His reputation in fascist circles was, according to a Home Office file on his career, that of an influential figure who 'gathered round him the more extreme members and was always known to be extremely interested in the acquisition of unlicensed firearms'.[33]

Geary did not take up any official position within the BUF: rather, according to an MI5 report on his activities, from 1935 onwards he used the anonymity of its ranks to infiltrate a respectable ex-servicemen's organisation, the Fellowship of the Services.

> We have received first-hand information that Geary was trying to recruit from amongst the members of the Fellowship of the Services extremists who would be prepared under certain circumstances to resort to violence in the event of a political upheaval in this country. Early in 1936 we learned beyond doubt that Geary was still interested in the collection of unlicensed firearms and was actually considering the possibility of obtaining machine guns or Lewis guns ...
>
> In March 1936 Geary asked an acquaintance of some years' standing to keep his eyes open for unlicensed firearms and ammunition and also for likely men who would keep their mouths shut. We learned also that Geary and his friends had a shooting range of some sort where they practised their shooting.

The Security Service's efforts to keep Geary under close observation had, however, been hampered by its shortage of funds and manpower.

Until May 1937 we could obtain no further information about Geary's activities as we had no-one in touch with him and he is a very cautious individual who never commits himself on paper. In May 1937 however there were indications that the Fellowship of the Services contained definitely pro-Fascist elements.

Finally, by March 1940, MI5 had managed to place informants inside his close circle of fellow fascists. What they reported was alarming.

It then came to our knowledge that Geary's 'boys' were trying to penetrate the British Union organisation and form in each branch cells of really reliable men who would, if necessary, actually fight. Later in the same month we learned directly from Geary that a member of his group in the Fellowship of the Services was trying to contact employees in the Enfield Small Arms Factory with a view to procuring arms and ammunition.

We also heard that in the earlier days of Geary's organisation some of the members joined the Territorial Army with the object of stealing bit by bit all the small arms, ammunition, and, if possible, Lewis guns which they could obtain.

In April 1940 Geary made a new acquaintance in whose reliability he had complete confidence. To this acquaintance he made no secret of the fact that he was interested in acquiring firearms. He told him also that he took elaborate precautions against government agents being planted in his organisation. He had avoided this for eight years as he thought the inclusion of one government agent might ruin his work.

In July 1940 Geary said that his organisation had two dozen motor cars which patrol about the country with four men in each car ascertaining the position of military strong points. There is more than a suggestion that these men may be disguised as members of the Home Guard. We are now informed that trustworthy members of the Fellowship of the Services who are at present in the Home Guard are to be instructed that when peace comes and they are told to return their firearms they are at all costs to keep them and not to hand them over.[34]

On August 13, Geary was arrested under Regulation 18B and swiftly taken to what a Special Branch report describes as 'the Ham Common internment camp'. Latchmere House was a large detached Victorian villa overlooking Ham Common in Richmond upon Thames; once a hospital caring for First World War officers suffering from shell-shock, in 1939 it had been redesignated 'Camp 020' and used to house captured enemy agents and high-risk domestic fascists.

The officer in charge of Camp 020 was Colonel Robin Stephens; known as 'Tin Eye' due to the monocle he habitually wore over his right eye, Stephens acquired a reputation for effective, if forceful, methods of interrogation[35] – though he denied accusations of torture which were subsequently levelled.[36]

MI5 records show that Geary arrived at Camp 020 on August 13 and was released fourteen days later, on the orders of the Home Secretary. There is no official explanation for this abrupt *volte-face* – and his stay at Latchmere House was unusually brief compared with other prisoners[37] – but from that date forward Geary disappears from official history. The decision, however, followed an appeal by his wife, Ivy, who complained about her husband's arrest 'without any explanation' and claimed he was 'a loyal ex-serviceman who even endeavoured at the outbreak of war to join his old Corps with the idea of having "another smack at the Germans" whom he hated – he is certainly no 5th Columnist'. Mrs Geary's plea concluded with the assertion that her husband had 'been treated like a criminal' and that his arrest would cause his family great hardship. Other than noting that Sir John Anderson had 'considered this case in the light of the evidence', there is no reason given for the somewhat rapid change of official heart on Geary.[38]

If the freeing of Geary only hinted at the Home Office's susceptibility to pressure, there was no such ambiguity about the release of John Ellis that autumn, and – given the clear evidence that he was a high-ranking fascist and that he had illegally stockpiled weapons and ammunition – it was a case which pointed to a serious and ongoing problem.

At the age of 40, Ellis was the very wealthy owner of several factories in Yorkshire – among them a foundry in Leeds producing shells for the Army. He was also an influential figure in the local BUF and had entertained Mosley over luncheons and suppers at his home in the Leeds suburb of Horsforth. West Riding Constabulary received a stream of complaints that Ellis was in the habit of pressing fascist literature on his employees and neighbours, and that visitors to the Ellis house observed him, his wife and their children giving the Nazis' straight-armed salute and ending conversations with a hearty 'Heil Hitler'.

The police passed this information on to MI5, along with intelligence which suggested that Ellis was a member of a violent breakaway section within the local fascist movement. Guy Liddell recorded the information in two entries in his journal; on August 8 he reported: 'There is an active pro-German group of disaffected members of the BUF in Leeds. ... The group is anxious to establish contact with Germany with a view to getting funds and possible arms.' Three weeks later the lead had been developed, and the new information was disturbing:

> There have been some melodramatic developments in the case of the BUF at Leeds. There is now a definite conspiracy to obtain military information ... and to pass this information to the Germans. There is also a scheme to obtain arms and explosives.[39]

The evidence for this alarming assertion – and its link to John Ellis – had accumulated over the summer. Between June 7 and 12, officers from the Kendal division of Cumberland and Westmorland Police had made a series of discoveries in woodland surrounding the small market town of Milnthorpe. The first was a package of BUF pamphlets and literature found in the woods; the third was a set of nine copies of Mosley's 1938 book *Tomorrow We Live*[40] recovered from a ditch four miles from the woodland itself. But it was the second bundle – unearthed from a shallow scrape in the heart of the woods – which was most disturbing: in addition to three further copies of Mosley's book, it contained 360 rounds of .22 calibre ammunition.[41]

Some of the material bore a name and address: Mr and Mrs J. Ellis, The Rookery, Horsforth. On June 15, alerted by their colleagues in the Lake District and armed with a search warrant signed by local magistrates, West Riding Constabulary arrived at the house.

The family was not at home, but their gardener unlocked the doors and watched as the police made an inventory of weapons, ammunition and Nazi literature found inside. The armaments included:

1 × .410 Stevens shotgun
1 × .410 walking stick gun
1 × Victor .410 smooth bore rifle
1 × .410 shotgun
1 × 12 bore shotgun
1 × German air rifle
1 × Webley service air rifle
1 × Webley air pistol
2 × Remington .22 rifles (1 repeating, 1 automatic)
1 × Winchester .22 rifle (repeating)
1 × Browning automatic pistol
690 rounds of .22 ammunition
285 rounds of .32 ammunition
400 rounds of B.B. caps [Bulleted Breech .22 rimfire
    ammunition]
'A quantity of shotgun ammunition'
1,371 × .410 shotgun cartridges
584 × 12 bore shotgun cartridges
30 × long range 12 bore slugs
250 × .22 rounds
3,000 × .22 [air rifle] pellets

Several of the weapons were unlicensed and therefore illegal; nor did Ellis have permits covering 1,369 of the bullets. The literature seized in the raid was equally revealing. Alongside BUF newspapers and leaflets, police found shelves of books about National Socialism, including Hitler's *Mein Kampf* in German, three further copies in English translation, books on the Fuehrer's genius by Goebbels and Hermann Rauschning, and Mussolini's autobiography. Tucked away in a cupboard, they discovered a large cache of maps – 205 in total – on which someone had marked strategically important towns, bays, harbours and ferries.

In the circumstances, it was hardly surprising that, on June 25, the Regional Commissioner for the North East, William Ormsby-Gore, 4th Baron Harlech, signed an order for Ellis' detention under Regulation 18B[42] on the grounds that he was known to be 'a member of, or to have been active in the furtherance of the objects of, an organisation [the BUF]' which had 'associations ... or sympathies with the system of government of, a power with which His Majesty is at war'; and that this was 'prejudicial to the public safety, the defence of the realm ... [and] the efficient prosecution of a war in which His Majesty is engaged'.[43] Ellis was arrested and taken to Liverpool prison.

He did not, however, remained locked up for long. Ellis had both the money to hire heavyweight legal representation – a firm of expensive lawyers based in London's Inner Temple – and political clout. On July 5, his local MP, Sir Granville Gibson, wrote to the Home Secretary demanding that his constituent be given an expedited hearing before the Advisory Committee; the request was granted (a privilege of timeliness not accorded to less well-connected detainees) and on August 22 Ellis appeared at a day-long appeal against his internment.

In advance of the hearing he was given facilities to prepare a lengthy typewritten statement in which he set out both his claims of innocence and his vital importance to 'the war effort'.

'In all about 900 workers are directly dependent on me and about another 750 only a little less so', he told the Committee, explaining that his brother, who had been left in charge of the family factories, dye works, laundry and fifteen retail clothing shops, could not cope alone and was 'now completely overwhelmed'. Nor could his father – 'semi-retired' and in ill-health – bear the burden 'of any heavy or long continued strain'.[44]

Since very little of the Ellis empire undertook war work, his plea to be released in the national interest was – at best – exaggerated. His explanations of his fascist affiliations, his stockpile of weapons and ammunition and the bizarre disposal of them in Lake District woodland were equally fanciful.

He claimed he had joined the BUF 'four or five years ago', having been 'induced to do so largely as a result of the publicity which was given to it at the time by the *Daily Mail*'. It was, he admitted, true that he attended Party meetings in Leeds – but only 'out of curiosity', and only when Mosley was due to speak – occasions which led to him entertaining the Leader to lunch or supper at The Rookery. In summary, he was a 'non-active' BUF member, one who did not 'bind himself to do anything at all to further the cause of fascism [whereas] an active member undertakes to give some part of his leisure time to furthering the cause'. Since among the documents seized from his home were BUF account books showing that he had paid £55 19s and 4d (the equivalent of £2,200 today) to repair its propaganda van, Ellis' claim was blatantly false.

As to the weapons he assembled, he airily told the Committee that he had 'developed a liking for shooting and decided to make somewhat of a hobby of it'. He amassed the large quantity of ammunition because he believed wartime restrictions would reduce his ability to buy live rounds. The maps, he said, were the innocent by-products of his other passion – motoring holidays – and the marks on them nothing more sinister than locations he intended to show his children.

There only remained the admittedly suspicious actions of dumping fascist literature and .22 calibre rounds in the woods: 'In a foolish fit of fear I decided to rid myself of the pamphlets which were in my possession ... and instead of handing them to the Police I dumped them in the country'; adding that he hid the ammunition because 'the fact that I had firearms in my possession was regarded ... as being somewhat suspicious'.[45]

The Advisory Committee weighed this testimony against the evidence provided by MI5 and the police. On September 5 it pronounced its verdict.

The business of the Committee was ... to decide whether Ellis is a truthful man and a trustworthy man. Having seen him and examined him, and studied his demeanour, the Committee are entirely content to record their view that he is a truthful and reliable man.[46]

On this advice, Sir John Anderson signed the necessary papers to release John Ellis from 18B internment.

The decision was greeted with anger and disbelief: MI5 protested that 'Ellis is in a position to supply an invading force with quantities of British uniforms, tractors and motor cars. If he is disloyal he is a person who is terribly dangerous. In our submission he cannot at this critical moment, be given the benefit of any doubt there may exist as to his loyalty.'[47]

Lord Harlech added his voice as Regional Commissioner, writing to Anderson's PUS, Alexander Maxwell, to report the 'bewilderment' of the police, and to warn that there had been 'the greatest uneasiness among responsible people resident in the district as to his being at large, and a corresponding relief when it was decided that an Order should be made against him, and the effect of his release upon local opinion cannot fail to be most unfortunate'.

In the bluntest of terms, Harlech reminded the Home Office that 'there is ... an underground Fascist organisation in this region upon which MI5 are keeping a close watch, and it is evident that a man of Ellis' beliefs, undoubted ability and great wealth is just the sort of person who is likely to be of assistance to a dangerous movement of this kind', before concluding:

> Leaving quite out of the account the question of the marked maps and the possession of large quantities of lethal weapons and ammunition, Ellis was admittedly an ardent Fascist who had on two occasions entertained Sir Oswald Mosley when he visited this part of the world, and if these facts are not sufficient to justify the conclusion that it is necessary that he should be under control, it would seem that recent prominence in the Fascist Party and active association with its leader, now under detention, are not sufficient ground for the maintaining of an Order under Regulation 18B(1a).
>
> I must confess that I share the bewilderment of the police and ... it is clearly unsatisfactory from every point of view for a regional Commissioner's decision under that regulation to have been reversed by the Home Office.[48]

For his part, Maxwell played Pontius Pilate. It was not for him to question the Committee's considered conclusion, he (incorrectly) informed Harlech,[49] especially since it had 'had the advantage of seeing Ellis in person' and reached the view that 'there is no danger of his doing anything contrary to the national interest'.

Of course should it be found that the Committee was mistaken in their opinion of Ellis and that he continues to promote Fascism, he would have to be interned immediately – but the Committee felt confident that there was no such danger.[50]

The best Harlech and the Security Service could achieve was a secret note, placed some time later on Ellis' vetting file, stating that he was 'not to be allowed into any of the Forces'.[51]

The case of John Ellis was a timely reminder of the internal battle still raging between the Security Service, the Home Office, and its Advisory Committees over the difficult balance to be struck between protecting the entire nation and penalising the individual. It was also a reminder, if one were needed, that the halls of justice would offer sanctuary to the wealthy and well-connected while proving unforgiving of lesser, equally dangerous, fascists.

In time this conflict would boil over into outright war: but that autumn all the opposing factions were facing renewed evidence that, away from the actions of individual pro-Nazis, much more organised plans for a violent fascist revolution had been hatched.

CHAPTER ELEVEN

The Kensington Conspiracy

'I should welcome a civil war with shots fired in the streets.'
Captain Archibald Maule Ramsay MP,
May 1940

On Tuesday, November 5, 1940, staff at the Central Criminal Court in London began taping up the glass. Diagonal white crosses were a familiar sight on windows all over the country, a protection against flying glass during air raids. But the windows being attended to that autumn morning were inside the Old Bailey, and the tape carefully fixed to them was intended to guard against prying eyes, not the Luftwaffe's bombs. As the *Daily Express* reported the following morning:

> During the trial of a woman at the Old Bailey yesterday thick brown paper was pasted over the glass panels of the doors, the doors them-
> selves were locked and police stood guard at them to ensure that nobody outside the court room would see a certain witness.[1]

The occasion for such stringent safeguards was a double trial: *R. v. Tyler Kent* and *R. v. Anna Wolkoff*. Both faced charges, under the

Official Secrets Act and Defence Regulations, of stealing top-secret military and government documents and of communicating with the enemy.

Over the course of eight days, a succession of undercover agents and MI5 officers testified that Kent and Wolkoff had hoped to bring about Britain's defeat by Germany. All their evidence was heard *in camera* and the Security Service asked the Director of Public Prosecutions to prevent newspapers from discovering even the most basic details of who was scheduled to take the stand. 'It seems to me most dangerous', Deputy Director General Oswald Harker complained, 'that the press should know who is giving evidence.'[2]

Harker's plea seems to have had an effect. There was very little further press coverage of the trials; and reports of the verdicts were remarkably brief for such a serious case. The dry, nine-paragraph account in *The Times* on November 8 was typical.

The trial ended at the Central Criminal Court yesterday ... of Anna Wolkoff, 37, daughter of a former foreign Naval Attaché, who was found guilty of offences contrary to the Official Secrets Act, 1911, and Defence (General) Regulations, 1939.

Also charged with her was Tyler Gatewood Kent, 29, a former clerk at the United States Embassy who, last week, was found guilty of offences contrary to the Official Secrets Act, and the Larceny Act 1916, judgement on him being postponed until the end of the case against the woman ...

After the jury, following an absence of two and a half hours, returned their verdict against Miss Wolkoff yesterday, the representatives of the Press were admitted to the Court.

Mr Justice Tucker said that Kent had been found guilty of five offences of obtaining and communicating documents which might be of use to an enemy for a purpose prejudicial to the state ... His Lordship then sentenced Kent to seven years' penal servitude.

Addressing Miss Wolkoff, the Judge said: 'You have been found guilty on two counts of a similar nature to those in Kent's case ... and also of a still more serious offence ... that with intent to assist the enemy you did an act which was likely to assist the enemy ...

You, a Russian subject who, in 1935 became a naturalised British subject, at a time when this country was fighting for her very life and existence sent a document to a traitor who broadcasts from Germany for the purpose of weakening the war effort in this country.

It is difficult to imagine a more serious offence but ... I take into consideration the fact that you undoubtedly have been led to do this by the anti-Jewish obsession on your part – a virus which has entered your system and destroyed your mental and moral fibre ...

The only useful sentence I can pass as a warning to others, lest there be others so minded as you, is one of 10 years' penal servitude.[3]

It was fine sentiment. But though neither Mr Justice Tucker nor the press knew it, there were many others involved in the conspiracy underlying the trial of Tyler Kent and Anna Wolkoff. Their identities, and that of the organisation to which they belonged, had been concealed just as effectively as the paper and tape had obscured the proceedings in court; they were, however, names which were all too familiar to MI5 – Captain Archibald Maule 'Jock' Ramsay MP and the Right Club.

*

In late June 1939, a middle-aged housewife set out from her modest home in Essex to take tea with one of Britain's most aristocratic ladies at one of the grandest houses in London. Marjorie Amor was 40 years old, short and stout; she was separated, but not divorced, from her husband and had for some years managed to raise the couple's son single-handed while simultaneously holding down a job giving public cooking demonstrations for a flour manufacturer.

In the summer of 1939 two events changed the course of her otherwise unexceptional life: her son's application to join the Merchant Navy was accepted, and she was approached by Maxwell Knight, head of a clandestine unit of amateur agents known as 'M.S.', within MI5.

Knight had met – and made use of – Amor several years earlier; now he sought to recruit her again for a new mission: the penetration of a group of diehard fascists based in the wealthy enclave of South Kensington. No. 24 Onslow Square, a pleasant four-storey building looking out over private gardens and boasting twin Palladian columns flanking its entrance, was the London home of Captain Archibald Maule Ramsay MP and his wife, the Honourable Ismay Ramsay. It was also the headquarters of the Right Club.

Knight had been trying to place an informant inside Ramsay's circle for some months, but the man he assigned had been unable to gain the group's confidence: a new approach was needed and Knight decided that, despite the Security Service's traditional antipathy to female agents, this mission required qualities which – to his mind – only a woman could offer.

'There is a very long-standing and ill-founded prejudice against the employment of women as agents', he wrote in a report on the activities of 'M.S.' just before the end of the war:

> It is frequently alleged that women are less discreet than men; that they are ruled by their emotions and not by their brains; that they rely on intuition rather than on reason; and that sex will play an unsettling and dangerous role in their work.
>
> My own experience has been very much to the contrary ... the emotional make-up of a properly balanced woman can often be utilised in an investigation ... A woman's intuition is sometimes amazingly helpful and amazingly correct ...
>
> On the subject of sex ... it is true ... that a clever woman who can use her personal attractions wisely has in her armoury a very formidable weapon ... However, it is important to stress that I am no believer in what may be described as Mata-Hari methods.[4]

Marjorie Amor was the polar opposite of the exotic courtesan-spy Mata-Hari. Her government-issued photograph shows her to have been plump-faced and rather plain; she was, however, intelligent and blessed with a warm personality – a quality Knight valued highly in his female recruits. 'Nothing is easier than for a woman to gain a man's confidence', he noted in his memorandum, 'by the showing and expression of a little sympathy.'[5]

She had one other vital attribute, qualifying her to infiltrate the Right Club: she knew the Ramsays personally, having met them during their mutual involvement in the Christian Protest Movement – an early-1930s group formed to combat the persecution of religious bodies in the Soviet Union.

At Knight's behest, Mrs Amor – now codenamed M/Y in MI5's records – telephoned the Ramsay household to rekindle their acquaintance: the Hon. Ismay promptly invited her to tea at 24 Onslow Square. According to Amor's subsequent statement:

> I went to tea a few days later and had a long talk with Mrs Ramsay on political topics; Captain Ramsay was not present. Her conversation was violently anti-Semitic and anti-Masonic. She talked at length about the Right Club of which her husband was the leader and ... explained that they would have liked to spread their views by means of public meetings, but owing to Jewish pressure they were unable, except on rare occasions, to get any halls or other suitable places in which to meet. They therefore had to rely on individual members to penetrate similar organisations such as the Nordic League, British Union, The Link etc.
>
> She explained the various grades of membership and told me that many of the names of the Right Club did not appear in any written record. The ones that did were kept in a special locked book ... This left me with the impression that membership of the Right Club was a secret matter.[6]

Over the ensuing weeks, Amor met Mrs Ramsay several times. She evidently played her role well, because by mid-August she had been invited to join the Right Club; on August 14, 1939 she received her membership card and the Club badge depicting an eagle killing a snake and bearing the initials P.J. – 'Perish Judah'.

Her membership should have been short-lived. Like other fascist organisations including the Nordic League and The Link, the Right Club was ostensibly mothballed on the outbreak of war. In reality, and under Ramsay's direction, it – and they – simply went underground.

On September 21, Amor had her first meeting with Ramsay himself. According to her statement, he made it clear both that the organisation continued to exist and that it was gaining useful recruits within the corridors of Whitehall.

He said that the Club would continue its activities in other organisations [and] ... that it was intended to carry on the work of the Club by the distribution of literature.

We ended the conversation by discussing the war and ... he told me that he had most of the Government Departments covered with the exception of the Foreign Office and the Censorship Department. He added, 'if you could help us here it would be very useful'.[7]

Marjorie Amor was not the only source of information on Ramsay's activities. The Metropolitan Police Special Branch had also been tapping its own agents within the fascist movement and, on September 22, its Chief Constable filed an alarming report on what they had discovered.

The activity of the pro-fascist and anti-Semitic Right Club ... is centred principally on the contacting of sympathisers, especially among officers in the Armed Forces, and the spreading by personal talks of the Club's ideals.

The talk has now reached the stage of suggestions that a military coup d'état is feasible and the leading Right Club enthusiasts seem agreed upon the fact that their views are received with a very satisfactory degree of sympathy by Service men.

Up to now, it should be made clear, nothing more than mere talk has taken place and no plans of any sort have been formulated – the subject is however being discussed seriously and not merely dismissed as a wild idea.

It is felt that should a leader step forward, the movement would make rapid headway. Naturally the name of the Duke of Windsor is mooted by some as favourable to the ideology behind the movement, but little hope is felt that he would lend himself to such an intrigue.[8]

The idea of a coup d'état, to be led by a coalition of British fascist groups, was certainly under consideration that autumn. A Special Branch intelligence memo from early November reported a gathering, held at Oswald Mosley's Pimlico home and attended by the Leader himself, Admiral Sir Barry Domvile of The Link, Aubrey Lees representing the Nordic League, and Lord Lymington, flying the flag for aristocratic fellow-travellers:

> This meeting was the result of tentative consultations that have been held between leaders of various pro-fascist or anti-Semitic groups and Mosley's contacts, aimed at securing a degree of collaboration between, if not complete unity among, them and the British Union of Fascists.
>
> For some days before, Mosley had been hinting to his intimates that the BUF would become the focal point of a vast secret revolutionary organization. In addition, it has been noted that since September, many of the pro-German and extreme anti-Semitic elements have inclined to the view that the BUF should be utilized to further their ends ... It is understood that Mosley did most of the talking and that a vague agreement on collaboration but nothing concrete was arrived at.[9]

Ramsay's own (subsequent) account of the coup discussions with the BUF suggested that they were more 'concrete' than Special Branch believed. According to this version, 'long before the outbreak of war' Mosley had asked Ramsay to throw in his lot with the Party and 'had promised Scotland ... as the area for which he would be responsible ... "Mosley said, we have nothing in Scotland. I wish you would take it over".'[10]

Mosley, however, had blotted his fascist copybook by previously reining in the naked anti-Semitism of the early BUF era. As a result he commanded neither the support nor the loyalty of more radically pro-Nazi organisations. Archibald Ramsay's aim in establishing the Right Club was to unify the movement in time for the much-discussed coup, while simultaneously marginalising Mosley. On September 23, 1939, Marjorie Amor had a revealing 'personal interview' with Ramsay in which she broached the subject of the coming uprising.

> In the course of conversation M/Y asked Captain Ramsay whether in the event of a Right Wing revolution breaking out in this country the Right Club members would be asked to follow Sir Oswald Mosley.

His reply was 'Certainly not: before such a situation arises I shall be in touch with all the members and you will then be told who is to be your leader.'[11]

This fascist uprising would not, according to MI5's reports of what Ramsay told Amor, happen spontaneously: rather, it would immediately follow the arrival of Hitler's troops in Britain.

> It is not that Ramsay anticipates successful revolution independent of German action. Ramsay has said to M/Y words to the effect that he expected Hitler would take the continent of Europe and leave Britain as a protectorate with Ramsay as a ruler. Mrs Ramsay is more modest. She anticipates that Jock will only be Commissioner of Scotland.[12]

He did, however, expect – and indeed look forward to – the prospect of violence, telling a meeting of trusted Right Club members: 'Personally, I should welcome a civil war with shots fired in the streets.'[13]

Ramsay was not the only fascist luminary getting ready to welcome a violent coup d'état. In January 1940, MI5 received a report from one of its informants inside the BUF about an incendiary speech given by General John Fuller. 'We know the present system of Government is rotten to the core', he told a meeting also graced by the presence of Lady Domvile on behalf of The Link. 'What we want is a bloody revolution and I am ready to start one right away.'[14]

In the meantime, Ramsay busied himself with placing more of his followers inside government ministries. Following up on the broad hint given to Marjorie Amor, Maxwell Knight arranged for her to join the staff of the Postal Censorship Department – a move which, when she reported it to Mrs Ramsay on October 25, was greeted as 'splendid' news, and with a request to keep her eyes open for useful intelligence. It also secured Amor's acceptance into what was described as 'the Inner Circle of the Right Club', a select group with some very familiar names: Lords Sempill and Tavistock, General John Fuller and Admiral Barry Domvile.

The Hon. Ismay Ramsay was clearly a co-conspirator with her husband and privy to the Right Club's most sensitive information;

she was also, usefully, somewhat talkative, letting slip to Amor the name of another Right Club informant inside the Military Censorship Department – Anthony Ludovici – and that it was also receiving useful intelligence from within the police.

> Mrs Ramsay mentioned an alleged contact of Captain Ramsay's at Scotland Yard and referred to a conversation between this man and some individual supposed to be in MI5 ... Captain Ramsay had received a warning that he was to take great care not to lay himself open to any risk of exposure.[15]

Over the course of the ensuing months, Mrs Ramsay expanded on the Right Club's penetration of Scotland Yard, MI5 and government departments. According to weekly summaries of Amor's reports to Maxwell Knight:

> The police of C. Division were all supporters of Captain Ramsay ... Mrs Ramsay stated quite definitely that the Right Club had a contact in MI5 and re-iterated her statements about contacts in the police. Referring to this she said, 'the main body are with us, but there is a bad patch up above, but even there we are not without help.'[16]

From other conversations Amor discovered that the Club also had contacts in the Ministry of Economic Warfare, the Air Ministry censorship branch and – most alarmingly – inside Churchill's War Cabinet.*

Throughout the months of the Phoney War, Knight placed two further female spies inside the Right Club: Hélène de Munck, a 25-year-old Belgian expat who had worked as the personal secretary of one of the Ramsays' aristocratic friends, became Agent M/I; and Joan Miller, a 22-year-old society girl somewhat down on her fortunes who became the spy-runner's secretary and later mistress (although the affair appears never to have been consummated sexually). Between them these three

---

* This was Francis Hemming, a member of the War Cabinet Secretariat. He subsequently admitted to his superiors that he was friendly with Right Club members – but was not, apparently, removed from his position.

agents gradually gained the full trust of both Captain and Mrs Ramsay and discovered the full composition of the Right Club's 'Inner Circle'.

This centred around a slightly bohemian 'set' of women living in the comfortable upper-middle-class streets of Kensington and Chelsea, and included Christabel Nicholson, the Hitler-worshipping wife of a retired admiral who had headed the Navy's submarine service; two internationally-famous racing car drivers, Fay Taylour and Enid Riddell; Ann van Lennep, a young Dutch expatriate; Archibald Ramsay's cousin, Dolly Newenham; and Anna Wolkoff, the daughter of the last Imperial Russian naval attaché to London, who now ran the Russian Tea Rooms off the Brompton Road.

All were diehard pro-Nazi fascists and should have been flagged on MI5's radar much earlier, since they were closely associated with Olive Hamilton-Roe – the young WAAF recruit who was convicted of breaking the Official Secrets Act in October 1939 and who was also, according to subsequent Security Service investigations, the lover of Anna Wolkoff's sister, Alexandra.[17]

Some of their more public activities seemed trivial, and occasionally bordered on the puerile. Fay Taylour organised trips to West End cinemas in which she and her coterie made a point of loudly booing newsreels whenever Winston Churchill was shown,[18] and led the disruption of anti-fascist protests outside meetings organised by groups with which the Right Club was associated.[19]

They also formed regular 'sticky-back' squads, posting anti-Semitic and anti-war leaflets ('This is a Jew's War!') on walls and street lights across London. This would turn out to be a rather more serious misdemeanour, since from the summer onwards a succession of more proletarian fascists would be given stiff prison sentences for following the Right Club's lead (and even for simply possessing the labels). And however prosaic, according to Joan Miller's account, the propaganda missions had a very definite aim.

> How did these people set about obstructing the war effort? They used to sneak about late at night in the blackout, groping for smooth surfaces on which to paste the pro-German, anti-Semitic notices they carried. ... These guidelines were issued to each member in the form of a printed sheet.[20]

Those guidelines – not, oddly, stored in MI5's files on the chief Right Club leaders but rather in the dossier on the lower-ranking Enid Riddell – make clear that Ramsay and his followers knew they risked arrest for posting the sticky-backs.

> Walk on the dark side of the road. Prepare your sticker in advance; it will stick the better and you will not miss your object. Don't stop walking while sticking if possible. Look out for dark doorways; police usually stand in them at night ...
>
> As a danger signal talk of the weather, for instance. 'Colder from the East' means someone is approaching from the right. Read your road indication by torch-light and memorise at least two streets in advance.
>
> Take turns in sticking, lookout and route reading. As we leave this house we do so in pairs at a few seconds' interval and are strangers until we meet at midnight at Paradise Walk.[21]

As Joan Miller noted, 'None of this could be said to constitute a serious threat to Londoners' morale', but other activities of the Right Club's Inner Circle were more sinister.

> With a German invasion expected at any moment, those who had all along supported Germany's claims, believed themselves to be in a strong position. The society was engaged in compiling a list of prominent opponents to the Axis cause: if your name got on to this list you could expect to be strung up from a lamppost once the country was in German hands. I was consulted, I remember, over who was to be classified as a fit candidate for lynching ... they kept pressing me to name the most vociferous anti-Nazis I had come across. They were adamant that an example must be made of these people to give the rest of the country a foretaste of the strong measures it could expect.[22]

None of this, however, was the real business of the Right Club's Inner Circle. Knight filed a memo in early spring 1940, reporting the latest intelligence gained by Amor and de Munck.

Anna Wolkoff, who describes herself as Captain Ramsay's chief staff officer, recently said that the Right Club had not done anything really dangerous yet. They were confining themselves to their sticky back and propaganda activities. She said, however, that these were merely a smoke screen for their real objectives.

She said that the Right Club were planning something which if it came off might mean life or death to some of them. It must be admitted that Anna Wolkoff is a Russian and rather temperamental but the circumstances in which this statement was made are such as to make our informant think that it was not entirely idle boasting.[23]

Anna Wolkoff was certainly volatile. The eldest daughter of Admiral Nikolai Wolkoff, she was born in Russia in 1902 and, with the rest of her family, had stayed in London after the Bolshevik revolution, becoming a naturalised British citizen in September 1935. Around that time she established a West End business – Anna de Wolkoff Haute Couture – catering to the needs of rich and aristocratic families for bespoke dresses, evening gowns and associated finery: Wallis Simpson was among her most prized clients.

Like her father, Wolkoff was an ardent anti-Semite and, throughout the 1930s, made regular visits to Germany. She developed a fierce passion for the Fuehrer, declaring (according to one of de Munck's reports): 'Hitler is a God ... He is of this century and it would be wonderful if he could govern Britain.'[24]

Joan Miller, who came to know Wolkoff well during the months she spent undercover inside the Right Club, described her as 'short and dark-haired, not very impressive in appearance, and displayed the intensity of manner which is often associated with those of a fanatical disposition. She took herself and her causes very seriously indeed. It was difficult to get close to her as she was filled with mistrust, but, once she'd accepted you, Anna was capable of impulsive and generous acts.'[25]

Early in March 1940 Wolkoff felt sufficiently sure of Hélène de Munck's loyalty to the Right Club cause to take her into her confidence.

Wolkoff informed [de Munck] that her groups were working against the Jews, and on the 20th March she said she had agents all over the place, not only in England, but also in America. She was anxious to know if [de Munck] was going to Belgium to visit her family, as, if so, she wanted her to ... smuggle into this country a document which she described as an anti-Jewish document, which the authorities were not likely to allow to be brought into this country in the ordinary way.

From time to time afterwards she referred to the possibility of [de Munck] going to Belgium, and on one occasion she explained that she wanted to convey information to other agents in Belgium. They (the group) had hitherto been communicating with these agents through the diplomatic bag, but had recently had no replies.[26]

The Right Club's contact with such useful access to secure methods of correspondence – the diplomatic bag is deemed inviolable – turned out to be Jean Nieuwenhuys, a Second Secretary at the Belgian Embassy in London, a man known to MI5 for being 'actively associated with pro-German and anti-Semitic activities in this country and in Belgium'.[27] In addition to sending Wolkoff's letters to pro-Nazis in the Low Countries, he was also using the diplomatic bag to pass her messages to an infamous British renegade in Berlin. According to Maxwell Knight's internal MI5 monograph on the case:

Wolkoff confided in Miss A. [Marjorie Amor] that by this means it was possible to communicate with William Joyce – Lord Haw-Haw – in Germany; and that the method was that the letters would be given to Nieumanhuys [sic], addressed to the Comte or Comtesse de Laubespin – an official at the Belgian Foreign Office in Brussels.[28]

Corresponding with an agent of the German regime – Joyce worked as a broadcaster for Goebbels' propaganda ministry – was unequivocally illegal. The problem facing MI5 was how to prove it. Not only was it impossible to intercept correspondence sent under diplomatic seal, but – from what Wolkoff told de Munck – the Belgian route now appeared to be broken. Faced with these twin impediments, Knight embarked on a course of action which was – at best – morally dubious.

He got in touch with James McGuirk Hughes – a long-time fascist who, under the pseudonym Captain P.G. Taylor, was also an MI5 informer. At Knight's direction, Hughes wrote a lengthy encoded letter to Joyce, and through a mutual friend, arranged to meet Wolkoff at the Russian Tea Rooms. He asked her if she could get the letter to Berlin, and Wolkoff agreed to try.

Simultaneously, Knight ordered de Munck to imply to Wolkoff that she had a contact in the Romanian Legation who might prove useful as a replacement for Nieuwenhuys. There was no such contact, but Agent M/I was evidently convincing; Wolkoff bit eagerly on the bait, and after a somewhat farcical interlude involving a back and forth with Joan Miller over Wolkoff's own additions to the Hughes document, the letter was duly 'delivered' to the non-existent Romanian go-between. According to de Munck's police statement, Wolkoff knew what the letter contained, since she opened the envelope in front of her, and was able to read the code.

> Anna ... showed me the contents of the envelope, a single sheet of quarto paper covered with a code consisting of letters and figures. It was typewritten and there was a diagram at the bottom of the back page ... She then explained the document consisted of an account of Jewish activities in England for the use of William Joyce (Lord Haw-Haw) in his propaganda broadcasts from Germany, and added that when he made use of the information, 'it will be like a bombshell'.
>
> She also gave me some explanation of the code ... she indicated that every fourth letter in the words at the top of the document provided the key to the code itself. She also referred to the diagram at the end of the document and said that this was to assist in the reading of the code.[29]

There were two notable aspects to this incident. The first was Knight's willingness to use *agent provocateur* techniques to encourage a suspect to incriminate herself; the second was that he failed to anticipate the legal problems this could cause when Wolkoff was prosecuted. The former would come back to haunt both him and MI5; the latter would come perilously close to derailing her trial.

In the event, Wolkoff was about to commit a much more serious crime than communicating with Lord Haw-Haw. In February 1940 she had been introduced to Tyler Kent, a handsome American diplomat who handled top-secret cipher messages at the US Embassy.

Kent had been on MI5's radar almost from the day he arrived in London in the autumn of 1939. On October 8, a watcher from the Security Service was keeping a suspected Gestapo agent, Ludwig Matthias, under surveillance, and observed him make contact with the American diplomat.

> Matthias was followed to the Cumberland Hotel where he met a man who subsequently was identified as Tyler Kent, holder of US Diplomatic Passport Washington DC, No. 405. Matthias paid a visit to Kent's room and on leaving Matthias was seen to be carrying a bulky envelope, approximately 10″ × 6″. Matthias and Kent spent the rest of the evening together, finishing up at the Park Lane Hotel.[30]

Between then and early May 1940, Kent stole thousands of top-secret documents from the American Embassy, storing them in a cupboard in his flat. Some of the most sensitive were telegrams sent by Churchill – who had not yet become Prime Minister but was First Lord of the Admiralty – and President Franklin D. Roosevelt. Their subject was a clandestine scheme for American shipping aid to Britain – political dynamite since the United States was then technically neutral and FDR was facing an election in which his opponent represented the dominant mood of isolationism within the United States. Others, however, were copies of War Office and Intelligence Service documents which had been shared with the American Ambassador, Joseph P. Kennedy.

Kent showed these first to Wolkoff then to Archibald Ramsay. Between them, they arranged to have some of the material photographed by a Russian contact of Wolkoff's; these copies were then given to Christabel Nicholson for safe keeping.

MI5 learned about the stolen documents in early April 1940 when, according to Knight's note on the case, 'a reliable source' – code for one of his three moles inside the Right Club – reported that Wolkoff was spending a great deal of time with Tyler Kent, whom she described 'as being pro-German in his outlook and as having given her interesting diplomatic information of a confidential nature'. Within a week, Wolkoff explained the nature of that information.

> In the middle of April 1940, another equally reliable source ... reported that Anna de Wolkoff had recently claimed that Kent had been able to give her confidential information regarding the sea battles off the coast of Norway and this information would appear to have been twisted in such a way as to make excellent anti-British propaganda.[31]

Wolkoff also said that Kent had given her information about 'confidential interviews ... between Mr Kennedy [the Ambassador] and Lord Halifax'. On April 22, Knight's agent reported that Kent had shown Wolkoff correspondence 'between a British Government source and the United States Embassy on the subject of the purchase of certain technical apparatus from the American Government'. That was followed by the news that Kent was using the US Embassy's diplomatic bag to smuggle Right Club correspondence out of the country.[32]

During the first week in May, MI5 began to turn up the heat; it executed a search warrant of the flat of one of the Right Club's Inner Circle, who had separately been in touch with William Joyce. The move clearly caused panic: a report filed by Marjorie Amor on May 3 noted that 'for the first time ... Anna is really frightened for her own position. Anna is by no means a coward and in no sense of the word is she hysterical, but she is talking in terms of her own arrest and trial.'[33]

On May 18, Knight went to the US Embassy to break the unwelcome news that it had a leak and asked Kennedy to waive Tyler Kent's diplomatic immunity. The Ambassador – not known for his support of Britain's war effort – agreed; at dawn two days later MI5 and Special Branch officers broke down the door of Kent's flat. They found him in bed with his latest lover, but more importantly they discovered a cache of 1,929 highly secret documents, including reports from MI5 to the American Embassy, copies of cables from Churchill to Roosevelt, and a book containing the names of pro-Nazi sympathisers under police surveillance. They also recovered a large red leather-bound ledger, locked with heavy brass clasps: the complete membership record of Archibald Ramsay's Right Club.

Later that day, Anna Wolkoff's flat was raided: both she and Kent were arrested under the Official Secrets Act. They were, as it turned out, lucky: had their offences been committed slightly later, they could have faced charges under the Treachery Act, for which the sole penalty was death. As Guy Liddell noted in his journal:

> Anna Wolkoff has come perilously near to high treason. She has obtained information of vital importance to this country from the American Embassy through Tyler Kent. She has had documents photographed by a man called Smirnov, and there is some evidence to show that she has passed this information to the Duca del Monte in the Italian Embassy.*
>
> She has moreover endeavoured to plant agents both in the censorship and MI5. There is little doubt that Captain Ramsay has been cognisant of her activities.[34]

The reports of Knight's three agents inside the Right Club, Marjorie Amor, Hélène de Munck and Joan Miller, clearly showed that both Ramsay and his wife and Christabel Nicholson were aware of – indeed had actively participated in – Kent and Wolkoff's activities. The Security Service was in no doubt that all three should also be prosecuted: an undated note in Ramsay's file stated:

> Papers dealing with ... a serious leakage of information from the United States Embassy are today being laid before the Director of Public Prosecutions for his consideration. It is thought by those who have investigated the matter that these papers disclose the existence of a traitorous and dangerous conspiracy to assist the enemy, and the Director of Public Prosecutions is being asked to examine the case

---

* Duke Francesco Marigliano del Monte was Assistant Military Attaché at the Italian Embassy. According to his own MI5 file (KV 2/1698; declassified February 7, 2005) Wolkoff had hand-delivered a letter to him, at his address in Cadogan Square, giving details of the telegrams between Churchill and Roosevelt. Shortly afterwards, on May 23, 1940, a telegram from the German Ambassador in Rome to the Reich's Foreign Minister, marked 'Most Urgent and Top Secret', repeated these details.

with a view to preferring serious charges against five persons ... Anna
Wolkoff, Captain Archibald Ramsay, Mrs Ramsay, Mrs Christabel
Nicholson, and Tyler Kent.

It is anticipated that all the above persons will be charged with
offences which in substance amount to espionage on behalf of
Germany or to something very closely akin to it.[35]

MI5 was not naive about the potential political considerations of charg-
ing a sitting MP, let alone his aristocratic wife and that of a celebrated
retired admiral. It noted that 'the proposed defendants take the view
that they are safe from trial and punishment because neither of the
Governments concerned dare to have these matters discussed', but suggested the problem could easily be overcome if the evidence against
them were to be produced 'behind locked doors in a cleared court'.[36]

What made the Right Club's treachery even more serious was the
revelation that it had inserted one of its members into the most closely
guarded establishment involved in the war. According to an MI5 file
note dated June 28, the search of Anna Wolkoff's flat had uncovered the
membership card of a woman named Muriel White. When they raided
her home in Ebury Street, Belgravia, they discovered that Wright had
left to join the top-secret Bletchley Park codebreaking facility where
she was 'employed by S.I.S. [MI6] in a confidential capacity in their
code and cypher department'.[37]

As Knight commented bluntly: 'It is important to note that this
discovery considerably strengthens the case against Anna Wolkoff, and
also the possible conspiracy charges against Captain Ramsay.'[38]

The government – in the shape of the Home Office and Law Officers
– was not, however, convinced. As the summer of 1940 dragged on –
and Britain steeled itself for the possibility of invasion and then the
start of the Blitz – letters slowly passed between Sir Alexander Maxwell
and Norman Birkett, now one of the great and good hearing appeals
against Regulation 18B internment:[39] these indicated that the Director
of Public Prosecutions was unsure whether a case could, or should, be
brought against Ramsay.

Finally a decision was reached: Kent and Wolkoff would stand trial
alone, with Ramsay subjected to the rather less onerous conditions of

internment in Brixton prison. Here, like his fellow fascist detainees, he was allowed regular visits from friends and his wife – left, without explanation, entirely free – who were permitted to bring their loved ones additional supplies of food and even wine.

There was no good legal reason for this. The evidence against both Archibald and Ismay Ramsay depended on the testimony of Knight's agents; all three testified behind the brown paper screening Kent and Wolkoff's successful prosecution – in the process becoming useless for any further undercover work on behalf of MI5: since their evidence was proved good in that trial, there was no reason to doubt its accuracy about the Ramsays.

In fact the only ripple in an otherwise uneventful trial was the problem caused by Knight's use of an *agent provocateur*. Understandably, Wolkoff's defence counsel demanded that James McGuirk Hughes be brought to court for cross-examination: MI5 compounded its sin by secretly flying him to a remote location in the north of Scotland and dishonestly pronouncing itself unable to locate him.

As Kent and Wolkoff began their prison sentences, the evidence of the Right Club's involvement in a scheme – however ill-formed – to bring about a violent fascist coup d'état was quietly buried. Ramsay was joined in detention by Admiral Barry Domvile, largely at the request of the Admiralty, which damned him with the words: 'If there be any British Quislings, then there are few more likely candidates for the role than Admiral Domvile and his wife.'[40]

Anthony Ludovici was dismissed from intelligence work in the Air Ministry; he was not, however, interned. Nor was General John 'Boney' Fuller: despite unease over his actions and political beliefs – Field Marshal Lord Alan Brooke, Commander of the Home Forces, noted high-level discussions about Fuller's 'Nazi activities' in his diary[41] – the man who was ready to start 'a bloody revolution' was left undisturbed.

This was a serious mistake. Archibald Ramsay's Kensington conspiracy was not the only scheme for a fascist coup uncovered during the dark days of 1940. The Security Service was aware of two other simultaneous plots: both were much further advanced than Ramsay's plan – and both involved Fuller as well as many other influential figures in British political and military life.

CHAPTER TWELVE

'A Revolutionary Dictatorship Should be Imposed'

'Intensive efforts have been made to obtain contacts
in HM Forces in order that when the time is ripe, they
will "turn their rifles in the right direction".'
MI5 report on John Beckett; March 3, 1940

On the evening of Wednesday, May 15, 1940, three seemingly ill-matched companions enjoyed a convivial dinner in a west London restaurant. One was a huge bear of a man – six feet eight inches tall, heavily built and of a slightly shambling gait, he appeared to be in his late thirties; the second was much younger – middle-twenties at most – and spoke with a distinctive German accent in keeping with his Aryan looks. The third diner, however, would have been a familiar figure, at least to those with an interest in politics: well-dressed and in his forties, he was dark-haired and suavely handsome in the manner of a Hollywood matinée idol.

The subject of their conversation, like countless others in the nervous atmosphere following the fall of Holland, turned to the likelihood of a German invasion and Britain's preparations to repulse it. The big man had been asked to join a volunteer corps preparing to fight off landings by parachute troops – an invitation he had indignantly rebuffed, apparently on the grounds of his unswerving dedication to pacifism.

This rejection attracted instant hostility from his older friend, who pronounced himself wholly in favour of the idea, since it would be 'too marvellous if one were able to obtain a revolver and ammunition at the present time'. Lest he be misunderstood, however, he made clear that he would not seek to employ these 'marvellous' weapons against German parachutists, but would instead use them to 'actively assist the enemy in the event of an invasion'.[1]

The two men openly discussing how to greet Hitler's forces were Benjamin Greene, a long-time peace campaigner and cousin of the more famous novelist Graham Greene, and John Beckett, once one of the most fiery and charismatic MPs sitting in the House of Commons. Both were then engaged in a new venture – an outwardly-respectable organisation dedicated to peace in Europe, but in reality a front for domestic fascism. What made their candour more disturbing was the identity of their dining companion: Harald Kurtz was unquestionably German and, in the minds of Greene and Beckett, an agent working covertly on behalf of the Nazi regime.

Kurtz was, indeed, an undercover agent. His employer, however, was not the Abwehr but Maxwell Knight's B5b Branch of MI5. The dinner conversation he reported, along with many others like it, would help uncover plans to replace – violently and with German assistance – the British government with a cabal of pro-Nazi fascists and fellow-travellers. He would also become a lightning rod in the war between the Home Office and Security Service and its investigations – and, in doing so, set MI5 on a course which tested the limits of legal and ethical investigation.

*

John Beckett had been on a remarkable political journey. He was born, in 1894, into comfortable circumstances in Hammersmith, west London; his father William was a resolutely respectable English draper, and his mother Dorothy was the daughter of a Jewish jeweller who had given up her faith and family to marry 'out' (as her father denounced it). Jack William Beckett, as he was then known, was sent to Latymer Upper School, the local educational establishment of choice for the sons and daughters of the well-off merchant class. At the age of fourteen, however, the family lost all its savings in an investment scam operated by the Liberal MP Horatio Bottomley, a jingoistic orator and unashamed swindler: young Jack was removed from Latymer's and required to make his way as an errand boy.

In August 1914 he joined the Army, enlisting originally with the 9th Battalion, Middlesex Regiment but swiftly transferring to the King's Shropshire Light Infantry – a decision taken, by his own account, because the Beckett clan had an ancestral connection to the county. True or not – and according to his son and biographer, Francis, Beckett's version of events is not necessarily reliable – the move 'almost certainly saved his life', since rather than serving on the Western Front, he was posted to the rather less lethal surroundings of India. Within two years he was discharged from the Army on account of a heart defect and declared 'no longer physically fit for war service'.[2]

After a year in hospital, he founded the National Union of ex-Servicemen, campaigning for better treatment of war veterans, and moved into politics. He joined the Independent Labour Party – an organisation to the left of the official Labour Party – serving on Hackney Council before being elected to Parliament, first as the member for Gateshead, then, in 1929, for the south London seat of Peckham.

A year later Beckett earned notoriety when he became the first MP in the history of Parliament to seize the ceremonial mace – the physical symbol of the monarch's authority in the House of Commons – during an ill-tempered debate. Parliamentary staff wrestled it from him as he tried to leave the Chamber; he was promptly 'named' by the Speaker for 'disorderly conduct' and briefly suspended.[3]

In 1931 he lost his seat and – notionally at least – retired from public life. He used the time to travel both geographically and politically, enthusiastically touring Mussolini's Italy and subsequently joining the British Union of Fascists. Mosley was evidently impressed with the young firebrand, appointing him director of publications – a post which put him in the editor's chair of both *Action* and *The Blackshirt* with, according to an MI5 memo, 'a budget of £210 per week to maintain BUF periodicals'. This was a substantial figure – the equivalent of £10,000 today – and it was not, therefore, surprising when the party found itself short of funds.

In December 1936 Beckett acquired a criminal record and a fine for creating a disturbance outside Buckingham Palace. The cause was the impending abdication of Edward VIII – a crisis the BUF believed to have been forced upon the King by the Prime Minister Stanley Baldwin. But for his own account of the context, Beckett's minor brush with the law would have been consigned to the backwash of history; Francis Beckett's largely sympathetic biography uses his father's own words to paint a picture of the fascists' plans to take the reins of power during the turbulence:

Mosley was in a great state of excitement. He claimed to be in direct communication with the court. The King, he said, was strengthened by the knowledge of the support of him and his movement, and for this reason would accept Baldwin's resignation and call upon Mosley to form a Government. Standing in the middle of the room, he detailed his plans for governing without Parliament until the budget ...[4]

According to this version of events, Beckett believed that Mosley's 'powers of self-delusion had finally conquered his sanity'. Certainly, the relationship between the Leader and his acolyte had cooled and, in March 1937, Beckett and his closest colleague, the BUF's director of propaganda, William Joyce, were sacked. Yet an excerpt from a draft of Beckett's own unpublished autobiography, obtained by MI5, suggests that the idea of ruling Britain without the encumbrance of Parliament had struck a chord.

It may be well briefly to set out my beliefs. Socialism, economic and political, is too well understood to need explanation, but the great dividing gulf between the Right and the Left is the difference between the believer in political democracy and the revolutionary. I have always been the latter, and that is probably why, when I lost all faith in internationalism in general and the British Labour movement in particular, I made a natural transition to the principles of Fascism, which is revolutionary but not democratic.

I believe that the only road to power is through the ballot box, but that once in power, a revolutionary dictatorship should be imposed, and every weapon used to ensure remaining in power until the task is accomplished. I do not believe in the 'ins and outs' principle so dear to the heart of the Parliamentary democrat.[5]

Within days of their dismissal from the BUF, Beckett set up the National Socialist League (NSL) with Joyce and sent a curious letter – intercepted by the Security Service – to a contact in Berlin. According to a report in February 1940, 'Beckett wrote to Dr Bauer, a German espionage agent, regarding his dismissal, saying that he and William Joyce were "most anxious that our German friends should know the truth"'.[6]

'Dr Bauer' was the alias of a man better known to MI5 as Friedrich Hugo Bernard Theodore Lieber, a full-time Abwehr officer;[7] Beckett's involvement with a known spy guaranteed him increased attention from British counter-intelligence. Maxwell Knight, then running MI5's belated attempts to monitor domestic fascists, took particular interest. He had been on friendly terms with Joyce since their mutual involvement in the British Fascisti, and the future Lord Haw-Haw appears to have been one of his loose network of informants.* After the NSL folded and Beckett set about forming a new vehicle, Knight began searching for a replacement source of intelligence.

Beckett's first post-NSL body was the British Council Against European Commitments – 'a front organisation for every fascist, neo-fascist and anti-Semite in London', according to his son.[8] This was rapidly subsumed into the British People's Party (BPP), funded by Lord Tavistock and led by Beckett, Ben Greene and Captain Robert Gordon-Canning, formerly the BUF's director of overseas policy and who had been best man at Mosley's 1936 wedding to Diana Mitford – an

---

* There is strong circumstantial evidence that Knight helped Joyce flee to Berlin just before he was due to be arrested in August 1939. 'William Joyce, alias Lord Haw-Haw'. National Archives file KV 2/245.

event which had taken place in the unusual surroundings of Joseph Goebbels' drawing room.

The BPP's manifesto proclaimed it to be dedicated to fighting for 'social security and justice ... the abolition of all forms of land speculation, the security of labour in its industrial organisation' and 'the abolition of class differences'. Beneath those progressive-sounding ideals, however, the party had a less well-publicised agenda: according to an advertisement it took out in *The New Pioneer*, these included 'the abolition of a financial system based on usury which perpetuates social and economic injustice' and 'safeguarding the employment and integrity of the British people against alien influence and infiltration'.[9] Both policies were barely disguised reworkings of the familiar dog-whistles of anti-Semitism and German fascism – unsurprising, perhaps, in view of Tavistock's open admiration for Hitler, whom he had praised for giving 'German youth faith and hope in the future, restor[ing] their self-respect, and [doing] much to reduce unemployment'.[10]

Notionally, the BPP suspended its activities on the outbreak of war. In fact, its leaders simply adopted a new disguise. On September 19, 1939, Beckett and Greene took lunch with Admiral Sir Barry Domvile, before all three headed off to the home of Gordon-Canning. Here they were joined by five other members of Domvile's The Link (in theory also disbanded) and planned a new organisation to lobby for a negotiated settlement with Hitler: the British Council for Christian Settlement in Europe (BCCSE) was born.

Its chairman – and prime financial backer – was once again Lord Tavistock; Beckett assumed the role of secretary, with Gordon-Canning as treasurer. Ben Greene provided the new organisation with headquarters in his comfortable home at Berkhamsted, Hertfordshire. It was, to all intents and purposes, the BPP under a new banner.

Within a month the BCCSE published its first pamphlet, 'A Statement on the European Situation', calling for an international conference to negotiate amicable peace terms with Germany. Twenty-eight public and semi-public figures attached their signatures; leading names in the pro-Nazi British fascist movement, including A.P. Laurie and Cola Carroll from The Link, were joined by the Reverend Donald Soper and Maude Royden, luminaries of the resolutely non-fascist Peace Pledge Union.[11]

Their involvement appears to have been induced by Beckett's deliberate insertion of the word 'Christian' in the organisation's title – a cynical ploy to disguise its underlying anti-Semitism – and due to their passionate belief that war was morally wrong. In neither case would their affiliation survive the BCCSE's first public outing.

The inaugural meeting was held at Conway Hall, Red Lion Square, on October 14. Contemporary press reports suggest that the Council's chief officers made little attempt to hide their pro-Nazi sympathies; the first paragraph of the *Sunday Express* story was blunt and to the point.

> About a hundred and fifty Britons met yesterday 'to bring peace to the world'. They praised Hitler. They reviled the British Government. They ended by sending a resolution to Mr Chamberlain calling on him to start peace negotiations.[12]

The report filed by Jimmy Dickson, an MI5 officer present in the hall, was more detailed and highlighted the contribution of Ben Greene.

> Ben Greene's speech was naked German propaganda. He sneered at those who said we could not trust Hitler, and asked which of our own politicians could be trusted. He referred to British policy as one of bluff and treachery, at which there was a loud shout 'And we shall know how to deal with traitors'.
>
> He explained that Hitler had been justified in all that he had done. It was not aggression for German troops to march into the German Rhineland; it was not aggression for them to occupy Austria which was predominantly German ('as German as Prussia' was his expression); it was not aggression to save the Slovaks from the misgovernment of Czecho-Slovakia, a state which should never have existed; and as for Poland, it was a small state which had no right to 'meddle in power politics' by concluding an alliance with France ...
>
> He referred to Hitler with great respect, using such phrases as 'Those of us who admire him' ... He expressed grave misgivings as to

the outcome of the war, as Germany could stand a long war but Britain could not. And when Germany had beaten us there was a frightful possibility to consider: 'Hitler is only human – he may die and be replaced by a German who has not Hitler's wise statesmanship'. He sat down to a storm of applause.[13]

Such overt extremism led Maude Royden, one of the more moderate speakers at the meeting, to write to the *Sunday Express* denouncing BCCSE and publicly disassociating herself from Beckett and Greene's organisation:

> When I was invited to speak I was told that the purpose of the meeting was to urge the Government to press for a European – and if possible wider than European – congress to discuss the conditions of a just and permanent peace. On these lines I agreed to speak.
>
> At the meeting, however, I was amazed to find that the other speakers, and the audience, seemed much less concerned with any such constructive policy than with denunciations of our own Government and praise of Hitler. I protested with intense indignation ...[14]

Rather more important than Royden's renunciation, the Security Service began to take a much closer interest in BCCSE's principal officers. Beckett and Tavistock were already firmly on MI5's radar, but it now extended its attentions to Gordon-Canning and Greene; very quickly B Branch discovered that both had existing files, and that the intelligence contained in them pointed towards treason.

Robert Gordon-Canning, known to his circle of aristocratic friends as 'Bobbie', was rich and extremely well-connected. Born into a military family in 1888, he had been commissioned into the Royal Gloucestershire Hussars at the age of eighteen and served with distinction in the First World War, winning the Military Cross for 'conspicuous gallantry and devotion to duty'.

His career in the inter-war years, however, was somewhat less respectable: as a dedicated advocate of Arab nationalism, from the late 1920s onwards his MI5 file began to bulge with reports of unsavoury weapons-dealing and espionage. Much of the first volume of that file was destroyed in the bombing raid which hit the Registry in September 1940, but a surviving memo from 1938 gives an indication of the concern he caused among intelligence agencies across Europe and the Middle East.

> This man, who was formerly concerned with gun-running for the Rifs,[15] has recently come under suspicion in various ways. He has been connected with Arabs who are opposed to the administration in Palestine. He is in touch with [a] well-known Italian agent. He has recently visited Tangiers where he aroused the suspicion of the French ... His pro-Arab interests bring him under suspicion of being concerned in subversive activities.[16]

Alongside a fervent anti-Semitism he also developed a deep respect for the Third Reich, enjoying two personal interviews with Hitler, whom he described as 'a person who has, I think, achieved very great things for the German people in many ways'. Nor did the Nazi persecution of its domestic opponents necessarily tarnish that admiration; Gordon-Canning subsequently airily explained that 'I am against the concentration camps – unless of the proper class'.[17]

He traded – with varying degrees of success – on his connections with the Nazi Party during the years he spent as a leading BUF official. According to an MI5 intelligence report (most likely based on information from Joyce) in April 1937, he passed 'secret information to Germany and Italy':[18]

> Gordon-Canning has been used on several occasions by Mosley as a go-between with the Germans ... Nazi opinion in Germany, however, is not very favourable to Canning, and on occasion, after a report written by Canning had actually reached Hitler, Hitler is alleged to have remarked: 'To be a true National Socialist one must have both an intellect and a heart; this man has neither'.[19]

At the end of December 1939, MI5 received allegations that Canning's support for Germany might go beyond forging links between British fascists and Nazi officials. According to the heavily-redacted statement of one of his friends in London society, he had pronounced himself willing to help German forces if, or when, they landed in Britain.

> On Xmas Eve ... Captain Gordon-Canning came to an egg nogg party at my house ... He said that he felt he would not be doing right to mankind if he did not doo [*sic*] all he could to help the Nazis. He praised the Nazi regime and said that if a submarine came and needed refuelling and revictualling they would know where to find a friend.[20]

The informant who provided this intelligence was adamant that she should not be identified: 'I do not on any account want ... to be involved in any way shape or form as a result of my making this statement', she told John Maude, the Security Service lawyer[21] who took it from her. It is a measure of MI5's less than rigorous approach to evidence-gathering that Maude cheerfully admitted that he had not even asked her to sign the statement, 'as I knew her word was as good as her signature'[22] – an error which would later come back to haunt the Service.

The trail of evidence against Ben Greene also began in the mid-1930s. Born, one of four children, in São Paolo, Brazil in 1901, his father was British, his mother German; on their return to England they set up home in the historic market town of Berkhamsted. Here, according to Greene's enormous Security Service files, his mother had attracted local opprobrium during the First World War and 'caused considerable trouble to Hertfordshire Police by her public expressions of pro-German sympathy'.[23]

Middle-class and comfortable, Ben Greene 'went up' to Wadham College, Oxford but left before graduating after suffering 'a religious crisis'. Like John Beckett, his political journey began on the left, before veering sharply to the extreme right – probably around the time he took the post of deputy Chief Returning Officer in the 1935 Saar Plebiscite – a referendum to determine the governance of the contested territory between France and Germany, marred by intimidation from Nazi agents.[24] According to a note in Beckett's MI5 files:

> Greene is another Fascist who has changed his coat, though not openly. In 1934 he was secretary of Hemel Hempstead Labour Party,

and in January 1935, when he was deputy Chief Returning Officer in connection with the Saar Plebiscite, he was prospective Labour candidate for Gravesend. He was not elected.

Ben Greene's conversion may have taken place in the same year, for in April 1936, SIS [MI6] passed on information that he was in Nazi employment and had received a sum estimated at £10,000* for Nazi propaganda purposes. It should be stated, for what it is worth, that local police enquiries failed to confirm this, but it is hardly likely, of course, that they would.

It may not be without significance that three days after we requested police enquiries, Greene burned a large quantity of German papers. He was then still secretary of the local Labour Party and also a JP and a member of the Herts County Council.[25]

The Security Service then lost sight of Greene; it would be more than two years before it intercepted correspondence showing that he was in touch with senior Nazi officials.

In January 1939, he wrote to thank Herr Bohle of Berlin, a relation of the notorious head of the Nazi *Auslands* organization,[26] for his advice, [and] informed Bohle that he was starting a Peace & Progress Information Bureau, and offered to send Bohle any information that he might need. The monthly bulletins of the Bureau were pure Nazi propaganda.

By August 1939, Bohle was writing to 'Dear Ben', and asking him to recommend a typist for a 'semi-official' post in Germany. Ben recommended Mrs Beckett.[27,28]

Greene appears not to have made much effort to hide his political opinions. In October 1939, Hertfordshire County Council successfully requested his removal from the bench of local JPs, citing concern over his pro-German sympathies. Three months later, he and the other leaders of the BCCSE came under attack in the popular press: on February 25, 1940, under the headline 'These Men Are Dangerous', the

---

* If accurate this was an enormous sum – the equivalent of almost £500,000 today.

Sunday Dispatch warned its readers about the threat posed by British pro-Nazis and fellow-travellers:

> We are now approaching the end of the first six months of the war, which means that, relative to the Great War, we have passed through one-eighth of the present conflict. Yet already we must guard against the danger of public opinion being warped in favour of a negotiated peace with Germany, which the world would regard as a huge victory for Hitler.
>
> For make no mistake about it, Hitler's Fifth Column has not been demobilized, despite the complete exposure by Sir Samuel Hoare in the House of Commons of The Link ...
>
> On the contrary, a kind of guerrilla warfare is being fought by the motley crowd of men and women, some of whom call themselves the British Council for Christian Settlement in Europe ... It has an innocuous sounding name, the kind that Hitler himself would have liked to choose. Yet its main duty seems to be to carry on from the point where the intensive German propaganda effort of last summer left off.
>
> The indirect method of propaganda was to encourage various organisations in this country to preach friendship with Germany and extol the virtues of Hitlerism. When the war broke out not only the Link but also the National Socialist League was dissolved. It is the British Council for Christian Settlement in Europe which has taken their place.[29]

The activities of Greene, Beckett, Gordon-Canning and Tavistock had, by then, attracted the attention of MI5's Maxwell Knight. He dispatched a succession of undercover operatives to penetrate BCCSE and feed back intelligence on its leaders. The first of these – from an agent code-named M/B – reported that, according to Beckett, 'the British Council for Christian Settlement in Europe, has a membership of 1,500 members, 300 in London and 1,200 in the provinces'. But more worrying than the rapid growth in membership was the indication that it was in the early stages of planning for an armed fascist uprising.

> Beckett has stated that he is making intensive efforts to obtain contacts in H.M. Forces in order that when the time is ripe there [*sic*] persons

will – to quote Beckett's actual words – 'turn their rifles in the right direction'.[30]

It was from another of Knight's spies that MI5 first learned of Lord Tavistock's mission, in February 1940, to secure agreeable peace terms from the German Legation in Dublin, and his hopes of persuading the Foreign Secretary to endorse them. On February 21 it sent an urgent note to the Foreign Office warning against giving any encouragement to the noble lord.

The BCCS[E] was formed towards the end of September 1939 and shortly after issued a public appeal to the Government to terminate the war immediately and to call an international conference for the peaceful settlement of German and Italian claims. This appeal was issued at about the same time as Hitler's speech on the conclusion of the war in Poland. In its general tendency it bore a strong resemblance to Hitler's peace offer. In view of this it did not appear far-fetched to regard both declarations as parts of one and the same 'peace offensive' inspired from Germany.

The leaders of the BCCSE are not merely well-meaning pacifists but are persons who have for long been involved in Nazi intrigues in this country. Lord Tavistock himself would seem to be a crank rather than a clear-headed political intriguer ... About a year ago he became associated with the British Union of Fascists and attended a BUF luncheon in February 1939. He has recently expressed his pro-Nazi sentiments in the form of an article in 'Action' of 11th January.

In this article, Lord Tavistock accused the British Government of responsibility for the war and closed with the words, 'Will the British people never wake up to the truth about the war and the men who made it?' It is thus quite clear that Lord Tavistock's sympathies are with the enemy ...

John Beckett is less of a crank than Lord Tavistock and gives one the impression of being an utterly unscrupulous political intriguer. In private conversations he is accustomed to display a liking for subversive and violent methods. Beckett has persuaded the Council to make extensive efforts to obtain contacts in H.M. Forces so that when the time is ripe they will – as he put it – 'turn their rifles in the right direction'. At about the same time Beckett made certain remarks at a confidential meeting which left no doubt in our informant's mind that he had recently been in touch with officials of the German Government.

Ben Greene is one of the most active members of the BCCSE and ... has particularly distinguished himself in producing certain propaganda sheets known as 'The Peace and Progressive Information Service' which are, in fact, National Socialist propaganda of a remarkably noxious kind. In this paper he has described one of Hitler's most violent attacks on this country as 'a great speech' ... There is no doubt that he has entirely allied himself with the German cause.

The above account of the BCCS[E] will, I think, serve to show that it is not what it appears to be on the surface. The innocuous sounding name is a cover for activities which are calculated to hamper the Government in the prosecution of the war and to assist the enemy. It is not a body of honest Christian peace-lovers but of rabid pro-Nazis.[31]

The warning seems to have played a part in the Foreign Office's rejection of the proposals which Tavistock brought back from his German friends in Dublin. That rebuff led BCCSE to publish a pamphlet reproducing his Lordship's correspondence with Whitehall on the issue – and, in doing so, spelled out clearly his pro-Nazi and anti-Semitic views. In a letter dated January 24, 1940, Tavistock sought to remind Halifax of the lesson men of their class had learned in childhood: 'We should not forget, also, that even in our boyhood the German Jew was a byword for all that was objectionable', he blithely asserted.[32]

Publication of this pamphlet coincided with an expansion of Knight's attempts to insert informants inside BCCSE. He had, by then, at least four agents providing intelligence which gave MI5 significant cause for alarm. A report from one of them – 'Agent M/D' – dated March 21 highlighted the potential threat posed by the organisation's secretary, John Beckett.

Today he said: 'To be quite frank, from the cold and logical point of view of the Party, the war is the best possible thing that could have happened. What I have done in ten months,[33] would have taken four years in ordinary times of peace.'

There is no doubt that Beckett will do all in his power to weaken the country's cause (within what he considers to be his legal rights) in order to further his own ends. And the fact that his ultimate aims are National Socialism, coupled with his intense admiration of Hitler, only strengthens my opinion that his activities ought to be checked before he obtains too much influence. The Tavistock fiasco seems to have done him little harm. Indeed, two prominent Conservatives have since promised him their complete support; and at the present rate of progress, Beckett will be playing a major part in seriously impairing the country's war effort.[34]

Knight's system for recording and filing his informants' intelligence was – to put it kindly – eccentric; as often as not, he would wait days or even weeks before writing up the reports himself, based on what his spies had told him. Nor is there any public record of their identities: 'Agent M/D', and his (or her) colleagues 'M/B', 'M/W' and 'M/M', remain anonymous to this day.

However, we do know the identity of the MI5 informant who provided much of the most damning evidence against Beckett and Ben Greene: his name was Harald Kurtz and the story of how he came to infiltrate BCCSE was indicative of both the concern with which MI5 viewed the organisation and the unconventional methods adopted by Knight to investigate it.

Harald Kurtz was born in Stuttgart in 1913, the middle child of three sons of a publisher who, shortly after Hitler's rise to power, became a staunch Nazi. In January 1937, while a student of languages and history at Geneva University, Harald came to London on vacation. He evidently preferred England to Germany, since he decided not to return home; he registered his presence at Bow Street police station, was issued documents showing him to be Alien No. 661286, and devoted much of the next eighteen months to ensuring he was allowed to stay.

He first worked for a firm of wholesale booksellers, before finding employment as private secretary to Lord Noel-Buxton;[35] then, in June 1938 he was hired by Maxwell Knight as a salaried agent of

B5b Branch. How the two men met has never been explained, though both were homosexual (then as illegal in Britain as it was persecuted in Germany) and the possibility exists that they encountered each other in the dangerous *demi-monde* of London's underground gay scene.

Nor is there any record of exactly what Kurtz did for the first year of his employment with MI5. His own subsequent statement specified only that he was engaged in 'the investigation of the activities of German espionage agents and members of the Gestapo operating in Great Britain'.[36]

In November 1939 Knight told Kurtz that there were 'several cases of suspected Gestapo agents'[37] inside Britain's internment camps for enemy aliens. Kurtz volunteered to go undercover inside the camps, posing as a Nazi sympathiser to smoke out the alleged spies. Knight quickly agreed and, to ensure the integrity of his cover story, arranged to have Kurtz officially interned; he entered the camps at the end of November 1939 and stayed there for three months. If this remarkable operation yielded any useful intelligence, there is no trace of it in the publicly released files covering the period.

On March 8, 1940, Kurtz emerged from detention and returned to a flat provided for him by MI5 in Ebury Street, Belgravia. The following day he met up with Knight who told him that the activities of Ben Greene, John Beckett and the other leaders of the British People's Party and its successor, BCCSE, 'were interesting the authorities very much indeed'. Together they came up with an elaborate plan to insert Kurtz into the organisations as an undercover informant. The key was to be Kurtz's old friendship with a member of the pre-war Nazi Party establishment in Britain, Ilse von Binzer, whom he had known since their school days in Germany.

Several months after arriving in England he encountered her again in the offices of Rudolf Rosel, the NSDAP official tasked with the organisation of 'a reliable Fifth Column' in Britain. Believing Kurtz to be loyal to the Party, Von Binzer and Rosel recommended that he made contact with Ben Greene – 'who is a great personal friend of Dr Rosel' and whose reputation (according to Kurtz) was 'as a man of definitely pro-Nazi views engaged in propaganda activities'.[38]

Both Ilse von Binzer and Rudolf Rosel had been sent back to Germany, making it safe for Kurtz to use their names as an introduction to Greene. Knight gave the scheme his blessing and told Kurtz to approach Greene 'with a view to finding out to what extent he was really implicated in activities which were prejudicial to Great Britain'.

By Kurtz's own account, the plan was successful. He met Greene on Good Friday, March 22, 1940, and Greene asked Kurtz if he 'was in a position to communicate with Fraulein von Binzer to ask her to convey to Dr Rosel the fact that the splendid work which he had done in this country was still being carried on'. This encouraged Kurtz to attempt to draw Greene into further damning revelations.

> I gave Mr Greene a brief sketch of my career, and although I was very careful never once to commit myself to a statement that I was a German agent, I told my story in such a manner as to leave him in no doubt whatever that my sympathies were completely pro-Nazi; that I had been working for some time on their behalf in some capacity which I did not specify; I was in some difficulty at the moment owing to the fact that my usual lines of communication with Germany were no longer available.
>
> Mr Greene showed no surprise whatever at my attitude, and he expressed some considerable sympathy for me in my difficulties. He suggested that I should make contact with his associates in the British People's Party and the British Council for Christian Settlement in Europe, whose offices are at 13 John Street, WC ...[39]

Over the following weeks Kurtz and his fellow agents supplied a series of reports on the activities – both public and private – of BCCSE and its leaders. Knight filed an account he received from them of a public meeting at Kingsway Hall, Holborn, chaired by Beckett and addressed by Lord Tavistock, BUF firebrand Ross Williamson and fellow-traveller John McGovern.[40]

> Three of my people who went to the meeting have all given the same impressions of it, namely that it was one of the most seditious

meetings they had ever attended in their lives, and the speech made by John McGovern was particularly treasonable.

One phrase which may be quoted was 'The people must refuse to fight! When the people refuse to fight we shall get peace on the people's terms!'

The Right Club attended this meeting in full force ... the booklet 'Hitler's British Dupes'[41] was distributed outside the hall and surreptitiously inside the hall [by anti-fascist protestors], but Fay Taylour discovered the source of supply and offered her services to distribute them, with the result that very few of them were actually distributed.[42]

Kurtz, in his adopted role as a Nazi agent, was then regularly dining with Ben Greene. According to Kurtz's statement, Greene told him over supper in Ebury Street that Germany would soon win the war and that 'the prospect of this was hateful to him because he did not want to see his country under foreign rule'.

He followed this up by saying that he would like me to convey to my friends in Germany that there 'were in this country men ready to take over the Government after a German victory; men trained in and filled with the proper spirit of National Socialism – a British National Socialism'.

Mr Greene said that he thought that the German Government had the wrong ideas about Sir Oswald Mosley, and he implied that he did not think that Mosley was the right person to lead the National Socialist movement in Great Britain. He hinted that he and his associates were better qualified than Mosley and his party to take over the government of this country.[43]

Buoyed by such promising intelligence, in late April 1940 Knight decided to add yet another undercover agent to the mix. Friedl Gaertner (sometimes spelled Gartner) was a 29-year-old Austrian cabaret singer, well connected in London's aristocratic circles and properly registered at Bow Street police station as the holder of enemy alien certificate No. 611918. Her father was a Nazi Party member in Berlin but, according to her subsequent sworn statement, she did not share her family's politics.

My sympathies are wholly and completely on the side of the Allies and in 1938 I offered my services to the British Military Intelligence Department. Since that date I have been employed by this Department in connection with counter-espionage work.[44]

Kurtz mentioned Gaertner to Greene, describing her as someone 'even more intimately connected with the right people in Germany than myself, and that I looked upon this person as almost a sort of "senior officer"'. Greene said that he 'would very much like' to meet her, and dinner was arranged for the three of them, *chez* Kurtz on Sunday, April 28. According to Gaertner, it turned out to be a revealing encounter.

> Mr Greene spent a considerable time trying to explain his own views in relation to the war on National Socialism. He stated he was a strong believer in National Socialism, but was careful to point out that he did not agree with everything Hitler had done, especially with regard to the Jews. ...
>
> He was convinced that in a year's time there would be practically nothing to do in England, and that German soldiers would be marching through London. He thought that only National Socialism could save the British Empire.
>
> Mr Greene claimed that he did not want to see his country ruled by anybody but Englishmen, and said that Hitler did not want this either ... He said that he personally would not fight in the war and would do everything possible to keep out of it. He went on to say ... such action as had been taken by the Germans against Great Britain was only a reprisal for what had been done to Germany ... he would take no part in it.[45]

Thus far Gaertner and Kurtz had been careful to avoid acting as *agents provocateurs*. Although they led Greene to believe they were German agents, they did not attempt to induce him to commit a treasonable offence. But halfway through dinner – and presumably acting on Knight's instructions – they stepped across the line into outright entrapment. Gaertner played out a morsel of bait by saying that she had a friend in Germany whom she wished to contact 'but that I had no desire to be known in this country as a friend of this person'. What, she asked Greene, did he recommend?

It was a clumsy – and probably unlawful – ploy and Greene appears not to have bitten, suggesting only that Gaertner might approach Thomas Cook, the travel agency which then offered a limited mail service to enemy countries; for good measure, he also warned her to be very careful. But if he avoided that somewhat dubious trap, Greene was evidently willing to incriminate himself in other ways.

> At some time during the evening, I am not quite sure when, Mr Greene told us that he had a few months ago seen in London a man whom he recognized as being a member of the German SA. This man Ben Greene had actually seen in Germany at the time of the handing over of the Saar, and he had been the first German to cross the bridge on that occasion. When Mr Greene saw this man in London he was sure that he too had been recognized, but that neither of them said anything to each other.
>
> This incident alone struck me as remarkable, for had Mr Greene been a loyal British subject he should surely have reported such an incident to the authorities at once. It was clear that he had not done so, and so one can only conclude that he was quite content to see a man about whom he should have been highly suspicious walking about at liberty in England after the outbreak of war.
>
> I should like to conclude this statement by saying that the whole course of the evening's conversation left me in no doubt whatever that Mr Greene was perfectly prepared to help people whom he must quite clearly have imagined to be agents of the country with whom Great Britain was at war.[46]

Kurtz's account of this dinner meeting largely – though not entirely – matched Gaertner's, but added a claim that Greene invited them to come to Berkhamsted and meet his wife 'whom he described as "an ardent admirer of Hitler", and in whose eyes Hitler could do no wrong'.[47]

With the evidence stacking up against Greene, Knight ordered Kurtz to redouble his efforts to befriend Beckett. On May 15, after a meeting at Holborn Hall organised by Lord Tavistock, Greene took Kurtz to meet Beckett and the three men set off to enjoy their supper at a nearby brasserie.

If Kurtz's account of Beckett's comments was reliable – especially on the importance of joining the parachute corps to obtain weapons (a question which would cause MI5 some difficulty in the months to come) – the BCCSE officials were guilty of serious offences. But even by their own subsequent statements, both men knowingly and willingly dined with a man they believed to be a German spy. 'Greene tells me he first knew him as a German refugee and that he then believed him to be a German agent', was Beckett's own description of the encounter with Kurtz. 'I promised to telephone him [later] because Greene invited him to Berkhamsted where both Greene and I lived.'[48]

Over the ensuing fortnight Kurtz and at least one other undercover agent provided further reports on their meetings with the leaders of BCCSE. Because Maxwell Knight did not record or even file them immediately, it is impossible to be sure of the exact chronology, but they nonetheless suggest that Beckett, Greene and Gordon-Canning were preparing for the much-anticipated German invasion:

> M/H reports that John Beckett and Gordon-Canning are very closely in touch, and according to Beckett, Canning would be perfectly ready to harbour pro-Nazi Germans if they were on the run in this country. Beckett is known to have offered facilities to a certain German in this respect.[49]

> It is confirmed, again by M/H, that John Beckett will be perfectly prepared to join the anti-parachute corps for the purpose of obtaining arms and ammunition.[50]

> John Beckett and Ben Greene have recently discussed the formation of a skeleton ex-serviceman's organization to be put into operation at the close of the present war. It is to be run like the British Legion and is to have people at the head of it who are, to quote John Beckett, 'above suspicion', and he himself will not appear on any list.

Their idea is to get an organization together with the object of collecting dissatisfied ex-servicemen and exploiting their grievances.[51]

In a conversation with M/M, Beckett openly referred to himself and his associates as the 5th Column. He says it is absolutely definite that the names and addresses of all 5th Column people have been sent to and received by the Germans.

These names and addresses are being listed and put into notebooks for future reference on arrival. Only names of thoroughly reliable people have been sent. This has probably been done through [William] Joyce but it is not certain.[52]

Between May 22 and May 24, Beckett, Greene and Gordon-Canning were all arrested and interned under Defence Regulation 18B; the orders – signed, as required by the Home Secretary – cited their 'hostile associations' and pronounced them to be a threat to the safety of the realm. Unaccountably, alone of the four leaders of BCCSE, Lord Tavistock was neither detained nor even questioned.

That the British Council for Christian Settlement in Europe posed a genuine danger was evidenced by a letter found in the raid on its offices. This document – written by Beckett on May 22 and addressed to Tavistock at his Scottish estate – detailed plans to replace the government with a Quisling cabinet of Nazi sympathisers once German troops conquered Britain.

I have had a series of conversations with key people who realize the situation and there is a general consensus of opinion that you are the only person around whom we could build an alternative government in time. I cannot say more than this by letter and have probably said too much, but I consider it vitally necessary that you should be here as soon as possible for consultation with various people.[53]

Beckett went on to list the names of the nineteen most senior figures in this putative 'Coalition Government of National Security'. Tavistock was to be Prime Minister, Mosley the Leader of the House and 'President of Council', while Greene was to be put in charge of Education and Gordon-Canning rewarded with the control of all British Dominions.

Beckett reserved for himself the crucial posts of Home Secretary and minister for 'National Security'.

Other familiar names from the fascist movement featured prominently in the roll-call of ministers-to-be. Lord Lymington and the Duke of Buccleuch were to take charge of Food and Agriculture and the War Office respectively, while Anthony Ludovici and the Right Club's Aubrey Lees were to be given junior ministerial posts.

What makes this document even more remarkable is its absence from the official histories of pro-Nazi fascists in Britain. Although Beckett, Greene and Gordon-Canning would all challenge their detentions – and, in the process, draw MI5 deeper into bitter conflict with Whitehall – Beckett's detailed plans for a Nazi puppet regime were never revealed.

The explanation for this strange oversight may lie in Maxwell Knight's administrative incompetence. Ostensibly the original letter was filed in MI5's dossier on Sydney, 1st Baron Arnold – a veteran pacifist, council member of the Anglo-German Fellowship and resolute opponent of war with the Third Reich.[54] Like the majority of those named in the proposed puppet government, Arnold's MI5 file – PF 62956 – is missing from the National Archives.[55] The only surviving copy of Beckett's proposal appears to have been misplaced and then added to his voluminous dossier at some later time. A handwritten note, scribbled on the top of the paper by someone whose initials are unreadable, states: 'I found this in a personal file of M's.'[56]

The most disturbing element, however, was the apparent involvement of two of Britain's most senior military leaders in Beckett's plan for a Quisling government. General John 'Boney' Fuller – the father of mechanised warfare who had helped Hitler develop his Panzer divisions (and celebrated the results at the Fuehrer's birthday parade) – was to be appointed Minister of Defence. Beckett was also expecting Fuller's long-time friend and sponsor in the military, General William Ironside, to join the coup. According to a report from Agent M/M (filed, inevitably, somewhat belatedly by Knight):

M/M had a long talk with Beckett shortly before he was detained under 18b order. Beckett discussed General Ironside and said that he knew the General favoured Fascism. Asked how he knew this, Beckett said he had been told so by Gordon-Canning and by a General 'who is one of us'. According to Beckett, General Ironside would not come out into the open until the moment comes, but may soon be approached.[57]

Since Ironside was, at that point, Chief of the Imperial General Staff – essentially the head of Britain's armed forces – his alleged involvement with Beckett's proposed 'revolutionary fascist dictatorship' suggested a significant problem. What made this even more troubling was that Ironside's name also featured in a second coup plot uncovered by MI5 that same spring.

CHAPTER THIRTEEN

Password 'Peter Leigh'

'Revolution is to take place after the total loss of the
Channel ports and defeat on the Western Front ...'
MI5 agent's report on Dr Leigh Vaughan-Henry,
May 28, 1940

No. 17 Stanley Crescent, in London's leafy Ladbroke Grove, was an unlikely command centre for the architects of a violent coup d'état. Its peevish and self-important owner was an equally improbable leader for a far-right revolution. Yet as the Low Countries fell to Hitler's Blitzkrieg and Britain braced itself for the prospect of invasion, the elegant three-storey house was the headquarters of a well organised and apparently disciplined organisation of Nazi sympathisers plotting to put armed fascists on the streets and conspiring to oust the government in favour of a British Quisling regime, loyal to the Third Reich.

The cabal involved a representative cross-section of the domestic fascist movement – members simultaneously belonged to the BUF, the Nordic League, Archibald Ramsay's Right Club, as well as fringe groups such as the Imperial Fascist League – but also had close links to Irish Republican Army activists in Eire who were forming armed 'legions' to fight in Britain 'when the revolution starts'.

What is most remarkable about this planned *putsch* is both the volume of intelligence collected by the Security Service about its innermost workings, and the complete absence of it, or its leaders, from the official histories of MI5 and the war on the Home Front. And yet, more even than the Beckett or Ramsay conspiracies with which it overlapped and shared some members, the scheme hatched inside 17 Stanley Crescent appears to have been the most advanced, the most serious and the most willingly violent of all the plots for a bloody pro-Nazi uprising in Britain. Its methods included 'illegal printing, a transport section to convey the members in their various activities, an extensive arrangement of accommodation addresses, and various aliases for leading members of the organization'. All of this was directed by 'a subversive organisation [intending] to establish an authoritarian system of Government'. Yet the details of the scheme are buried in an obscure legal file held not by MI5 or even the Home Office, but instead lost for decades in the vaults of the Treasury Solicitors' Department.[1]

*

Stanley Crescent was one of three crescent-shaped streets built in 1850 on the site of the former Hippodrome racecourse. Each boasted graceful, stone-faced houses gathered around well-laid communal gardens filled with shrubs, trees and lawn tennis courts.

Named after Edward Stanley, 14th Earl of Derby, then Prime Minister, its position, close to Kensington Gardens and a short carriage ride from Buckingham Palace and the Houses of Parliament, attracted wealthy, often artistic, buyers: lawyers, politicians and respectable publishers paid handsomely for the right to live there. No. 17 was at the end of a short terrace on the north side of the Crescent, backing directly on to the gardens. In the 1920s, it had been converted into spacious apartments: by the end of the decade the ground-floor flat was occupied by a celebrated composer, conductor, music critic and author.

Dr Leigh Francis Howell Wynne Sackville de Montmorency Vaughan-Henry claimed a direct familial lineage to Celtic druidry, and had been a member of the Welsh National Gorsedd.[2] In the 1920s he had been director of music at the Theatre Institute in Florence, and such was his reputation that he had been chosen to conduct concert performances for the British royal family. To the general public he was known for his regular appearances on BBC wireless programmes in which he discussed his particular areas of expertise: the Welsh bardic tradition in poetry and song.

To the police and to MI5, however, Leigh Vaughan-Henry was better known as a pro-Nazi fascist and violent anti-Semite. They had been monitoring him and the secret fascist organisation he commanded for five years – and for very good reason.

Henry was born in Liverpool in 1889, the son of a moderately famous singer and composer of Welsh songs. When the First World War began, he was working in Florence but was invited to visit Germany; when he arrived there he was promptly arrested and interned as an alien in the Ruhleben camp for civilian prisoners of war, near Spandau. The conditions were humane and the site well run, and his incarceration there apparently left Henry with an abiding respect for the country. Throughout the 1930s he visited Germany regularly and married (albeit bigamously) a German woman, Hedwig Steinborn. He also became a diehard fascist and devoted admirer of Adolf Hitler.

In December 1935 he requested an interview with the Fuehrer and his propaganda chief, Joseph Goebbels. Henry sent his letter via the London correspondent of the *Völkischer Beobachter*: Dr Hans Thost was an agent of influence for the Nazi Party, who cultivated 'persons who appeared to be sympathetic to Germany in general and Hitler's policies in particular' and who was subsequently expelled from Britain in 1935 on suspicion of espionage.[3] Henry told Thost he believed the Nazi Party leaders 'are the means to carry out what I wish to do for your people with the right cachet'. For good measure he signed the request 'Heil Hitler'.[4] This, together with his membership of the British Union of Fascists, where he worked in the policy department and for whom he was a regular public speaker, brought him to the attention of MI5. According to a surviving memo from his once-substantial files:

> [Henry] made no secret of his pro-Hitler sympathies, and associated with Otto Bene[5] and Dr Hans Thost, who had been sent to this country to spread Nazi propaganda. His flat was frequently visited by Germans. He was friendly with certain Nazi Government officials in Berlin, and used to give letters of introduction to them to any of his friends who were intending to visit Germany.[6]

In the years immediately before the war, Henry himself was a frequent visitor to Berlin, where he was entertained by Nazi Party officials and, on at least one occasion, made a radio broadcast for Goebbels. According to intelligence reports reaching MI5 he used these trips both to bring back propaganda and to carry messages between the German government and its supporters in Britain.

> In the summer of 1939 Vaughan-Henry visited Germany ostensibly to conduct his orchestra. But according to our information he was closely associated with the Nazi leaders ... He visited Berlin on 1st September 1939, and met Goering before he left. His wife is still in Germany and he corresponded with her through Amsterdam.[7]

Nor did the outbreak of war limit his efforts: in mid-September 1939, Special Branch officers reported that Henry 'had been addressing Fascists in Trafalgar Square' and 'had boasted of his associations with the Reich'. The following month a police intelligence report sent to the Security Service indicated that these contacts had enabled Henry to establish a covert Nazi beachhead inside a middle-class pressure group, originally founded to campaign against left-wing activism.

> In October 1939 Special Branch reported that the centre of pro-German anti-war activity was at the premises of the National Citizens Union,[8] 56 Victoria Street ... Vaughan-Henry, Captain Ramsay and A.T.O. Lees[9] were present at a meeting of this society. This society was originally an anti-communist organization, but later became pro-German and used to carry on defeatist propaganda on the same lines as the British Union.[10]

Henry had, by then, parted company with Mosley and the BUF and flirted with Arnold Leese's Imperial Fascist League, as well as the Imperial Socialist League, a small but vociferous organisation which received 'its instructions and funds from Germany via Holland',[11] and the Anglo-Irish Fellowship, a 'pro-German' organisation established by John Webster, a maverick former communist who campaigned for an alliance between London and Berlin to undermine the Soviet Union.[12]

Henry's involvement with these wilder fringes of the British fascist movement, his association with German Intelligence and his rabidly pro-Nazi oratory, led Maxwell Knight to send two of the undercover informants he had deployed on the Beckett conspiracy to infiltrate his circle of friends and supporters. The efforts of Agents M/M and M/W were evidently successful since Henry's MI5 file, listed as PF 42909 in the Registry, ran to at least three volumes.

That file, however, no longer exists. MI5 says it 'has been destroyed' – though has given no indication of when or why. It may have been one of the hundreds of intelligence dossiers destroyed[13] in the September 1940 German bombing raid when a stick of incendiaries severely damaged MI5's Registry in Wormwood Scrubs prison.*

However, the official history of the Security Services records that much of the information was eventually 're-constructed' from microfilms and files held in other locations.[14] With this in mind – and in the context of the sensitivity surrounding some of Knight's more dubious methods as well as the file's apparently extraordinary contents – it is equally possible that it has simply been withheld from public view.

That the dossier's contents were extremely disturbing emerges from the surviving fragments to be found in the Treasury Solicitor's docket and in the files on John Beckett and Ben Greene. Pieced together, they reveal what the government and the Security Service discovered about Henry's work as an agent of German Intelligence, and his plans for a violent fascist revolution. In a memo for the Home Office, apparently written in November 1940, an unnamed MI5 officer noted:

According to our information in March 1940 Vaughan-Henry was waiting for instructions from Holland to leave for Constantinople where he was to work under the German Legation against British interests. He was specially interested in persons whom he believed to be connected with the British Secret Service, and used to pass on

---

* The Registry was housed in the remarkably vulnerable former prison laundry – a glass-roofed workshop offering little or no protection to the collection of vital national security information.

information to a secretary in the local Italian Embassy, from which it reached the Germans through the German Embassy in Rome.[15]

Evidently those instructions did not materialise, because the following month Henry was charged with causing a breach of the peace in London. On April 8, he addressed a lunchtime meeting of the English National Association, an offshoot of the BUF, funded by Lord Tavistock, in Finsbury Square. It was this appearance which landed him, a week later, before magistrates at Old Street Police Court: according to the evidence of Special Branch detectives present at the meeting, Henry told his audience that Jews were 'a lot of dirty lousy Yids' and 'a menace to Britishers'. He then 'challenged those of Jewish beliefs or the Jewish race to come up to the platform and resort to force'.[16]

The bench gave him the choice between a £250 fine[17] and three months in prison. Henry paid the fine and was additionally bound over to be of good behaviour for six months – an injunction he chose promptly to ignore.

Someone less arrogant than Leigh Vaughan-Henry – in one fragmentary report MI5 described him as 'bumptious'[18] – might have realised that his high-profile anti-Semitic and pro-German statements all but guaranteed close observation by the Security Service and would have lain low, at least for the period of his binding over.

Whether from hubris or because his plans were too well advanced to be interrupted, Henry pressed on. He failed to grasp that his correspondence was being opened under a Home Office warrant, much less that his inner circle of co-conspirators had now been infiltrated by two MI5 undercover agents.

The mail interception revealed that Henry was communicating with German Intelligence through his wife, who had remained in Germany on the outbreak of war and to whom he wrote regularly, now using a female cut-out in occupied Norway.[19] Agents M/M and M/W meanwhile reported that a month after war was declared, Henry openly discussed meeting an Abwehr agent who, in the guise of a Dutch merchant, visited Britain 'as a courier' between the Fifth Column and its masters in Berlin.[20] They also filed memos listing the most senior members of a secret organisation he had established: chief

A 51-year-old Scottish hairdresser and German spy, Jessie Jordan
was the unrepentant centre of a pre-war transatlantic Nazi
espionage network. She was jailed for four years in 1938.

Crown Copyright

A 55-year-old conman, bigamist and thief, Edwin Heath sold British military secrets to the German Secret Service. He was arrested six days after war was declared and interned under Defence Regulation 18B.
Crown Copyright

Donald Adams, a 58-year-old freelance journalist and racing tipster, spied for the German Secret Service for two years. In September 1939 he was jailed for ten years.
Crown Copyright

In 1934 Serocold Skeels (on the left) unsuccessfully fought a by-election on behalf of the fascist New British Party. A virulent anti-Semite and devoted admirer of Hitler, in February 1941 he was jailed for four years for conspiring to assist the enemy.
Acme News Agency/Topfoto

A pro-Nazi fascist and founding member of the Nordic League, Oliver Conway Gilbert was interned under Defence Regulation 18B on the outbreak of war after MI5 discovered he was communicating with German and Japanese spies.
Crown Copyright

(LEFT) A diehard fascist and admirer of Hitler, in 1940 Hastings William Sackville Russell, 12th Duke of Bedford, tried to negotiate peace terms with Germany. Despite this, and his funding of pro-Nazi groups, his privileged status protected him from prosecution or internment.
Crown Copyright

(ABOVE) A former Director of Naval Intelligence, Admiral Sir Barry Domvile was a close friend of Heinrich Himmler, and praised 'the great work done by Hitler'. His organisation, The Link, disseminated Nazi propaganda. He was interned under Defence Regulation 18B.
Alamy

(LEFT) Lord Sempill admitted selling military secrets to Japanese Intelligence for more than fifteen years. Despite this he was never prosecuted or interned, and retained his seat in the House of Lords.
Alamy

A convinced anti-Semite and leading conservative intellectual and writer, Anthony Ludovici enjoyed personal friendships with the leaders of Nazi Germany. Although he published articles and books praising Hitler, he was employed by MI6 until 1940.

Getty Images

Captain Archibald Ramsay, a Conservative MP, fascist and anti-Semite, founded The Right Club and with his aristocratic wife Ismay plotted one of three violent coups d'état uncovered by MI5 in 1940. He was interned under Defence Regulation 18B but allowed to retain his seat in the House of Commons.

Getty Images

The daughter of a White Russian diplomat, Anna Wolkoff – seen here in the uniform of the Auxiliary Fire Service – was Ramsay's chief lieutenant in The Right Club. In November 1940 she was jailed for ten years for sending British military secrets to Nazi Germany.
Getty Images

(BELOW) Tyler Kent (second from right), a cipher clerk at the US Embassy, conspired with Wolkoff to obtain British military secrets and smuggle them to Berlin. He was jailed for seven years in November 1940.
Alamy

A former Independent Labour MP, John Beckett became a fascist in the 1930s. Backed by the Duke of Bedford's money and influence, he formed a succession of pro-Nazi groups and, in 1940, MI5 undercover agents uncovered his plans for a revolutionary coup d'état. He was interned under Defence Regulation 18B.

National Portrait Gallery

(LEFT) A celebrated conductor and musicologist, Leigh Vaughan-Henry was deeply anti-Semitic and a pro-Nazi fascist. In 1940 MI5 discovered that his highly-organised group of traitors was plotting an armed coup d'état. He was interned throughout the war.

(RIGHT) Dedicated fascists, Molly Hiscox (second from right) and Norah Briscoe (centre) were members of Archibald Ramsay's Right Club. In 1941, an undercover MI5 sting operation caught them passing military secrets to a man they believed to be a Nazi Intelligence agent.

In August 1942 George Johnson Armstrong, a petty thief who offered his services and military information to German Intelligence, became the first British man to be hanged for treachery during the Second World War.
Crown Copyright

A former prostitute and petty criminal, Dorothy O'Grady (aka Pamela Arland) sabotaged telephone lines and made maps of defence facilities on the Isle of Wight. In December 1940 she was convicted of treachery and condemned to death, but her sentence was mysteriously commuted to fourteen years' penal servitude.
Crown Copyright

A twenty-year-old drunkard and thief with a weakness for sex workers, in 1942 Duncan Scott-Ford was recruited by German Intelligence and induced to sell British military secrets. He was convicted of treachery and executed in November 1942.

Crown Copyright

A German-born clerk and naturalised British citizen, in November 1941 Irma Stapleton was caught in an MI5 sting operation in which she handed over military secrets and an anti-aircraft shell to a man she believed to be a German spy. The following February she was jailed for ten years.

(ABOVE) A 57-year-old German Intelligence officer, between 1938 and 1939 Hermann Simon travelled throughout Britain collecting military information and setting up a network of British 'Fifth Column' sub-agents. Although he was caught with spy equipment and sensitive material, he was only briefly jailed before being expelled.

Crown Copyright

A German-born cook, Josephine 'My' Eriksson worked in some of Britain's leading aristocratic households while leading a double life as a Nazi spy. She was Simon's pay-mistress and like him was only briefly jailed in December 1939.

Crown Copyright

(LEFT) A Whitehall veteran, aloof and deeply set in outdated ways, as Home Secretary Sir John Anderson failed to grasp the unique nature of the Nazi threat, and was responsible for the chaos of internment policy in the first year of the war.
Getty Images

(RIGHT) As Anderson's Permanent Under Secretary at the Home Office, Alexander Maxwell regularly clashed with MI5 over the threat posed by British fascists. His obduracy was a key factor in the breakdown of relations between Whitehall and the Security Service.
National Portrait Gallery

A leading Liberal barrister who became the head of the Home Office Advisory Committee on internments under Defence Regulation 18B, Norman Birkett distrusted the Security Service. In November 1941 he savaged the evidence of an undercover MI5 officer, causing the Security Service to abandon internment applications in favour of a long-term *agent provocateur* scheme.
National Portrait Gallery

MI5's first Director, by the outbreak of the Second World War Sir Vernon Kell was 65, outdated and out of his depth. He was sacked, on Churchill's orders, in June 1940 and died eighteen months later.

Getty Images

Guy Liddell joined MI5 in 1931 and in June 1940 became Director of B Branch, the section responsible for counter-espionage. Throughout the war he dictated a revealing daily diary – a journal so sensitive that it was locked in a safe in the Director General's office until it was declassified in 2002.

Getty Images

MI5's chief, and most effective, spycatcher for more than a decade, because of his German birth and accent Colonel William Hinchley-Cooke's first MI5 pass was inscribed with the words 'He is an Englishman'.

After the Battle

A former member of an early British fascist party, Maxwell Knight joined MI5 and ran a string of often amateurish undercover agents. Recently praised as 'Britain's Greatest Spymaster', Knight was chaotically disorganised, undisciplined and sometimes caused severe problems for the Security Service.

National Portrait Gallery

A middle-class English housewife recruited by Maxwell Knight, Marjorie Amor became a highly effective undercover agent. She infiltrated Archibald Ramsay's Right Club and provided clear evidence of its plans for a fascist coup.

Courtesy of Stephen Mackie

Joan Miller was a young society girl recruited by Knight, first as his secretary, later as his mistress and live-in companion. The Security Service attempted to ban her memoirs, which offered a revealing insight into Knight and his stable of agents.

The heir to the Barony of Clanmorris, John Bingham was Maxwell Knight's protégé and ran one of MI5's earliest entrapment operations against British Nazi sympathisers. He remained in the Security Service after the war and was one of the inspirations for John Le Carré's fictional spymaster, George Smiley.
National Portrait Gallery

A gifted polymath and Labour peer, Victor Rothschild joined the Security Service shortly after the outbreak of war. In addition to carrying out bomb disposal missions, he masterminded MI5's elaborate 'Jack King' *agent provocateur* scheme.
Getty Images

A former bank clerk, Eric Roberts joined MI5 in 1940 and became its most successful undercover agent. As the supposed Gestapo officer 'Jack King', he uncovered several hundred British pro-Nazi spies, saboteurs and traitors.

Crown Copyright

As part of Eric Roberts' cover legend, MI5 created an exact replica of a Gestapo officer's identity card in the name of 'Jack King'.

Courtesy MI5

among them was Captain Archibald Maule Ramsay MP, founder of the Right Club.[21]

On May 9, 1940, according to information supplied by Agent M/W, Henry summoned five members of the organisation – two women and three men (all unnamed) – to a meeting in the drawing room at 17 Stanley Crescent.

This group was, apparently, one of eight 'cells' working under Henry's command: he told them that they were each to obtain 'an accommodation address and that each member should be prepared to distribute propaganda leaflets in pillar boxes, restaurants and other public places. All those who were present at the meeting gave the Nazi salute. Henry left the meeting at 10.15pm and later returned bringing a typewritten copy of the German wireless bulletin.'[22]

Henry also made clear that his chief lieutenant in the organisation was Samuel Darwin-Fox, formerly Professor of English Literature at the University of Freibourg, Switzerland, but better known to MI5 as a member of BCCSE and 'one of the more extreme and unbalanced of Nordic League members'.[23] Two weeks after the meeting on May 9, Agent M/W called on Darwin-Fox at his office in Drake Street, Bloomsbury; the former academic expanded on Henry's immediate plans, explaining that:

> Italy would declare war almost immediately, that France would then give in and that Britain would follow before the end of the week. There would be a short civil war, the Government would leave first for Bristol and then for the Colonies, General Ironside would become dictator and after things had settled down Germany could do as she liked with Britain.[24]

If this report, once again naming Britain's most senior military Home Front chief* as part – or at least the proposed beneficiary – of a fascist coup, caused any anxiety, there is no record of it in either MI5's files or any government documents released to public scrutiny in the National

---

* Ironside was appointed Commander-in-Chief, Home Forces on May 27, 1940.

Archives. Nor is there any direct evidence that Ironside either knew or approved of the plots. Nonetheless, he was on record as a champion of General John Fuller (and had seriously considered appointing Hitler's favourite British general to a sensitive role under his command[25]) and was rumoured to be a secret member of the BUF.[26] Rather more concrete information showed Ironside to have been a member of the Anglo-German Fellowship and that in November 1939 Fuller was confident enough of his mentor's support to advise Admiral Barry Domvile, 'Ironside is with us'.[27] Either way, in July 1940 he was summoned to the War Office and dismissed – ostensibly on the grounds that the Cabinet wanted a man with more recent combat experience in charge of preparations for the expected German invasion.

Leigh Vaughan-Henry was eagerly anticipating the arrival of Hitler's troops. In late May he called another, larger meeting of his organisation – the last, he told them, to be held before the planned coup d'état. This time sixteen members were present in the drawing room – the leaders of what Henry said were individual 'cells' spread across London.

In addition to Darwin-Fox, there were representatives of Ramsay's Right Club, John Beckett's British People's Party, the BUF and the Imperial Fascist League. There was also a familiar figure from the Nordic League – Takuidi Egushi, the Japanese journalist who combined his role as London correspondent of *Tokyo Shimbun* with work as a spy.[28] According to the report from Agent M/W (saved for posterity in MI5's files on John Beckett):

Elaborate precautions were taken for escape by the back way in the event of a raid and on one occasion when the doorbell went, a man started playing the piano and half the people cleared out into the garden. This was the last meeting to be held, after this they are only to communicate with their two 'contacts'. It is to work like a chain, when one man is arrested the next will take his place.

Certain people will continue to have direct contact for the moment with Henry, and he is to be accepted as leader by all, his instructions to be obeyed implicitly. Only a certain amount [is] to be told each person, and all to be kept in watertight compartments ...[29]

Henry had evidently accepted M/W as a genuine fascist revolutionary, since the report he (or she) gave to MI5 described clearly 'The Leader's' secret plans for a violent coup:

> Revolution is to take place after the total loss of the Channel ports and defeat on the Western Front, and an effort is to be made to link up with the enemy in Holland ... The next plan is the [in]filtration into the C.P. [Communist Party] and chiefly the I.L.P. [Independent Labour Party]. This to be done by Darwin-Fox. Intimidation of certain people by threat, and possible action against their wives and children; bumping off certain people (this to be organized with great care).[30]

But Henry was also aware that his plot might be discovered before the coup was launched. He told his cell leaders that in the event of trouble, plans had been put in place to hide his revolutionaries from the police and then to smuggle them away to safety in the Irish Republic.

> Arrangements are being made for the allocation of hide-outs for the women of the party and their children if necessary. These will be reached in 10 minutes and ... the point to go will be imparted to each person, and from there he will be escorted to an unknown destination.
>
> A getaway out of London is to be by river, and out of the country to Ireland via S. Wales, a route which has been tried successfully; there is a second route. Two people have already used the first route, one apparently injured a policeman who is now dying.[31]

Unknown to Henry, Oswald Mosley, Archibald Ramsay and John Beckett had all been arrested earlier that day. When Agent M/W returned to Stanley Crescent on June 2, he (or she) found The Leader in defiant – but apprehensive – mood.

> Henry said he had been up nearly all night destroying incriminating papers ... [He] spoke about the war news and said that the German broadcast had said that Mosley and Capt. Ramsay had been detained. In Vaughan-Henry's own opinion the Government would never have the nerve to liquidate these people, adding that he was sure that

British troops in Belgium had already capitulated and that Germany has all but won the war.[32]

Five days later, the second of Knight's undercover agents – 'M/M' – reported on a meeting with Henry in Stanley Crescent in which he made clear that his organisation had not been affected by the round-up of other fascists.

> There are 18 cells already organized. Each cell has 25 members who are responsible for the district in which they live or work. Henry says he has many phone numbers; instructions are to be given to each member who will destroy them when committed to memory. No call is genuine unless 'Peter Leigh' is mentioned in the conversation on both sides.[33]

Agent M/M also reported that Henry had obtained a printing press to churn out the revolutionary government's instructions. This 'has been moved and will continue to be moved by a baker in his bread van every few days. It does not wait for an emergency to be moved.'

Nor was this Henry's sole involvement with illicit printing. A note in MI5's Statement of Case against him, prepared in November 1940, suggests that he was forging identity documents.

> According to information which we obtained from a reliable source, Vaughan-Henry had a large stock of inner pages of passports, and a Foreign Office embossing stamp. He said he could replace the photograph in a passport with that of someone he wanted to smuggle to Ireland, and stitch in blank pages for endorsements.
>
> He then sends such persons to a place in South Wales and thence to Ireland. In a period of ten days he has smuggled six persons to Ireland in that way, and members of the I.R.A. have come to England by that route.[34]

Henry was clearly aware that he might soon be arrested and was making plans to protect himself when the authorities caught up with him. He told Agent M/M that when the time came he planned 'to be apparently very frank' with the police, while in reality withholding the details of his organisation: this, he predicted, would ensure that it survived and that 'there will be a legion formed in Ireland (by those who go over by the secret route) who will return to fight when the revolution starts'.[35]

These reports gave MI5 more than enough evidence to arrest Henry. But for more than a week it waited, in the hope that The Leader would reveal the names of more of his followers to its undercover agents. There are no reports, in any of the surviving files, indicating that he did so, and at 7.45am on Monday, June 10, four Special Branch officers led by Inspector Arthur Cain and Jimmy Dickson from Knight's 'M.S.' section of MI5, raided the flat at 17 Stanley Crescent. According to Henry's own pompous and somewhat melodramatic account, they were armed and aggressive:

> My small dog being in my bedroom since my wife was away, [was] unable even to ejaculate one bark before every panel of my door was kicked out and an absurd spectacle of four arms holding revolvers appeared through the panels and I am then shrieked at to open to the police in the King's name ...
>
> I said I had been for a considerable time in Hollywood and these gentlemen as supers in a 'G' film would not get a job from me, would they please come inside, which they did. It was not perhaps a happy opening but it was as happy as the genteel announcement of their presence ...[36]

Cain handed Henry a copy of warrant number 401, issued under the Defence Regulations. When (according to his version of events) Henry asked the detectives, 'what does all this mean?', one of them replied, 'you can shut your bloody mouth you shit, we are going to go through your place' and then, 'bloody well shut up and hold your tongue'.[37]

The search of his flat took several hours and yielded a variety of typewritten fascist slogans, a portrait of Hitler, several 'obscene' paintings, and photographs of Hedwig Steinborn in the nude.[38] But other papers, detailed in Cain's report of the raid, revealed the extent of Henry's treachery and the seriousness of his coup plot.

In London Vaughan-Henry has organized district 'cells' under 'sergeants' who use code terms and keep in touch with him by telephone. He claims that when all the Government defence authorities in England have been disorganized, his group would come on the streets and assume control.

Amongst the documents was a code, which [Henry] stated he had devised for communicating with his wife in Germany. There were also draft plans for a subversive organization to establish an authoritarian system of Government.

The methods to be adopted included illegal printing, a transport section to convey the members in their various activities, an extensive arrangement of accommodation addresses, and various aliases for leading members of the organization. Among Dr Henry's chief associates in these political activities have been Captain Ramsay, M.P., Jock Houston, Samuel F. Darwin-Fox and Norman Hay.[39]

Those four names were significant, since all had been separately documented as involved in plans for a fascist uprising. Darwin-Fox and Ramsay's schemes had been laid out in the reports from Knight's agents, and their co-conspirators were equally deeply immersed in pro-Nazi plots. Richard Alister 'Jock' Houston, a member of the BUF, the Nordic League, the Right Club and the BCCSE, was a street-level fascist activist and notoriously violent anti-Semitic rabble-rouser; within a year he would feature in the prosecution of two other British fascists on attempted espionage charges.

Norman Hay, meanwhile, was known to the Metropolitan Police Special Branch as one of the conspirators involved in a series of secret meetings, convened by Ramsay and Oswald Mosley between March and May 1940 and attended by representatives of most of Britain's pro-Nazi fascist groups. According to a report of these meetings, written by the police on the basis of intelligence received from 'a very reliable informant', the purpose of the gatherings was to prepare for an imminent coup d'état.[40]

The papers found in Henry's flat would, therefore, have added much to MI5's knowledge of the various strands of the plots. Cain attached copies of these incriminating documents to his report, marking them

Exhibits A and B. Oddly, however, they are missing from any of the publicly available files, making it impossible to assess the breadth of the scheme, or the names of all his co-conspirators.

Also missing is Exhibit C, which, according to the Special Branch report, provided unequivocal proof that Henry had been trying to obtain a sizeable arsenal of weapons to equip his army of revolutionaries. All that remains is a tantalising summary of this evidence, set out in Inspector Cain's statement.

> A small piece of notepaper torn out of a notebook was found on which was written '£250,000 Lee Enfield made 1917, 1920. 41 dollars complete F.O.B. U.K. Port. 1939 Ammunition 303'.[41]

Lee Enfield .303 bolt-action, magazine-fed rifles were then the standard arms issued to British infantry. The apparent price of £250,000 – equivalent to £15 million today – would have purchased several thousand weapons and significant quantities of ammunition. The acronym FOB, standing for 'Free On Board', was a shipping term indicating that the purchaser had agreed to pay the cost of freight on arrival at the port.

Other documents found in the flat tied Henry to this attempted arms deal; but, true to the plan he had discussed with Agent M/M, when Cain and Dickson questioned him The Leader was evasive, claiming that he was merely an intermediary for two European governments.

> Vaughan-Henry stated that he was only acting on behalf of an emissary of General Franco who could obtain surplus arms from Spain for the purpose of an arms deal with Turkey.[42]

MI5 was sceptical of this explanation – not least because Henry was not a licensed weapons or ammunition dealer, and because reports from its undercover agents suggested that he 'intended to smuggle some of the arms into this country'.[43] Special Branch then set off on a lengthy trek round the various companies and individuals named in the documents and with whom Henry claimed to have been working: three had no firearms licence and claimed they passed on all requests for assistance in importing ordnance to a firm of consulting engineers in Westminster. The owner of that company, who was a licensed arms dealer, recalled being approached by one of Henry's contacts but said he 'couldn't be bothered' to pursue the opportunity because 'the persons dealing with it had little knowledge of the business involved and were not the type to deal with armaments'.[44]

Since all of those named in the documents denied any involvement with The Leader or his plans, the Security Service needed Henry himself to open up about the arms-running and the coup plot: on August 7, 1940 it arranged for him to be transferred to Latchmere House on Ham Common for interrogation.

'Camp 020' had opened for business two months earlier. Notionally under the jurisdiction of the Home Office and intended to handle captured German spies, it was in reality managed by Guy Liddell, by now director of MI5's B Division, and the first occupants of its 30 cells – all equipped with hidden microphones – were British fascists.

According to one of them, the former BUF director of policy, Alexander Raven Thomson, the house and its outbuildings were 'completely surrounded by a double-row of barbed wire with patrolling guards carrying fixed bayonets', and inmates were treated to distinctly robust questioning. 'Some of us were pulled from our beds in the middle of the night', he complained in a post-war article in a fascist journal, '[and] brought before a secret tribunal of men, sitting at a table behind glaring lights'.[45]

Whether MI5 stepped across the line from vigorous, if legal, interrogation to outright torture is open to question. Some historians have argued that prisoners were subjected to sleep deprivation, physical violence and mock executions,[46] but Camp 020's commander, Colonel Robin 'Tin Eye' Stephens, claimed to be resolutely opposed to the use of physical or psychological violence – albeit on practical rather than ethical grounds. While acknowledging that his officers' orders were to obtain 'truth, in the shortest possible time', Stephens' own, subsequently published account insisted:

Violence is taboo, for not only does it produce answers to please, but it lowers the standard of information. Never strike a man. It is unintelligent, for the spy will give an answer to please, an answer to escape punishment. And having given a false answer, all else depends on the false premise.[47]

Henry plainly encountered the habitually-monocled Stephens during the four weeks he was held at Latchmere House. Surviving fragments of his files show that he made a succession of remarkably petty complaints about his treatment at the hands of 'a man in plain clothes with an eye-glass' ('Tin Eye' evidently called him 'Henry' rather than according him the more dignified 'Vaughan-Henry'). But even though he admitted provoking his captors by throwing a chair across the room during one interrogation, he never offered any claims of physical mistreatment. Despite this – and notwithstanding the irony of his being a Nazi sympathiser who had been planning to 'bump off' opponents – the would-be leader of the fascist uprising denounced the regime to which he was subjected.

'While I do not wish to be melodramatic', he wrote in one of several complaints to the Home Office and (eventually) the courts, 'it begins to approach the methods alleged against the Gestapo, the Checks [sic] and the OGPU,[48] and it is very un-British.'[49]

True to his boast to Maxwell Knight's undercover agents, Henry appears to have held out against his interrogators: there is no indication in his surviving files that he revealed the names of any members of his organisation, or details of his attempts to obtain rifles and ammunition. He appears, however, to have been rather less cautious in his conversations with a fellow inmate – a highly improbable informant working for MI5.

William Wishart, the pre-war spy for the Abwehr, had been languishing in prison as an 18B internee for more than a year. Records of Camp 020, declassified in 2007, show that he was brought to Latchmere House on August 7,[50] the same day as Leigh Vaughan-Henry; and a few fragmentary reports in his very heavily-weeded Security Service files reveal that MI5's B7a Branch[51] had recruited him as a 'stool-pigeon' with instructions to befriend Henry.

The ploy appears to have been at least partially successful. Wishart fed back to his handlers the names and addresses of four previously unidentified members of Henry's organisation. An internal MI5 letter from B7a section to Captain Stephens on October 1, 1940 reported:

> The persons named, in north London and Leeds, were not known to us and I have not received a reply to the requests for information which were sent to Special Branch and the Chief Constable of Leeds. It now appears however that Wishart is accurately reporting Henry's statements, even though these be sometimes stale or exaggerated.[52]

A second note the next day showed that Special Branch was working with MI5 to follow up the leads. But it also revealed that, according to the (unnamed) writer, the original investigation into Henry's conspiracy had been curtailed:

> I fully agree with Captain Stephens' estimate of the importance of this case and have always regretted that the necessity for protecting an agent has prevented us from following up the alleged underground route to Ireland. In my opinion it is this upon which we should now concentrate, and Wishart appears to be capable of doing good work in this connection.
>
> The report of his work ... is most interesting, and he has included a number of names and addresses which are, so far as they are known to us, correct. We now have an opportunity to pursue the question of the alleged route to Ireland without jeopardising an agent who is now engaged on still more important work, and I hope that the utmost use will be made of Wishart.[53]

Unfortunately, all subsequent reports on Wishart's intelligence – and on the investigation into Leigh Vaughan-Henry's plot to launch a violent fascist coup – have either been destroyed or remain withheld. Yet given the surviving evidence of his conspiracy, the failure to prosecute him under the (then) new Treachery Act is puzzling. The detailed and damning statements reported by Agents M/M and M/W provided more than enough to support a prosecution: other British traitors had been tried on lesser evidence – and, before long, two would be sent to the gallows for their crimes.

The surviving documents suggest one of two explanations. Either Henry's plot involved such senior figures in Britain's political and military establishment that even proceedings *in camera* posed too great a threat; or the Security Service took a pragmatic view that internment proceedings under Defence Regulation 18B were less legally rigorous and posed a lower risk of exposure to its undercover agents.

The vigorous weeding of the relevant files, and the abrupt ending they appear to disclose of the efforts to uncover the extent and seriousness of his coup plot, seem to imply the former explanation. However, the Treasury dossier on Henry's repeated attempts at litigation could point to the latter. The would-be 'Leader' made a succession of appeals for release from internment to the Home Office Advisory Committee: all were turned down after MI5 presented statements detailing his involvement with German Intelligence and his plans for a fascist coup d'état. Unusually, given the Committee's increasing reluctance to accept the unsupported claims of Security Service officers, there is no record of it asking to hear evidence directly from Agents M/M and M/W.

Nor was such testimony sought when Henry applied to the High Court for a writ of habeas corpus. Mr Justice Humphreys and Mr Justice Cassels roundly dismissed the application, describing it as 'a waste of time, money and paper'.[54]

For the duration of the war, Leigh Vaughan-Henry remained behind barbed wire fences on the Isle of Man. If his ambition to be the leader of an armed and violent revolutionary fascist uprising had been foiled, there was strong evidence that at least some of his organisation remained intact: within a year one of the members of his eighteen 'cells' would be caught in a new bid to help Germany vanquish Britain.

But by then MI5 was facing a new front in its bitter war with Whitehall – and was under attack from the highest levels of government over its investigation into domestic spies, saboteurs and traitors.

CHAPTER FOURTEEN

Witch-finding

'If we are found out we might get ten or 25 years. We are
only women. But you will have your heads chopped off'
Molly Hiscox, spy, March 13, 1941

On Saturday, January 25, 1941, Winston Churchill sat down to compose a memo to the two newest members of his War Cabinet. The previous October he had moved Sir John Anderson from the Home Office, replacing him with the politically more progressive (but administratively superior) Herbert Morrison; two months later, just before Christmas, he finally managed to ease Lord Halifax out of the Foreign Office, dispatching him to Washington, DC as Britain's US Ambassador and appointing the distinctly more hawkish Anthony Eden in his stead.*

The subject on the Prime Minister's mind that morning was the Fifth Column – and more specifically, the efforts of the Security Service to uncover and neutralise it: he was not happy about either, advising the Home and Foreign Secretaries that, in his opinion, 'the witch-finding activities of MI5 are becoming an actual impediment to the more important work of the department'.[1]

---

* Eden had been Foreign Secretary between 1935 and 1938, resigning in February that year in part due to the government's policy of appeasing Hitler.

Churchill's memo was strangely timed. Between the outbreak of war and January 1941, 36 men and women had been successfully prosecuted for offences under the Official Secrets Act or Defence Regulations; each was convicted of espionage, sabotage or aiding the enemy, and given a prison sentence ranging from two months to twenty years. More pertinently, at the very moment the Prime Minister communicated his displeasure, Security Service agents were preparing to give evidence in three new and very serious trials of British fascists working on behalf of Nazi Germany.

Those cases would reveal the involvement of the Nordic League, Archibald Ramsay's Right Club and Leigh Vaughan-Henry's unnamed group of plotters in what were unequivocally acts of treachery. But their outcomes also exposed the deepening fault-lines undermining the war against Hitler's British Fifth Column.

*

Opposition to MI5's investigations had been growing for six months inside the Cabinet and Whitehall. The first indication that the government was beginning to pull back from its commitment to unearthing and detaining British Nazi sympathisers had been signalled by Churchill in the summer of 1940. In a House of Commons debate on August 15, the Prime Minister sought to assure MPs that the threat had been overstated and had now passed:

'I am glad to tell the House that a very great improvement has been effected in dealing with this Fifth Column danger. I always thought it was exaggerated in this Island, and I am satisfied now that it has been reduced to its proper proportions, and is being gripped and looked after with very high efficiency.'[2]

Since it had been Churchill himself who had led the charge for mass internments of both domestic fascists and enemy aliens, this statement showed a remarkable degree of chutzpah. But the speech – on the government's creation of a new Security Executive to oversee MI5's work[3] – also hinted at a softening of the Prime Minister's previously hard-line approach.

'I should not have felt I was doing my duty by the National Defence, if I had not taken these special steps to cope with Fifth Column activities, and I can assure the House that the powers that Parliament has given to the Executive will not be used consciously in any unfair, oppressive, or, if I may use the expression, un-British spirit.'[4]

Six days later, the Minister of Aircraft Production, Max Aitken, Lord Beaverbrook, made the point more forcefully to MI5's Victor Rothschild. In a meeting memorialised in Guy Liddell's diary he attacked the Security Service for its investigation of suspected Nazi agents – both German and British – employed in Beaverbrook's aircraft factories.

'I am surprised that somebody with your name, your liberal views, your position and reputation, should go in for this witch-hunting', he complained. 'You should not be involved in this persecution and you should not be in MI5 witch-hunting. You should be leading your people out of the concentration camps.* When Rothschild asked if the minister thought that 'MI5's investigations into Nazi agents in industry are of no value?', Beaverbrook replied: 'No value at all.'

Liddell's account of the rest of the interview was equally revealing:

ROTHSCHILD: So really you are quite happy about having these people about. You remember what happened in France and Holland?

BEAVERBROOK: I was in France at the very last moment before the government fell, and I can tell you it was nothing to do with so-called Fifth Column activities. The French were a decadent and beaten race ...

ROTHSCHILD: Well, if you are quite happy about having dangerous people in your employ, I will say nothing more about it.

BEAVERBROOK: You produce your case. You have not produced anything yet ... You should not be in that organisation with witch-hunters.

---

* Victor Rothschild had been a member of the left-wing Cambridge [University] Apostles and was, of course, Jewish.

It ought to be abolished. I do not think there is any danger from Nazi spies in this country. I do not think it matters if they are at large.[5]

Since, by the time of this conversation, MI5's efforts had led to the prosecution of two spies within the Air Ministry itself – William Downing and Thomas Beckett, sentenced to six and three years in prison respectively for offences under the Official Secrets Act – and had also revealed that Lord Sempill, the unrepentant intelligence agent for Japan, was employed there, Beaverbrook's attitude was as obtuse as it was inexplicable. It would not, however, prove to be unique.

Proof that the threat from pro-Nazi British fascists was not abating emerged in the Central Criminal Court in February 1941. In the now-familiar conditions of secrecy – the *Daily Herald* reported that 'police guarded the entrances to Court No. 1 ... and the glass panel doors were covered with dark paper'[6] – a grey-haired, 66-year-old tutor and his bespectacled seventeen-year-old pupil were charged with three counts of conspiring 'to assist the enemy'.

The older man in the dock was Serocold Skeels, a leading figure in Beckett and Joyce's National Socialist League and a member of the Nordic League's ruling council. He had come to MI5's notice for volunteering his services to the German Embassy in May 1939: the evidence presented at his three-day trial showed that since then he had recruited David Esmé Vaughan, a vulnerable young man placed in his care, to the cause. Skeels' methods would today be recognised as classic terrorist grooming and radicalisation, but even without the benefit of hindsight it is clear that what he induced his young charge to do posed a very real danger.

Vaughan was born in Biarritz on May 2, 1923, the only child of a British father (a veteran of the Royal Hussars cavalry regiment) and a French mother. When he was nine, his parents brought him to England and promptly sent him to boarding school in Folkestone. This does not appear to have been a happy experience, since he became so severely ill that he was taken out of school and home-tutored.

By 1934 Vaughan's parents had divorced and his father had remarried. The boy left England with his new family and spent the next three years living in Cannes, before being sent back to school in

Gloucestershire. This venture seems to have been as unsuccessful as the one which preceded it, and at the beginning of 1938, Serocold Skeels was engaged as a private tutor for the fourteen-year-old.

Financially, Skeels was on his uppers. He was admitted as a 'Poor Brother of Charterhouse', an historic City of London charity supporting ex-soldiers and which provided him with free board and lodging, free meals and an allowance of £60 a year.[7] Politically, however, he was extremely active, and he pushed Vaughan to become involved in fascism. According to the young man's sworn statement:

> Under Mr Skeels' tuition I began to take a keen interest in politics and encouraged by him I joined the National Socialist party, the directors general of this concern being William Joyce and a Mr Beckett ...
>
> Mr Skeels took a keen interest in this party and ... as a result of belonging to this concern, which I joined in September 1938, I began to take a keen interest in German affairs.[8]

Skeels knew that Vaughan was mentally fragile, since the young man was treated over two months by a psychotherapist for 'a bad state of nerves'; nonetheless he used his position to indoctrinate his pupil thoroughly in the Nazi cause.

> I spent the daytime, every day, with Skeels at Charterhouse ... he told me he had a very great admiration for Germany ... He talked to me a great deal about racial theory and taught me that the Nordic people were the good influence in the world ... He called Hitler a symbol of World hope and held him up as the one I should follow.[9]

Nor was this 'education' limited to theory. During the early months of the war, Skeels persuaded Vaughan that Hitler's troops would shortly land in Britain, and that when they did both men would be promoted to senior roles in a Quisling regime.

> He ... told me that when the invasion came there would be a German Army of occupation here, that the Government would resign, and that with the introduction here of National Socialism he would be a leader

of the people. He told me I would be his secretary ... I firmly believed that a National Socialist Government would come into power with Skeels as the leader, with or without German help.[10]

To help bring this about the veteran fascist ordered his charge to write to William Joyce in Berlin, giving 'Lord Haw-Haw' details of the effects of German bombing raids, and suggesting strategic targets in London to be passed on to the Luftwaffe. Throughout the course of 1940 – including during the first weeks of the Blitz – Skeels dictated letters 'about once a week'; some were handed to a contact in the Spanish Embassy for onward delivery to Berlin in the diplomatic bag.

Strangely, since MI5 was plainly involved in monitoring these activities and played a role in their eventual trial, there is no Security Service file on either Skeels or Vaughan in the National Archives. The file relating to their prosecution, however, does contain an example of one letter they sent to Joyce in September 1940.

The raid by the German pilots last Monday 9th Sept at 6.30pm over Fulham was a failure. They completely missed 'The Prize' and instead they demolished Fulham Hospital in Fulham Palace Road. There were no casualties.

They must have another try for the Fulham Electrical Power Station, also Duckham's Oil Stores and the Petrol Pool Store. These three objectives lay [sic] on the Thames and can be clearly seen if approached from the river. If this is properly tackled we will have no petrol or electric light.[11]

The diagrams attached to this note gave the location of an Army Service Corps barracks in Church Street, Kensington, a power station in Chelsea, and the Southall gas works; they also disclosed that St Paul's School in West Kensington had been taken over by the Army and that several departments of the War Office had been evacuated there.

At some point Vaughan realised, according to his sworn statement, that he was committing a serious offence, since the purpose of the letters was to assist Germany; but he claimed that Skeels threatened him if he betrayed 'the cause'.

> With Skeels' 'guidance' I began to ... give vital information to the
> enemy regarding vital military objectives in this country, to help them
> in the conquest of this country. Mr Skeels told me that I must continue
> in my activities or else I should be shot by the Party.[12]

Later in this same statement Vaughan accused his mentor of being 'a
hypnotist, and I now believe I was hypnotised into doing these things
against my will'. Given the young man's delicate mental health – and
the very real risk he faced of being charged with treachery – the claim
should be treated with some scepticism. Nonetheless, and however it
was achieved, what followed was very clear evidence that Skeels so successfully indoctrinated Vaughan that the young man decided he should
leave Britain and travel to Germany to work with William Joyce; the
idea was both unrealistic and dangerous, but Skeels actively encouraged it.

'Skeels said he could help me but that I would first have to offer my
services to the German Reich', Vaughan told Special Branch and MI5
officers in his interview. The first draft of his application was deemed
'unsuitable' by Skeels, who promptly wrote out a replacement version, addressing it to the 'Leader of The German Volk and Supreme
Commander of the German Armies'; he promised to deliver this to
the First Secretary at the Spanish Embassy for onward 'transmission
to Lord Haw-Haw, Radio Deutch [*sic*], Berlin, Germany'. The letter,
headed 'I, David Esmé Vaughan', was unequivocal evidence of an
offence which carried the death penalty.

> Like my tutor I became a convinced and fervent National Socialist,
> and consequently became on Sept 24, 1938, at the time of the Munich
> crisis, a member of the National Socialist League under the direction
> of the leader, Mr William Joyce ...
>
> I hereby express my heartfelt desire to enlist as a good soldier in
> this struggle between the good principle and the evil principle, under
> the Swastika banner of Herr Hitler, the great Leader of the German
> Volk ... I hereby request permission to become naturalised as a citizen
> of the German Reich, the new Germany of Hitler in order to live in,
> to fight for, and if necessary to die for, Germany ...

Should the authorities of the Reich, however, be of the opinion that
my services in the great fight might be better utilised in England or in
France, I place myself unreservedly at their disposal.[13]

There is no indication in the surviving files of the precise reason that
MI5 and Special Branch raided Skeels' rooms in Charterhouse, nor the
exact date on which they did so. However, it is clear that they found
the original of Vaughan's letter among Skeels' possessions. Both men
were arrested.

When he was interrogated on December 27, Skeels attempted
to lay all the blame on his pupil. 'That document was written at the
request of David Vaughan to satisfy and pacify him and to amuse
myself', he claimed in his signed statement. 'He repeatedly expressed
an ambition to get into the German Secret Service ... The whole document was an elaborate joke and I do not know what became of it
afterwards'[14] – a claim somewhat undermined by the fact that it was
found in Skeels' room.

Unsurprisingly, the judge at their joint trial expressly rejected this
defence. Mr Justice Wrottesley[15] appears to have decided that Vaughan
was mentally ill and ordered his detention in a secure psychiatric facility;[16] but in his summing up he laid the blame squarely on Skeels:

'Everything that could conceivably be said on your behalf has been
said by your learned counsel, but I do not find myself able to take the
view that you were not responsible for misleading and poisoning
the mind of that young man who I have just dealt with ...

'You did dominate that unfortunate young man ... and that is the
grave part of your offence, and it is because of that – it is not because
of your opinion[s] – that I am going to send you to prison. It is because
of the way in which you poisoned the mind of that young man. Two
years to run concurrently on each count.'[17]

Skeels appealed against this conviction – a bid rejected by the Court of
Appeal in May 1941. Nor did he fare better following his release from
Wandsworth prison in October 1942; he was immediately rearrested
and interned in Brixton prison under Regulation 18B.

His applications to the Home Office Advisory Committee were equally unsuccessful; the Committee (which, by then, recommended release almost as a matter of routine) was compelled to report to the Home Secretary that: 'Attempts ... to get Skeels to answer questions were met by violent protests on his part and it proved impossible to conduct any satisfactory examination of him.'[18] He remained in detention for the duration of the war.

There would, two years later, be an odd coda to the story of Serocold Skeels. In February 1944 the Home Secretary faced hostile questions in the House of Commons, in which the continuing internment was denounced as being so 'dangerous' that it could lead to a breakdown in the detainee's 'mental, nervous or physical health'.[19] The MP who championed Skeels' cause – Captain Archibald Maule Ramsay – had himself been held under 18B before being somewhat curiously released. What made his own freedom controversial – indeed inexplicable – was that he and his Right Club featured heavily in two trials of British traitors immediately following that of Skeels and Vaughan.

MI5's investigations into Leigh Vaughan-Henry had thrown up the name of a journalist who occasionally worked for him. Norah Constance Briscoe was a 40-year-old widow; in 1936, four years after the death of her husband (a clerk in the Ministry of Labour) she had taken their son Paul – then aged six – on a trip to Germany and developed a profound admiration for Hitler and the Nazi regime. This passion was so great that when the time came to return to England she left her child behind to be brought up by a German nanny and educated in the National Socialist school system; her outlook was evidently so extreme that Vaughan-Henry, when writing a letter commending her to a leading Dutch fascist in June 1939, felt the need to give his contact advance warning.

This is to introduce you to a journalist friend and author, Mrs Briscoe ... she is politically well-informed ... quite Jew-wise and aware of much of the machinations which are worked by international finance. You may find her views proceed further in the direction of totalitarianism than your own, as do my own ideas, as you are well aware.[20]

In the years leading up to the outbreak of war, Briscoe made regular trips back to Germany and at some point met a fellow British Nazi enthusiast, Gertrude Blount Hiscox, then running a travel agency providing tours of the Reich.

Hiscox, the daughter of a journalist and usually known as Molly, was eleven years younger than Briscoe but even more dedicated to the fascist cause. She had joined the BUF in 1934 and in 1937 became a 'foundation member' of Admiral Sir Barry Domvile's organisation, The Link. She also met and fell in love with Richard 'Jock' Houston, the sometime house-painter and violently anti-Semitic street orator; the two set up home together, where they were shortly joined by Norah Briscoe. Paul Briscoe subsequently painted a vivid account of this fascist *ménage-à-trois*.

> Mother immediately fell under [Jock's] spell. The fascination wasn't sexual, it was political. Jock, then aged 31, was a fanatical admirer of Hitler and a frenzied activist who fizzed with energy. Fast-talking, short-fused and histrionic ... he was never more at home than when he was standing on an East End pavement on a soapbox, ranting at a crowd in the odd accent of a cockney who had spent much of his life in Glasgow.
>
> Jock told them what he told anyone who would listen: that he, they, and the nation were being kept down by an international conspiracy of Jews. The unemployed were told that the money that should be creating work for them was being hoarded by Jewish financiers, and that their jobs would be stolen from them by 'refu-Jews' from the only country that was dealing with the Jewish menace, Hitler's Germany ...
>
> The analysis was crude, hateful and false – but Mother embraced it uncritically ... But there was another reason for Mother's enthusiasm. Jock saw himself as a leading figure in English fascism. He boasted that when England had a Fascist government, he would be a Gauleiter and his friends would be figures of influence. Mother's admiration for him was genuine, but it was not without self-interest.[21]

Houston was, like many British fascists, promiscuous in his party affiliations. In addition to the BUF, he was simultaneously involved with

Vaughan-Henry and with the Right Club, and he appears to have introduced both Hiscox and Briscoe to the 'Inner Circle' of diehard fascists who kept the Club going after Ramsay's internment. According to a memo in March 1941, reporting intelligence gathered by two more of Maxwell Knight's undercover agents over a period of three months, the group included Molly Hiscox, Mary Stanford, the Hon. Ismay Ramsay, Aubrey Lees, and a member of the Nordic League, the BUF, and The Link called James Emerson MacDonald Mogg; all were 'carrying on, or endeavouring to carry on, the activities of the Right Club and to impede our war effort'.[22]

The accounts of these 'activities' ranged from petty acts of anti-Semitic spite to planning for violent insurrection. At a meeting on November 21, 1940, Stanford explained that she was employed by the Public Assistance Board for Refugees in Bloomsbury and 'that she took great delight in being as hard as possible to German Jewish refugees, refusing them assistance if possible. ... She said she was using her job as a means of spreading Nazi propaganda and anti-British defeatist sentiments.' A month later, on December 30, Hiscox addressed the group, suggesting that 'they should immediately round up all pro-German sympathisers and meet weekly in public houses so that they could get on with obstructing the Government in small ways ... they should commence rumour campaigns about food, sinkings of ships and bomb damage ...'[23]

All of this was to be done in anticipation of an impending German invasion: Hiscox claimed to know that this would happen in the middle of January 1941, and that it would last only about two weeks. 'She continually referred to Hitler as "my beloved Führer"', the agent's report noted. A day later, this 'news' was passed to other members of the Inner Circle.

'Miss Stanford was in high spirits because she believed a German invasion to be imminent', recorded a file note on New Year's Eve. 'She was compiling a list of refugees who held anti-Nazi sentiments with a view to handing it over to the Germans.'[24]

By mid-January – despite the absence of the expected invasion – Hiscox and Stanford were noted as being 'the brains and driving force' behind the group. Hiscox announced that she had joined the

Communist Party since it was less heavily monitored than fascist groups, and that she was going to 'work under that cover towards [the Right Club's] aims of helping the Nazis and hindering the successful prosecution of the war'.[25]

Then, on January 21, the Inner Circle members began plotting violence. Just before the group's meeting James Mogg met Knight's agent at a local pub: over drinks he put forward a plan to bring in Irish Republican gunmen to attack the prison where Archibald Ramsay was then detained.

[Mogg] said that he had killed a man called Potter in Ireland during the Irish rebellion. He had, he said, shot Potter on the instructions of the IRA whilst Potter was in a car with his wife. Whether this was true or not is perhaps irrelevant in view of Mogg's statement that he felt no qualms at all about murder ...

He proposed a plan which he intended to carry out to try to get together six IRA men who were known to him. In case of invasion these men were to break into Brixton Prison to rescue Captain Ramsay.[26,27]

If this seemed far-fetched – the stuff of frustrated fascist fantasy – it was not the only such scheme reported by Knight's agents inside the Right Club. According to a subsequent digest of this intelligence (the actual reports are missing from the various publicly released Security Service files):

After her husband's arrest Mrs Ramsay's first reaction was to plot his escape from Brixton. She hoped that advantage might be taken of the disruption resulting from air raids, revolution or invasion, to force the gates of the prison with bombs. She hoped for the help of Fascist sympathisers and the Army and added ... 'We shall not fail, and I long to see the Home Office people swinging and hanging from lamp posts'.[28]

The identity of Knight's agents – replacements for Marjorie Amor, Hélène de Munck and Joan Miller – has never been revealed. However, it is probable that one of them was John Hirst, a former colleague of

Knight's in the British Fascisti and whom he used as an occasional informer: what is certain is that it was Hirst – recorded in the files as 'Special Source' – who set in train the events which would lead Molly Hiscox and Norah Briscoe to the dock in the Old Bailey.

At a meeting of the Inner Circle on March 7, 1941, held at a flat in Stanhope Gardens, South Kensington, Hiscox introduced the group to her friend, Norah Briscoe, whose position as a shorthand typist at the Ministry of Supply offered the prospect of access to secret documents. Hirst's wife, who had accompanied him to the tea party, expressed surprise that Briscoe had been able to get the Ministry job 'in view of her German connections'. (Mrs Hirst had, she said, been turned down for 'a very minor Government job' because of her parents' German nationality.) Briscoe was happy to report that the Ministry had been easy to penetrate.

> Mrs B. said that she had lied in her application for the job; she had told them that she had never been in a regular position, but had been a freelance journalist. She was, however, able to give three very good personal references, and as she has a brother and several relations holding high positions in the Army and Navy, she had been able to get in quite easily.[29]

Nor was Briscoe the only known pro-Nazi fascist to find employment within the Ministry.

> She informed us that Major General Fuller and his wife are also working and sleeping at the Ministry: that they have access to the most confidential information, such as the position of our submarine bases, and our most important secret munition and aircraft factories. She said that she was very pleased about that because the General was a personal friend of Hitler's.[30]

Briscoe, too, had access to these sensitive war papers, since two months after she joined the Ministry 'she had been selected to do secret and confidential work ... and she now has access to most important documents and letters ... When she gets what she describes as a "real hot one" she takes an "extra carbon copy" in case it might be "useful".' The news was received enthusiastically by the Inner Circle.

> Molly H. was most anxious to get all this information into the hands of a German Agent if possible; the trouble was that they did not know one. ... Molly H. said that it was essential that all the actual work in this direction should be done by the women, and that I was not to touch it, because if this went through as they hoped, it would mean that if caught they would serve a long term of imprisonment, whereas I would be executed.[31]

Over the following days Hirst and Maxwell Knight concocted an elaborate scheme to entrap Hiscox and Briscoe. Hirst offered to introduce them to 'a young German friend' of his – by implication a Nazi intelligence agent – who could smuggle the documents out to Berlin: the women took the bait and a meeting was arranged for Wednesday, March 12.

The 'friend' in question was Harald Kurtz, Knight's undercover 'Agent M/H', who had penetrated the British Council for Christian Settlement in Europe and whose evidence had resulted in the internment of John Beckett and Ben Greene. At the rendezvous, Briscoe said that she and Hiscox were determined to find a way to smuggle information to Germany. According to Kurtz's report, Briscoe 'spoke in glowing terms of Hitler, remarking that he was one of the men of the century. In reply to a question as to why she wanted to help Germany she said "I have been in Germany regularly since 1935, and since then I could not live in England for more than two months at a time" ... She also remarked that had she known that war would break out she would certainly have offered her services to somebody in Germany to help Germany.'[32]

Hiscox also again made clear that the women realised the dangers in what they were planning.

> During our conversations the question of taking risks was discussed, and she said 'Nora and I will be all right. If we are found out we might get ten or 25 years. We are only women. But you (meaning 'Special Source' and myself) will have your heads chopped off.'[33]

Knight decided that a successful prosecution of Hiscox and Briscoe, however, required something technically more sophisticated than the old system of dictating often-belated reports describing incriminating encounters: MI5 acquired an apartment in Swan Court, Chelsea, and, two days before the next rendezvous, concealed microphones in the living room.

Around lunchtime on Saturday, March 15, two Special Branch officers squeezed themselves into the flat's kitchen; here they would use headphones to eavesdrop on the conversation, taking verbatim shorthand notes of what was said. At 3.00pm Kurtz met Hiscox and Briscoe outside the apartment block, then led them upstairs into the trap. His account of the meeting included transcripts of the women's words.

We went into the sitting room, where Miss Hiscox and her friend sat on the sofa, and I sat in the armchair opposite to them. Before sitting down they inspected the bomb damage outside the window. Miss Hiscox asked me if I had seen the big bomb crater at the Bank, saying 'Wasn't it marvellous?'.

In order to conform with the pose which I had been instructed to adopt, I replied 'Yes' ... The general trend of their remarks showed quite plainly that their sympathies were with Germany and not with this country.

A few minutes after this, Mrs Briscoe said, 'We might as well get down to business'. She took from her handbag a card, which I saw was some sort of pass for the Ministry of Supply; she shewed* me this for the purpose of satisfying me that she really did work in the Ministry.

She told me that she worked at the Headquarters of the Ministry of Supply, and that although she had a comparatively unimportant job, she saw a lot of official files in the course of her work. Just after this, Mrs Briscoe appeared nervous, and said 'Can anyone hear us here?' I reassured her by saying that the block of flats was very quiet since the bombing, and was not much frequented. Mrs Briscoe seemed

---

* This old-fashioned spelling of the word 'showed' was a notable feature of Maxwell Knight's memoranda and reports, suggesting that, once again, he rather than Kurtz had actually typed up the document.

satisfied, and she then produced a bundle of papers from her hand-bag. She placed these on a small table which was between the sofa and the chair.

She referred to the various documents, and explained to me some-thing of their importance and contents. I think the first document she shewed me concerned Factory Sites and Contracts for Northern Ireland: I think this was in connection with an aerodrome. I remember the document, because there was some discussion over the date of it, which was the 8th January.

She also shewed me another document concerning supplies for Turkey. When talking about this, she remarked that sometimes the dates of shipping were given. She said quite voluntarily that she could not always find out the ports from which shipments were made, but she said that such information would, she thought, be 'very useful'.

This appeared to be a clear indication that there were no secrets within her reach which she was not prepared to pass on to me, as a supposed German Agent. I certainly gathered that she imagined that I could arrange for the shipments to be destroyed.

Referring to another document, also about supplies in Ireland, she pointed out to me that it seemed clear from the document in ques-tion that supplies for Northern Ireland were coming from Southern Ireland, and she added the significant remark, 'I suppose you want to do something about that?'

Briscoe also handed Kurtz a list of power plants and described delays in the delivery of radio masts which, according to the documents, were then troubling the Prime Minister. A few minutes later, the trap well and truly sprung, the sweating police officers emerged from the kitchen and arrested both women; to maintain his cover story, they also uncer-emoniously bundled Kurtz into a waiting car.

Special Branch and the Security Service wanted both Briscoe and Hiscox charged under the Treachery Act and, if convicted, sentenced to death. As Guy Liddell noted in his journal, 'the documents ... are voluminous and cover a wide field. If the information had leaked it would certainly be a very serious matter. They relate to the location of factories, shortage of materials, establishment of submarine bases in Northern Ireland, etc.'[34]

The government's Law Officers, however, decided to wait for the outcome of a forthcoming trial of another member of the Inner Circle before confirming the final charges.

Mrs Christabel Nicholson was 50 years old, a successful doctor and married to (retired) Admiral Wilmot Nicholson, a veteran of the First World War who rose to become head of the Royal Navy's submarine service. When in the 1920s he married Christabel, the best man at their wedding was Admiral Reginald Hall, former Director of the Intelligence Division at the Admiralty War Office.

The couple were wealthy and moved in London's privileged aristocratic social circles. Archibald and Ismay Ramsay were among their closest friends and associates, and the Nicholsons shared the Ramsays' fascist beliefs; both were founding members of the Right Club. As Liddell noted in his journal:

> The Admiral is rather a passive member and strongly anti-Semitic and with a bee in his bonnet on the subject of corruption in high government circles. Mrs Nicholson on the other hand is a much more active member of the Right Club and has a strong pro-German background.[35]

An indication of Mrs Nicholson's Nazi sympathies emerged in the reports of Marjorie Amor, Knight's original undercover agent who penetrated the Club's Inner Circle. In her sworn statement of evidence for the Tyler Kent and Anna Wolkoff case, she wrote:

> On 17th March 1940 I went round to the Ramsays' house, 24 Onslow Square, after dinner, and I was there introduced by Mrs Ramsay to Mrs Nicholson and her husband Admiral Nicholson, both of whom had dined with the Ramsays. ... Mrs Nicholson said that this country was in a hopeless position and that if we had someone like Hitler at the head of the State there would have been no war – but what could be expected from a Methodist like Chamberlain? ... She went on to say, 'But it will be one step worse this time if that Jew-ridden Churchill takes charge'.

Addressing herself to me she explained that she had met Hitler personally as one of a small delegation of Britishers who had been received by him in Germany (I gathered that this delegation was connected with a Nazi event of some sort) ... She said that Hitler was undoubtedly a genius and ridiculed the idea, which she said was prevalent in Britain, that because of his sudden spasms of violent rage he was not quite sane. She, as a doctor, knew that this was untrue.[36]

Mrs Nicholson was arrested as a by-product of MI5's investigation into the Kent and Wolkoff case in 1940, after it received evidence that she had actively helped them copy and then conceal the documents stolen from the US Embassy intended for onward transmission to Germany. According to a statement sworn by her housemaid, Catherine Welberry, Nicholson had given her an envelope containing the papers and asked her to keep it secret.

On Thursday, the 23rd May, Mrs Nicholson came to me in the kitchen and offered me a sealed envelope and asked me if I could keep it in a safe place. She said I could bury it in the garden or poke it behind the lavatory. She said if it was found by anyone, I was to say I thought it was Admiral Nicholson's will. She wanted me to keep it for about a fortnight or three weeks ...

Mrs Nicholson put the envelope into my handbag which was hanging on the knob of the kitchen door. She asked me to leave it in the bag until I got home and then put it into a safe place. I brought the envelope home and while listening to the news on the radio that night, I heard that Capt. Ramsay had been arrested. I remembered that Mrs Nicholson had told me that Capt. Ramsay had often been to dinner at her house. I mentioned this matter to my husband and asked him if I should take the envelope to the police. He suggested waiting until morning when I saw Mrs Nicholson, and to see how she was and what she had to say.

Next morning, Friday the 24th May, I was late in arriving at Mrs Nicholson's house and when I went in, she came out of the bathroom saying 'You made me sweat, Kitty.' I said 'Why', and she said 'I thought you had been seized by the police or someone, with the papers. For goodness sake either stick them in your corsets or bury them in the garden'. She repeated again 'It will only be for a fortnight or three weeks'.[37]

After talking this over with her husband, Mrs Welberry decided to open the envelope. The couple discovered two sheets of paper covered with notes written in pencil. They did not understand the contents, but when they saw references to the British Naval Fleet they promptly took the documents to Walham Green police station, Fulham; its officers handed them on to the Security Service.

On May 26 Knight and a senior Special Branch officer arrived at the Nicholsons' fashionable Kensington address. Christabel appeared unconcerned at their presence and reacted calmly to being questioned under caution. Knight's subsequent statement before trial recorded the encounter.

> I shewed her a Right Club membership card and asked if the handwriting and signature thereon were hers. She replied 'Oh yes, rather.' I shewed her the pencilled document and asked if she could offer any explanation of it. She said, 'That was something I copied from something I saw and I thought it was very important' ... I asked Mrs Nicholson who had shewn or given her the matter from which the copy was made and she said, 'I'm afraid I won't say' ... Mrs Nicholson persisted in her refusal to divulge the name of the person and said, 'I think it would be most disloyal to my friend. You are trying to intimidate me and get my friend shot.'[38]

The documents, together with Mrs Welberry's account of being asked to hide them and Mrs Nicholson's refusal to cooperate, made prosecution unavoidable. To provide additional evidence of Christabel's motivation, Special Branch took an additional and seemingly damning statement from her 'daily'.

> Since I have been employed by Mrs Nicholson she has often told me that she had met Herr Hitler and that he was a very good man. On one occasion – I think it was the second week in May – she asked me

what the poorer classes thought of him. I told her that they would like to have him for five minutes and they would know what to do with him.

She then said that I was to tell all my working class friends that their views were all wrong, that Hitler didn't intend to harm any of them at all. He was the kind of man we needed in England. On the same day Mrs Nicholson also told me that the Germans would be sure to invade England and get to London by Christmas and would march through all the streets. She told me that when that time came I must be sure to stay indoors and I would be quite all right.[39]

On May 1, 1941 Christabel Nicholson appeared in the dock at the Old Bailey facing four charges, two each under the Official Secrets Act and Defence Regulations. The trial was once again held *in camera* and there is no transcript of the week-long proceedings in the publicly released official files.

There is, however, a Special Branch memo recording the verdicts – not guilty on all counts – and the police's account of how they were secured.

Under cross-examination, Mrs Nicholson made many inconsistent and inaccurate statements, the most glaring of which were brought to the notice of the jury by the Judge in his summing up. She could give no explanation at all of her action in handing the copy of the telegram to her charwoman and instructing her to hide it for her, or of her expressing fear that, because the charwoman came to work a few minutes late the following morning, she had been 'seized by police with the paper ...'

[Defence counsel] Sir Patrick Hastings made no defence on the charges under the Defence Regulations, and contented himself with trying to disprove 'the purpose prejudicial to the safety or interests of the State' in the Official Secrets Act charges.

He put it to the jury that, if they found Mrs Nicholson guilty on these latter charges it would be tantamount to finding that she was a traitress and if they did this they would have branded the distinguished Admiral who was her husband as a traitor, for he had seen the telegram and had taken notes of the private letters sent to President Roosevelt by Mr Kennedy.

The whole of Sir Patrick's speech consisted of variations on this theme, plus the contention that it was incredible that a woman of Mrs Nicholson's standing and background would be guilty of treachery.

The jury retired at 1pm and when the Court resumed at 2pm, his Lordship read a note which they had sent him asking if they could find Mrs Nicholson guilty of copying a secret document and not guilty of doing anything against the safety of the Realm. His Lordship again explained the nature of the charges to them and after a further short retirement they returned their verdict of 'not guilty' ...

No evidence for the prosecution was challenged. In view of this and of the fact that no defence was made to the charges under the defence Regulations, the verdict on these charges was quite incomprehensible. The same can be said in a slightly less degree about the Official Secrets Act charges ...[40]

The acquittal managed the rare feat of uniting opinion within Whitehall and MI5. Liddell's diary entry captures the incredulity of both.

Mrs Nicholson has been acquitted in spite of the fact that she admitted that she had made notes from cipher telegrams which she had received from Anna Wolkoff. Her husband went into the box and admitted that he had also taken notes ...

The former Attorney-General, Sir Patrick Hastings KC, made a clever move in putting the husband into the box and bamboozled the jury into thinking that a British Admiral could not possibly commit an act of treachery and that therefore his wife must be innocent. The Solicitor-General regards the case as one of the worst miscarriages of justice that he has known since he was at the bar.[41]

The acquittal raised the question of whether the Security Service could thereafter persuade the Home Secretary to keep Christabel Nicholson in Holloway prison under Regulation 18B, and the prospect of a new battle with the Home Office Advisory Committee. More immediately, however, it made a Treachery Act prosecution of Molly Hiscox and Norah Briscoe politically impossible. A memo in their file by Knight in June noted:

> In view of the recent disastrous verdict in the Nicholson case, the law officers of the Crown ... decided that, as Hiscox and Briscoe were ready to plead guilty to the charges under 2.1.a of the Defence Regulations, the charges under the Treachery Act would be withdrawn.
>
> The Law Officers feared that it was quite possible that, if a Jury failed to convict under the Treachery Act – owing to their reluctance to be responsible for the Death Penalty for women – a judge might say that as the offences under the D.R. were substantially the same as those under the Treachery Act, they could not be Not Guilty of one and Guilty of the other.[42]

In early June 1941 Hiscox and Briscoe pleaded guilty at the Old Bailey to two charges each of 'doing acts likely to assist the enemy ... in communicating information from the files of the Ministry of Supply', contrary to Defence Regulations. As usual, all but the sentencing took place in secret – 'behind the blue-curtained windows of the closely guarded court', as the *Daily Mirror* informed its readers[43] – but MI5's notes on the case show that Hirst and Kurtz gave evidence (under the pseudonyms 'Witness Q' and 'Witness X'), and that the jury was shown material seized from Hiscox's flat. This included membership cards for the BUF and The Link, photographs of Hitler, and a letter she had written to 'den Führer des deutsches Volkes, ... Reichskanzler Adolf Hitler' on August 31, 1939. This included the statement, 'As an Englishwoman who was very often in Germany I wish you to know that I have unlimited trust in you'.*

In mitigation, defence counsel St John Hutchinson KC evidently attempted a repeat of the successful tactic used to secure Christabel Nicholson's acquittal. According to Knight's account, the barrister:

---

* The letter had been intercepted and returned to Hiscox by the GPO Censorship Department.

... stressed the fact that both Hiscox and Briscoe were neurotics, and ... he put the primary onus of the responsibility for the acts of Hiscox and Briscoe on the shoulders of persons like Oswald Mosley and Captain Ramsay, who played upon the emotions for their own ends ... He asked the Judge to bear in mind that a heavy sentence might confirm these two women in their wicked ways, whereas a just but salutary sentence might have the desired effect.[44]

But neither woman belonged to the same privileged class as Ramsay or Mosley; nor did they enjoy the protection afforded Christabel Nicholson by her marriage to a former Admiral of the Fleet. They were sentenced to five years' penal servitude each, a considerably more lenient punishment than they would have faced under the Treachery Act – and one at which, according to a *Daily Herald* report, 'the faintest flicker of relief passed across the older woman's face [while] the other smiled'[45] – but more than their co-conspirators of the Right Club Inner Circle ever had to suffer. Before sending them down, Mr Justice Asquith[46] gave his opinion on their offences:

'Your crime is a political crime, and it is sometimes suggested that political crimes ought to be treated with greater leniency than other crime. I entirely dissent from that view. It seems that, of all forms of crime, that which affects the State at whose heart it is directed can be least tolerated.'[47]

Asquith's *obiter dictum* reflected the fact that, in 1941, there was still a Victorian-era provision establishing a class of political prisoners who were sentenced to incarceration in the 'First Division' rather than the more commonplace 'Second Division' for regular criminal offences. His imposition of a relatively compassionate sentence, however, nodded towards something equally outdated: that while the foot-soldiers of British fascism were (if caught) subjected to the law's full sanction, their rich and better-connected accomplices were often not punished at all. A suspicion that social status could be the factor which determined freedom or imprisonment was already causing ripples of unease in Parliament: soon, it would prove to be the difference between life and death in the courts.

CHAPTER FIFTEEN

Humble Tools and Real Criminals

'I can quite understand the bitterness as regards Domvile, who
deserves P.S. [penal servitude] far more than this woman.'
Home Office file memo on the trial of Olive Baker,
June 10, 1941

At 10.30pm on Sunday, February 25, 1940, British wireless listeners turning their dials to seek out broadcasts across the
shortwave radio spectrum were greeted by the strains of the traditional Scottish folk song, 'The Bonnie Banks of Loch Lomond'. The
signal at 51 metres announced itself to be the first transmission of
the New British Broadcasting Station, ostensibly a clandestine operation by loyal British citizens who were opposed to the war, based
at an undisclosed location somewhere in England. In reality NBBS
was a 'black propaganda' station, run by Büro Concordia, a division of
Goebbels' misinformation ministry run out of the offices provided by
the Reichs-Rundfunk-Gesellschaft (Reich Broadcasting Corporation)
in the Charlottenburg district of Berlin.[1]

Black propaganda – false information purporting to emanate from
one side in a conflict while actually being produced by the other – was

deployed by both Germany and Britain: its value was as a psychological weapon intended to lower morale and undermine the will to fight among the enemy's domestic population.[2]

Radio – particularly shortwave broadcasts which could be beamed several thousand miles – was the dominant medium for disseminating disinformation; NBBS was one of four stations run by Büro Concordia, each targeting a different segment of the population. Its nightly transmissions, which ended with a rendition of 'God Save The King', were aimed at the working class and were entirely separate from William Joyce's widely-mocked broadcasts; but like Lord Haw-Haw's operation, the station also used a British 'newsreader', Leonard Banning, a former teacher and BUF activist who gave his name as (variously) John Brown or William Brown.[3] Surviving copies of typical programmes show it to have denounced capitalism and – with varying degrees of subtlety – the 'international Jewish financiers' who allegedly ran it.

> 'Seventy per cent of the national income has been spent on the war. This year the cost of the war has meant £126 per head of the population: now that gives you something to think about. We all know that this war has cost thousands of millions of pounds and the great mystery is, where did all the money suddenly come from? In peacetime there was never any money for vitally-needed projects for the good of the nation; but when there is a war, as if by magic the money suddenly becomes available. So why is that? Because the big bosses control the money; they control the banks which control the whole flow of money ...'[4]

The station's existence was not in any way a secret. The *Daily Express* was the first to report its arrival, on February 28; a week later the *Sunday Dispatch* followed up by publishing the exact frequency on which it could be found. Then, on March 20, Archibald Ramsay used the House of Commons to publicise it further, asking the Minister of Information, Sir John Reith, 'whether his attention has been drawn to the nightly talks at 10.30 on a short wavelength of 51 metres broadcast by a new station, whose signature tune is "Loch Lomond", to the effect that international Jewish finance and Continental freemasonry are pursuing a policy of world domination by wars and revolutions and credit monopoly ...'[5]

Despite this, between June 1940 and October the following year, six men and women would be jailed for between six months and seven years each for advertising NBBS' frequency; their cases highlighted the disparity between the treatment of 'establishment' pro-Nazi fascists and less elevated foot-soldiers of the movement – a manifest injustice which came to trouble at least some officers in the Security Service.

*

MI5's initial fears over NBBS were, however, focused on suspicions that it was transmitting covert messages to German agents in Britain. On May 22, 1940, Guy Liddell noted in his diary:

> A representative of the B.B.C.* came here this morning to say that in his opinion the New British Broadcasting Station, which is of course a German one, was putting over information in code. He had made a careful study of broadcasting methods when the Germans took Poland and also when they took Holland. They had destroyed the Polish broadcasting stations and had taken their wavelengths. In the case of Holland they had left the stations standing and had taken them over. There were strong indications that in the event of an attack on this country the New British Broadcasting Station would try and monopolise the air and issue instructions and misleading information to the public.[6]

There is no conclusive proof that NBBS broadcasts contained coded messages – although an internal report by Lord Swinton's Security Executive on June 15, 1940 suggested that 'in addition to cypher communications with high grade agents, the Germans were almost certainly using plain language in this way for Fifth Column purposes'[7]. But the station's ability to undermine morale on the Home Front with rumours

---

* MI5 enjoyed an occasionally fractious working relationship with the BBC on technical issues relating to broadcasting. The Corporation seconded one of its senior engineers, Malcolm Frost, to head a new division within the Security Service tasked with searching out enemy black propaganda stations.

and lies – on August 14 it broadcast 'news' that parachute troops wearing British uniforms or civilian clothing had landed near Birmingham, Manchester and Glasgow, and that they were being hidden by British Nazi sympathisers – was viewed as a serious threat to the war effort.

The front lines of this propaganda war were walls and lamp-posts across the country, and the munitions 'fired' in it were 'sticky-back' labels plastered on to them; these advertised the frequency on which NBBS could be found, sometimes accompanied by slogans denouncing the fight against Germany as 'The Jews' War'. These stickers were clearly produced either professionally or semi-professionally, and their distribution appears to have been handled by local offices of the BUF and other fascist groups. Yet efforts to limit their spread concentrated exclusively on those posting them in public places. Rex and Violet Freeman were typical.

Rex Wilfred Freeman was 21, a railway porter and member of the BUF; he lived with his similarly-minded mother, Violet, in Stoke Newington, north-east London. In late spring 1940 streets in the area had sprouted a rash of NBBS sticky-backs, advertising the station's frequency and pronouncing it to be 'Uncensored News – Hear the Truth!' The Freemans' neighbours denounced Rex as the most likely culprit, and on June 1 two local police officers arrived on their doorstep: they were not well received.

'Do you call this a free country?' Mrs Freeman shouted at DC Fred Gribble. 'Why shouldn't we tell people where to hear the truth. You don't get any truth from the BBC. You think that because the British are beat [sic] you can do what you like but you can't. There will be more justice when Hitler comes. It is a bloody shame that they put Mosley in prison ... I am a Fascist and my son is a Fascist.'[8]

A search of the house unearthed a swastika pennant, a 'fascist badge', a selection of NBBS sticky-backs and Rex's passport showing he had visited Germany less than two weeks before the outbreak of war. It amounted to very little – penny-ante fascism by a pair of clearly unimportant activists; yet both were charged with four counts of 'Encouraging members of the British public to listen to a wireless station in Germany then broadcasting in English by communicating the wavelength of the said station', contrary to Section 2A(1) of Defence

Regulations, and were brought to the dock of the Old Bailey. There, on July 5, 1940, Lillian Freeman was jailed for twelve months; Rex fared even worse – sentenced to seven years' penal servitude for his actions.[9]

Evidence that this was not an isolated case of judicial overreaction emerged the following month when a 42-year-old professional violinist received an identical sentence for the same offence.[10] William Saxon-Steer had been caught in the act of putting up an NBBS sticky-back in a phone box on the Brompton Road, Chelsea. He pleaded guilty, claiming only that he had 'no idea that the station was in any way connected with Germany ... I was given to understand that the station operated in England and was sponsored by the Peace Pledge Union'.[11]

Saxon-Steer was – at least – a fascist fellow-traveller; a search of his rooms unearthed papers showing he was both actively publicising the NBBS wavelength and vehemently anti-Semitic. 'Dictator Churchill and his rotten gang can go to Canada as soon as they like and take their gold with them', he had written to an unidentified friend. 'Once gone, they don't come back. The Jew boys will follow soon.'[12]

But neither anti-Semitic opinions nor dislike of the Prime Minister were criminal offences, and while promoting the frequency of an enemy propaganda station was prohibited by Defence Regulations, the fact that Ramsay had been allowed to do so in the House of Commons without any sanction suggested that the law was being selectively applied. The prosecution of Olive Evelyn Baker, a 40-year-old registered nurse from Bath, reinforced the point.

Baker was a member of both the BUF and Sir Barry Domvile's The Link. In the summer of 1939 she had arranged the group's trip to Salzburg – a visit curtailed by the Home Secretary's parliamentary denunciation of The Link as an instrument of German propaganda – and had become close friends with the Admiral and his wife.[13] In May 1940 she was arrested for distributing NBBS sticky-backs and charged with 'assisting the enemy'.[14]

When police searched Baker's rooms they found 'a large quantity' of material published by the BUF and other right-wing organisations, documents revealing that she was simultaneously involved with the British Council for Christian Settlement in Europe, as well as photos of Nazi leaders.

Letters she had written to her similarly-minded friends showed that she was an unrepentant admirer of Hitler. In one, sent to a woman of German origin living in Watford, Baker wrote:

> I have so many friends there (in Germany). What a tragedy it all is and so unnecessary. You must, though, be proud to have such a wonderful Führer. I have seen him often and am convinced that he really has been divinely sent to make the world a cleaner and better place, and the world is crucifying him. Yours sincerely in B.U. and National Socialism.[15]

But it was her correspondence with the Domviles which strengthened the impression that well-connected fascists were being treated with legal kid gloves while their more proletarian counterparts faced severe punishment. In late March 1940 Baker wrote to the couple, describing her despair at the government's refusal to make peace with Germany. On April 1, Sir Barry Domvile replied, telling Baker to keep up her spirits in anticipation of the long-promised uprising by pro-Nazi British fascists:

> There is nothing to be done until the general clean up comes – we have sunk to such depths of degradation and depravity under our Jewish teachers that nothing can surprise me.[16]

In the meantime, he suggested that she should tune in to 'the New British B.B.C. [*sic*]', pronouncing: 'it's grand. Ramsay asked questions about it in the House and gave it a good adv[ertisement].'[17] Three weeks later, Lady Domvile added her own recommendation. 'I think most people find the New British Broadcasting Station quite easy to get, but not always clear to hear', she told Baker, before giving precise instructions for locating it on her wireless and adding, 'there is something wrong with your shortwave if you cannot get it'.[18]

Such support proved to be of little material comfort to Baker. While awaiting trial she slashed her wrists and daubed 'Hail Mosley' and 'Heil Hitler' in blood on her cell walls. When she was tried at Bristol Assizes on Thursday, July 4, there was no sign of her aristocratic friends in the public gallery and no character witness to speak on her behalf: she was convicted on all three counts and sentenced to five years' penal servitude.[19]

The injustice of low-ranking fascists receiving lengthy prison terms, often with hard labour, while the wealthy or politically-connected were either interned or, more commonly, left entirely free, evidently registered inside Whitehall. An extract from one of Baker's original Home Office files,[20] dated June 1941, noted:

> There is no doubt whatever that this woman ... was rightly convicted ... She has certainly behaved like a traitor to her country and done her best to assist the enemy – and her friends must know that well enough. I can quite understand the bitterness as regards Domvile, who deserves P.S. [penal servitude] far more than this woman.[21]

Six months later the Home Office went further, recording that 'Baker's interest in the NBBS was largely due to the incitement of Am [Admiral] and Lady Domvile'.[22] Even the Security Service was moved to suggest that, under the circumstances, Baker's offences should be treated with a degree of compassion. The unnamed Home Office bureaucrat reported on discussions in which MI5 officers made clear that 'it is no part of their functions to suggest the exercise of the Prerogative of Mercy but it seems clear they would raise no objections on security grounds if Baker were released'.*[23]

The growing unease over the disparity in sanctions taken against pro-Nazi British fascists was pointedly highlighted by the judge in yet another NBBS-related trial. William Bruce Tomkins, a 27-year-old accountant from Kingston upon Thames, appeared at the Old Bailey on July 24, 1940; the evidence against him was not that he had posted sticky-backs in phone boxes or on walls, but that he had shown them to his landlady and thus 'communicated information likely to be of assistance to an enemy'.

Tomkins was a self-professed National Socialist: he had joined the BUF as early as 1934 and told the magistrate at one of his remand

---

* Despite this, Olive Baker was only released, on licence, on October 30, 1943.

hearings that he was 'proud to be a Fascist', though he 'repudiated the charge that he was other than pro-British ... [but] also said that he thought the country would be better governed under the totalitarian system'.[24] His defence at trial was that he believed NBBS to be a station run by the British People's Party – the pro-Nazi organisation funded by Lord Tavistock and run by John Beckett and Ben Greene. Whether true or not, the claim did not save him from a guilty verdict; but it prompted a telling response from the judge, Mr Justice Atkinson.[25]

> 'I ought to punish severely anyone who helped to disseminate this poison, but I am not going to punish with severity a humble tool when the real criminals responsible have not been brought to justice.'[26]

The question also slowly began to exercise Parliament. The following summer, in the wake of the Kent and Wolkoff convictions and the seizure of the 'Red Book' – the leather-bound ledger listing the names of the great and good who had joined Archibald Ramsay's organisation – Liberal MP Geoffrey Mander asked the Home Secretary 'whether he will publish the list of members of the Right Club in possession of the Home Office; and what supervision is now exercised by his Department?' Herbert Morrison initially tried to placate the Commons with a general defence of secrecy and an assurance that the government had the situation under control.

> 'I do not think it would be in the public interest to publish the names of the members of this organisation, or to state what steps have been taken from the point of view of national security. Appropriate steps are taken to watch all kinds of people about whom there may be grounds for suspicion ... To publish the names of people who are being watched would be most unwise: to publish the names of people who are not being watched would be unfair. Secrecy is the essence of any system of supervision.'

This attempt at a straight-bat defence did not satisfy the Honourable Members. Mander pointed out the high proportion of Right Club members drawn from aristocratic and political circles:

'In view of the fact that it has been stated that a number of distinguished persons, including Members of this House, belong to this
rather remarkable organisation, does not the right hon. Gentleman
think it would be in the public interest for everyone to know who
belongs to it?'

Morrison replied that 'it would be very interesting, but there is much
interesting information in the Home Office which we really must keep
to ourselves' – a response so bureaucratically smug that it drew a
sharp follow-up from Labour's Emanuel Shinwell: 'As regards the
allegation that several hon. Members belong to this questionable
organisation, will my right hon. Friend give an assurance that this
is not so, or, if they have belonged to it, that they have resigned?'
When Morrison refused to do so, Shinwell pressed the point: 'Does
that mean that my right hon. Friend does not wish to give such an
assurance or that there are no hon. Members belonging to this organisation?' Evidently flustered, Morrison simply refused to provide any
further information: 'It does not mean either of those things. It means
that I do not propose to give any indication of what names there are,
or are not, on this list.'[27]

The Red Book would remain under wraps for more than 50 years.*
Since MI5's publicly released files disclose no evidence of any serious
wartime investigations into the Right Club, the government's purpose
in keeping its membership secret can only have been to protect the
reputations of those who belonged to it.

This evidently troubled the Security Service, which noted that
many of Ramsay's most senior acolytes continued to sit in either the
Commons or the Lords – a freedom which allowed them to continue the pro-Nazi movement's efforts at undermining the war with
Germany. A December 1941 memo by Edward Stamp on the activities
of Lord Tavistock – now seated in the Upper Chamber as the Duke of
Bedford – pointed out both the injustice and the danger of this policy.

---

* The leather-bound ledger was finally released to the Wiener Archive in London,
and made available to researchers, in 2000.

The history of the past two years has shown that Hitler's boast, that his invading Armies would not have to fight any battle since he could rely on the forces of disruption within the enemy countries which he planned to attack, was not an idle one. Wittingly or unwittingly, wickedly or in child-like innocence of purpose, the Duke has become an instrument of Nazi propaganda. He is doing what the New British Broadcasting [Station] is imploring its listeners to do – he is pressing for peace ... He is going further than the NBBS ... dares to go. He is excusing and defending Hitler and his Nazi system and accusing and condemning his own countrymen ... The poison is spreading.[28]

Throughout 1940 and 1941 a succession of prosecutions confirmed MI5's belief, and with it the threat posed by the distribution of pro-Nazi propaganda. In October 1940, Ray Leonard Townsend Day, a BUF member who ran an underground printing press, was sentenced to eighteen months in prison on five charges of 'assisting the enemy'. The evidence in his remarkably threadbare criminal file (there is no matching MI5 dossier in the National Archives) shows that Day bypassed government censorship regulations to publish a duplicated weekly news-sheet; since he headed this 'The Uncensored News Bulletin' there was little doubt that he was deliberately flouting the law.

Its contents were unquestionably dangerous: as well as publicising the NBBS frequency and extolling the Fuehrer's virtues ('The Germans are not completely devoid of common sense, you know. Herr Hitler wants to exercise the controlling influence in a peaceful Europe'[29]), Day's *samizdat* effort provided first-hand accounts of bomb damage across south-east England and details of a secret session of the House of Commons held on July 30, in which the Prime Minister reported military setbacks.

Exclusive Information. We have been fortunate in obtaining certain details regarding the Secret Session of Parliament last week [concerning] diplomatic reverses in Rumania and Japan. Another point which caused considerable concern were [*sic*] our merchant shipping losses which Churchill admitted were larger than had been revealed. One member suggested we were losing 200,000 tons a week, a figure which Churchill neither confirmed nor rejected.[30]

Day's account of this secret Commons debate – held behind locked doors and which the press was prohibited from reporting – was extremely accurate, suggesting that it was fed to him by one of the fascist sympathisers still drawing their £600 annual MP's salary. There is no indication that any attempt was made to discover the identity of his source: by default or design, prosecutions were almost exclusively focused on those Mr Justice Atkinson described as 'humble tools'.

Some of these trials were for offences which, by any definition, were pitifully minor. Five low-ranking fascists – three men and two women – were charged with 'endeavouring to cause disaffection' among British forces. In June 1940 Peter Farmer, Alexander Hancock and Doris Conley were sent to prison for three months each after a particularly inept 'action' in which they threw BUF 'Stop the War' leaflets in the vague direction of troops stationed in Northampton.[31]

The following month Llewellyn Cadwallader and his nephew, Thomas Jackson, were treated considerably more harshly at Manchester Assizes for buying drinks for soldiers in a pub in Preston and trying to turn them against the war effort; in sentencing them to two years each, Mr Justice Oliver pronounced that 'It is shameful that any two men calling themselves Englishmen should fall so low as to commit offences of this kind', and complained that since they had 'only' been charged with breaches of Defence Regulations, 'the sentences I am able to pass are completely inadequate'.[32]

Evidently this problem was not insuperable, since the following year one of Oliver's fellow judges found the means to impose a much stiffer punishment for identical offences. On June 24, 1941, Elsie Orrin, a 48-year-old BUF member and private teacher, was convicted at Hertfordshire Assizes for attempting to cause disaffection; she had ventured into a pub in the village of Little Easton and told troops drinking there that 'Hitler was a good ruler, a better man than Mr Churchill', that the government was 'corrupt ... and ruled by Jewish financiers ... and that if they were men they ought to kick the present Government out'. Mr Justice Humphreys sent her to prison for five years.[33,34]

If these were very minor offences, other prosecutions showed that lowly individual British fascists posed a genuine threat. On May 28, 1940 Cyril Stephens, an eighteen-year-old metal press operator from Edmonton, north London, who (according to sworn statements by his colleagues) 'expressed pro-German views', deliberately sabotaged a machine making ammunition boxes for the Army. He was sentenced to three years' penal servitude at the Old Bailey on June 25.[35]

The following September George Mace Wall, a 28-year-old electrical mechanic whose openly pro-Nazi sympathies had not stopped him from obtaining a job at the Air Ministry's sensitive experimental research station on the Isle of Wight, was jailed for six years for offences under the Official Secrets Act.[36] He had stolen 'highly secret details of receivers and transmitters ... of great use to the enemy' – apparently in anticipation of receiving a reward from Hitler's forces. According to evidence given by his co-workers, Wall habitually adopted the Nazi salute, and warned them what would happen to non-fascists when Germany won the war. 'When they do I will be in charge up here ... The people who look after the Führer now will get the cream of the jobs when he comes over here'.[37]

Albert Munt, a sixteen-year-old errand boy living with his parents in Edmonton, took rather more direct action to bring the glorious day of German victory closer. At the height of the Blitz on London, in September 1940, he set fire to six houses in the neighbouring streets to guide the Luftwaffe's bombers on their way. According to his police statement:

> I sympathise with Hitler and I thought I could help by starting the fires ... Each time an air raid was on when I started the fires, and I started the fires to make a big glow to help the raiding German planes if they were low enough to see it ... I had to be very careful ... as I could hear the people talking in their [air raid] shelter ... As the guns banged I crept forward a few paces each time.[38]

Munt's case seems to have worried the police and courts (there is no indication of any Security Service involvement in the case) since someone arranged for him to be given a psychological examination before his Old Bailey appearance. The resulting report by the medical officer at Feltham prison revealed that Munt's intelligence was 'quite normal for a youth of his age', and there was no indication of 'mental deficiency'. There was, however, an indication of what led him to light the makeshift beacons.

> Concerning the offences, which he has admitted, he explains that they are the result of listening to German broadcast propaganda, combined with general anxiety over the war situation recently. Then he states that he met an older man recently at the local public library who was largely responsible for putting Fifth Column ideas into more concrete shape in his mind. He does not appear to realize the seriousness of his conduct ... and if his present attitude persists, it seems likely he will continue to be a menace to the community.[39]

It was a neat encapsulation of the potential impact of NBBS propaganda and pro-Nazi proselytising on an impressionable young fascist, and – since it was laid before the judge hearing the case – may explain the unusually lenient sentence for what were genuinely serious offences: on October 16, 1940 Mr Justice Tucker sent Munt to borstal* for three years.[40]

Against this backdrop, it was inevitable that at some point an innocent member of the British pro-Nazi movement would be convicted simply on the basis of his association with it. That moment came on December 11, 1940, when Peter Louis Revill, a nineteen-year-old former public schoolboy, was convicted at Birmingham Assizes on two charges under the Official Secrets Act.

On the outbreak of war, Revill had abandoned his studies at the University of Birmingham and started work at Vickers Armstrong aircraft works, then finalising production of the top-secret Halifax heavy bomber. His crime – such as it was – was making rough traces of the plane's wing section and taking these home to study. That home

---

* 'Borstal schools' were detention centres for serious youth offenders under the age of 21. Their regimen was designed to be educational rather than simply punitive, with the aim of rehabilitating inmates and interrupting their cycle of offending. They were abolished in 1982.

– 88 Holyfield Road, Sutton Coldfield – was the crucial factor in all that followed.

He shared the comfortable detached house with his widowed mother, Louise. She was a middle-class pillar of the local community: a welfare worker and 'honorary collector' for Sutton Coldfield Hospital and Nursing Home, secretary of the Mothers' Union and member of the local St Chad's church. But in the eyes of some of her neighbours – and, more pertinently, Warwickshire Police – she was not truly British.

Louise Agnes Baettger, as she once was, had been born in Germany in 1884. On the eve of the First World War she met a British expatriate businessman, Reginald Revill; in 1913 the couple were married and managed a few months together before Reginald was interned in one of the Kaiser's camps for 'enemy aliens'. When he was released in 1918, the Revills returned to England and Louise acquired British citizenship. Two years later Peter was born in Sutton Coldfield.

Throughout the 1930s the family took a succession of holidays in Germany, meeting up with Louise's family and Reginald's former business acquaintances; after his death, Louise continued the tradition, each time taking Peter with her. She was evidently disturbed by the growing persecution she witnessed, because from 1938 onwards she worked – 'untiringly', according to one of her respectable English colleagues – to find foster homes in England for the children of Jewish refugees, and to deposit, in a dedicated Post Office account, money sent out of Germany for their upkeep. That year, however, she also made the error which would lead to her internment and to Peter's arrest: she became a member of Admiral Sir Barry Domvile's The Link.

With good reason, Warwickshire Police regarded Domvile's group as 'a subversive organisation':[41] less reasonably it believed, by extension, that anyone belonging to it – especially a woman 'of German origin' – was guilty by association and should be targeted for investigation. Nine days after the outbreak of war, the Chief Constable forwarded to MI5 the case for a Home Office warrant to intercept letters sent to or from the house in Holyfield Road. A note on the Registry Minute Sheet of her Security Service file reported this 'evidence':

> Mrs Reville [*sic*] is a German by birth and both husband and wife have strong Nazi sympathies. Mrs Reville is reported to have frequently changed Money Orders at the Post Office and when acquaintances have been present she has appeared nervous and has conducted her business in a surreptitious manner. Mr and Mrs Reville have both been very secretive about their correspondence, posting letters at post boxes some distance from their house. Mrs Reville has paid fairly frequent visits to Germany and has also visited the German Consulate in Birmingham. It seems, therefore, very likely that they have been in some way working for the Germans.[42]

There was much wrong with this supposed information – not least the misspelling of the suspect's name, and the fact that her 'secretive' and 'pro-Nazi' husband had died some years previously. Nor did the Home Office warrant unearth any incriminating correspondence. It was, however, enough to bring Peter Revill under suspicion. A second entry on the Registry sheet, dated September 29, noted the nature of his new job and suggested that a delicate approach be made to his employers.

> We have reason to believe that the Castle Bromwich Aeroplane Factory may have engaged P.L. Revill. We have no very definite evidence with regard to Revill's pro-Nazi proclivities and we do not think he should be barred from employment in an aeroplane factory.
>
> In view, however, of the undoubted Nazi sympathies of Revill's parents and their somewhat suspicious activities it would not seem advisable for Revill to have access to any confidential or secret information.[43]

In denouncing Louise and the late Reginald as Nazi sympathisers, MI5 was relying on Warwickshire Police's intelligence – a trust that was sorely misplaced. It appears to have taken a unilateral decision to have Peter Revill sacked from the aircraft factory and to have demanded the internment of his mother; both requests were granted in November 1939.

There is an unexplained six-month gap in the official accounts of what happened next to Peter Revill. His Home Office file[44] remains closed to public scrutiny until January 1, 2027. However, the Security Service files on mother and son, declassified in 2003, show that for unexplained reasons Warwickshire Police raided the Revills' home on July 7, 1940: in a cupboard in Peter's room they found a collection of (perfectly innocent) model aircraft and 'three or four' tracings of the Halifax bomber wing. He was arrested, charged under the espionage provisions of the Official Secrets Act and, in December, appeared before Mr Justice Oliver at Birmingham Assizes.

The trial was once again held *in camera*, but MI5's files show that a Sergeant John Dodridge testified that both Peter and Louise Revill were members of The Link, and that Peter had attempted to lie when questioned about the tracings, allegedly claiming that they were plans for a new addition to his collection of model aircraft – an admission Peter denied making and which does not appear in his police statement. Nonetheless, the jury chose to believe Sgt Dodridge, and Mr Justice Oliver duly sent the young man to prison for four years.

'I have', the judge pronounced, 'in the public interest, to pass sentence on you, a thoroughly dangerous person, which will prevent you from further betraying your country during this war. What you did was to make drawings of one of our newest and most secret war 'planes for a treacherous purpose. That is certain. What use you made of them, if any, no one but yourself knows, but the point is this – you are very young and just at the irresponsible age which the Nazi regime seeks to exploit.'[45]

The case clearly troubled MI5 – not least because Louise was released from internment in February 1941 after the Home Office Advisory Committee issued a report declaring that she was innocent of any Nazi sympathies, and that 'what she had done she had done out of the purest of motives and the rest of her public services in Sutton Coldfield corroborates her'.

In Peter's case, according to a succession of lengthy memoranda and internal reports, the Security Service noted the complete absence of any genuine evidence against him.

'The case of this young man presents considerable difficulties', an MI5 officer wrote to the Air Ministry in August 1943:

As far as we were, and have been, able to ascertain there was and still is <u>no evidence</u> [emphasis in original] that the drawings were made for a treacherous purpose. His reasons for making them were somewhat obscure but can, I think, be explained by the fact that he was keen on his work and did not realise the seriousness of what he was doing ...

One fact which probably greatly inflamed his trial was that his mother had by that time been interned, but very shortly afterwards she was released without restrictions. I feel that had there been no evidence of German associations and background, Revill's offence would have been treated as a technical one and a serious view of it would in all probability not have been taken ...[46]

Other MI5 reports clearly suggest that both Peter and Louise Revill had effectively been targeted as proxies for the genuinely pro-Nazi leadership of The Link.

She was a member of 'The Link'. This can hardly be regarded as surprising or suspicious. Whatever some of its hierarchy may have been, the rank and file members were people who wished to substitute Anglo-German friendship for Anglo-German enmity and suspicion. To a woman who was Anglo by marriage and German by birth, nothing could have seemed more desirable.

But in September 1939 'The Link' was the object of grave suspicion – especially the Birmingham branch of it ... and it was in this connection that the Warwickshire Chief Constable first reported to us on the Revill family on 4.9.39.[47]

The internment and trial, respectively, of Louise and Peter Revill, together with the severe sentences given to the 'humble tools' of the pro-Nazi fascist movement, formed a disreputable chapter in the war against the British Fifth Column. It showed that justice was partial at best, rough at worst, and that those whom Mr Justice Atkinson labelled 'the real criminals' were treated much more leniently – if they were punished at all – than those whom they inspired to commit offences. And it was a disparity which would be thrown into stark relief by the cases of three men and one woman facing execution for the crime of treachery.

CHAPTER SIXTEEN

Treachery and Death

'Scott-Ford is frankly terrified ... he is quite certain that
the Germans would liquidate him. On the other hand,
he knows that he faces a traitor's death in this country.'

MI5 interrogation report,
August 27–29, 1942

At precisely 9.00am on Wednesday, July 9, 1941, Thomas Pierrepoint stepped into the condemned cell on E Wing, Wandsworth prison. Pierrepoint was a veteran executioner: in a career which began in 1906 and lasted 40 years, he hanged 294 men and women, and was renowned for the speed with which he dispatched his victims.

He bound the prisoner's arms behind him, walked him swiftly through a connecting door into the execution chamber, and positioned him at the centre of the polished wood trapdoor in the floor. He quickly placed a white cotton bag over the man's head, tightened the noose over the bag, stepped back and pulled the trapdoor lever set into the planks on his left.

Less than a minute passed between Pierrepoint entering the cell and the moment the knot in the rope snapped the condemned man's neck. At 9.01am George Johnson Armstrong became the first British traitor of the Second World War to die for his crimes.

All national newspapers carried brief reports of the execution in their first available editions. These were based on a press release issued by the Home Office and were sparse in the extreme: most simply noted the name, age and occupation of the hanged man – a result of the secrecy in which George Armstrong had been tried and the paucity of information about what he had done. The left-leaning *Daily Herald* alone managed to slip a few glimpses of colour past the censor's blue pencil.

> George Johnson Armstrong, a 38-year-old British engineer who was executed for treachery at Wandsworth Jail yesterday, carried his family secrets with him to the grave. If he had any relatives living, he never spoke of them from the time he was arrested until the warm sunlit morning when he walked to the gallows. Nobody made application to see him during that time. Nobody wrote to him ...
>
> This Home Office statement, issued yesterday, threw a little more light on Armstrong's crime. 'A few months ago he offered his services to the German espionage organisation operating against Britain, through the intermediary of one of the German consuls in the United States. On his subsequent return to this country he was arrested and put up for trial.'[1]

There were a number of ambiguous aspects to Johnson's case – not least his real name; there was also a lingering uncertainty about whether he had, in fact, betrayed his country. But the most serious (and unanswered) question was why he was charged, tried, convicted and hanged while other British men and women whose guilt was much clearer received considerably more lenient punishment.

*

The execution of George Armstrong was not the first under the Treachery Act. The previous December three Axis spies – Jose Waldberg, Carl Meier and Charles van den Kieboom – were hanged at Pentonville prison. They had landed by rowing boat on a beach near Dymchurch in Kent, in September 1940 and were arrested by military patrols within hours of their arrival; they initially claimed to be refugees escaping Nazi oppression, but since they were caught with radio transmitters, a compass, £130 in British banknotes and a loaded revolver there was very little doubt of their guilt.[2]

They would not be the last foreign agents caught in Britain (Waldberg was German, Meier and van den Kieboom Dutch) to be convicted of espionage. Between August 1941 and July 1944 ten further German spies – Werner Waelti and Karl Drueke,[3] Josef Jakobs,[4] Karel Richter,[5] Alphonse Timmerman,[6] Johannes Dronkers,[7] Franciscus Winter,[8] Oswald Job,[9] Pierre Neukermans[10] and Joseph Vanhove[11] – were tried in secret hearings at the Old Bailey. All but one were hanged, at either Wandsworth or Pentonville prisons; Jakobs was shot by a firing squad at the Tower of London – the last such execution in British legal history.*

Neither was Armstrong the first British traitor to be condemned to death. That distinction was claimed in August 1940 by a 42-year-old petty criminal who had been caught in the act of sabotaging telegraph wires on the Isle of Wight and in possession of detailed maps of military defences along the south coast. What distinguished this case, and ultimately proved the difference between life and death, was that the offender was a woman.

Dorothy O'Grady had a lengthy docket in the Criminal Records Office at New Scotland Yard. Born – parents unknown – in the south London suburb of Clapham on October 25, 1897, at the age of three months she was adopted by George and Pamela Squire. The couple were unusually old to take on such a young baby: George was a 50-year-old clerical worker at the British Library, Pamela, a 47-year-old housewife. Nonetheless – and despite being sent away to boarding school when she was eight – Dorothy's early childhood appears to have been trouble-free: a psychological report in her prison files noted:

---

* An eleventh Abwehr agent, Engelbertus Fukken, alias Jan Willem Ter Braak, committed suicide in an air raid shelter in Cambridge at the end of March 1941. Since he had operated, undetected, in England for five months, it suggested that MI5's ability to identify and arrest German spies was not wholly successful. 'Engelbertus Fukken'. National Archives file KV 2/114; declassified September 9, 1999.

Up to the age of eleven she was happy with her adopted parents but the mother then died, the father re-married and she was sent first to school then to a domestic service training and finally put into service. She says she has never seen or heard of her father since.[12]

Dorothy's own (not necessarily reliable) account, in a 1981 interview with the *Sunday Times*, painted a slightly more complex picture:

I loved my mother so very much. She was so good to me. I never liked my father; he was never kind to me. And after a year he married the housekeeper, Miss Bird.

She was wicked, very cruel to me. She'd bully me, pull my hair and say 'Now go and tell your father and see what good it will do you'. Then the following year she took me aside and said, 'They're not your real parents you know. They adopted you.' It was a terrible shock. I hated my father and stepmother. I was never really happy after my mother died.[13]

She entered domestic service in 1913. Within five years, however, she was in the dock at the Old Bailey – under the name Pamela Arland – charged with forging banknotes. On January 29, 1918 she was sentenced to three years' imprisonment in Aylesbury borstal. An entry on her record by the institution's governor noted:

Prisoner is intelligent and bright. Her past history shews that she is dishonest and not industrious or of good character ... has strong criminal tendencies and ought to be detained for her own reformation.[14]

The report was prophetic, and when she was released on licence on December 1, 1919, her file recorded her status as 'incorrigible'. Unsurprisingly – employment for women was contracting in the immediate aftermath of the First World War and the return of men from the trenches – Dorothy turned to prostitution to pay for food and lodging.

By January 1920 she was to be found in the care of the 'Friendless and Fallen London Female Preventative and Reformatory Institution', on Euston Road. This attempt at saving her from a life of crime was evidently unsuccessful: the following June she was back in court, this time for stealing clothes: she was sentenced to two months' hard labour. Three years later she was charged with prostitution at Marlborough Street Police Court – the first of four prosecutions for the same offence between 1924 and 1926.

Details of her life from then until her arrest in 1940 are, unfortunately, sketchy. They were originally recorded in the Home Office account of her prosecution and trial under the Treachery Act – a file declassified in January 2006. Four years later, however, the file disappeared – 'misplaced when on loan to [a] Government Department', according to the National Archives.[15]

By her own account, at some point shortly after her final conviction for prostitution, Dorothy married Vincent O'Grady, a 49-year-old London fireman and former naval rating. When he retired the couple moved to the Isle of Wight and she opened a guesthouse – Osborne Villa – in Sandown. On the outbreak of war Vincent was recalled to the London Fire Brigade, leaving Dorothy to run the business alone.

In the summer of 1940 the Isle of Wight was on the front line of Britain's defences against the expected German invasion. The island was heavily fortified and its beaches had been designated a 'Prohibited Place'; despite this, O'Grady regularly entered the forbidden areas, ostensibly to walk her dog. By her own subsequent account, published ten years later in the *Daily Express*, she did so deliberately and in the knowledge that she risked arrest.

When the war began all my guests left Osborne Villa, and ... I was all alone except for my black retriever, Rob. The island was full of soldiers and most of the seafront was prohibited to residents. But the summer was hot and I continued to take my dog for his swim. I walked miles to get the better of the soldiers in order to reach the beach.

Gun emplacements were everywhere, and one day in July I got to the beach at Whitecliff Bay, near Bembridge. I was sitting reading when two soldiers appeared. They asked me what I was doing there, and then one of them noticed a small swastika pinned under the lapel of my coat. It came from the *Daily Express* war map, with which little coloured flags were provided for marking the changes in the front. The swastika flag must have stuck to my hair as I bent down to pick something up in front of the map. As I walked I found it in my hair and quite naturally pulled it out and put it under my lapel.[16]

O'Grady was taken to the nearest army base, interrogated and then released with a warning to stay away from the forbidden zone. News of her brief detention, however, was passed to the local police; a few days later it sent an officer to question her at Osborne Villa. Her version of what transpired is impossible to corroborate in the absence of official files, but its tone of irresponsible insouciance matched the rest of her *Daily Express* interview.

A young policeman came to question me. He asked me my views on Hitler. I realised that they thought I was a spy. I said to myself, 'Very well, I'll give them something to think about.' So I told the constable that I thought Hitler was a fine man, and if he wanted to make Germany greater I didn't see why he shouldn't. To my huge delight he wrote all this down.[17]

Unaccountably, the police did not immediately arrest O'Grady – a decision which allowed her to return to the seafront. She used the freedom to draw up a series of detailed sketches of the island, marking them to show gun emplacements, searchlights and the disposition of defensive forces. Some of those maps survived long enough for the *Daily Express* to reproduce them, and the notes O'Grady wrote on them offered explicit evidence of espionage:

'Bembridge School – troop headquarters'; 'Whitecliff Bay – powerful batteries on point. Concealed between garden and corner of monument is Wireless Station on top of Culver Cliff (Most important in the Kingdom!)'[18]

The timescale of what followed is fractured and incomplete. At some point in August 1940 she was caught cutting telegraph wires, arrested and summoned to appear before Ryde magistrates. She promptly went on the run.

> I packed a bag, locked up the villa and went to stay at Alum Bay. It was three weeks there before they found me. When the police took me to Yarmouth Police Station they found my maps and sketches and also a false identity card.

On remand, O'Grady was held at Holloway prison and interrogated by MI5's veteran spycatcher, Colonel William Hinchley-Cooke; he was evidently unable to determine whether she was a genuine Nazi spy and, if so, to prise from her the names of her contacts. Two entries from the middle of September in Guy Liddell's wartime journal recorded:

> She admitted that the drawings were hers but refused to disclose the identity of the person for whom she was working ... Her maps and drawings are quite good and the details of gun emplacements etc. are correct [but] she still refuses to say whether she was acting for anybody in particular.
>
> She evidently dislikes this country. I am a little inclined to think that she may be the type of person who has to be in the limelight.[19]

In the absence of any innocent explanation for her actions, the Attorney General sanctioned a prosecution under both the Official Secrets Act and the Treachery Act. On December 16, 1940, O'Grady appeared at Hampshire Assizes in Winchester, charged with nine counts of 'having approached a prohibited place; having made a plan which might be useful to the enemy; having made a plan likely to be prejudicial to the defence of the Realm with intent to assist the enemy; having possessed a document purporting to contain defence information; and of sabotage by cutting a telephone wire'.

The trial, held completely *in camera*, lasted two days. O'Grady's barrister offered no evidence in her defence, instead arguing that while she was 'a foolish woman' she was not truly a spy. It was a plea for leniency largely undermined by her own admission to Hinchley-Cooke that she had been motivated to cut the telegraph wires 'so that the guns could not go into action'. The jury found her guilty and the judge imposed the only sentence allowed under the Treachery Act:[20] according to her own account, O'Grady found the moment amusing.

> The excitement of being tried for my life was intense. The supreme moment came when an official stood behind the judge and put his black cap on for him before the death sentence. The man didn't put it on straight. It went over one of the judge's eyes and looked so funny that I was giggling inside and had a job not to laugh ...
>
> My only fear was that I would be taken away one morning to be hanged without being told about it the night before. Sometimes I dreaded going to sleep in case this happened. I was terrified but I enjoyed being terrified.[21]

Enjoyable or not, O'Grady's fears proved groundless. On February 10, 1941 the Court of Criminal Appeal sat to consider an application to overturn the Treachery Act conviction. As with the original trial, the hearing was held entirely in secret, but the following morning the *Daily Mirror* carried a report of the outcome.

> At the conclusion of the judgement, which was delivered *in camera*, Lord Caldecote announced in open court: 'The conviction under the two capital charges has been quashed ... This court has passed a sentence of fourteen years' penal servitude on the counts other than those under the Treachery Act.[22]

Caldecote, the Lord Chancellor and thus the most senior appellate judge in England, gave no reason for the decision and, since O'Grady's Home Office file has been lost, it is impossible to know exactly how she escaped execution. She unquestionably committed acts of both sabotage and espionage, and there remains a reasonable inference that the judiciary was uneasy at the imposition of the death penalty on a middle-aged woman. Whatever the reason, Dorothy O'Grady spent the next ten years in Aylesbury prison[23] while two other, male, traitors were hanged; tellingly, the evidence against the first of them was much less clear.

Like O'Grady, George Johnson Armstrong – who also went by the name of George Hope – was a petty criminal. Born in 1902, by his mid-twenties he had accumulated separate convictions for stealing a bicycle and a raincoat as well as for obtaining money by false pretences and 'uttering a forged document'. His file in the Criminal Records Office – No. 9368/25 – shows him to have been sentenced to a total of two years and two months in prison.[24] The docket also shows that on February 1, 1940 he was convicted at Willesden Police Court of another offence of obtaining money by false pretences and sent to prison for three years and three months.

He evidently did not serve this sentence, since in July that year he was to be found at the Chelsea Hotel on West 23rd Street in Manhattan. He had arrived at New York harbour on the MV *Britannic* transatlantic liner, listing his occupation as a 'marine engineer',* and was waiting to join the merchant steam tanker, *La Brea*. With money in his pocket but little to do, Armstrong took advantage of New York City's nightlife. According to his subsequent MI5 statement:

> We stayed there about a fortnight and during that evening [*sic*] we had nothing to do except to run around and enjoy ourselves ... I met a woman named Alice Hahn, who was a German ... I was talking to her one day in a bar near the Chelsea Hotel when Carl Klein came in.[25]

Carl Klein was a spy. Armstrong said he knew this because he had met him at a club in London before the war and someone 'who was in the party at that time told me he was a German agent'.[26] There is no record of a Security Service file on Klein in the National Archives, nor on Alice Hahn; but in the version of events Armstrong provided, he claimed to have discovered that the two were working together in America.

> In view of the fact that I knew he was an agent, reputedly a German agent, I was rather curious to know the connection between them ...

---

* Armstrong had no qualifications for this position. His surviving files show that MI5's spycatcher William Hinchley-Cooke complained about press reports describing Armstrong as a marine engineer since, in reality, he had only 'served at sea for two short periods of seven and eight weeks'.

I found out that Alice Hahn was making a point of getting in the company of merchant navy officers and was particularly interested in the matter of convoys.[27]

Armstrong never boarded the *La Brea*: on August 24, 1940 she was torpedoed by a U-boat in the North Atlantic and sank immediately. By this time, however, Armstrong had already left New York for Boston, where he was arrested by US Immigration and, in October, interned in a holding centre on Deer Island, Massachusetts. Before long he was joined by a familiar figure: Carl Klein had also been arrested, charged 'with being a German agent and being illegally in the country', and was scheduled for deportation back to the Reich. Armstrong told William Hinchley-Cooke that he had decided this presented him with an opportunity to discover the extent of Klein's spy-ring.

I got very friendly with Klein because I was sure and am still sure, in fact I know, that he has got British agents here in England and it was my intention to find out who they are or who they were. I had many conversations with him and he admitted to me that he was a German Nazi agent in the Far East but he claimed to have had no such activities in the United States.

But in view of what I had seen in New York, and been told by Alice Hahn when she had had too much to drink, I knew he was. I questioned him in many ways closely without arousing his suspicions, as to who his contacts might be in England, and in a roundabout way from his conversation I gathered that there was a particular ring of them in the United States.[28]

Among these agents was Dr Herbert Scholz, the German Consul at Boston and the second most senior official in the Reich's US-based diplomatic corps.* Scholz regularly visited German inmates at Deer Island, and Klein allegedly told Armstrong that the diplomat was the

---

* Herbert Scholz, later given the rank of SS-Oberfuehrer, was the US-based director of the Sicherheitsdienst – the Nazi Party's own secret service which operated independently of (and often as a rival to) the Abwehr. He was expelled when America declared war on Germany in December 1941.

organiser of a Nazi spy network which stretched from California to Boston – and across the Atlantic. Scholz also gave Klein a bundle of papers which Armstrong managed to examine. These included 'a reference ... to the American bomb sight' and sensitive information about a 'tool steel experiment' carried out by the Tungsten Steel Corporation on behalf of the US government. Armstrong also saw a list of names; he said he had been unable to copy it, but did manage to remember a few tantalising details.

> There was one particular fellow, but I don't remember the name. This man had been employed at Buckingham Palace and is now in the employ of the Earl of Athlone.[29]

Buoyed by his success in winning Klein's confidence, Armstrong claimed he decided to approach Scholz directly, posing as a disloyal English seaman in the hope of discovering the identities of German agents in Britain. On November 19, he wrote the letter which would send him to the gallows.

> Please excuse this somewhat unusual method of address, this letter may come to you by messenger; or failing in his effort to do so, it will reach you by mail. I am an officer of the British Service, an engineer at recent date attached to the Inspection of Aircraft Dept. (AID) in England.* Latterly I was transferred to the Marine Dept. under control of the British Admiralty.
>
> My intention is to make German contacts here in the US which may be beneficially used on my return to England. Naturally in the various capacities in which I was employed in England, I have information which would be very valuable in the proper sources. You will no doubt agree with me that it is not advisable to enter into any written discussion upon this subject here at this time, but if you could have someone contact me who was reliable then the matter could be more fully gone into.

---

* There is no evidence in any of Armstrong's files to support this claim.

I was detained by the US Immigration authorities before I could make any such contacts here in the US and have been transferred from East Boston Immigration Station to Deer Island to be held pending deportation proceedings.

I feel that the information which I have and the value of someone so placed in England in these times would be greatly appreciated by yourself or those who you would put in contact with me.

The letter never reached Scholz. It was intercepted by US immigration officials and sent on to London; when Armstrong was deported, Special Branch officers met his ship on its arrival at Cardiff docks on March 2, 1941. They arrested him and bundled him into a car bound for New Scotland Yard.

Hinchley-Cooke was waiting for him there, and had prepared a small but ultimately significant trap. Rather than immediately confronting Armstrong with the letter to Scholz, the spycatcher merely asked him to write out a short note explaining the reasons for his deportation. Armstrong's statement made no mention of the German Consul, the supposed international spy-ring or his attempt to unmask it – an inexplicable omission since he knew he was speaking to an officer of the Security Service. As soon as Armstrong signed the document, Hinchey-Cooke sprang the trap.

I then showed him the letter [to Scholz] and asked him if he had seen it before. He was silent for about a minute and changed colour and then said 'Yes; yes. I know what this is. That was from Deer Island. I wrote it. I am surprised you have got it ... I wondered why he did not contact me'. There was again a pause and he then volunteered a [second] statement which was taken down in shorthand.[30]

It was only in this second statement that Armstrong put forward his claim to have been working as a volunteer undercover agent.

I would like to state at this time that my interest in this affair has always been and is solely with a view to trapping these people into some admission upon which I could procure concrete evidence which would be of definite value to my Government.

I am sure that if given the opportunity to do so I, and perhaps I only, through these contacts would yet be able to procure a complete list of the agents at present working in England, the coastal ports of USA and the convoy base at Halifax, Canada.[31]

Armstrong's reference to the convoy base in Nova Scotia served only to incriminate him further. Halifax was then the gathering point for Merchant Marine ships and their Royal Navy escorts; in recent months both the British and Canadian governments had become aware that details of these convoys had been leaked, and potentially passed to the German U-boat fleet patrolling the Atlantic. When Armstrong was searched, police found a sheaf of notes he had made about the base and the ships gathered in it: to MI5, this was additional evidence of his attempts at espionage.

Armstrong, however, told a different story. He admitted recording details of arrangements for the convoy pool at Halifax, but claimed that this had been part of his efforts to penetrate Scholz's spy network. In a third signed statement, he wrote:

My observations made at Halifax N.S. Central Convoy base for British ships crossing the Atlantic with war materials, have only served to verify the fact that this aforementioned Nazi ring is operating in conjunction with agents in this country and in Canada ... I learned that it was common knowledge just when the convoy conferences were being attended by the various Captains of ships in Bedford Basin to make up convoys. Further, it was known just what each cargo ship carried and how much; the names of the ships in the convoy; whether steam or motor ship; the speed of the convoys; the number of vessels; the Commodore [lead] ship; the armament of these ships and what is more important the sailing time and the circle upon which the course was laid.

Many lives are lost [and] thousands of tons of shipping and millions of dollars worth of valuable war materials simply by the gross carelessness and wanton neglect of officials responsible for the suppression of such conditions.

My interest is and has been solely from a Merchant Navy point of view; it is with this purpose in mind at all times that I have jeopardized my own security to produce some concrete evidence that would lead to an investigation of the officials concerned and the apprehension of the agents who use the information so procured.[32]

It was a plausible explanation, but fatally undermined by Armstrong's failure to make any mention of his unofficial information-gathering until confronted with apparently incriminating evidence. At 9.20am on March 5, he was charged at Cannon Row police station with one count of breaching Defence Regulations; five days later the Attorney General signed the required *fiat* to add a charge under the Treachery Act.

His two-day trial at the Old Bailey was held entirely *in camera*, and Armstrong's Home Office files do not contain a transcript of proceedings, only fragmentary extracts. These show that he gave evidence from the witness box, denying that he had been a spy, and telling the court that had he planned espionage, he would hardly have written so openly to the German Consul.

'If I had wanted to become a spy, I would certainly not have gone about it in that way. If I had wanted to have a visit to Dr Herbert Scholz during the three months I was in Boston I could have gone and seen him for that matter. What I wanted was Dr Herbert Scholz to come and visit me and give me any information that would be of value.'[33]

The jury was evidently unimpressed by this defence: fifteen minutes after the judge ordered them to retire they returned with guilty verdicts on both counts. An usher placed the traditional black cloth on top of Mr Justice Lewis's wig as he read out the only sentence allowed under the Treachery Act.

'You shall be taken from this place to a lawful prison and from there to a place of execution where you will be hanged by the neck until you are dead and thereafter your body buried within the precincts of the prison and may the Lord have mercy upon your soul.'

Armstrong's subsequent appeal was rejected by the Court of Criminal Appeal on June 23, Lord Caldecote pointedly noting that despite his claims to have been working on behalf of his country, 'the fact was that neither during the time of his detention in America, nor during the time of his arrest in this country, did he take advantage of the opportunities which he had to indicate that he had any information which would be of assistance to the British Authorities'.[34] Sixteen days later Thomas Pierrepoint swiftly dispatched him at Wandsworth prison.

If there remained a lingering sense of unease at Armstrong's fate – he had, after all, not actually passed any intelligence to Germany, merely (at most) offered the Consul unspecified assistance – there was no such unease about the execution which followed it a year later.

Duncan Alexander Croall Scott-Ford was a drunkard, braggart and thief, with a weakness for foreign prostitutes which led him into the welcoming arms of German Intelligence. He was born in Devonport on September 4, 1921; eleven years later his father, a naval sick bay attendant, committed suicide by taking an overdose of morphine. Despite this, his mother entrusted her son to the Royal Navy, sending him as a boarding pupil at the Greenwich Training School in London.

In September 1937 Scott-Ford was formally accepted into the ranks as a Boy Seaman, First Class, and spent the next two years on board warships sailing the Pacific and South Atlantic oceans. In June 1939, with war on the horizon, his ship put into port at Dar-es-Salaam, in what was then Tanganyika (now Tanzania); here, over a shore leave of ten days, he met a seventeen-year-old German girl and promptly fell in love.

Ingeborg Richter was, according to a memorandum from the local Commissioner of Security and Intelligence, slightly built, with fair hair, blue eyes and a 'very pleasant manner; attractive to men; speaks good English'.[35] Less promisingly, she was a member of a 'Nazi Youth Organisation' and her father, ostensibly the manager of a car company, was an NSDAP official for East Africa. According to Scott-Ford's own sworn statement, the young couple were deeply (if rather chastely) attached to each other, but realised that their relationship faced a substantial hurdle.

She was dead straight and I was never intimate with her, in fact until the last two days I never made love to her.* When I did tell her how I felt, she told me it would be impossible for us to carry on unless one of us would change our nationality.

We agreed to correspond but agreed her father should not be allowed to know of the depth of our friendship because he was a Nazi and would not have approved.[36]

Consummated or not, Scott-Ford's passion for Ingeborg Richter would be noted by German Intelligence and ultimately used to lure him into a classic blackmail trap. In the meantime, however, his ship sailed to Egypt and the 21-year-old sailor comforted himself throughout the latter half of 1940 by taking up with a local prostitute, Nahid Mohamed. She operated out of a cabaret bar in Alexandria and may have been both a German asset as well as an (evidently expensive) sex-worker: there is a fleeting note in Scott-Ford's MI5 file which suggests that Ms Mohamed used him to obtain information as well as cash.

He apparently spent a good deal of money on this girl and he maintains that it was because of this fact that he was held responsible for a leakage of information from the cypher [sic] room which was traced to Nahid Mohamed and led to his Court Martial.[37]

The official account of that court martial records that Scott-Ford was convicted on March 3, 1941 for crimes of embezzlement: to finance his relationship with Ms Mohamed, he had repeatedly altered the balances shown in his Post Office savings account book and then withdrawn more money than it held. He was jailed for two years and given a dishonourable discharge.

Both rulings were subsequently overturned after an emotional plea by his mother: Scott-Ford served only six months in prison and his record was altered to remove the word 'dishonourable' – a remarkably

---

* This may have been an archaic idiom meaning 'romanced' or 'courted' – though given Scott-Ford's subsequent carnal activities it could equally have meant that the couple had sex.

rash decision which would have far-reaching consequences for the Navy – and by September 1941 he was back at sea, this time serving with the Merchant Marine on convoys on the transatlantic and Mediterranean routes. On May 10, 1942 his ship, the SS *Finland*, docked at Lisbon.

Portugal was notionally neutral, although its 600-year-old treaty with Britain* remained intact. Due to its strategic location, however, its ports were major centres of activity for both MI6 and the Abwehr. Duncan Scott-Ford's weaknesses for drinking binges and commercial sex made him an obvious and easy target for German spies on his first shore leave.

On May 15 he walked from the docks into town and quickly picked up a local prostitute, spending the night with her in a cheap flophouse. The following evening found him alone, deep in his cups, in a sailors' bar. According to his own extremely frank account, after 30 minutes' solitary drinking he was approached by a friendly German 'businessman'.

A man came in and sat on the next stool. I had had two or three beers and was a bit muzzy. I afterwards learned that this man's name was Rithmann.

Rithmann entered into conversation with me, talking about the war in a very general way. He said that he had travelled on the East Coast of Africa, at which I said that I had been to East Africa and had met a German girl there at Dar-es-Salaam. He asked me who she was – I told him, Ingeborg Richter. He asked me whether I had been able to write to her and I said no – that my last letter had been sent back with a note saying that she had gone to Germany.

After this, Rithmann began to pay greater attention to me. He said that to marry a German girl was the best thing you could do, because of the splendid training they had. He did not actually refer to the Hitler training, but I understood him to mean that.[38]

---

* The Anglo-Portuguese Alliance was signed in 1386, guaranteeing that neither country would wage war against the other. It is the oldest such surviving agreement between nations.

When Scott-Ford said that he was an able seaman on the *Finland*, Rithmann began probing for information, claiming that a friend of his had mentioned the date of a gathering of ships for a new convoy.

> Rithmann then asked me if I knew what was happening on the 28th June as this mate had told him that all British ships had orders to be in port on that date. This was the first I had heard of the 28th June and I said that I could not confirm or deny anything like that. Rithmann said that if I could confirm what was happening on that date he would pay me 1,000 Escudos and also get a letter for me into Germany to Ingeborg Richter. I said that I would see what I could do ...[39]

Even to someone as drunk as he undoubtedly was, Scott-Ford must have realised that Rithmann was a German spy, and the information he sought had only one purpose – the sinking of Allied shipping. Despite this – and the fact that Scott-Ford had no history of fascist or pro-Nazi sympathies – he willingly agreed to talk with the agent's superiors.

Between May 17 and May 21 he met Rithmann and his handlers on at least five occasions. At one rendezvous, in the offices of the Portuguese branch of the Krupps military combine,* the senior agent, who identified himself as 'Captain Henley',[40] first plied him with whisky and vermouth, then bribed him for convoy information.

> They gave me plenty to drink and then Henley cut the cackle and started asking questions. He asked me about shipbuilding and if Americans were in England and Scotland. I couldn't tell him anything except they were in Belfast and he said 'that's not news, that's history' ... Henley said he would pay me a very large sum of money for charts showing the positions of our mine fields, but I told him that I did not have access to the charts.[41]

---

* Krupps was then a vital part of the Reich's war machine. Its agency in Portugal was run by Kuno Weltzien, a businessman who was also a spy-runner for the Abwehr, focused, according to an MI5 memo in Scott-Ford's file, on 'recruiting as agents seamen upon Allied or neutral ships bound for British ports'.

After 'Henley' handed him 1,000 Portuguese escudos – worth approximately £10 then, and equivalent to £350 today – Scott-Ford again agreed to get the information and to provide copies of manuals on British shipping. They arranged to meet up again on Sunday, May 24, at a flat above a wine shop, hours before SS *Finland* was due to leave Lisbon.

> Henley opened the door, it was a flat furnished in pink and was obviously his residence. Henley asked me if I could confirm any places where there were American troops in Britain and the extent of their training and efficiency, also their numbers.
>
> He asked me to try and find out the American naval base in Britain and about the three new battleships which were being built and the approximate date of completion. I told him I would try and he gave me two hundred Escudos.[42]

Henley also wanted information about British warships anchored at Gibraltar: Scott-Ford willingly told him that a battleship and a light cruiser were berthed there in readiness for the next convoy;* for good measure he handed over details he had obtained about military preparations to defend the Rock against a gas attack. He also agreed to obtain ration books and identity cards on his next trip home – a clear indication that his handlers were planning to send agents to Britain. At the end of the meeting, he carelessly signed a formal receipt for all the money 'Henley' had given him: 1,800 escudos, worth £18.[43]

SS *Finland* left Lisbon later that day, docking at Liverpool on June 20. The next day all crew members were summoned for standard intelligence interviews and asked if they had been contacted in Lisbon by German agents. Scott-Ford admitted that he had been approached, but insisted that he had rebuffed them.

The ship was not due to sail again until early July; Scott-Ford stayed on board during the days, but spent his nights in a room at the Avoca Hotel. He shared this agreeable accommodation with Molly Gallagher,

---

* One – HMS *Hermione* – was tracked and sunk by U-boat 205 in the Mediterranean three weeks after Scott-Ford revealed her location. Eighty-seven crew members died.

an alleged member of the Irish Republican Army* whom he picked up in a local bar; according to MI5's subsequent 'Liquidation Report' on the case, he boasted to Gallagher about his contacts with German Intelligence and his prospects for advancement within the Abwehr once the war was over, and he roped her into the mission 'Henley' had given him.

> During this period Scott-Ford seems to have made a somewhat deter-
> mined effort to obtain clothing coupons and identity cards. On one
> occasion he went to the International Café and indeed did succeed in
> obtaining clothing coupons, for which he paid the sum of £1. He gave
> these to Molly Gallagher. Scott-Ford saw in this adventurous character
> a potential recruit for the German S.S. and one capable of working
> under him as a sub-agent. He sounded her out on the subject and at first,
> because of the monetary gain, she was willing to co-operate with him.
>
> At a later date, however, he admits that she had expressed some
> doubts about accepting work on behalf of the Germans which might
> result in the bombing of women and children.[44]

SS *Finland* arrived again in Lisbon on Sunday, July 26. Scott-Ford was met on the dockside and ordered to go straight to a meeting at the Krupps Agency. Over the course of a 90-minute 'stormy' interview, 'Henley' demanded the naval manuals, information about military bases, and ration and identity cards which his agent had been paid to provide; when Scott-Ford admitted he did not have them with him, his handler grew angry.

> Upon learning that he had failed to secure these, it is plain that the
> mask of good fellowship rapidly dropped from them. Henley was
> extremely annoyed and commenced questioning Scott-Ford regard-
> ing his voyage out in convoy, and in particular the number of ships
> torpedoed and their names.[45]

---

* It is impossible to be certain whether Gallagher was a member of the IRA. She was subsequently interned as such under Defence Regulation 18B, but her Home Office file – HO 144/23190 – is closed until January 1, 2042.

'Henley' made it plain to Scott-Ford that he was in real danger. As MI5's report on the encounter noted, he 'was completely in the hands of the German Secret Service':

> He had been paid 1,000 Escudos at the first meeting with Rithmann and Henley and later had received three other sums of 200 Escudos, 500 Escudos and 100 Escudos respectively. Scott-Ford had signed a receipt for each of these sums ...
>
> He found that he was met with the suggestion that unless he did better next time the receipt would be handed to the British Consul ... He was told further that he would get Ingeborg Richter into trouble if he did not produce [the material].[46]

In desperation, Scott-Ford blurted out classified intelligence about the sinking of five British ships. 'Henley' was evidently unimpressed and ordered him to come back the following Wednesday night, bringing with him the books and coupons which Scott-Ford claimed to have left on board the *Finland*. He evidently handed at least some of these over at the rendezvous, and his handler appeared somewhat mollified; a further meeting was arranged at which 'Henley' said he would give Scott-Ford £50 – funds which were to be delivered to one of his agents in Scotland.

Scott-Ford never kept that appointment (and thus never discovered the identity of 'Henley''s spy in Britain): his ship sailed out of Lisbon, bound for Salford, this time with Scott-Ford as its helmsman. Anxious for something to give 'Henley' at their next rendezvous, he used the position to make detailed notes on the course steered and the type of warships which guarded the convoy.

In reality, he had more to fear from British Intelligence than its German counterpart. Unknown to Scott-Ford, an MI6 agent had been watching him in Lisbon and sent reports of his meetings with Rithmann and 'Henley' back to Hinchley-Cooke at MI5. When the *Finland* docked on August 18, he was questioned again about contacts with enemy agents.

Initially he tried to bluff his way through the interrogation, but when confronted with the times and locations of his meetings with

'Henley', he evidently realised he had been kept under observation throughout his stay in Lisbon. According to a report by MI5's regional security officer:

> At this point, and this point only, Scott-Ford was completely non-plussed. For a very brief space he showed terror and soon after this confessed to taking money from Enemy Agents in Lisbon ... [But] he steadfastly refused to give the name or description of this man ... and gave the impression, almost, that in confessing to his traitorous activities he was hoodwinking the interrogator or rather turning him away from the really dangerous part of his story.[47]

The Security Service sent him for more rigorous enquiries at Camp 020. With an eye to a likely prosecution under the Treachery Act – and a likely capital sentence – Colonel Robin 'Tin Eye' Stephens gave his prisoner a thorough examination.

> During the course of these interrogation[s], some difficulty was experienced in extracting the exact truth from Scott-Ford. He is given to somewhat fanciful embroider [*sic*] of his story, and endeavours to pose in a bombastic way as a clever agent. When he finally 'broke' and cried it was obvious that, contrary to the above, he is no more than a scared rat, who had been threatened by the Germans with physical violence, and told that he would be denounced to the British Embassy ...
>
> The one redeeming feature in this traitor's character is his affection for Ingeborg Richter. This may be incomprehensible, in view of his affairs with other women, but I am certain that it exists ...
>
> Scott-Ford is frankly terrified of the Germans and is now equally terrified of the authorities in this country. As he has stated, he does not know where to turn. In addition, he states that if he were at liberty, and returned to Lisbon, he is quite certain that the Germans would liquidate him. On the other hand, he knows that he faces a traitor's death in this country.[48]

Duncan Scott-Ford appeared in the dock at the Old Bailey on October 16, 1942. His trial – held entirely *in camera* – took just a day.

He pleaded not guilty and gave evidence in his own defence, but no other witnesses were called by his barrister.

'I had no intention of assisting the enemy', he told the court. 'I was frightened by the threats made by the German agents in Lisbon that they would give my receipt for money I had had from them to the British Consul. My reason for mixing with these German agents was so that I might write a letter to Ingeborg Richter in Germany.'[49]

Neither the judge nor the jury was impressed by this plea for understanding; Mr Justice Birkett[50] caustically noted its 'inadequacy' and the jury retired for only a few minutes before returning with a guilty verdict. At 9.00am on Tuesday, November 3, 1942, Albert Pierrepoint* entered the condemned cell at Wandsworth prison, bound the prisoner's hands behind his back, marched him through to the waiting scaffold and swiftly pulled the lever to spring the trap doors. Later the same day, Duncan Alexander Croall Scott-Ford was buried in grave 76 inside the prison's walls. He was 21 years old.

The official history of British traitors condemned to death during the Second World War begins and ends with the three prosecutions of Dorothy O'Grady, George Armstrong and Duncan Scott-Ford. There was, however, a fourth case: a never-publicised court martial of a serving soldier who was sentenced to die by firing squad in February 1942.

The files on Gunner Philip Jackson were quietly released to the National Archives in 2010; they received no publicity, yet they provide a revealing picture of the disparity with which justice was meted out to those who betrayed their country, and of a growing trend in MI5's techniques to unearth them.

Philip Jackson was born in Nottingham on May 10, 1905. At some point in 1940, he either volunteered or was conscripted into the Army, and was posted to a Royal Artillery anti-aircraft battery in Wolverhampton. Military life did not, however, agree with him and by the following September he was sufficiently discontented to offer his services to Germany via a handwritten (and less than literate) letter, addressed to the Spanish Embassy for onward transmission to Berlin.

---

* Nephew and successor to Thomas Pierrepoint in the family's execution business.

Considering the condition's [*sic*] in the Army, Navy and Air Force and the country generally I am of the opinion the quicker Churchill and his Rotten Gang are out, and his Brass Hats of the War Office, ... the better to make way for Moseley [*sic*] and National Socialism.

If you can get me an interview with the German Minister to Eire I would be pleased to be the means of ending this reign of hypocrisy and rotteness [*sic*] under the present regime. I can give conclusive evidence that civilians and military personnel of all services are on the verge of mutiny owing to mismanagement.

It doesn't need bombing or invasion to win the war. If I could get to Eirie [*sic*] I could tell the people the truth over the radio and the Government would soon fall: built as it is on corruption and inefficiency.

I have written to your Embassy three times during the last three months when on leave but was unable to get an interview. But I am so disgusted with conditions as they are I am sending this letter by post, a very dangerous procedure as you will admit. But I'd sooner be shot than fight for such scum ... If this does reach you would you please send to the German Minister in Eirie [*sic*] ...[51]

Spain was technically a neutral country. Although Franco's regime supplied material and military support to Germany and Italy, it never formally joined the Axis powers; as a result, MI5 was prevented from intercepting general correspondence sent to its London Embassy (although it did obtain Home Office warrants allowing it to examine mail sent by individual British fascists). The Post Office duly delivered Jackson's letter to the Embassy, where it was seen by an English civilian employee; he secretly copied it out and took the text to the War Office.

The note posed a number of problems. The first and most obvious was that there was no means of preventing the Embassy passing on Jackson's offer to the German Legation in Dublin; the second was how to handle the case.

On the surface, there was little to distinguish Jackson's attempt at treachery from similar bids by William Craven or Serocold Skeels, and he could, in theory, have been interned like Craven or prosecuted like

Skeels. Against this was the very real risk of exposing the mole inside the Embassy, and the fact that Jackson was a serving soldier.

After more than a week in which the letter was unaccountably shuttled between in-trays at MI19 and MI11,[52] the case landed on the desk of Major 'Jock' Whyte, head of MI5's B4 Branch. He decided to initiate an elaborate 'sting' operation in which he wrote back to Jackson posing as 'John Browne', a British-based German intelligence agent who had been ordered to follow up the Gunner's offer of assistance.

> A copy of the letter which you recently sent to London has been brought to me by a sure hand from Dublin (you probably know where) and I have been asked to get in touch with you. Will you let me know to what extent you are prepared to co-operate with us in bringing about the overthrow of C. and his gang. Our ultimate victory is certain. We already have the whole of Europe in our hands and the sooner Englanders are crushed the better it will be for all ...[53]

'Browne' suggested meeting in Birmingham as soon as Jackson could get leave from his unit; the soldier responded positively and MI5 began working out the details of its entrapment scheme. Whyte was careful to record very clear rules of engagement: 'no inducement of any sort should be offered or even hinted at', he stressed in a memo in November, the sole aim being to establish whether Jackson was a genuine Nazi sympathiser or merely a disgruntled soldier.

He faced two immediate hurdles. The first was the need to document every word spoken at the proposed meeting; unlike London, where it could easily place microphones in apartments for sensitive meetings, MI5 had very few resources outside the capital – which meant hiring hotel rooms and drafting in local police officers to eavesdrop on the conversations.

The second hurdle was finding someone to play the role of 'John Browne'. MI5's authorised histories do not include a description of Jock Whyte, but he evidently spoke no German and realised that he could not pass as a 'stay-behind' Nazi agent. He turned instead to Maxwell Knight and asked to borrow one of his stable of 'M.S.' undercover assets.

The officer selected was Eric Arthur Roberts, a 34-year-old former bank clerk who had joined the Security Service in July 1940.[54] Within a year he would go on to play the central role in MI5's most remarkable and extended *agent provocateur* operation, but in winter 1941 he was largely untested in undercover work.

Whyte felt the need to issue him strict instructions for the meeting with Jackson, and his pose as a German spy.

If our friend maintains that he wants to assist in pro-German and anti-British propaganda, and not espionage, it should be pointed out to him that there are thousands of others who wish to do that and that such appointments are only given to those who have proved their desire to help Germany by providing information of value. We have to remember the tremendous risk involved in trying to get 'right minded people' over to Germany in time of war. Facilities are only given to those who have already proved their worth ...

We are particularly interested in the ceiling which can be reached by anti-aircraft shells, in the details of the fuses used and in the type of shells used ... We are also interested in where shells for each battery are stored and ... in the arrangements which are made to co-ordinate the activities of the anti-Aircraft Batteries and the night fighting aircraft ...

If this fellow really wants to co-operate with us, what pay or compensation does he want? We usually start by paying by results, until we find the real value of an agent, and from then onwards we usually pay him on a very generous scale commensurate with the risk involved. We are unable to make any definite arrangements at this meeting, as we have to refer the matter back to ... Dublin.

It is still of the utmost importance not to offer him any definite inducement in order to make him incriminate himself. I can see no harm in saying what we usually do in the matter of paying by results, in order to get him to say what he is prepared to do, or to try to do.

If he does not react in that manner, it would be better not to pursue the matter further, because he must not be offered any inducement to get him to offer to engage in treachoroous [*sic*] activities.[55]

The planned entrapment was delayed for more than a month by a faintly farcical series of crossed letters and missed meetings. In the interim, MI5 intercepted Jackson's correspondence, which included a revealing exchange with a familiar aristocratic name: Lord Tavistock, now fully ennobled as the Duke of Bedford. One letter showed that Bedford appeared to be aware of the soldier's disloyalty. On October 29, he wrote to Jackson from his Scottish estate:

> Many thanks for your intriguing letter ... With regard to your political views, tut! tut! man. Do you not know that a soldier who says anything calculated to weaken the conviction of a Member of the House of Lords, that Mr Churchill is our Great White Hope and Lord Beaverbrook our Great Red One, is liable to be shot at dawn for the crime of spreading despondency and alarm in our more or less free country (always providing, of course, that the Ministry of Munitions hasn't mislaid the cartridges for the firing squad)![56]

Since no action appears to have been taken against Bedford, this raised – once again – the uncomfortable suspicion that well-connected Nazi sympathisers were accorded privileged treatment compared with their less elevated fascist brethren.

'John Browne' (alias Roberts) finally sat down with Gunner Jackson in the Woolpack Hotel, Birmingham, at 9.15pm on Thursday, December 4, 1941. Throughout the encounter, captured on concealed microphones and recorded in shorthand by a local detective constable sitting in an adjoining room, Jackson repeatedly expressed suspicion and concerns for his own safety.

> 'You will have to understand. I am thinking this may be a police trap or something like that ... I know it sounds silly but there is a means of recording a conversation. What do they call those talking things? They make records ... I don't want to be suspicious but I'm taking a big risk.
>
> 'As I say I'm willing to take a certain amount of risk ... so give me an idea of what information you want ...'[57]

He also stressed that what he really wanted was to be smuggled out to Germany from where he would, like Lord Haw-Haw, make radio broadcasts exposing the British political and military leadership which was 'rotten to the core'.

> 'I want to tell you my idea ... I have the idea to support a certain regime and it would be better than the one in this country at the present time, and I know I am taking a big risk in doing so ... Is it possible through your organisation for me to get across to Germany? It sounds bloody silly, but I hope to get across to Germany and do a broadcast instead of the fellow who is doing it at present.'

When 'Browne' pushed for information on anti-aircraft defence, as a test of Jackson's willingness to help Germany, Jackson was initially reluctant, saying, 'I believe I could give you details of gun-sites but it is not going to serve any useful purpose'. He also made clear that he was worried that in doing so he would enable the Luftwaffe to bomb British women and children, not just military targets. 'They could not guarantee the accuracy of the bombs, could they?' he asked Browne. Nor, in his view, would this help the German cause.

> 'Suppose I arrange to let you have that information about how many guns were in a particular area so that your people would know places that were not properly protected, the range of the guns and exactly where they were situated – that is not going to win the war.'

By the end of the interview, however, Jackson's attitude evidently hardened.

> 'I would come over with your pilots over this country in their planes and risk my life like that. That is the enthusiasm I feel for a cause when I take it up. I would show them the sites where they could drop their bombs.'

Since the statement was damning, 'Browne' sought confirmation, asking Jackson if he was prepared to 'help us in an invasion?'. He received an unequivocal answer: 'Yes, all the way includes invasion.' And he stressed that he was 'not doing this for money, but to get the bloody rotten Government changed ... I want no pounds shilling and pence ... I am not out to make money. I believe my country's future lies in lining up with Germany and building a new order.'[58]

Jackson's words provided enough evidence to arrest him. The Security Service, however, decided that to do so would require 'Browne' to give evidence in court, and thereby expose his true identity as MI5 officer Eric Roberts. Instead, 'Browne' told Jackson that he had passed the initial examination and would next be interviewed by his boss in the German Secret Service, 'Harry Marshall'.

Marshall was ostensibly a Dublin-based businessman who worked closely with the German Embassy in Eire; in reality he was a Chief Inspector Sanders from Birmingham City Police. At 6.00pm on Monday, December 29, 1941, Jackson met 'Marshall' at Birmingham's Imperial Hotel; he repeated the offers of assistance and treachery he had made to 'Browne'. The conversation was once again captured on hidden microphones and taken down in shorthand, and at 7.38pm, Inspector Sanders made the arrest. The next day Jackson was bundled, under military escort, on a train to London, taken to Military Police HQ, Great Scotland Yard and charged with treachery.

Because Philip Jackson was a serving soldier, he was tried in February 1942 in a court martial. All proceedings were held in secret and there is no report in any of Jackson's files disclosing his plea, defence case or mitigation. There is, however, a record of the court's sentence: death by firing squad.

That sentence was never carried out. Although the evidence and legal basis for Jackson's conviction were exactly the same as those which sent George Armstrong to the gallows – a memo by one of MI5's legal officers specifically noted that the court had reached its decision 'on the authority of *R. v. Armstrong*'[59] – either the Army, the government Law Officers or the Security Service arranged for a commutation to life imprisonment.

The reason for this appears to have been a determination to protect MI5's original informant within the Spanish Embassy, and more importantly, to keep secret its reliance on undercover *agents provocateurs* to secure the evidence of Jackson's crimes. The timing of this decision was interesting. At the same time as news of Gunner Jackson's entrapment, trial and sentence were being withheld from the press, MI5 was enduring the fallout from a very public and embarrassing scandal over exactly that technique.

CHAPTER SEVENTEEN

'Most Frank and Attractive'

'The chairmen of the Advisory Committee have repeatedly
made clear that they are profoundly mistrustful of
the evidence of "agents", whether anonymous or not.'
Complaint by MI5 to the Home Office,
January 6, 1942

On Friday, November 14, 1941 Harald Kurtz was summoned to No. 6 Burlington Gardens, Mayfair, the imposing Italianate wartime home of the Home Office Advisory Committee on Internment. Kurtz was then the star agent in Maxwell Knight's 'M.S.' stable of undercover operatives; his impersonations of a Nazi intelligence officer had led to the internment of a string of British Nazi sympathisers, as well as the conviction of Molly Hiscox and Norah Briscoe for attempting to pass military secrets to Germany – efforts for which he received considerable respect and fulsome praise from his masters in the Security Service.

His reception that Friday morning, and on the following Monday, was very much less congenial. The 28-year-old agent was subjected to a searching, sometimes hostile, cross-examination by the Advisory Committee over his evidence in the most high-profile case to come before it; within days, it would accuse him of 'ingenious ... [and] very considerable lying'. Kurtz's career as an intelligence officer was destroyed; more importantly, the very public debacle which followed would convince MI5 that legal proceedings could not contain the threat of British Fifth Columnists – and set it on a course which would effectively bypass both Whitehall and the courts.

*

The Advisory Committees on Internment were always going to be a problem. The bureaucratic fudge which gave birth to them downgraded the original plan for full-scale judge-led tribunals of enquiry, replacing this with a panel of barristers and establishment worthies, whose woolly and ill-defined remit was to provide (ostensibly) non-binding recommendations to the Home Secretary, rather than to make absolute findings of fact. This sidestepped traditional rules of evidence: there was no cross-examination of witnesses and no opportunity to challenge any statement they chose to make. For a purpose so serious – the attempt to preserve at least a basic semblance of justice in cases where a citizen's liberty could be snatched away by executive order – it was flawed from the outset.

Within a month of the outbreak of war, the Home Office made a bad situation worse. On October 16, 1939 it replaced the Committee's first overall chairman, Walter Monckton, with Norman Birkett KC, a leading criminal defence barrister and former Liberal Party MP. An internal memorandum by Permanent Under-Secretary Alexander Maxwell shows that the Home Office knew exactly what it was signing up for.

> The Home Secretary agrees that Birkett would do the job admirably. His only doubt was whether some of the more conservatively-minded people would think (though I have no doubt mistakenly) that Birkett would be inclined to take too liberal a view.[1]

Maxwell must have known that those 'conservatively-minded people' would include British Intelligence, whose remit was to investigate – and, where appropriate, recommend the detention of – domestic Nazi sympathisers. By appointing Birkett, Whitehall was setting the Advisory Committee on a collision course with MI5; over the course of the first three years of war, a succession of overlapping and bitterly-fought cases turned that collision into a disaster. An entry in Guy Liddell's diary for August 1940 recorded the Security Service's early concern.

> At the board meeting today[2] Toby [Pilcher][3] raised the question of Birkett's attitude towards members of the BUF. In spite of the fact that he had agreed to keep in internment proven members of the BUF since their organization had now been proscribed, he had been letting them out whenever he thought they had an attractive personality. Evidence did not seem to count for very much. In one case the man denied that he was a member of the BUF in spite of the fact that his black shirt was found in a drawer and that he was wearing a Fascist belt. I forget what excuse was offered about the shirt, but as regards the belt he said that he wore it for his lumbago. This was readily accepted by the Committee.[4]

The first major flashpoint came six months later, over the internment of William Craven, the ardent young British fascist who, a year before war broke out, had volunteered his services (and loyalty) to the Third Reich. Craven had been one of the earliest 18B detainees, but in October 1939 had persuaded the Advisory Committee to recommend his release. He had applied to join the Army – a move blocked by MI5 – and had subsequently been swept up and re-interned in the round-up of BUF members which followed the fall of France in the summer of 1940.

He appealed against this second detention and, on February 19, 1941 presented his case to the Advisory Committee at its occasional offices in the Berystede Hotel, a comfortable resort in the affluent Berkshire town of Ascot. With no MI5 representative to challenge him, Craven persuaded Birkett that he was the victim of the Security Service's prejudice. The Committee recommended his release, which the Home Secretary duly arranged.

The decision – greeted with anger inside MI5 – was followed, over the next two years, by a succession of events which, had they not been so serious, would have been farcical. At the end of June, Craven arrived in Gloucester, notionally to start work as an agricultural labourer on a nearby farm; as required by the terms of his release, he reported to Gloucester police station and promptly announced that his loyalty to Hitler remained intact: 'If I can do anything to help Germany, I will do it', he informed the desk officer.[5]

Within a week, he moved to a different address and, since he failed to report this to the authorities, was summoned to appear at the local police court. He pleaded guilty and cheerfully told the bench that he had no intention of abiding by any of the conditions governing his release from detention. The magistrates were clearly unsure how to deal with Craven, passing the buck on to the Regional Commissioner; he in turn wrote to the Home Office, recommending re-internment. The Home Office, however, felt otherwise and insisted on giving Craven another chance to redeem himself; in a letter to MI5's new Director General, Sir David Petrie,[6] Alexander Maxwell explained his reasoning:

> I cannot help feeling that the real trouble with this man is his embitterment and disappointment by the refusal of his offer to serve with His Majesty's Forces ... In such cases I am inclined to the view that the Security Service should not oppose the man's enlistment.[7]

The suggestion provoked the Security Service to respond with a forcefully worded memorandum from MI5's legal branch. This argued that Craven was 'a fanatical Fascist with very strong German leanings ... His whole history for the last few years shows that he is obsessed with Fascist and Nazi doctrine and we do not think that he should in any circumstances be permitted to join the Armed Forces of the Crown'; Petrie, in barely more measured tones, protested to Maxwell that leaving Craven at large was a serious mistake.[8]

The Home Office refused to be pressured into authorising a new internment; in an internal memorandum on September 20, 1941 Maxwell lamented what he saw as the intransigence of the Security Service: 'I am afraid we shall never be able to make MI5 recognise the advantages of a bold and liberal line in this matter', he wrote to an unidentified fellow bureaucrat.[9]

The results of this 'bold and liberal' approach followed swiftly. Craven joined the British National Party, a fringe fascist organisation founded by Middlesex fishmonger Edward Godfrey,[10] and on November 8, 1942 wrote to the Home Secretary expressly repudiating all the commitments and professions of loyalty to Britain which he had made to Birkett's Committee.

> I desire to inform you that I no longer consider myself bound to the statements I made before the Advisory Committee in February 1941, which resulted in my release from detention the following April ... The news of the German attack on Russia* ... was welcome, and dispelled any doubts I may have had concerning Hitler and Germany, the Crusade for which I had worked and to which I had looked forward had begun ... I am working to achieve the ending of this suicidal and useless struggle between Britain and Germany.[11]

A month later, in a signed statement to a Gloucester Special Branch officer, he openly challenged the Home Office to rearrest him.

> I have resumed political activity. I am a supporter of the British National Party. I have a statement of their policy and I intend to put that across the public [sic] as far as possible. I know this is against the conditions of my release ... It is my intention to carry on my political activities in spite of the conditions laid down, and it's up to the Home Secretary whether he decides that I'm not allowed to, and puts the Suspension Order into effect ... I'm prepared to accept it and to return to the barbed wire ...
>
> I have always been ... a strong admirer of the Germans and Adolf Hitler. I've held these opinions since 1933. I've studied Fascism since 1935 ... and I got in touch with our British Fascists and had various contacts with people in Germany ... I think it is Germany's rightful place in Europe to maintain peace. Britain has no place in Europe ... I think the German Army was very generous when they left part of France unoccupied.
>
> I am prepared to be re-interned on account of my views rather than be free under conditions which forbid me to voice my opinion ...

---

* Operation Barbarossa, the Axis powers' invasion of the Soviet Union, began on June 22, 1941.

If they transferred me to a munition factory I should refuse to make munitions for Russia.[12]

Predictably, the Home Office ignored this; it also turned a blind eye when Craven wrote to the head of the Swedish National Socialist Party the following February, once again professing his pro-Nazi loyalties.

Comrade, I, a section leader of the proscribed 'British Union' write to you in the spirit of our common philosophy. An invasion of Norway is imminent; Britain and America are waiting like jackals to pounce on the body of Germany, now sorely stricken after nearly two years of magnificent achievement, fighting alone as a nation against the barbaric hordes of Stalinite [*sic*] Russia.

Should Germany fall, struck from behind by those who are traitors to our civilization and serve their Jewish masters in the interests of the Comintern, chaos will descend upon Europe and our people will become the vassals of Asia. As a member of the Finnish Volunteer Force of 1940[13] in whose veins flow the blood of your land I urge you to rally Sweden in support of Germany and against Russia ... With you in spirit as I wish I could be in body, I am at your service.[14]

Since other British fascists were then behind bars for identical or, in many cases, rather more minor actions, the Home Office's refusal to re-intern Craven was inexplicable. It also evidently encouraged him, since three weeks later he sent another declaration of loyalty to the Reich, this time addressed to the German Legation in Dublin.

As one who has been, and still is, a friend of Germany, and accepts Adolf Hitler as the leader of Europe, I am deeply grieved over the present situation of the Fatherland. By her refusal to consider the Führer's repeated offers of peace, especially after the consolidation of Europe and the opening of the crusade against Bolshevism, Britain has lost all moral justification for continuing this fratricidal struggle in the name of justice and humanity ...

The people, their minds poisoned by the lies and insinuations of those who hate 'the creed of the modern age' because they see in it the end of their exploitation of Europe for the benefit of Jewry, turned a deaf ear to our warning and exhortation ...

Germany, alone, stands as the guardian of Europe and, in the agony and suffering which that guardianship has imposed, I join with you in sorrow, and glory with you in triumph and look forward to joining with you in victory. With best wishes to my friends in Germany, especially to Herr Reinhardt, former Consul-General in Liverpool, my home town. Heil Hitler![15]

This letter, intercepted by government censors, finally prodded Whitehall into action. On April 6, 1943, Craven was tried at the Old Bailey on two charges of 'communicating with the enemy with an intent to assist him'; it took the jury just 21 minutes to return guilty verdicts on both counts and rather less for Mr Justice Singleton to impose a sentence of penal servitude for life.[16] Three days later, Guy Liddell noted the verdict – and the lessons to be drawn from it – in his journal.

Craven's release was strongly opposed by ourselves, and Sir Alexander Maxwell minuted the file to the effect that it was a pity that MI5 took such an unbalanced view, and had not got a liberal outlook. The effect on Craven of the Home Office's liberal outlook has been to get him a life sentence instead of merely internment for the duration of the war.[17]

Had the sorry and absurdly drawn-out saga of William Craven been an isolated instance there might have been less cause for concern: unfortunately, it wasn't. Between 1941 and 1943 the Advisory Committee recommended the release of all the interned Inner Circle members of Archibald Ramsay's Right Club – counsel the Home Office was moved to accept despite remarkably clear evidence that each had repeatedly lied to the Committee. The transcripts of Christabel Nicholson's appeal, on October 14, 1941, were typical.

Throughout the hearing she easily tied Norman Birkett in knots, forcing him to apologise for asking leading questions and 'putting words in my mouth'. She was, by turns, evasive and dismissive, claiming at one point that she had only joined the Right Club because she liked the 'uniforms' made for its leading members by Anna Wolkoff.

> NICHOLSON: 'The manner in which I joined the Club was accidental and it was done in order to get a cocktail outfit I liked. I knew nothing of its aims or organization, nor do I believe it to be anything but a loose collection of names, some of which are irreproachable ...'
>
> BIRKETT: 'Do you really say you joined the Right Club to get a cocktail outfit which you liked?'
>
> NICHOLSON: 'Yes. I have brought the hat if you would like to see it ...'[18]

Nor was Birkett much troubled by the evidence, provided by Knight's undercover agents, of Mrs Nicholson's admiration for Hitler; the most his gentle questioning elicited was a blithe statement that she thought the Fuehrer was 'not as bad as he was painted', and – at most – considered him 'a nuisance'. Even her admission that she had received – and attempted to conceal – the top-secret documents which had sent Tyler Kent and Anna Wolkoff to prison was disregarded on the basis of her own claim that she had not 'deliberately intended to injure the nation and [its] enemies'. On these assurances, Birkett decided that her detention should be cancelled.

> The Committee are quite satisfied that whatever decision is taken Mrs Nicholson, after her experiences, will be no danger to the security of the state ... it was impossible to avoid being struck with her intense desire not only to be freed from internment but to avoid by word or deed anything which would be likely to bring her into any further trouble ... The experiences of the last 17 months will also protect her from any such conduct in the future.[19]

Archibald Ramsay, Mrs Nicholson's leader and founder of the Right Club, also appealed to the Advisory Committee for release from internment, and the tangled saga of his determined battle for freedom and eventual restitution to the House of Commons encapsulated many of the widening fault-lines between the Home Office's strange reluctance to pursue British Nazi sympathisers and the attempts by MI5 to contain them.

Ramsay first appeared before Birkett and his colleagues on July 4, 1940. It allowed him to testify, largely uninterrupted, for the entire day and to argue that his intention had only ever been 'to inform the people of this country of the control exercised in public life by that part of Jewry which is really the international financial power of the world' – a claim which was hard to reconcile with his admission that he had, as MI5's agents alleged, been prepared to mount a fascist uprising should there be any sign of communists taking to the streets. At the end of the session he thanked the Committee for giving him 'such a very liberal and lenient hearing'.[20]

Despite Ramsay's acceptance of all the allegations contained in the reports of MI5's main undercover informant, the Committee decided that the evidence was 'in a rather unsatisfactory state', and insisted – over the Security Service's strenuous objections – on hearing directly from Marjorie Amor. She was brought to Burlington Gardens on July 9, 1940 and since she was – in the Committee's words – 'an agent of the Intelligence Service' for whom 'the temptations ... to provoke incidents which may lead to the evidence with which she is particularly concerned, are no doubt great', it resolved to examine her testimony 'with the most scrupulous care'[21] – a scruple not evident in Birkett's account of Ramsay's interview.

Amor evidently passed the test, since the Committee reluctantly came to the conclusion that it would be unwise for the Home Secretary to release Ramsay from internment. In reaching this decision, Birkett specifically endorsed MI5's concerns about the plot for a pro-Nazi revolt, noting that 'the activities of the Right Club were not solely concerned with combatting the power of Jewry but were also concerned with other steps which might conceivably be taken at some crisis in the affairs of the country, whatever that crisis might be'. He softened this, however, by accepting, unchallenged, Ramsay's claim that the fascists would not strike first.

It is important to keep in mind that any discussion between Captain Ramsay and Mosley was on the basis that a Communist rising had taken place and the ordinary constitutional machinery had broken down.[22]

As to his involvement with Kent and Wolkoff, the Committee reached an apparently damning conclusion:

> A Member of Parliament has knowledge that a servant of the United States Government is stealing confidential documents. That servant is introduced to him by a Russian girl, who has been engaging in very extraordinary activities since the outbreak of war.
>
> With knowledge that these confidential documents have been obtained in this most dishonourable way, Captain Ramsay not only countenances this dishonourable conduct but himself becomes an accomplice by inspecting the documents for his own purpose.[23]

Given Birkett's findings – evidently reluctantly drawn – it is hard to understand how Ramsay escaped prosecution. It is even more difficult to explain what the Home Office did next.

On August 22, 1940, the *New York Times* published the first of a series of reports on the activities of British Fifth Columnists. One paragraph directly accused Ramsay of working on behalf of Germany.

> The fact that the British police found it necessary to arrest a Member of Parliament, Captain Ramsay, on the charge of having transmitted to the German Legation at Dublin, treasonable information given to him by Tyler Kent, cipher clerk at the American Embassy in London, would seem to show that some of the finely-spun threads from Berlin to London remain.[24]

From his cell at Brixton prison, Ramsay issued proceedings for libel, engaging King's Counsel to represent him in the High Court. The action posed a substantial problem for the British government, since the paper's story was based on a briefing given by MI6 and Lord Swinton, head of the Security Executive, to President Franklin Roosevelt's personal intelligence representative, Colonel William J. Donovan.[25]

Ramsay's libel writ caused panic inside Whitehall. Although, as one of MI5's legal officers noted, the *New York Times* article had gone beyond what Donovan had been told, the newspaper was determined to defend the action and sought the assistance of the British government. This posed a difficult diplomatic problem and one which the Home Office was deeply reluctant to address. MI5's memo spelled out the dilemma.

The New York Times and Colonel Donovan are, as might be expected, extremely worried about this action and ... the Solicitor General agreed that in any event it would be tragic for the Americans to get the impression that we were not co-operating with them over this matter after all the trouble they took to help in the Wolkoff and Kent prosecution.

This appears to be even more desirable in view of the fact that, quite wrongly, the Americans take the view that the passage in the article was based on something told them in official quarters in London ... The matter does not, however, rest there, for the following consequences would inevitably ensue if the action is left to be handled by the solicitors to the New York Times without any assistance from us.

1. Ramsay will go into the witness box and deny, not only the precise allegations contained in the offending passage, but that he has ever been guilty of any treasonable, unpatriotic or subversive act of any sort. The defence will have no material for cross-examination and, therefore, Ramsay's word will go unchallenged and the picture which the general public will gain from the press reports will be that of a political martyr.

2. The inevitable result of the foregoing must not only be an increase in the agitation which is ongoing in some quarters against DR 18B, but as a result of the libel action it seems likely that a large number of persons who would otherwise be indifferent to any such agitation must inevitably be drawn to follow the lead, because the only evidence they have will be that of the innocence of Ramsay himself.

3. Not only are the damages to be awarded likely to be very substantial, since it is difficult to imagine a more grievous libel than to say of

a man that he is a traitor, but it is quite clear that there must be some alienation of the friendly feelings of the Americans, and many of them are likely to be influenced against Britain and her Government by the considerations affecting Ramsay's guilt or innocence which are set out in (2) above.

It is therefore submitted, with respect, that the question of assistance to the defence should be considered again in the light of the above matters. The only argument of principle which has so far been raised in favour of the refusal to help the Americans is that it is contrary to established practices that secret information should be made public during the continuance of the war. This would appear, however, to be a double-edged weapon in this case. If the information which we have is not disclosed to the public, Ramsay will be left with a clear field to make what statement he likes without fear of contradiction.

It is realised of course that no evidence which we could supply would enable the New York Times to defend the action successfully, but it is suggested that the proper course would be that ... every effort should be made to mitigate the damages so that, if possible, they should be reduced to a contemptuous sum.

If all our information is placed at the disposal of Messrs Culross & Co [the *New York Times*' London solicitors] there appears a very reasonable chance that the sum awarded will show that although the precise libel could not be justified, nevertheless it was very nearly true ...

I have discussed the above, in principle, with my legal colleagues in B7 who agree that it would be disastrous if Ramsay was able to obtain substantial damages without a case against him being put forward at all ...[26]

The lawyer's memo went on to suggest that if the Home Office agreed to 'careful and covert' cooperation, 'there would be a very healthy stiffening of public opinion in favour of the executive action in detaining such persons as Captain Ramsay and perhaps those in high authority would be less worried by the complaints and appeals of those acting in sympathy with them'.

The Home Office had, in American argot, 'skin in the game'. Another of Donovan's original sources was Alexander Maxwell, the Permanent Under-Secretary of State whose concern for 'liberal' values had put him at odds with the Security Service. The declassified files on Ramsay have been heavily weeded, but it appears from them that despite their complicity, Maxwell and his fellow Home Office mandarins initially refused to back up their briefings with evidence from intelligence reports on Ramsay.

Only after Whitehall belatedly realised the importance of keeping American public opinion on side was the information in MI5's files quietly provided to the newspaper's lawyers. On July 31, 1941, Ramsay's action came to an ignominious end in the King's Bench Division of the High Court.

He did not technically lose. Mr Justice Atkinson pronounced that the *New York Times* had indeed libelled Ramsay; he tempered this, however, by awarding only 'contemptuous damages' of one farthing, and issuing a stinging attack on the Right Club leader.

'He was disloyal in heart and soul to our King, our Government and our people – people fighting and dying, not for appeasement or for the preservation of Nazidom, but for victory and the destruction of Nazidom ... I am convinced – as I believe that a jury would have been convinced – that Captain Ramsay's claim to loyalty is false.'[27]

In a nation less dominated by tradition and the deference accorded to its ruling classes, Ramsay's pyrrhic victory – denounced in court as a friend of the dictator against whom Britain was fighting – would have caused an urgent reassessment of why he had never been prosecuted. None took place. Instead, for the duration of his internment he retained the salary and privileges of a serving MP, frequently submitting parliamentary questions to the government's ministers from his prison cell.

When he was finally released, on September 26, 1944, he resumed his seat in the House of Commons as if nothing untoward had happened. 'On the whole', he wrote to his fellow fascist plotter Sir Barry Domvile about the attitude of his fellow MPs, 'they have been very nice to me, and some have gone out of their way to be so.'[28]

Throughout this period MI5 was having to come to terms with the political reality that status and influence could be the decisive factor in whether pro-Nazi British fascists were freed or kept in detention. The case of Robert Gordon-Canning, the BUF's former director of overseas policy, treasurer of the British Council for Christian Settlement, would-be provider of 're-fuelling and revictualling' to German U-boat crews, and putative minister for the Dominions in John Beckett's planned Quisling regime, highlighted the problem.

Gordon-Canning was interned in June 1940 and appealed almost immediately. On August 28 he made his first appearance before the Advisory Committee: the transcript of his testimony shows that he made no effort to hide his admiration for the Reich and its Fuehrer.

> I saw Hitler twice ... Hitler is a person who has, I think, achieved very great things for the German people in many ways ... If I ever praised the Nazi regime it has always been limited to what it has accomplished for the poorer classes in Germany, on account of its economic and social work there – the Strength Through Joy movement and the Labour Camps.[29]

Nor did he deny outright MI5's evidence that he had boasted about his willingness to provide assistance to any German forces invading Britain.

> I will tell you exactly what I said. I said: 'If any parachute troops come along here, what am I to do? What I shall do is to invite them into my house and give them some beer'. It was said purely as a joke ... I told my solicitors: 'If they are frightened of me as a Quisling, the last thing I or anybody with any sense would do would be to act as a Quisling while the Germans have troops here occupying my country'. The last thing anybody with any sense would do I imagine would be to serve in a Government in a country occupied by foreign troops.[30]

It was hardly the most ringing protestation of innocence, and somewhat undermined by his appearance on Beckett's list of future leaders of exactly this sort of puppet regime. Nonetheless, the Committee accepted his word and recommended release. The proposal outraged the Security Service; its in-house lawyer, Edward Blanshard Stamp, made a succession of increasingly vehement protests.

> We have serious positive evidence of an intention on the part of Gordon-Canning to assist the enemy ... The report that he had said he would do all he could to help the Nazis and refuel or revictual a German submarine came from [REDACTED] who heard him say it in the presence only of [REDACTED]. She was examined about her statement and there is no reason to doubt the truth of what she said ...
>
> Gordon-Canning's position, his history, his wealth, his power of leadership, his known pro-Nazi views, all combine to render him a very dangerous man ... There is at least, we submit, a serious doubt as to his loyalty ... and in the existing critical state of this country, we should be failing in our duty if we did not oppose, as strongly as we can, a proposal to release a man who at least may possibly be a fifth columnist and whom we regard as such.[31]

The Committee, however, was unimpressed and, in what was to become the focus of bitter conflict with MI5, demanded to know the identity of the informant who had provided the damning evidence about German submarine crews.

> What is the proof that the 'source is most reliable'? ... Why is the Committee to accept without question the report of an [REDACTED] as against the evidence of a man whom the Committee has interviewed at length and examined about this incident? A man whose word the Committee felt could generally speaking be relied upon.
>
> Why can we not see the statement made by [REDACTED] and why can we not be told who examined her upon it and why may we not see a note of the examination? For example, if Mr Stamp himself conducted the examination I would be prepared to accept it, but I would still like to see the notes; so much depends on the type of person conducting such an examination. If it were conducted by a Detective Sergeant, I should be disinclined to attach any importance to the examination unless I knew the Detective Sergeant or was satisfied as to his ability – to say nothing of his impartiality.[32]

Disclosing the identities of informants was a red line for the Security Service and one which it was not prepared to cross. Finally, the Advisory Committee backed down, but only after being given assurances that one of the witnesses to Gordon-Canning's remarks was 'the wife of a well-known Member of Parliament'.[33] This proved, however, to be only a temporary truce, and the following August the Advisory Committee gave Gordon-Canning a second chance to request release from internment.

The transcript of this hearing shows that he remained unshaken and unapologetic in his admiration for the Third Reich. He admitted 'taking the Fascist uniform' and when asked about Germany's network of concentration camps, he remarked blandly, 'I am against the concentration camps unless of the proper class'.[34] Despite this, Birkett and his colleagues once again recommended Gordon-Canning's release.

> The Committee have most anxiously studied Gordon-Canning's character. They are of the opinion that he is a truthful man and that his statements ... should be accepted. They are indeed satisfied that he is a man of high character and sincere patriotic intentions.[35]

The Committee had also, according to its report, been swayed by letters of support that Gordon-Canning had secured from his friends among the great and good, including a peer of the realm, an MP, and the Secretary of State for War, Anthony Eden.[36]

Once again, MI5 fought back, though a remarkably frank letter from its legal section to the Home Office shows that it was beginning to realise this was a losing cause. 'It seems, at this stage, hardly worth while to attempt to clear up the question of the part played by Canning in ... obtaining subsidies for British Union from Germany', one of its lawyers, Captain S.H. Noakes, wrote on October 6:

> Other leading Fascists, such as ... Major-General Fuller, played an equally important part in British Union at that time and acted as intermediaries between British Union and Germany, but no action has been taken against these individuals ...[37]

For the moment, the dam held: Herbert Morrison rejected the Advisory Committee's recommendation and Gordon-Canning remained in detention. It is a measure both of the relatively relaxed conditions enjoyed by 18B internees, and of Gordon-Canning's connections, that in December he was able to contact and secure the tentative support of the King's younger brother, Prince Henry, Duke of Gloucester.[38]

A year later he added to this the overt backing of the Cabinet minister and Chancellor of the Duchy of Lancaster, Duff Cooper. On January 5, 1943, Cooper wrote to MI5's Director General putting the case for Gordon-Canning's release.

My reasons for doing so are first, that he is an old acquaintance of mine, in whose loyalty I believe despite his many errors. Secondly, he had, unlike Mosley, an admirable record of service in the last war, when he earned the Military Cross and the respect and affection of his brother officers ... and, so far as I am aware, he did nothing after the outbreak of worse than openly advocate a patched up peace and express the view that Germany was not more to blame than Great Britain. Many people equally guilty, such as the Duke of Bedford and General Fuller, are still at liberty ...

I feel confident that if he gave an undertaking on his word of honour to abstain from politics and from giving interviews to the press during the duration of the war and promised to live on his own estate in the country and to inform the Police whenever he left it that he would be as good as his word.[39]

Faced with this barrage of establishment special pleading, the Security Service threw in the towel. Seven months later Gordon-Canning was released from internment on condition that he did not stray outside a five-mile restriction zone placed around his country house in Gloucestershire.

There was a further reason MI5 abandoned its efforts: the previous year it had suffered a humiliating and uncomfortably public denunciation of its agents' honesty, and had thereafter given up any hope of persuading the Advisory Committee to maintain the detention of known British Nazi sympathisers. The case which caused the debacle centred on the coup plot involving the three principal officers of BCCSE – John Beckett, the Duke of Bedford, and Benjamin Greene.

The first skirmishes in what would become a protracted and bitter struggle came in July 1940, two months after Beckett and Greene were interned, when both men appeared (separately) before the Advisory Committee to contest their detention. Beckett went first on July 10. Norman Birkett put to him the reasons for his internment – that he 'had been recently concerned in acts prejudicial to the public safety and defence of the Realm, and in the preparation and instigation of such acts'. Specifically, he was accused of 'taking steps to get members of his organization in touch with members of the armed forces so that "when the time was ripe they would turn their rifles in the right direction"'. Beckett denied this, claiming that he suspected the man who had allegedly overheard the remark was an MI5 agent, who had tried to provoke him.

He also denied the second key allegation, that he 'had stated that he would like to join the local Defence Volunteers so as to obtain a rifle and ammunition ... [and] that he had reproved his associate, Ben Greene, for refusing to join the local Defence Volunteers and so obtain a rifle and ammunition'. As to the final plank of the case against him, that he had boasted of having sent the names and addresses of British Fifth Columnists to Berlin in anticipation of an imminent German invasion, Beckett admitting saying 'something like this', but argued that: 'If disapproving of the present government means you are in the fifth column, the fifth column must be a very big column indeed and I am certainly a member of it.'[40]

Birkett and his colleagues plainly found themselves torn between admiration for Beckett and a lingering suspicion that, if MI5's evidence was accurate, he might pose a very real risk. The Committee's report, on July 30, decided to hedge its bets.

The Committee considered the whole of the evidence in this case with most anxious care. They were not unimpressed by the personality of Beckett who gave his evidence in a very frank and attractive way ... [but] there can be no doubt that up to the 12th of May at least, he had been engaged in activities which were detrimental to the efficient prosecution of the war ...

The conclusion to which the Committee came was that whilst they did not regard Beckett as a highly dangerous man, or one who would willingly do injury to the country's effort, they yet felt that if they were to recommend his release, it would be done with very considerable misgiving ... [and] recommend that, in all the circumstances of the case, the detention of Beckett should continue.[41]

But it also added a substantial caveat over the reliability of MI5's written evidence detailing the reports of Maxwell Knight's undercover agents. This did not augur well for the future.

The Committee considered the evidence with regard to these allegations and Beckett's denials, and they came to the conclusion that in the circumstances it would be proper to make no conclusion adverse to Beckett on this part of the case. The evidence came from an agent who was not before the Committee and whose evidence could not be tested. In those circumstances the Committee thought it fair and right to ignore these allegations entirely.[42]

Greene's hearing, on July 23 and 24, seemed – at first glance – to go rather better for the Security Service. The Committee was less than impressed by his somewhat unreliable memory – he denied, then was forced to admit, having made pro-Nazi remarks at a public meeting – and, initially at least, it was prepared to take seriously the written statements of Knight's two agents, Harald Kurtz and Friedl Gaertner (though MI5 redacted their names and key identifying details).[43] By early August, however, it had undergone a change of heart, and sent a formal request that the Security Service produce both agents for examination. MI5 refused point blank, telling the Committee 'that it has been decided by the highest authority here that in no circumstances will we consent to agents going before the Committee'.[44]

The conflict highlighted the fatal flaw in the Advisory Committee system. Natural justice – and centuries of legal precedent – required that an accused man or woman facing contentious allegations had the right to challenge the evidence against them; that was impossible if the identity of the accuser was withheld. Weighed against this – especially in a war which threatened the country's very existence – was the practical need to safeguard the intelligence services' ability to uncover those threats. By fudging the issue, the Home Office had pushed on to the Advisory Committees the responsibility for balancing these conflicting interests and, essentially, to act as arbiters between an existential danger and a moral evil. It was an unresolved – and ultimately unresolvable – tension, and one which was guaranteed to end with either injustice or peril.

Ben Greene proved to be the case which exposed this fault-line to public view. After the Advisory Committee reluctantly endorsed his continuing detention, in March 1941 he issued a writ in the High Court for habeas corpus. This challenged the Home Secretary's right to keep him under lock and key on the basis of allegations from MI5 agents whose identity had been withheld and whose evidence he had been unable to challenge.

The case dragged on for four months until it reached the Court of Appeal. The judges there found themselves in the uncomfortable position of having to rule on the vexed questions which the Home Office had been so anxious to avoid. On July 31, *The Times* carried a detailed account of Mr Justice Scott's dismissal of Greene's writ.

The whole [18B] Regulation dealt with a topic which was necessarily of a highly confidential character; it invited a decision ... by an executive Minister of the Crown who occupied a position of utmost confidence; who had at his disposal much secret information which ought not to be made public – above all during a war; who was under a duty to keep that information and its sources secret; and finally who could not be compelled in any Court to divulge what he considered ought not, in the national interest, to be divulged. All the King's Courts recognized that inhibition and enforced it ...

He attached great importance, and he was sure the Home Secretary did also, to the most careful observance of every precaution provided by the regulation for the protection of any person detained under

Regulation 18B. The liberty of the subject was only one degree less important than the safety of the nation.[45,46]

Away from the Courts, Greene's energetic lawyer, Oswald Hickson,[47] had been pressing the Advisory Committee to divulge the identities of his accusers. MI5 once again objected forcefully, telling Birkett that 'both Kurtz and Fraulein Gaertner were still active on behalf of this office and that Fraulein Gaertner was in particular engaged in certain delicate work where there might be very serious consequences if the information reached the Germans'.*[48]

The Advisory Committee evidently heeded this warning and, initially, refused Hickson's demand. The lawyer then appealed over its head to the Attorney General and the Treasury Solicitor's department, who overruled Birkett; without warning the Security Service, Birkett duly handed over Kurtz's name and the address of his flat in Ebury Street. It was an extraordinary betrayal of trust, and one which would cause serious problems for MI5 and its agent.

Hickson asked Greene's brother, Edward, to contact Kurtz; when he did, the agent, unaware that his cover had been blown, agreed to meet for lunch at Simpson's-in-the-Strand. The meeting, on October 21, was uneventful, but just before they parted Greene sprang the trap which Hickson had planned. According to Kurtz's statement, made later the same day:

Mr Greene said that his only hope for Ben's release was now 'wire-pulling behind the scenes' and that reminded him that I might be able to help in one small point. It had been alleged that Ben had been in touch with a great many German refugees, a fact which had partly caused his detention [and that] ... there was one story in particular which the authorities had taken a grave view of. This was that

---

* Friedl Gaertner had by then joined the XX Double Agent network under the codename Gelatine (apparently because her handlers thought she was 'a jolly little thing'). But, according to her MI5 files, 'Gelatine showed very little aptitude for acquiring useful political information via her social contacts. As an agent and DA ... Gelatine's overall contribution was modest.' 'Gelatine – Double Agent'. National Archives files KV 2/1275–1280; declassified September 26, 2003.

I had introduced to Ben Greene an Austrian girl whose fiancé was still in Austria and was, therefore, in great personal distress. I had approached Ben Greene with a view to getting his help.

By this time we were walking along the Strand. I replied at once that the whole story was certainly untrue, and I had never approached Ben Greene on such a matter. About here Greene said 'Ah I see this is Surrey Street. Would you mind repeating this to my solicitor? He lives in this street.' The time was approximately 1.30 and I saw no possibility of pleading another appointment so we went to Mr Hickson's office.[49]

Once there Hickson ambushed Kurtz, accusing him of using subterfuge to secure the internment of his entirely-innocent client.

Mr Hickson's almost first words were 'Are you aware that Mr Ben Greene has been detained at Brixton Prison for 16 months on your evidence? The implication is that you are an agent provocateur'. I expressed my utter amazement and asked who alleged that I am such an agent, to which Mr Hickson replied 'From the Government'.

Mr Hickson then proceeded to read out the charges made against Mr Greene. After he had finished this I said 'I presume that the whole thing amounts to a charge of treason'. [Hickson said] 'That is so'.[50]

Kurtz was caught completely off-guard. Unsure of whether to admit to being an undercover agent, he tried to play for time by claiming he had to speak to his own solicitor: since he did not actually have any legal representation, he gave the name of a notable advocate who he had read about in the newspapers. It was a clumsy and, given the circumstances, an unfortunate lie.

Hickson then pressured Kurtz into recanting all the evidence he had given against Ben Greene, recording the *volte-face* in a new statement and setting a 72-hour deadline by which he wanted it signed, sworn and entered on the record. Its contents destroyed MI5's entire case.

Mr Kurtz denied that subsequent to the outbreak of war Mr Benjamin Greene attempted to communicate through him with persons in Germany, whom Mr Greene knew or suspected to be in association with persons concerned in the government of Germany. Mr Kurtz further denied that Mr Greene counselled, assisted, or advised him, Mr Kurtz, as to the best means of sending messages into Germany by illicit channels.

Mr Kurtz further denied that subsequent to the outbreak of war Mr Benjamin Greene endeavoured through him, Mr Kurtz, to make known his sentiments in regard to the establishment of a National Socialist regime in Great Britain to those in control of the German Government.

Further, Mr Kurtz denied that he was an agent of the German Government, or had given Mr Benjamin Greene reason to think he was an agent of the German Government or that Mr Greene had offered to assist him, Mr Kurtz, by any means in his power to avoid detention by the authorities in Great Britain, so that he, Mr Kurtz, could continue his work on behalf of Germany.[51]

MI5 reacted angrily to the incident. Guy Liddell grumbled that 'Kurtz had been lured into making a rather foolish statement' and that 'the whole matter was obviously a trick by Hickson, aided and abetted by Edward Greene'.[52] Petrie went further, sending an angry letter to the Home Office in which he denounced (evidently without irony) the use of subterfuge to entrap an undercover agent.

If Hickson had employed these tactics in judicial proceedings his conduct would have been open to very severe criticism. No doubt, however, he feels that in dealing with an 'agent' in a case of preventative detention he is justified in using methods which would certainly not commend themselves to the Courts or the Law Society.[53]

Unethical or not, Hickson used the document to put pressure on the Advisory Committee; in December it overrode MI5's objections and summoned Kurtz for examination. He was not helped by Maxwell Knight's distinctly lax methods of recording information gathered by his spies: it emerged that, despite the seriousness of the original conversations with Greene, Kurtz had not committed them to paper for days, sometimes weeks, after they happened – and then only with guidance, editing and rewriting by Knight himself.

Worse, for unexplained reasons, Kurtz had not been given the opportunity to reread his statements in advance of his evidence to the Committee; the result was that he was hazy about some of the details and misremembered others.

But it was the Hickson document which posed the greatest problems. Under cross-examination by Birkett, Kurtz essentially recanted the recantations of his original evidence which it contained, arguing that Hickson had wrung them out of him under what amounted to duress; and that he had been forced to lie to the solicitor to protect his role as an officer of the Security Service. The argument did not impress the Committee, and Birkett's ensuing report was savage.

On any view of the case Mr Kurtz was guilty of very considerable lying, and somewhat ingenious lying also ... If the practice of one's calling necessitates the habit of lying, it is not to be wondered at if the evidence one gives in grave matters is looked at with especial care. So the main allegations against Mr Greene rest on the uncorroborated evidence of a German in the employment of the Intelligence Service, who has admittedly told deliberate lies on several occasions, and most particularly to the solicitors for Ben Greene, on the essential matters in this case ...

[The Committee] formed a very favourable view of Greene himself ... and they are satisfied that he is a man of strong beliefs, but they did not believe he would say to the Committee that he would do nothing to hamper the war activities and then use the occasion of his release to do so ... Greene is entitled to be freed from charges which amount to treason, and not to labour all his life under the cloud which otherwise will remain.[54]

After delivering what amounted to a formal reprimand, Birkett added a coda in which he warned MI5 that from then on it would be expected to produce its informants for cross-examination.

The rule that only in exceptional circumstances can agents be seen and examined by the Committee is most unsatisfactory. It leads to possible injustice and places the Home Secretary in a most difficult position.[55]

The Security Service was appalled. Edward Blanshard Stamp, its in-house lawyer chiefly responsible for liaison with the Home Office and the Committee, wrote a lengthy denunciation of Birkett's behaviour – and his conclusions – for the Director General.

> The report of the Advisory Committee is the most partial document I have ever seen ... it gives altogether a false impression of the evidence, and in certain instances disregards important facts ...
>
> It is of course true that the Advisory Committee should view the evidence of an agent with some suspicion, bearing in mind the possible temptations for such a person to exaggerate or distort his evidence for the purpose of justifying his existence, but it seems to me equally necessary to regard an appellant in the same light: an appellant has not only his livelihood at stake but his freedom, and if by a lie or by a suppression or distortion he can make his case better there is every incentive to do so ...
>
> Unless Kurtz deliberately falsified the events of his interview with Greene ... or Major Knight was guilty of impropriety in exaggerating or distorting Kurtz' story to him, I do not see why very great reliance should not be paid to the written statement [Kurtz's original reports] ...
>
> Kurtz is further attacked by the Committee on the ground that in the course of his duties he made statements which were not in fact true, but this, I suppose, is an almost indispensable necessity if the agent is to have any success in his duties.
>
> Should it be held, as the Committee seem to think, that deliberate falsehoods of this type render a witness' evidence subject to suspicion, then I cannot see why any agent is worthy of belief, and the same sort of stigma must be attached not only to agents but to a great many officers of the Security Service who have to work under what is usually known as 'cover'.[56]

Sir David Petrie followed this with a strongly-worded complaint to the Home Office. He condemned the Advisory Committee's attack on Kurtz as 'grossly unfair' and argued that it reflected Birkett's prejudices rather than the evidence.

The chairmen of the Advisory Committee have repeatedly made clear that they are profoundly mistrustful of the evidence of 'agents', whether anonymous or not. Although the chairman in this case professed to understand the work carried on by Major Knight through his agents, I cannot, in the light of experience, but feel that he has failed to grasp at least some of the principles of our work and in particular of the work of secret agents ...

It does not seem to have occurred to the Advisory Committee that such officers employed on security duties often have to live a life which is a complete 'lie', but do so from the highest motives and often at the risk of their lives.[57]

Greene was released, under strict residence conditions, in January 1942; but he was not yet finished with MI5 or the Home Office. The following month he and Hickson persuaded Labour MP Richard Stokes to denounce the internment on the floor of the House of Commons, demanding an assurance from the Home Secretary 'that no persons are detained under Regulation 18B on false evidence, as in the case of Mr Benjamin Greene?'. Herbert Morrison rejected the accusation, but Stokes was after a bigger scalp.

May I ask my right hon. Friend whether it is not the fact that the evidence of the single witness against this man was admitted to be false by the man himself; and would not unfortunate detentions of this kind be avoided in the future if persons detained were told the names of the persons who give evidence when they are not members of the security police?[58]

The debate, fully reported in the next day's newspapers, severely damaged MI5's reputation and destroyed its already limited faith in the Advisory Committee's ability to balance the conflicting wartime interests of the state and the individual. As Guy Liddell noted in his journal:

The whole business of Greene shows only too clearly how hopeless it is to establish any reasonable degree of security under this quasi-legal system by which the prosecution and its witnesses are subjected to severe cross-examination whereas the word of the accused is accepted without question.[59]

From then on, barring one last legal hurrah, the Security Service would abandon its commitment to the judicial system; instead, it would direct most of its investigative efforts into an extensive and extraordinary scheme to divert British Nazi sympathisers and would-be traitors down an intelligence cul-de-sac. The operation was simultaneously technically pioneering and ethically ambiguous; and at its core was a whole-hearted embrace of *agent provocateur* techniques.

'Rosebud' and the Road to Entrapment

'We were to some extent forced to adopt these
methods because if we interned people under
18(b) ... they were almost invariably released.'
Guy Liddell, diary entry,
November 18, 1941

Irma Stapleton's handbag was suspiciously heavy. She pushed it across the table and invited her dining companion to feel it. She would not – yet – let him look inside, since the couple were waiting for the room service waiter to deliver their supper and what the bag contained was evidence of treachery.

The dinner, in Room 513 of the Cumberland Hotel opposite Marble Arch, was the third occasion on which she had met the urbane and handsome man known to her as John Brunner. He was in his early thirties, slim, his hair swept back and neatly Brylcreemed; his spoken German was impeccable, with only the barest hint of an accent – less pronounced, in fact, than Stapleton's own. It was easy for her to believe that he was a Gestapo agent working undercover in London at great personal risk.

'John Brunner' was not, however, German; nor was he a spy – at least not for the Gestapo. His real name was the Honourable John Michael Ward Bingham, and he was the raffish but slightly impoverished heir to the Barony of Clanmorris in County Mayo. He was also Maxwell Knight's deputy in the 'M.S.' section of undercover MI5 agents.*

'At the time when I first met him', Knight wrote in his internal report on the section's work, 'Mr Bingham was the art editor of the *Sunday Dispatch* ... [He] had volunteered for the Army before the outbreak of war, and had seen military service, but owing to bad defects of eye-sight he would never have been able to serve in the field ... His transfer to us was consequently arranged.'[1]

Although Bingham was married and had a young son, he had earned a reputation within MI5 as something of a Lothario, bedding his fellow agent Hélène de Munck (an unhappy liaison from her viewpoint and one which contributed to her alleged dependence on narcotics[2]). His good looks, charm and fluent German made him the ideal candidate to seduce – politically if not physically – Irma Stapleton.

She had been born in Zwickau, Saxony, on December 18, 1904. Her parents, Erich and Gertrude Troejer, were theatrical performers who toured Europe's capitals with a music hall revue of 'lightning caricatures'.

The act – billed as 'Democratus' – was evidently successful, since the Troejers could afford to send Irma to high school in Munich, then to Hamburg to learn singing and dancing, and finally on to Paris to study French. She initially joined the family business but at some point in the 1920s abandoned the stage for a job as a shipping clerk in Antwerp. It was there, in 1928, that she met Patrick Laurence Stapleton, a radio operator serving on a merchant ship. They began a relationship, married three years later and settled in England; when Patrick got a job as a wireless repair technician with EMI, the couple took out a long-term mortgage on a modest terraced house in Greenford, Middlesex.

---

* Bingham worked for MI5 for two decades and was, according to John Le Carré, one of the inspirations for his fictional spymaster, George Smiley. He became the 7th Baron Clanmorris on the death of his father in 1960.

Although Patrick was evidently devoted to Irma, whom he routinely called 'Rosebud', she was rather less starry-eyed: 'He is serving my purpose all right as regards nationality', she later told Bingham. 'I am covered. It is very convenient. No-one can touch me.'[3]

By 'covered', Stapleton was referring to a substantial hole in the regulations, imposed by the Home Office in the lead-up to war, on non-British citizens. Germans who acquired UK nationality through marriage before Hitler came to power in 1933 were exempted from the need to register as aliens and were not considered as candidates for internment: they were, to all intents and purposes, invisible.

Irma Stapleton did not, however, go completely unnoticed. Her docket in the Criminal Records Office at New Scotland Yard – No. 27140/36 – shows that between November 1936 and July 1941 she appeared before magistrates at three separate police courts to answer charges of petty theft from West End shops: for stealing a lady's hand-bag, two pairs of silk stockings and £10 in cash she was fined a total of £16[4] and placed on probation for two years.

Despite this she managed to secure a succession of clerical jobs in firms across north and west London and in 1941 she started work at Wade's Chain Works in Ealing, which had contracts to produce Oerlikon anti-aircraft shells for the Admiralty. Here she met and befriended Helmut Eduard Husgen, a fellow exile from Germany.

At 27, Husgen was ten years Stapleton's junior, but he had crammed a great deal into his young life. After leaving school he had worked, variously, as a mechanic and government clerk in Koblenz; in parallel to this humdrum daily life, he had also been a Storm Trooper with the Sturmabteilung (SA), the original paramilitary wing of the Nazi Party, before moving on to work for the Gestapo. He fled to England in May 1937 after badly injuring a man in a café brawl.

Given his clear Nazi background, Husgen should have been a strong candidate for automatic internment on the outbreak of war. His MI5 file – original reference PF 45663 – has either been destroyed or remains withheld from public scrutiny; there is no trace of it in the National Archives, only a Home Office record of his post-war naturalisation as a British citizen.[5] But it is clear that by the time Stapleton met him, he was one of Maxwell Knight's collection of occasional informants; this may explain his reprieve from preventative detention.

In early November 1941, Stapleton confided in Husgen – who, by implication, had told her about his Gestapo connections – that she had previously worked for the German Embassy, and that just before the outbreak of war she had been ordered to stay on as a sleeper agent in England. Now she wanted 'to place her services at the disposal of the German Reich for purposes of espionage, sabotage and occasional political assassination. Her motive ... was pure idealism.'[6] He played along, saying 'that her offer would be referred to Berlin for approval'.

That approval – emanating from Knight's offices in Dolphin Square rather than Prinz-Albrechtstrasse in Berlin – followed swiftly. On November 10, Husgen met Stapleton at the Café Royal on Regent Street, and introduced her to his supposed boss in the German Intelligence Service, 'John Brunner'. According to Bingham's account of the meeting, she reaffirmed her desire to serve the Reich.

> Stapleton at once expressed her eagerness to help the German cause, pointing out that for two years she had been hiding her true feelings behind a façade of patriotism for this country. She said that she was known among neighbours and workmates as a most loyal subject and an enthusiastic fire-watcher, and had, in fact, a perfect cover.[7]

MI5's initial intention was to discover the names of any other stay-behind agents who were working with Stapleton – a suspicion provoked by the fact that she had once briefly worked for Siemens Schuckert Ltd, known to have been a significant component in the Nazi intelligence network in Britain. With this in mind, Bingham arranged a second rendezvous – an intimate dinner in a private suite at the Cumberland Hotel – and Post Office engineers installed covert microphones to relay the conversation to Special Branch officers in an adjoining room. On November 14 the two took supper in 'an atmosphere of considerable cordiality' in Room 513. The shorthand transcript of that meeting[8] shows that although Stapleton was unable to provide any names of German agents, she was determined to volunteer her own services, whatever the cost.

I know what it means. It means my life blood ... if you start working for the German Secret Service [there] are mighty risks. Our soldiers are taking grave [risks] and I think it is the least we can do ...

It is in the blood. It is just a question of loving my country and I would do anything for Germany against this lot here ... I am all consumed with hatred. My marriage has been an absolute failure ... my dear husband called me several little horrible names and I swear definitely to have my own back. I tell you frankly that I am not stopping at murder ...[9]

When Bingham asked her to confirm for the record that she was willing to work for the German Secret Service she said, 'Oh yes ! ... I shall never disobey any instructions. Yes. Discipline – that is the way I have been brought up. It is a quality lacking in this country.' She then suggested she could sabotage the production of shells at Wade's Chain Works.

Why not do a little bit at the machines to hold them back ... It is not difficult. Every little bit helps ... and I could throw in a chuck or something. It would stop work for an hour.[10]

Bingham's sting was working well but, in an error which typified the sloppy nature of Knight's undercover operations, he had forgotten to bring with him a typed questionnaire – supposedly produced by his masters in the Gestapo – on which Stapleton was to state exactly how far she was willing to go. Undeterred, he wrote it out, longhand, over supper; as she filled in the blank spaces, she suggested an additional way to serve the German cause.

In order to cope with several of the points on the questionnaire, Stapleton offered to steal an Oerlikon shell, magnanimously stating, indeed, that she could steal dozens if so desired.[11]

Bingham readily agreed to the proposal, and arranged to meet Stapleton at the same time and location the following week. Before they parted he offered to pay her expenses – a suggestion she refused, insisting that her actions were 'absolutely idealistic'.

The Stapleton operation unequivocally involved an element of entrapment, and was the cause of some discussion within MI5. On November 18, Guy Liddell recorded this concern in his journal.

> We had a Directors' meeting and I raised the question of Irma Stapleton. From the transcript notes taken by mike [*sic*] of her last interview with John Bingham, posing as a representative of the German Secret Service, there seemed no doubt that she was prepared to go to any lengths and that she could quite easily bring out a whole shell from the factory where she works. She has swallowed our bait hook, line and sinker. If we went on with the case there seemed little doubt that we could get her seven years' at the Old Bailey.[12]

This meeting took place in the same week that Ben Greene appeared before the Advisory Committee and as the Security Service braced itself for Birkett's inevitable attack on Harald Kurtz and the *agent provocateur* methods he had been ordered to employ. Liddell, however, was in no doubt where the blame for this lay.

> We were to some extent forced to adopt these methods because if we interned people under 18(b) because we felt they were a potential danger they were almost invariably released.
>
> There are various other arguments, namely that it has in the past been said about people that we intern under 18B that if our facts were as stated we should have prosecuted. It is also for consideration whether some use could be made of this case in the coming debate in the House on 18B. The public and MPs are generally rather reluctant to believe that such people as Irma Stapleton exist.[13]

The following day – just hours before the proposed third rendezvous at the Cumberland Hotel – Sir David Petrie decided to remove the case from Knight's control, handing it over to the Deputy Director General of MI5, Oswald Harker. He also enlisted the support of the Director of Public Prosecutions, securing an undertaking that if Stapleton did, as she had promised, give Bingham an Oerlikon shell, he would sanction a criminal trial.

At nine o'clock that evening Stapleton arrived for another intimate supper in Room 513; as before, a Special Branch officer was installed in an adjoining room and listened in on headphones connected to the concealed microphones. There is no transcript of the conversation in Stapleton's MI5 file, but a report by Bingham detailed what was said.

> The first thing she did was to ask me to feel her handbag. I said it felt suspiciously heavy and she laughed. I concluded that it contained shells and she suggested that we should not examine them until later lest we should be disturbed by the waiter ...
>
> I asked her whether she had had any difficulty in obtaining them [the shells] and she said ... that she had 'pinched the lot' and that she had put the shell up her sleeve and later into her handbag.

Stapleton went on to explain that Wade's produced between 25,000 and 35,000 shells a week, and handed over production plans to accompany the shells. Shortly afterwards, at 10.00pm, the Special Branch inspector walked in and arrested her.

Bingham was plainly delighted and championed the effectiveness of the sting operation in his report:

> Had the initial causes for investigation not been so clear-cut, and had purely formal police inquiries been made amongst this miserable woman's neighbours, workmates, and employers, there seems not the slightest doubt that the resulting picture would have been one of an intensely loyal, patriotic, hardworking woman, sacrificing her leisure in fire-watching, and longing for the day of Hitler's defeat.[14]

Liddell, however, remained more sceptical, sending a cautious memo to Petrie the next day.

> As stated at the Director's meeting yesterday, I rather wonder how far it is worthwhile to have a full dress party with this woman and get her 7 years at the Old Bailey. If the trial was going to be a public one

there might be something to be gained but since this is impossible it would save an immense amount of trouble if the woman could just be interned under 18B.

What to some extent leads us to the methods we are now employing is our lack of confidence in the Advisory Committee, although I do not think that if they accepted these transcribed notes they could possibly recommend her release.[15]

In the end, MI5 had its 'full dress party': on Thursday, February 5, 1942, Stapleton appeared in the dock at the Old Bailey, charged with four counts of 'doing an act with intent to assist the enemy'. Over a four-day trial held, inevitably, *in camera*, Bingham gave evidence and presented the transcripts of his meetings with her.

Husgen did not testify, an internal Security Service memo having noted that 'it would ... be rather awkward if our principal witness was a German, late Gestapo. The fact might not emerge, but if it did it would certainly create a great deal of prejudice.'[16]

Stapleton's defence called no witnesses but she gave evidence on her own behalf, claiming that far from being a traitor, she had been trying to entrap 'Brunner', whom she knew to be a Gestapo agent; and that she had planned to turn him over to the police as soon as she secured enough evidence. It was the same defence that George Armstrong had attempted and it met with a similar lack of success: on February 9 she was convicted on all counts. In sentencing her to ten years' penal servitude, Mr Justice Hallet told her: 'They are extremely serious charges ... In the country whose interests you serve, such charges would be punished by death.'

There was a sad little coda to the proceedings: as warders led Irma Stapleton from the dock, her husband ran down towards her from the spectators' gallery, shouting, 'I don't believe you are guilty, Irma. You are not guilty in my eyes.'[17,18]

The verdict and sentence came as some relief to MI5. It arrived less than a week after the Service had been savaged in the House of Commons over the Ben Greene debacle, and the fulsome reports in the national press helped restore a little of its lost prestige. On February 12, Petrie sent a letter to Lord Swinton, head of the Security Executive, highlighting the success and contrasting it with the way undercover agents had been treated by the Advisory Committee.

> So far as I can judge, we seem to fare much better before the Courts of Law than before the Committees. The reason may be that testimony can usually be given as to acts done, instead of as to the precise words used in conversations which may have taken place quite a long time before.[19]

Within Whitehall, however, the entrapment tactics used by Maxwell Knight's section were already causing unease – concern which was shared by, and would soon lead to a schism within, the Service's own ranks. The row had begun in September 1941, when Knight sent Marjorie Amor – alias Agent M/Y – to conduct an undercover sting operation on a vicar in Bristol.

The Reverend Henry Dymock was an unapologetic fascist who had regularly used his pulpit at St Bede's church (as well as the pages of the BUF newspaper, *Blackshirt*) to peddle vehemently anti-Semitic rhetoric. Local police had attempted to investigate, with a view to having the 62-year-old priest interned, but when this failed to produce results, they sought help from MI5. According to Liddell's diary, Amor was duly instructed to approach Dymock and tempt him to incriminate himself.

> She provoked the old man by suggesting that they should compile a seditious pamphlet and circulate it secretly. She also hinted that in time of invasion there might be a possibility of cutting up telephone wires and blowing up bridges. She got quite a strong reaction and in the course of conversation ... it emerged that Dymock had a number of Fascist uniforms concealed on church property so the police decided to search. The uniforms were discovered and the Regional Commissioner made an order for internment and submitted it for confirmation to the Home Office.
>
> M/Y had arranged a special code and pseudonym for corresponding with Dymock before his arrest. He got frightened when she sent him a telegram and gave a copy of it to the police saying that he knew

nothing about its contents or the sender. In the meantime, he telephoned to M/Y instructing her not to come near him.[20]

Dymock's anti-Jewish rants were unquestionably vile, and the fascist uniforms concealed in his church suggested that he might be willing to break the law banning the wearing of them in public;* neither, however, was justification for the entrapment scheme Knight had devised, and the Home Office mandarin Frank Newsam was appalled, roundly denouncing 'the agent provocateur methods of MI5'. In this, he was not alone: Gonne St Clair 'Toby' Pilcher, a barrister in MI5's legal section who more usually despaired at Newsam's habitual intransigence, argued with Liddell 'about the lengths to which provocation should go, and [said] he thought that there was a limit'.

Liddell agreed in principle, but maintained that Dymock had hidden the uniforms long before Mrs Amor's attempt to entrap him; he also decided that the specific wartime threat posed by pro-Nazi British fascists required MI5 to set aside legal qualms over *agent provocateur* tactics to ensure the defence of the Realm.

> I put up a strong minute to Director-General saying that if these methods cannot be employed to investigate the Fifth Column field we cannot be responsible for its investigation at all. Quite clearly, the ordinary methods will lead us nowhere, and it is clearly part of our duty to find out exactly where doubtful elements would stand in time of invasion. This can only be achieved by provocation.[21]

Against this backdrop, and despite the successful resolution of the Stapleton case, the use of entrapment and the public criticism which followed the Greene saga led to significant changes in the Security Service's investigation of domestic Nazi sympathisers. Together they marked the end of Maxwell Knight's hegemony over undercover operations: from the start of 1942 he became an increasingly isolated figure

---

* The Public Order Act 1936 banned the wearing of political uniforms 'in any public place'.

and before long would be accused by his own staff of 'going slightly fascist'.[22]

Rather than putting a stop to his much-criticised methods, however, MI5 decided to embrace them wholeheartedly (albeit without Knight's involvement). Although Hinchley-Cooke continued to pursue clear-cut cases of espionage, Irma Stapleton's conviction was the last attempt by the Security Services to use the courts or 18B internment to fight the Fifth Column. Instead, it embarked on an elaborate scheme to lure Nazi sympathisers and would-be traitors into an intelligence cul-de-sac – one which required neither Home Office approval nor the *post-facto* blessings of a successful trial. According to Liddell's journal, the plan was hatched in March 1942.

> Victor Rothschild has brought me a scheme by which Jack [Bingham – though possibly 'King': the entry is ambiguous] is to organise the Fifth Column as an agent of the Gestapo. His various friends and connections naturally look to him to give them a lead. It seems that certain of them already know about the invasion list* and if and when the time comes they do not propose to be just where the police can find them.
>
> It may therefore be a good thing to get them organised so that we know where to put our fingers on them. A difficulty arises over the Home Office Order since it will be based solely on the information of one informant. They will have to face up to this if we are to go on with the scheme.[23]

Victor Rothschild was then, in theory, head of the Service's counter-sabotage section, BI(c), and had distinguished himself by defusing unexploded bombs. There is no indication in any publicly available file that his audacious plan was ever discussed with the Home Office; there is, however, clear evidence that it was quickly taken out of the hands of Bingham and – by extension – Maxwell Knight. Instead, Rothschild and Liddell cast about for a reliable agent to embark on a long-term

---

* The register of pro-Nazi British fascists and fellow-travellers who were to be arrested before German troops landed.

undercover mission. They quickly settled on the officer who had proved his ability to impersonate a Gestapo officer during the entrapment of Gunner Philip Jackson.

Eric Arthur Roberts was a most unlikely spy. To his neighbours in the modest street of 1930s semi-detached houses at Tattenham Corner in Epsom, he was an unassuming father of two young daughters, who had worked as a clerk for the Westminster Bank since leaving school at the age of eighteen. In May 1940 he was 33 years old and awaiting an imminent call-up to military service.

But beneath his rather dull image as a middle-class suburban pen-pusher, Eric Roberts had been living a double life for more than a decade. In 1924 he had joined the British Fascisti, where he was recruited by Maxwell Knight to infiltrate the Communist Party. On Knight's instructions, Roberts went on to join the BUF and to feed scraps of intelligence on the fascist movement back to MI5. He also took regular holidays – including his honeymoon – in Germany, providing reports on conditions in the Reich. He did this work largely unpaid, receiving only a token emolument of £1 per week but, according to Knight's biographers, with some success.[24] In spring 1940, with a German invasion expected within weeks, the Security Service's budget expanded sufficiently to take him on as a full-time agent. An internal note on May 31 set out the proposal:

> Roberts is thoroughly familiar with everything connected with the various pro-Nazi organisations in this country and Maxwell Knight has the highest opinion of his character and abilities.
>
> As the sudden increase in the volume of B.7. work has created a very serious situation I should be very grateful if steps could be taken immediately to procure Roberts' transfer from the Bank to this office. Roberts has stated that he will be called up in October and the Bank would in that case be paying the difference between his army pay and his normal salary.[25]

On June 8, Harker wrote to the Westminster Bank's head office, asking for Roberts to be 'spared to my organisation for the duration of the war'. The approach evidently baffled his employers: in a letter three days later, the bank's Assistant Controller agreed to the request, but gently queried whether MI5 was sure it had the right man.

> If the Bank were satisfied that the release of Mr Roberts were of real national advantage they would release him at once ... However, what we would like to know here is – what are the particular and especial qualifications of Mr Roberts – which we have not been able to perceive – for some particular work of national importance which would take him away from his normal military call-up in October.[26]

Roberts formally joined MI5 as a salaried officer on July 4. He was assigned to Knight's 'M.S.' stable and was one of the undercover agents placed inside the outer circles of Archibald Ramsay's Right Club, before winning plaudits for the quiet efficiency of his work in the Jackson investigation.

But his major mission began in March 1941: under the direction of Lord Rothschild and his assistant, Theresa Clay,* Roberts was given a new identity – 'Jack King' – together with a cover story as a 'stay-behind' agent and recruiter for the Gestapo. His orders were to locate and befriend German sympathisers who 'might be capable of forming a fascist 5th Column'[27] in Britain. It was an extraordinary, daring and extended operation, involving fake identity cards, bogus NSDAP medals and the most technically advanced intelligence-gathering methods yet deployed by MI5. Over almost three years 'Jack King' would uncover 'scores and probably ... hundreds' of domestic Nazi supporters.[28]

From the outset there was never any intention of mounting prosecutions or of seeking their internment; instead MI5 would defuse – 'canalise' in the Security Service's jargon – their repeated attempts to smuggle some of Britain's most secret military information to Berlin. And it began with a lonely-hearts advertisement.

---

* Theresa Clay was a celebrated entomologist and world expert on the *Mallophaga* species of chewing lice. She was introduced to Rothschild by their mutual friend (and Clay's alleged lover), the First World War intelligence agent Richard Meinertzhagen.

CHAPTER NINETEEN

Dorothy, Dormouse
and Jack

'No-one suspects Dorothy of being an agent for the British
Secret Service, the fear which is constantly in the minds of all
Nazi sympathisers, because she is so stupid and so obvious.'
MI5 report on 'Plan Dorothy', November 19, 1941

Dorothy Wegener was 35 years old, single and lonely.

In the summer of 1940 she was living alone in Kent, a long way from the comfortable London house she once shared with her brother, and nervous exhaustion had taken its toll on her small blouse-making business. In the hope of finding a future husband, she had joined a correspondence club.

Her five-shilling annual subscription provided her with the names and addresses of five possible partners: each claimed to be looking for a wife, though since at least one was already married they were probably seeking rather more physical – and temporary – solace. The fourth man she corresponded with was seemingly interested in a platonic friendship, but he recommended her to a friend of his: Jack King, a London-based businessman who travelled extensively throughout the home counties.

Over a period of three months Dorothy Wegener and Jack King corresponded regularly, initially sharing their reactions to the Luftwaffe's air raids; Dorothy confided that she 'had some very narrow escapes and suffered very severe shocks' and found the bombing 'too terrible for words'.

It was King who first broached the subject of anti-Semitism. ''The firm for which I work is owned by Jews', he told her in an early letter, 'and sometimes when I have time to think I remember what one hears about them.' She responded positively:

> From the contents of your letter, I assume that you do not like Jews. Well, neither do I. What I do so dislike about them is the way in which they exploit people ... you can feel very proud of your dislike ... for it only goes to prove the keen sense of proportion you must have over things ... To be absolutely frank, I utterly loathe and detest them, and I feel more than certain that the Jews and nobody else are responsible for this war. If England had not had such an influx of Jewish refugees, she would not have entered this war.[1]

As the letters passed back and forth, their tone grew ever more anti-Semitic and Dorothy became openly pro-Nazi.

> Why Germany and England must always be at loggerheads is beyond me ... You are quite right when you say you doubt the alleged ill-treatment of the Jews in Germany, for it was not as we were made to believe.
>
> What your German friend said about the leaders of Germany is quite right and if only common sense had prevailed here, this awful war would never have taken place. But there is not the slightest doubt this war was made for the last stand for Jewish Capitalism and Imperialism. Sometimes I think that the British Empire is in pawn to the Jews. I know only too well how they exploited Germany to the utmost degree ...[2]

By September 1940, Dorothy Wegener and Jack King had still not met in person. Their letters had, though, taken on a more intimate tone and it was plain that she was becoming attached to her pen pal; the time was fast approaching when a romantic rendezvous was inevitable. This, however, posed something of a problem, since 'Jack King' did not exist; in reality he was an undercover agent for MI5, and his interest was not in Dorothy, but in her younger brother.

*

Walter Ernest Oscar Wegener had been on the Security Service radar since the beginning of the war. On September 28, 1939, an inform-ant told Special Branch officers at New Scotland Yard that 'Wegener had pronounced Nazi sympathies, had gloated over the sinking of HMS *Courageous*,* and was visited by people who appeared to him to be typical Nazi Party members'.[3]

The report was typical of the thousands of vague (and often inac-curate) allegations passed to the police by members of the public in the first weeks of war; two points, however, caught MI5's attention. The first was that Wegener, although born in London, was half-German; his father, Hermann, was a Berlin hairdresser who had arrived in England in 1900, married a London woman, Maud Landon, and set up business as a barber in the City. He had, though, not taken British nationality – an omission that ensured he was interned during the First World War, and which his children repeated; both Walter and Dorothy had German passports, issued by the Reich's Embassy in Carlton House Terrace.

But it was Walter Wegener's place of employment which most interested the Security Service. After spending three years teach-ing English in Germany – where, according to a subsequent report, he was recruited by the Abwehr[4] – in 1938 he had joined Siemens Schuckert Ltd as a clerk in its sales department. Since this was – in the words of an MI5 report – part of 'a vast espionage organisation for the German Government' encompassing 'the distribution of pro-Nazi propaganda ... the organisation of fifth column activities ... espionage regarding armament programmes, [and] the setting up

---

* HMS *Courageous* was a 'hunter-killer' cruiser. On September 17, 1939 she was on patrol off the west coast of Ireland when she was torpedoed by U-boat U-29, and sank within twenty minutes. Her captain and 518 crew members died.

and servicing of illicit wireless stations',[5] Wegener potentially posed a danger and, more importantly, might provide an opportunity to penetrate the company.

On October 23, the Home Office granted a warrant for the interception of mail to and from his home in the south London suburb of Thornton Heath. If this revealed any evidence of spying it has been removed from his heavily-weeded MI5 file in the National Archives; it did, however, reveal that he shared the pleasant, double-fronted detached house in Brigstock Road with his sister – and that she was seeking companionship through the correspondence club.

There is no indication in Wegener's file which branch of MI5 concocted the plan to target Dorothy as a means of investigating Walter, but what followed bears all the hallmarks of Maxwell Knight's section. These shabby, ill-thought-out and deeply unethical beginnings of the 'Jack King' entrapment scheme may also explain why the Security Service file on Dorothy Wegener – PF 55495 in its Registry – has either been destroyed or withheld. Fragments, however, remain in the declassified dossiers on subjects of the later – and much better-run – operations; they show that MI5 investigated each of Dorothy's pen-pals before settling on the (unnamed) fourth correspondent and asking him to recommend his 'friend' to Dorothy.

When it finally became unavoidable, the prospect of a meeting between the two posed a substantial hurdle. Whoever the letter-writing 'Jack King' was (his identity has never been revealed), he was apparently entirely unsuitable to play the role, in person, of an anti-Semitic, British pro-Nazi. According to a contemporaneous note in the Service's files:

It was decided that Jack King himself would not be able to meet Dorothy, being too busy in his job and not being trained, and it was therefore decided to substitute a trained agent, 'Jack King', for the meetings. This caused one difficulty which had not previously been foreseen. Jack King had written letters to Dorothy in his own handwriting, but when it was realised that 'Jack King' would have to attend the meetings, some time before the meeting was arranged to take place, King hurt his hand, and had to type his letters. At the present moment 'Jack King' is learning to copy King's signature, but it is evident that at any moment this may cause serious difficulties.[6]

The new 'Jack King', so assiduously learning to imitate his predecessor's signature, was Eric Roberts, then still working in Knight's branch. By the time he was brought into the case Walter Wegener had been interned, for 'hostile associations' with Nazi officials, on the Isle of Man,[7] and Dorothy had moved from London to Kent. Despite this, King was tasked with posing as a would-be conduit to German Intelligence in the hope of uncovering stay-behind agents sheltering inside Siemens.

> We often thought that an organisation like Siemens Schuckert (Great Britain) Ltd, which had been so well organised before the war, might perhaps have left some form of Kriegsnetz* behind. For this purpose, Jack King frequently told Dorothy that although he was most anxious to help the Germans in every way and really would do anything, he was completely impotent because he did not know what to do now or how to get in touch with anybody who might advise on this point.[8]

It did not take him long – 'one or two meetings', according to MI5's memorandum – to determine that while she was unquestionably anti-Semitic and instinctively pro-German, it was 'very doubtful' that Dorothy knew any genuine Abwehr agents, and she posed no real threat to security.

> It became evident that she herself was not a dangerous person in the sense of actively helping the enemy now, and we were not and are not particularly interested in her, though she has of course been placed on the Invasion List because in those circumstances she would be only too pleased to assist the enemy in every possible way. She has, in fact, announced her intention of hoisting a Nazi flag on her house when the German troops get near ...[9]

---

* Before the outbreak of war the Abwehr had created a number of Kriegsorganisationen, known as KO for short, which were branch offices of the German Secret Service located in countries expected to remain neutral. Kriegsnetz was the term for its sub-branches.

Despite this, 'King's' superiors decided to step up the *agent provocateur* plan. In the summer of 1941 he was provided with the blueprints – ostensibly stolen from one of the companies he visited, but in reality handed over by MI5 – for a secret new tank, then under development by the Army. He was ordered to give them to Dorothy, and to ask her to think of a method of sending them to Berlin. It was naked entrapment and, on the evidence of MI5's own reports, a task so completely beyond its target's capabilities that 'King' had to feign anger at her incompetence.

> Dorothy has found considerable difficulty in doing this and on occasion Jack has become rather annoyed, feeling that although he has taken considerable risk for the sake of the Fatherland, nothing ever seems to come of it.[10]

At King's behest, she hid the plans in 'a container in the middle of a large pot of marmalade'. She was still unable to think of how to smuggle them out of the country but, to MI5's evident satisfaction, suggested that she ask Walter on her next visit to him on the Isle of Man. 'Dorothy ... is going to ask his advice as to the best way of getting the tank plan to the enemy', the burgeoning reports on the Wegeners recorded.

The faintly hare-brained scheme appears not to have yielded any tangible results; it did, however, open up a new line of enquiry.

MI5 had long harboured suspicions that security in the internment camps was slack, and that pro-Nazi Fifth Columnists detained there were able to send intelligence out to the German Secret Service. In October 1941, a request from Wegener seemed to confirm this, and to offer the prospect of uncovering those responsible. Guy Liddell noted the news in his journal.

> There has been an interesting development in the Dorothy case. Her brother has asked us to supply him with a small American wireless set. This is to be passed into I.O.M. camps at the bottom of a tin of biscuits. If such a thing is possible it discloses considerable laxity. It is also quite certain that letters are going in and out uncensored, since Dorothy took out three for her brother in the lining of her coat.[11]

The plan was complex, requiring the cooperation of both the military authority in charge of the camp, and the local Manx police force; initially, at least, Sir David Petrie refused to give it his blessing. On December 2, Liddell recorded the Director General's intransigence:

> He has made up his mind that there is nothing to be gained by allowing the wireless set to go in in the biscuit tin, since Walter Wegener was already interned. I tried to explain that the project had a definite intelligence value.
>
> If Walter started to transmit we hoped to learn firstly whether there was any subversive organisation among the internees in the Isle of Man and secondly whether Wegener would communicate to the Germans that certain of his former collaborators in Siemens Schuckerts were now at large and could be made use of. The Director-General felt that if Wegener used the set he would ultimately have to be arrested and that our connivance in the whole matter would then come out.[12]

Liddell, however, was not deterred. Two days later he convinced Petrie to sanction the scheme, and by February 1942 'Operation Quasi-Dormouse' (the inexplicably obscure codename given to the plan) had succeeded in getting the wireless into Peel Camp on the Isle of Man. There remained, however, an additional problem: since the set ostensibly originated from representatives of German Intelligence, it should have been accompanied by an encryption code and a specific frequency on which Wegener was to transmit information.

MI5 knew that these were some of the Abwehr's most closely guarded secrets and would not have been provided to a stay-behind agent, much less passed on by the planned intermediary, Dorothy Wegener. It was, as Liddell noted, 'difficult to make the scheme plausible'. More fundamentally still, there was absolutely no evidence of Walter Wegener using the set he had been given. 'We have had a van working in the vicinity but he has so far not been picked up', Liddell reported on February 14.[13]

There is no indication in Wegener's surviving files that he ever used the wireless set, or that he sent messages to Germany from the Isle of Man. Whether he was an active agent or, more probably, one who was abandoned by the Abwehr, there remained sufficient suspicion about his sympathies for even the liberal-minded Advisory Committee to deny both of his applications for release.

The first hearing elicited from him an admission that 'I am pro-German in view of my connections', and that if asked to choose between Germany and Britain, 'I should find it exceedingly difficult'.[14] The Committee's second report, in July 1942, was unusually harsh in its verdict.

> The Committee were unable to escape the conclusion that Wegener was potentially a dangerous man whose continued detention was necessary ... The result of the examination was that a strong suspicion was left in the mind of the Committee that, in fact, Wegener was a whole-hearted Nazi, that he was well aware before the war started that the London centre of Siemens Schuckert was an espionage centre, that he had deliberately spread Nazi propaganda, and that he was not averse from doing other work for Germany, if suitable opportunity arose.[15]

There were no such reasonable grounds for suspecting Dorothy Wegener of working on behalf of Germany; but MI5 decided that her growing attachment to 'Jack King' could be exploited to yield introductions to those who were – or who, at least, wanted to.

> Dorothy is not an intelligent woman, nor a trained German agent, and the approach has therefore been much easier and progress much quicker than would have been the case if she had been a trained agent whose suspicions might easily have been aroused.
>
> No action is contemplated against Dorothy for her treachery, as it is obvious that she has been provoked. She is merely being used as a channel through which contact can be made with other Nazi sympathisers and through which it is hoped that contact with real agents may be effected.
>
> The satisfactory feature of this set up is that no-one suspects Dorothy of being an agent for the British Secret Service, the fear which is constantly in the minds of all Nazi sympathisers, because

she is so stupid and so obvious. On the other hand, Jack King can put ideas and queries into her mind which she, in her own suitable way can [use to] deal with stickier and more experienced Nazi sympathisers with whom she comes into contact.[16]

The Security Service evidently realised the cynical and deeply amoral deception on which 'Plan Dorothy' (as Liddell described it) depended. An internal file note warned of the inevitable consequences:

Dorothy is a neurotic and lonely woman who has unfortunately become much attached to King. It is obvious that at some future date their relationship will have to be severed and we do not want to do this in a way which will cause her unnecessary distress.

But however unethical, the scheme began to produce results. By the end of 1941, Dorothy had introduced King to an ever-widening circle of British Nazi sympathisers, vouching for him as an undercover agent 'most anxious to help the Germans in every way'.[17] One of these contacts would shortly become the central figure in what MI5's Registry filed as 'The S.R. Case' – Victor Rothschild's extraordinary and ambitious plan to set up an entirely fictional London 'cell' of the Gestapo, and to lure into it would-be spies, saboteurs and traitors.

We know relatively little about Mary Marita Margaret Perigoe. Her original Security Service file was, for unexplained reasons at an unstated date, destroyed, and the version of its contents made public in 2014 was reconstituted from a poor-quality microfiche, with many of the documents removed.[18] This shows that she was originally Swedish or German-Swedish – her maiden name was Brahe – and at some point during the 1930s she married Bernard Perigoe, a former communist who had joined Mosley's BUF.[19]

According to a description of her, based on reports by Eric Roberts (in his adopted role as 'Jack King'), she was 'not a neurotic nor feminine type; she is a masterful and somewhat masculine woman. Both in appearance and mentality she can be described as a typical arrogant Hun.' She was also 'violently anti-British and ... anxious to do anything in her power to help the enemy', and was contemptuous of mainstream domestic fascism.

She despises the BUF and without any advice from Jack came to the conclusion that somebody who really wanted to help Germany should have little to do with them. Her reasons were sensible. She realised that the BUF has many stupid and unreliable though occasionally dangerous persons within it. She found to her surprise that even members of the BUF had some sort of loyalty to this country on occasions, and for this reason she could not trust them completely.

At the same time she believed that the BUF, the Duke of Bedford's group, Ackworth's group,* Jehovah's Witnesses** and other Fascist or quasi-Fascist and pacifist organisations represented nuclei of subversion and disloyalty within this country and might therefore be of use to the enemy.[20]

When 'King' was first introduced to Marita Perigoe, it was clear that she was a very different prospect to Dorothy Wegener.

This crafty and dangerous woman seemed of such interest that it was decided to pay a good deal more attention to her ... A woman of this type, with so much misdirected ingenuity, might do great harm to the security and war effort of this country, unless she were controlled.

But she also offered the prospect of access to a wider group of potentially dangerous pro-Nazis than either Dorothy or Walter Wegener.

Someone like Marita would clearly have friends with similar disloyal sympathies ... From a knowledge of conditions in other countries attacked by Germany, we considered it possible that there might be a significant number of persons in this country who, though not in touch with the German Secret Service, might be willing to help the

---

* Captain Bernard Ackworth ran the Liberty Restoration League, a front group for the Nordic League. 'Disturbances 1933–1943: Liberty Restoration League'. National Archives file HO 144/21823; declassified January 1, 2004. In May 1939, Leigh Vaughan-Henry spoke at one of its meetings.
** During the Second World War Jehovah's Witnesses were interned, due to their refusal to bear arms. 'Internment of Jehovah's Witnesses'. National Archives file HO 213/2373.

enemy in time of invasion. We were particularly thinking of persons
who might give food, hiding and lodging to parachute troops and
invading forces in general. Such people were of use to the Germans in
invaded countries. We thought that through Marita we might find out
whether such persons existed in the U.K. If they did, arrangements
could be made for their neutralisation.[21]

Unfortunately, Perigoe was also a great deal less gullible than the
Wegeners; to allay her instinctive suspicions and develop her as a viable
source of information, MI5 had to radically restructure the entire 'Jack
King' operation.

Jack's role with the employees of Siemens Schuckert (G.B.) Ltd was
that of a disloyal Englishman anxious to help the enemy but not knowing how ... Marita ... was found to be a very different proposition, and
it was decided that Jack would have to change his role.

Bearing in mind the general dangers of provocation techniques
and the bad psychological effects that certain unfortunate episodes in
another case have had on MI5 agents who are now nervous of being
accused of being agents provocateurs it was decided at the start to
obviate any possibility of this accusation by the following method.

Jack, after weeks of cautious preparation, stated that he was an
English representative of the Gestapo. He said that he was not a representative of the German Secret Service, which is concerned with
the acquisition of intelligence, and he was not interested in espionage
nor sabotage. His job in this country was to check up on persons who
might be loyal to the Fatherland.

On instructions from Head Office, he had carefully avoided any
suggestion that Marita or other persons with whom she is in touch
should engage in espionage, as it was not his job. All he requested was
the names of persons who were believed to be a hundred per cent loyal
to the Fatherland; he would relay these names to Germany for use in
time of invasion, particularly from the point of view of giving food,
lodging and hiding to invading forces.

Although this was satisfactory for MI5, in that we could never be
accused of provocation, it had disadvantages. One person in touch

with the Duke of Bedford's group pointed out to Marita that the technique employed by Jack, as if he were a Gestapo agent, was exactly the technique that an MI5 agent would use. An MI5 agent would dissuade persons who were loyal to the Fatherland from committing any acts which might endanger the security of this country, though at the same time such an agent would attempt to find out who <u>was</u> disloyal, with a view to interning them in time of emergency.[22]

Internment proceedings were, however, never considered as an option in Jack King's undercover activities. From the outset, and with the experience of the Harald Kurtz debacle uppermost in his mind, Victor Rothschild designed the operation specifically to bypass the courts and the Home Office. Rather than collecting evidence to be used in a prosecution, or before the Advisory Committee, Eric Roberts was instructed that in his role as Jack King he was to 'canalise' the information given to him by his targets.

The logic behind this was straightforward and pragmatic. Perigoe and her friends were so determined to aid the German cause that they would, so Rothschild reasoned, eventually find a way to send information to Berlin; if Jack King could convince them that he was a genuine Gestapo agent, he could divert this flow of dangerous intelligence safely into the arms of MI5.

Rothschild was considerably more meticulous than any previous agent-runner inside MI5. To support King's new 'legend', or cover story, the Security Service's in-house document forgers created an exact copy of a genuine Gestapo green membership card; the resulting document – Durchlaßschein No. L 2/033 – bore an authentic Nazi eagle and swastika stamp and showed 'Jack King' to have been appointed to Gestapo-Einsatzgruppe London on March 25, 1939.

The next step was even more ambitious. Rothschild's section hired a flat in a substantial apartment block, half a mile from Marble Arch in a discreet neighbourhood just off the Edgware Road, and had it wired for sound with covert microphones. But unlike previous operations in which Special Branch officers had to make an instant shorthand note of the conversations they heard on headphones, No. 499 Park West was equipped with the latest in recording technology.

Although magnetic recording tape had been invented – by the German company BASF – around 1930, the recorders themselves were huge, unwieldy and slow to warm up, while the tape reels were enormous, extremely expensive and prone to breaking: neither quality was suitable for the operation Rothschild planned.

The fundamental point of renting a permanent base was to enable King to receive guests at short notice. More pertinently, the long-term nature of the scheme meant that there was to be no pressure put on those who volunteered their services, and therefore meetings were likely to be long, meandering and difficult to control; that, in turn, demanded a recording system which was cheap, relatively quick to switch on, and which yielded easily-portable results.

None of the S.R. Case files released to the National Archives describe the system Rothschild chose for King's flat. They do, however, show that his conversations were captured on a succession of records; and from documentary evidence describing the way MI5's sister service, MI6, was simultaneously recording conversations between senior German PoWs,[23] it seems likely that the same technology was installed in Park West. If so, it was an extraordinarily well planned operation – it took the Secret Intelligence Service four months to install its bugging equipment in the much less exposed surroundings of a country house estate – involving pressure microphones and double-sided 12-inch acetate recording discs. Over the next three years MI5 would capture an extraordinary series of encounters in which a diehard group of Nazi sympathisers provided Jack King with military intelligence and some of the most secret war technology. Eric Roberts' successful impersonation of an undercover Gestapo agent led to the discovery of 'scores and probably hundreds'[24] of British fascists eager – and able – to betray their country to Germany; and at the very heart of its inner circle was Marita Perigoe.

The Marita Network

'It has been found impossible to control her. On more
than one occasion she has spontaneously committed
acts of espionage ... against our instructions'
MI5 memorandum on the Marita/'SR' Case, July 1942

'I've brought it complete with all the figures and everything', Marita
Perigoe told Jack King. 'I thought it seemed a pity not to bring it ...
I don't know what it means, but I dare say someone will know.'

'It' was the pump from a Rolls-Royce Merlin aircraft engine, one of
the technical innovations which helped make Spitfires and Hurricanes
faster than the Luftwaffe's Focke-Wulf and Messerschmitt fighters; 'the
figures and everything' turned out to be blueprints of the component,
as well as a top-secret government report on companies producing
other trial prototypes for the War Office, which she had obtained from
an engineer employed as 'a liaison officer between the Air Force officials
and the factories'.

> It's frightfully technical – it conveys nothing to me at all – but what is
> so useful about it is that it gives you exactly what every firm is experi-
> menting on; it gives exactly what they've reached in the experimental
> line ... it's all there.[1]

It was a little after 9.00pm on Wednesday, May 5, 1943. Perigoe had been meeting Eric Roberts for more than eighteen months and had so completely swallowed his 'legend' as Jack King, Gestapo officer, that she now thought of herself as his deputy and had accepted a weekly stipend, ostensibly sent from Berlin via British cut-outs, to cover her expenses. An early MI5 progress report spelled out the elaborate details of the arrangement.

She is paid £2 a week,[2] the money being sent in a double envelope, the inside one being blank, in pound notes. Letters are posted from different parts of London every Thursday evening. Although Marita is fully aware that the British authorities impose HoWs [Home Office warrants], she was persuaded by Jack to accept payment through the post. She feels secure because the money is sent in a double envelope, so that if any curious person at the GPO were to hold the letter up to the light, he would not see the pound notes inside.[3]

She had also recruited a number of 'sub-agents', fellow fascists eager for a German victory who provided her with information gleaned either from their workplaces or from acts of espionage in towns and cities across southern England. Some of these contacts she passed on for King to deal with himself, but an inner circle of three women – Hilda Leech, Nancy Brown and Eileen Gleave – were personally brought to Apartment 499, Park West, where their reports were captured on the ever-growing pile of acetate discs.

Although only a handful of the thousands of pages – at least 'a sheet of foolscap' was generated every day – have been released, they show that all three women were providing highly-sensitive war intelligence, and intending it to be sent on to Berlin.

Hilda Leech was a clerical worker for the Petroleum Board,[4] where she had access to maps showing the location of Britain's petrol and aviation fuel stocks; according to the progress report in July 1942, she was an eager, if somewhat volatile, recruit to Perigoe's group of Fifth Columnists:

This woman is unstable and neurotic ... violently anti-Semitic, had BUF sympathies, was in touch with persons associated with the

English Mistery,* and at present appears to be in touch with Jehovah's Witnesses. When she heard that Marita was in touch with the Gestapo, she said that she would like to send information and have it transmitted to the appropriate quarters. She is employed in the Petroleum Board Headquarters and reports regularly every week on the location of fuel dumps all over the country.[5]

Initially, at least, MI5 viewed Leech as too severely unhinged to be taken seriously. That changed when she brought King details of the then top-secret research on a new type of jet engine for fighter aircraft.

She reported that a friend of hers working in Handley Page told her that experiments were going on a new type of tail-less aeroplane which ran on low-grade fuel. Although neither she nor Jack understood the implications of this, we immediately realised that she was referring to the highly secret experimental research work on the propeller-less jet propulsion aeroplane which many authorities believe will revolutionise air warfare, as this type of aeroplane runs on paraffin, fights as well at an altitude of 40,000 feet as at 20,000, and will be capable of enormous speeds. This is a good example of the need for paying attention even to women of this type, as there is no doubt that the enemy would be extremely interested to hear of these experiments, which are in the most secret category.[6]

Unlike Leech, whose MI5 file was released in 2014,[7] there is no trace of the Security Service dossier on Nancy Brown; but transcripts of her meetings in Apartment 499, found in other declassified volumes relating to the Jack King network, show her to have once been a secretary with John Beckett's British Council for Christian Settlement in Europe. By the summer of 1942 she was working for Brighton town council,

---

* The English Mistery was a small, quasi-fascist group, founded in 1930 and dedicated to restoring the feudal system under which a narrow aristocratic elite would rule over a racially-purified nation; among its luminaries was Anthony Ludovici.

where she had access to 'a lot of civil defence stuff' and used her position to gather intelligence on military establishments in the area. Nor was there any doubt about her intentions in passing this to King; a recording on August 29, 1942 of what appears to be their first meeting, arranged by Perigoe, includes the following exchange:

JACK: 'Had you any idea that you were going to be asked to become a German agent when you came up this morning?'

NANCY: [laughs] 'Not in the slightest! ... But that is really what I'm being asked to do, isn't it? ... People say "Wouldn't you like the Germans here?" I know I would ... The majority of our people, honestly, are such fools that they're really worth nothing unless to be ruled by the Germans. I think they'd make a better race of us ... I'm fed up of seeing these Americans and Canadians coming over ... I'd much rather see Germans here.'[8]

Among the information which Brown passed to King was the location of anti-aircraft gun batteries recently dug in to the grounds of two schools – Roedean and Brighton Grammar – and details of military camps around the town. Excerpts from the reports he fed back to MI5 show that Brown had convinced herself that this played a part in guiding German bombers to their marks.

Nancy Brown was thrilled by the recent tip-and-run raids on Brighton. She seemed to think that her information (which she thought had gone to Germany) was the reason for the German choice of targets, and deplored the fact that there had been so many near misses. She described how a nearby school clinic was hit, and said with a grin that one expectant mother was killed, two girls badly injured, a clerk and two children killed.

There was not a sign in the faces of these three women (Nancy Brown, Eileen Gleave and Marita Perigoe) of contrition, and it was obvious that the deaths of these people meant nothing to them. Nancy Brown was very pleased and happy to think that the news she had given resulted in the deaths and damage of the last raid.[9]

Eileen Gleave, the third member of the inner circle, had been on MI5's radar for more than a year before she was recruited by Marita Perigoe. Born Eileen Lesley Cragg in 1907 (there is no exact date listed in her evidently weeded Security Service file), in 1934 she married Edward Gleave, a wireless engineer, and the couple set up home near the Wembley Exhibition Grounds in north London. They also became enthusiastic members of the BUF, and when (despite his fascist history) Edward was posted to Lancashire 'on special war work', she transferred her affections to the party's district sub-leader, Ronald Stokes. He moved into the Gleaves' flat in Danes Court – a development which quickly attracted a Home Office warrant intercepting all correspondence to or from the address. 'It looks as though we have come across a little nest of Fascists', the Service's in-house lawyer, Edward Blanshard Stamp, noted in making the application.[10]

There is no evidence that the mail intercept yielded any useful intelligence on Mrs Gleave's activities; nor is there any trace of a file relating to Ronald Stokes. But by the time Perigoe introduced her to Jack King in early summer 1942 it appears that Eileen had fallen out of love with him and with the BUF – the latter on the grounds that 'the members are not active enough in assisting Germany'.[11]

Like Hilda Leech, Nancy Brown and Marita Perigoe, Mrs Gleave evidently found working for the Gestapo rather more to her tastes. She, like them, began touring the area near her home and making maps showing military targets for bombing. A recording, made in King's flat on September 4, captured her handing over a sketch of the road between Watford and King's Langley in Hertfordshire, where there was a heavy concentration of troops and defensive emplacements.

'I went all around here', she told her handler, pointing at the map. 'There's a pill-box with tank traps in front of it, and then the barbed wire starts ... now there's a big hangar [but] it's not a hangar at all, it's a factory [with] four huts ... the usual type of army huts ... there's a big bomber there and two fighters at the side.' Playing his role to the hilt, King replied: 'When you hear of that place being wiped out later on ... you'll be able to pat yourself on the back and say, "well, I had a hand in that".'[12]

As MI5's progress report that summer made clear, Perigoe was also making her own maps of militarily-sensitive factories and actively seeking intelligence on Britain's home defence.

Marita Perigoe herself, though head of the organisation, has been unable to resist indulging in certain forms of espionage, for which she has a remarkable aptitude. In fact, Major Maxwell Knight said that he would very much like to have her as one of his own agents.

She works for Fortifone Ltd, the manager of which is an enthusiastic member of the Home Guard. Marita heard him dictating instructions about certain impending Home Guard manoeuvres, including details of equipment. Marita noticed that the carbons used for this memorandum, which was on folio paper, were new and therefore concluded that they would have a good imprint of the memorandum. She asked the manager's secretary if she could lend her some folio carbons, knowing that the only ones available were those which had been used for this memorandum.[13]

The alacrity with which Perigoe and her sub-agents took to spying evidently alarmed MI5. Its early progress report noted that they were running ahead of the rules of engagement that Rothschild had agreed with Director General Sir David Petrie, and that this was causing problems.

Another disadvantage that the decision to discourage all forms of espionage has incurred is that Marita and certain of her contacts are so anxious to take a more positive role than the mere acquisition of information about sympathisers all over the country, that it has been found impossible to control her. On more than one occasion she has spontaneously committed acts of espionage, involving considerable ingenuity, against our instructions.[14]

For this reason, King was instructed to remind his growing band of Fifth Columnists that the Gestapo's instructions were – for the time being – only to identify and contact Nazi sympathisers. 'Actually', he told Perigoe in a conversation recorded on August 29, 'the department does not do much in the way of espionage proper, do you see? That's the job for the Abwehr, but our job is to – we're the forerunners you see. We have to find out our friends and our enemies, but all this [military information] is passed on. I shall pass it on tonight myself.'[15]

This warning worked, at least to some degree. The transcript of meetings in King's flat show that both Eileen Gleave and Marita Perigoe contacted two pro-Nazi organisations which had gone underground following the mass internment arrest in May 1940.

Perigoe, who seems to have been assigned the agent code number 12560, acted as a liaison between her own growing network and Arnold Leese's Imperial Fascist League. According to the report she gave King, the IFL's anti-Semitism – and its ability to plan for a Jewish pogrom – had not been adversely affected by the detention of its founder.

> The IFL is a much better bunch on the whole than the BU ... Leese is supposed to collect together a list of the first two thousand names of Jews and converted Jews ... Leese apparently has all these people's life histories and everything written down; all their crimes and everything. A good beginning isn't it? The first two thousand of the complete wipe-out – I mean they're not even to be deported, these people.[16]

Meanwhile Gleave – agent number 12563 – reported back on a new group being formed by some very familiar names. An S.R. Case memo dated July 11, 1943 recorded that she was now involved with 'an organisation being formed by the Duke of Bedford and his friend Captain Rogers'.* The latter was 'pro-German and determined on the overthrow of the present government ... 12563 stated emphatically that the Duke of Bedford was spending very large sums of money on what he called his intelligence service':

---

* Captain Arthur Rogers OBE was a member of the Imperial General Staff during the First World War, and later worked for British Military Intelligence. He was a close friend of Admiral Barry Domvile, was secretary of the Liberty Restoration League, a front organisation for the Nordic League, and became a prominent member of A.K. Chesterton's post-war fascist party, The League of Empire Loyalists.

12563 alleged that the Bedford Group numbered about thirty people ... and the Duke of Bedford was very pleased with the results of an expenditure which had appeared to be on the large side. 12563 assured 12560 that the Duke of Bedford had so many helpful friends in various key places that he was well informed of what was being said against him but contended that the authorities were afraid to take any definite action because they were not certain of the extent to which he was supported within their own ranks. 12563 claimed that if the Government knew the identities of some of the people who got in touch with the Duke they would be very frightened.

Gleave evidently met Bedford several times, concluding that he was nothing 'more than a harmless lunatic'. Those who joined his group and supported his nascent plans for a fascist uprising, however, were rather more troubling.

12563 told 12560 that certain important changes are in progress in the Bedford Group. Major General J.F.C. Fuller has been officially nominated as Leader of the embryo movement and is reported to have accepted the position.[17]

Given the regularity with which his name cropped up in intelligence reports on pro-Nazi groups plotting for a Quisling regime on behalf of Germany, Fuller's continuing freedom was – to say the least – puzzling. There is no indication that Gleave's information was developed, but the Bedford organisation's plans for direct and violent action evidently accorded with her own intentions. Another S.R. Case report noted that 'Eileen Gleave would, in time of invasion, be prepared to raid the Wembley Home Guard arms depot in order to assist the enemy. She is ardently pro-Nazi and the sort of person who would really carry out what she said she would do.'[18]

Ultimately, however hard King tried to control his growing network of Nazi sympathisers, many were determined to become fully-fledged spies. Edgar and Sophia Bray were typical of those brought to his door by Gleave and Perigoe.

Edgar Thoreau Whitehead was a veteran of the Communist Party in the 1920s and, as secretary of its west London branch, had attracted the attentions of the Security Service – not least since he appears to have served a short prison sentence for organising a 'mutiny' in the Army Labour Corps. By the mid-1930s, however, he had moved across the political spectrum to join the BUF; he had also abandoned his wife and set up home in Wembley with Sophia Bray – formerly Sophia Voznesennsky, a Russian exile who had obtained British citizenship through marriage to a (now-absent) Englishman.

The couple were ardent fascists and unashamed anti-Semites. In the years before the outbreak of war, Edgar – who adopted his mistress' name in preference to his own – wrote to Dr Hans Thost, the German 'agent of influence' operating under journalistic cover in London, offering his services as a propagandist on behalf of the Reich.

> I have recently been in communication with the German Embassy in reference to assisting to checkmate the Jewish Lie campaign against the Nazi Party in this country ... I am a skilful and experienced political publicist, lecturer and contraversialist [*sic*] and have for some time carried on a local campaign in favour of the Nazis against the Jews and for Fascism in general.
>
> It is quite evident however that the campaign of distortion and calumny just now being directed against Nazi Germany is so powerful that uncoordinate [*sic*] local efforts are not enough to check it and I should welcome the opportunity of cooperating in a more effective campaign ...
>
> It appears to me that there is a wide field for a skilfully prepared publicity explaining the position in Germany, the <u>reasons</u> action has been taken against certain Jews in Germany and the underlying justice of Nazi ideology.[19]

Although this letter was intercepted at the time, there is no indication in the declassified files on Edgar and Sophia Bray that the Security Service monitored the couple once the war started. Given their intense Nazi sympathies, it was perhaps unsurprising that they were found by Marita Perigoe and became eager recruits to the network she was building on behalf of Jack King. The S.R. Case files show that from June 1942 the Brays began providing reports on a new experimental amphibious tank undergoing trials at Hendon, north London. According to a memo King filed on June 27, Edgar Bray reported that:

> The amphibian [*sic*] tank he saw practising contained thirty people at the trial. He counted them when they came out. The tank had two wing floats which extended when the tank entered the water. He did not think that the tank could be heavily armoured nor carry much ammunition.[20]

There was something faintly farcical about the ease with which the couple had obtained this highly-sensitive information. The tank trials were held in the very public setting of Brent Reservoir, known locally as 'the Welsh Harp', with no attempt made to prevent spectators looking on. Bray's reports to King, as an internal MI5 memo noted, 'reveal gross lack of security in what must be a highly secret matter, and this is being taken up with the Director of Armoured Fighting Vehicles, War Office'.[21]

Sophia Bray appears, initially at least, to have been reluctant to pass this valuable intelligence to King for onward transmission to Berlin, arguing instead for a route which she knew from previous experience to be reliable.

> Mrs Bray stated that the only German espionage organisation functioning in this country was not German at all but Spanish. The Spanish consuls and officials passed on any scraps of information that came their way.
>
> Naturally their uses were limited and when specialised knowledge was required the Germans sent an agent over ...[22]

Eric Roberts' skills of persuasion evidently convinced the Brays that Jack King was just such an agent, and that he was well placed to ensure their information reached German Intelligence. By the end of July 1942, the couple had abandoned the Spanish Embassy route and, as fully committed members of the Perigoe network, were anxious to do anything they could to assist the Nazi cause.

Mrs Bray offered to give any help in her power and said that age prevented her from doing much but that she was willing to hide German agents and give them food. She stated that it would not be the first time that she and her husband had hidden people in whom the authorities would have been interested. On two previous occasions they hid people for considerable periods. On both occasions the men got away safely.[23]

Meanwhile, her husband fed back reports on troop movements and accidents at nearby air bases, still seemingly untroubled by local security.

Mrs Bray said that Northolt Aerodrome is now under American control. When Edgar Bray heard that a bomber had crashed at Northolt he set off immediately to see the damage and to make enquiries ... He was told that the crashed bomber was an American machine.

Edgar Bray takes great interest in accidents of a military or air nature and is always keen to make enquiries ... [but] it was thought [by the authorities] that Edgar Bray's interest was merely idle curiosity ... it was thought that if Bray was really sinister he would not spend so much time working on his allotment. A man would not be interested in gardening and espionage at the same time.[24]

By the start of 1943, the group of agents reporting to Jack King was growing increasingly active. While Marita Perigoe was collecting information about military emplacements in north London, and cultivating the contacts from whom she would shortly obtain the Merlin engine pump, Eileen Gleave was travelling further afield. In January she set out to investigate troop locations and suitable industrial targets for German bombers across north and south Wales. On her return she gave the details to King, explaining that she had obtained her information by flirting with soldiers and airmen, and specifically suggesting that the Luftwaffe should concentrate its efforts on the iron and steel works at Port Talbot.

'[It's] a lovely target. It's just right bang past the railway station ... only got to find the railway station and drop a few bombs round it, and you are bound to hit the place', she told her supposed Gestapo boss.[25]

There was also a growing rivalry within the network, with the self-identified agents vying to provide ever more damaging secrets to their handler. Perigoe, in particular, saw herself as in competition with one of the recruits she had originally brought to King.

Hans Kohout was born in Austria, but had emigrated to London in 1936, where he quickly joined the BUF. At the behest of the NSDAP he obtained British citizenship, and on a trip back to Vienna in 1938 was recruited by the Abwehr to work as an occasional informer on British industry. On the outbreak of war he was working for John Dickinson, a north London firm which had secret Admiralty and Air Ministry contracts to produce materials for the RAF.[26]

When Perigoe tapped him as a potential recruit he 'willingly agreed' to join – but on condition that he was allowed to run his own cell, with the assistance of his co-worker, Adolf Herzig.*[27] By summer 1942, Kohout was roaming the military zones around Hertfordshire, marking important locations on a scale map with a numerical code. On August 29 he presented this to King.

No. 2 is Pill-boxes. No. 3 Minefields. No. 4 Searchlights. No. 5 Anti-Aircraft guns. No. 6 Camouflaged factories. No. 7 Explosive factories ... No. 8 is the places where the Army and Air Force is stationed. No. 9 Aircraft factories and Nought – just a plain Nought – is tank traps, and a cross is wireless stations, Army wireless stations.[28]

At the same meeting he also handed over intelligence, gleaned from a contact who made military equipment for the RAF, about the development of one of Britain's most effective new aircraft. 'I heard about a dive-bomber. It is still on the secret list, named a Mosquito ... two engines, 15 to 1600 horse power', he said, before giving technical details of its landing speed and passing on the highly-sensitive information that the company was working on an experimental version which could – to

---

* Despite Herzig's presence at several meetings at King's flat, captured on the covert recordings, there is surprisingly no trace of an MI5 file on him in the National Archives.

a degree – hover. 'It is not in production yet. A hundred have been built for experimental purposes', he told King.*

Kohout's success clearly irked Perigoe. In a September meeting she complained that he was a womaniser and a black marketeer and insisted there should be no place for him once German troops arrived in Britain. 'He ought to be exterminated. Such people shouldn't live', she told King. 'He doesn't make any disguise of the fact at all that his concern is simply from a money point of view ... He should be exterminated: there's no doubt about it.'

King responded with a mixture of gentle chiding and encouragement: 'Don't be too bloodthirsty about it, Marita, we'll exterminate him in due course.'[29]

The following month Kohout's espionage yielded an even greater coup. Since the start of the year, British scientists had been developing a system to confuse German air defences with 'chaff' – a cloud of small, metal-coated paper strips which, when dropped by aircraft, would appear on ground radar screens as a cluster of false targets. The scheme, codenamed 'Window', was the brainchild of the Telecommunications Research Establishment, but manufacture of the aluminium-backed paper was parcelled out to firms working on government contracts; one was John Dickinson.

Test production revealed that the most effective material was black paper coated on the reverse with aluminium and then cut into strips. On October 8, 1942, the acetate discs recording conversations in 499 Park West captured Kohout giving King precise details of the experiments.

'Last week was very important, on Tuesday there were some Admiralty trials ... They brought down a solution with them for something that is inflammable cellulose varnish and they had to treat that paper with the varnish ... [it was] black paper ... with the tinfoil on the

---

* The Mosquito, made by de Havilland, was a fighter-bomber and night-bomber and one of the fastest aircraft in the world when it entered service late in 1941; the fighter-bomber variant entered service in 1943 and played a vital role in preparations for the D-Day landings. The experiments for a hovering version do not appear to have been successful.

other side ... Now here are the papers actually pasted together. Then in the middle comes some kind of chemical.'

The Admiralty, Kohout reported, had ordered 7,000 yards of the paper, with another order for 35,000 yards to follow.

'The whole order is worth over a thousand pound [*sic*]. That means, actually quite definitely, it's out of the experimental stage.'[30]

Three weeks later Kohout was back, this time with both the specific Admiralty order number – A125835 – and a sample he had stolen from the factory.[31]

'Window' was one of Britain's most closely guarded secrets and would not be deployed for another nine months.* Had it leaked to Germany – as Kohout intended – it would have been a devastating setback and could have caused the deaths of hundreds of RAF aircrew. On this basis alone, the Jack King scheme to 'canalise' the efforts of domestic spies and Fifth Columnists was an outstanding success.

Yet inside MI5, Rothschild, his assistant Theresa Clay and their boss Guy Liddell were beginning to run into opposition from their colleagues. In particular two of the Service's coming men – Dick White and Roger Hollis, both of whom would go on to become successive Directors General – were deeply distrustful of the operation.

On August 24, 1943 – less than a month after 'Window' was first used – Liddell recorded the first of the skirmishes in his daily journal.

I had a discussion with Dick, Victor and Miss Clay about the Marita case ... Dick, I think, has still got a general impression that the case is not of much importance and that we are dealing with a pack of hysterical women ... [and] was rather in favour of liquidating the whole business with a prosecution, which he felt would act as a deterrent.

---

* It was first used in Operation Gomorrah, the Allied bombing of Hamburg in July 1943. Its success in confusing German air defences was credited for the relatively small number of losses incurred by the RAF's 35 Squadron.

There are various difficulties to this course: firstly it could not be taken without putting Jack [King] in the box, secondly I am strongly of [the] opinion that it would create a bad impression both with the public and also with the H.O. [Home Office]. Although to my view there is nothing to which exception can be taken in war time, I am quite sure that defending counsel would make a great song and dance about the whole case and that we should be dubbed as the Gestapo Dept. ...

Quite apart from this aspect of the case I cannot see that we stand to gain very much, since the Marita organization in its present form does not really constitute any danger. The information is handed to us and goes into a cul-de-sac. The advantage that we get from the case is that it supplies us with information about people who would if they could do this country harm.[32]

For the time being, Liddell's argument won the day. But three months later, the scheme came under renewed fire, this time from Roger Hollis, then running MI5's counter-subversion branch, F Division.

Roger evidently does not like it. He cannot get out of his liberal mind that this is a serious form of provocation. In a very mild sense it is, but in the absence of any other methods I do think it is desirable to ascertain something about evilly-intentioned persons. Roger's view is that the country is full of evilly-intentioned persons but there is no necessity to drag them out of their holes. They had much better be left to rot in obscurity, and will be swamped by the common sense of the community as a whole.[33]

Despite Eric Roberts' continuing success in his role as Gestapo agent Jack King – Perigoe, Gleave, Herzig and Kohout continued to deliver reports, and the latter also handed over a revolver he had acquired – the discontent rumbled on. In January 1944, Rothschild felt obliged to mount a lengthy defence of his entrapment operation.

It is agreed ... that a prosecution in this case would not be possible for the following reasons.

(a) The requisite corroboration and evidence is not available, and in order to get it many of the cases would have to be started again from the beginning.

(b) The case would undoubtedly create an unfavourable impression in court and the Security Service might be liable to severe attacks on the grounds of the methods used ...

The view of this section ... is that this office should have as much information as possible about these movements [British pro-Nazis and fascists] ... The Marita case can be adjusted at will to cover larger sections of what will be called for the sake of shortness the Fascist community; and apart from this, our agents have in some cases penetrated into Headquarters organisations which is in itself a more profitable method of gaining general intelligence than by local penetration.

Rothschild was acutely aware that the use of *agent provocateur* methods made his colleagues suspicious of the information uncovered by Jack King, and of the risks of creating, rather than neutralising, an organised Fifth Column.

The question arises as to whether the agents under the influence of Jack do not become more interested in and more proficient at subversive work than they would be if they were left alone. The answer is yes, to a limited extent, but it is known that these people would have started reorganising and becoming interested in subversive matters in any case; and though there may be some disadvantages in someone like Marita being a better agent now than she would have been if she had not come into contact with Jack, it is submitted that this light disadvantage is worthwhile in view of the large benefits in the way of intelligence that accrue to the Security Service.[34]

It is a measure of the persistent unwillingness of the British establishment – both White and Hollis were alumni of Oxford University in its gilded inter-war years – to grasp the Nazis' adoption of total war, that the Security Service found itself in the unexpected position of having an internal philosophical debate over the same issue which had led to the fractured relations with the Home Office and its Advisory Committees. Nonetheless, the battle of memo and counter-memo raged on for much of 1944.

In September 1944 – three months after D-Day and as Allied troops fought their way through the Low Countries of Belgium and Holland – Hollis's deputy in F Division, Thomas Shelford, penned a deeply equivocal assessment of what he termed 'The Fifth Column Case'.

> I think that the question of the usefulness of the organisation must stand or fall on the organisation's value as a source of intelligence. It is sometimes said that it is a useful means of canalising or controlling the activities of pro-Germans. I have, personally, doubts about its value in this respect.
>
> It seems to me on the whole fortuitous what pro-Germans are contacted and I am convinced that there are more pro-Germans and pro-Nazis throughout the country than is generally realised. I do not think, therefore, that the organisation serves as a very capacious drain for these undesirable activities ... The usefulness of the organisation from the point of view of intelligence has to some degree been diminished by the fact that the information it obtains is for obvious reasons of such secrecy that it cannot be used as much as we would like ...
>
> The Fifth Column organisation raises in the minds of many people an instinctive mistrust, which is, I think, largely irrational under the present circumstances, although there is a basis in reason. The suspicion is that the subjects of our enquiries are subjected to provocation.
>
> I understand that in fact a very close control is exercised by the agent Jack in preventing a provocation. I have little doubt that his efforts have been very largely successful. I do not, however, believe that it is possible, having regard to the very nature of the organisation, to exclude provocation altogether ...
>
> I am, however, not sufficiently familiar with the details of the workings of the organisation to be able to estimate the exact degree of this danger ...[35]

In fairness to Shelford, his memorandum reflected a serious dispute within MI5 about the ethics of *agent provocateur* tactics. Spread throughout the disparate files on the ever-growing number of recruits to the Jack King network, reports and correspondence from Security Service officers reflect both sides of the argument. The slim volume on Alwina Thies offers a perfect encapsulation of the tension between protecting the public from potentially dangerous Nazi sympathisers and the fundamental dishonesty of entrapment.

To her employers, friends and fellow bomb damage volunteers, Thies was the very model of a 'Good German'. Born in Bad Salzuflen in 1905, she had come to England in May 1935 and had worked as a domestic servant in London ever since. She had no criminal record, no known association with the German Embassy, the NSDAP or domestic British fascists; she was, in modern policing terms, 'a clean skin'.

She was introduced to Jack King's network at the start of 1944 by another equally obscure member of the network, an Austrian woman called Fini Donko[36] who appears to have been recruited by Hans Kohout. According to one of Roberts' 'S.R. Case' reports on January 19:

> I arrived at Brent station at 1.20pm and Fini Donko at 1.35pm. Fini said that she had seen her friend Alwina Thies, who had from time to time, given her items of information intended for Germany. Alwina told her that she had heard from a friend who worked at an important secret factory at Waltham Cross. The friend had to work all through the Christmas period and although Alwina was not enlightened as to what was being made at the factory she was advised that there were two factories and that their production was essential to the smooth opening of the Second Front.
>
> Alwina Thies suggested to Fini Donko that a concentrated bombing of the Waltham Cross area might have excellent results. Fini stated that Thies subsequently remarked that she wanted to be placed in contact with us and she had accordingly done her best to arrange a meeting between the three of us for this day. I agreed to meet Thies and Donko at Baker Street station at 8.15pm.[37]

Unlike some of Maxwell Knight's undercover agents, Roberts was assiduous in submitting thorough and immediate accounts of meetings conducted in his role as Jack King. His reports on Alwina Thies show that over the ensuing three months he patiently won her trust by never pressing too hard, and in doing so allowed her to reveal her determination to help the German war effort. The account of their first encounter, in a café near Baker Street tube station on January 19, set the tone.

> Thies gave a first impression of considerable intelligence. Her English is surprisingly good. She was not keen to talk about herself and ... I was most impressed by Thies' method of conveying information in an apparently artless sentence. She would mention a place X, say something in its praise or to its detriment and then add details of every factory and aerodrome in the vicinity of X. To me there was no mistaking her intentions, but to any listener the conversation would have appeared completely harmless.
>
> To the best of my memory she made only one slip ... when she said directly to me 'I have every reason to believe that a saturation raid on the Waltham Cross locality would repay you handsomely.' This phrase told me that she knew what I was supposed to be and that she was placing her knowledge at our disposal.
>
> She permitted herself to express strongly anti-Semitic sentiments but did not refer to or praise the National Socialist regime ... She told me that she had a number of English friends, including a Squadron leader ... and that she was completely trusted by them all. The trusting nature of the British was a matter of constant amazement to her ... I formed the opinion that Alwina Thies is a person who could be a grave danger to this country if in contact with the enemy. Her intelligence is above average.[38]

That, in essence, was the point of the entrapment scheme: to prevent previously unidentified Fifth Columnists from passing secrets to German Intelligence by sending it down the cul-de-sac of the bogus Jack King Gestapo network. And it worked perfectly on Thies. Two months after their first meeting, she was regularly giving information to King, believing that it would be forwarded to Berlin. The final report in her file, dated March 18, 1944, shows that, over an agreeable afternoon tea in Twickenham, she described the way in which she had infiltrated herself into British society.

Thies ... describe[d] how, at the start of the war, she was viewed with 'suspicion and hostility' in the neighbourhood, and how several people told her bluntly that 'She should be interned' while others threatened to complain to the police about her. She decided that the only course open to her was to work hard to win the trust and the liking of the British.

She said that in the nature of my duties I must have found that although the bulk of the British were detestable people owing to their insularity and conceit, yet they were soft hearted and often soft headed. Her opportunity came during the Blitz in 1940. Thies lent a hand in dealing with incendiaries and made coffee and cooked for the local defence workers. She said that it was amusing to see how these stupid people reacted. On several occasions she overheard them say to one another 'Here at least is a decent German'.

She also maintained this facade with her employer, an evidently benevolent widower who held a senior position in the Civil Defence service, and told King that her role as his housekeeper and cook had given her access to sensitive documents he left lying around the house.

She spoke of his many kindnesses and generosity ... She had always been careful to persuade Mr Martin that she was pro-British and if he knew that she had passed on his Civil Defence secrets to the German S.S. it would break his heart ... Thies remarked that the English found it impossible to appreciate the fact that whatever political opinions were held by a German, there could only be one loyalty and that was to Germany. Whilst she was helping the British she was hoping all the time that one day she would have the opportunity of doing something for her country ... I looked at the amiable Thies and wondered ...

By the time of this meeting the war had begun to turn against Germany. Thies saw this and – while seeking to help the Reich for as long as it lasted – had begun planning for the future.

Thies proceeded to give me a number of items of information which she thought would be of use to the German Secret Service eg: a recent raid heavily damaged an aerodrome at Feltham, several 'planes being destroyed, the RAF have opened a new bomber station at Scarborough etc etc. I listened to the lengthy list without comment.

When she concluded, Thies said she wanted to help the German Secret Service if it continued after the war. If she was not allowed to do so, she intended to visit Germany to see if she could contact anybody carrying on the struggle.[39]

The same thought had, according to an internal MI5 memo headed 'Post-war Applications', already occurred to other members of the network, and to its hidden controllers.

> The recent Allied successes have had a profound effect upon the group and its members are beginning to realise that Germany may lose the war ... They are therefore beginning to formulate tentative plans to enable to make the best of what to them is a major tragedy.
>
> The simplest cases are those of persons of German origin, such as Kohout and Herzig ... Kohout, with the realisation that Germany may now lose the war, has already started planning post-war espionage, considering that in another twenty years Germany will again be ready for war and will be in need of an espionage organisation. Kohout's scheme, which he is working out in considerable detail, deals with industrial espionage and plans to penetrate industry with Germans or persons of German origin. Kohout, who himself works in a firm engaged on secret Government contracts, realises the amount of vital information people, placed such as himself, can obtain. Herzig's ideas are similar, and he has suggested organising the Germans in this country on a secret basis.[40]

'When the war is over' had become a familiar refrain in Britain by the beginning of 1945; it was one of the main topics of conversation in pubs and clubs, civilian homes and military bases across the country – and it was also preoccupying the Security Service. In the months after Germany surrendered, MI5 faced the difficult task of evaluating the likelihood of a fascist revival now that Hitler and the Nazi Party had been eliminated, and the extent to which the members of the Jack King/

Marita network posed a significant threat. It commissioned an internal evaluation of the 'S.R. Case' by Gonne St Clair Pilcher.

'The position today', he wrote in a report submitted to Sir David Petrie in September 1945, 'is that some six men and women, British subjects with only one exception, believe S.R. to be an agent of the Gestapo having facilities for communication with Germany and entrusted by the Gestapo with the task of identifying Nazi sympathisers in this country. The six men and women make it their business to report to S.R. on persons who have German or Nazi sympathies and on the personnel, formation and development of Fascist movements in the UK. In doing so these six are of course conscious agents of Germany and are aware that by their activities they are incurring a risk of very heavy penalties.'

Pilcher's detailed account also recorded the remarkable insight which Eric Roberts' impersonation of Gestapo agent Jack King had provided into the extent of pro-Nazi Fifth Columnists in Britain.

> The number of persons who have been the subject of S.R. reports, either as direct contacts of one of the six or as friends or associates of such direct contacts, has grown steadily throughout the past three years. It now amounts certainly to scores and probably to hundreds. Most of these persons live in London or its neighbourhood, but there are groups in some of the provincial cities. ... Of those British subjects in or near London who from other sources have been known to harbour pro-German sentiments or a Fascist political outlook there is almost none on whom S.R. has not supplied something relevant, detailed and vivid.
>
> The volume of material now reaching F.3 [counter-subversion branch] through S.R. is very considerable and may be computed at a sheet of foolscap at least per diem. There is no excess verbiage in this material: it is all condensed and it is immediately relevant to F.3 work. Not only is it relevant: it consists also of a record of the sayings and doings which the persons concerned would be in the highest degree anxious to keep secret from the authorities.[41]

Both the volume of material and the dramatic uncovering of would-be traitors it revealed had, Pilcher noted, caused some Security Service officers to question its authenticity; from his review of the recordings and reports, those fears were groundless.

> When, about two years ago, the S.R. Case began to extend from its earlier limited sphere into wider Fascist-minded groups, the spectacular nature of some of the reports and the vivid light which they threw on the disloyal outlook of so many British subjects naturally created doubts in some quarters as to the validity of the information or at least some of it. But it gradually became apparent that the bulk of the S.R. material could be relied on as substantially accurate. In very many points of detail it was possible to check it by reference to other sources or to facts already established and when checked it was nearly always found to be true.
>
> From this the inference was inevitably drawn that the additional information, which in its nature was not capable of confirmation from other sources, was also substantially true; and in the entire history of the case no facts have come to light which suggest the contrary.[42]

To those in MI5 who believed in the Jack King scheme, it was vital to maintain the network for the foreseeable future. With this in mind, Rothschild arranged for King's two most effective agents, Marita Perigoe and Hans Kohout, to receive a remarkably realistic forgery of the Nazis' War Merit Cross, the Kriegswerdienstkreuz (2nd Class). Pilcher set out the intelligence value in the new, post-war environment.

> If S.R.'s services were to be lost, F.3 would be deprived of its most valuable single source of information. It would lose much of the knowledge which at present it possesses about the current attitude and future fascist plans of Mosley and his lieutenants; of Ramsay and his circle; of Arnold Leese and his attempts to revive a new form of the Imperial Fascist League ... and of disloyal persons and Hitler-worshippers ... too numerous to mention.
>
> Further if S.R.'s services were to be lost, there would be released to the possible danger of the State the energies of the six conscious agents whose activities are at present canalised into harmless channels. Finally the loss of S.R.'s services would jeopardise future security,

not only in respect of a native Fascist revival, but also in respect of the growth of a long term German underground movement preparatory to a third attempt at world domination.[43]

The tide, however, was turning against Pilcher, Rothschild, Theresa Clay and the remarkable Eric Roberts. A new order was coming inside the Security Service, and its attention was increasingly claimed by the emerging Cold War with communism rather than the 'old war' with fascism.

CHAPTER TWENTY-ONE

After the War

'Even if the stories about the Hitler régime were true
– and we know most of them to have been propaganda
– they would not have justified the war'
John Beckett, British People's Party, October 9, 1945

On Wednesday, May 2, 1945 the front pages carried almost identical banner headlines: 'Hitler Dead'. The stories reported a proclamation by Admiral Karl Doenitz that the Fuehrer had committed suicide in his Berlin bunker, and were universally joyful: the *Daily Express* described the announcement as 'the news everyone hopes is true'.

The *Express* verdict was – albeit marginally – overstated. While most of Britain celebrated the inevitable precursor to the war's end,* many of the British Nazi sympathisers who had sought to bring about a German victory were dismayed. The Duke of Bedford wrote a column for Guy Aldred's monthly journal, *The Word*, mourning the passing of the leaders of international fascism.

The assassination of Mussolini** and the death of Hitler remove from
the stage of international politics two figures with whom I prophesy

---

* Germany formally surrendered five days later on May 7, 1945.
** Mussolini was executed by Italian partisans on April 28, 1945.

that future historians will deal more leniently than present-day war propagandists.[1]

Oliver Conway Gilbert, formerly of the BUF and a founding member of the Nordic League, was even more forthright. According to a report from the 'S.R. Case' files, lodged the day after the announcement:

> Gilbert took Hitler's death very seriously and referred to it as 'this tragic drama ... this modern Twilight of the Gods' ... the Führer's death had put the clock back twenty years ... He shook his fist in the air and demanded vengeance against the Jews and their friends in Whitehall. Gilbert said that the Führer had died a hero, true to his ideals to the last ... The cry of the future was 'Vengeance'.[2]

The demand for vengeance by British Fifth Columnists was, in the first weeks and months of peace, a genuine concern. With hindsight, it is clear that the death of Hitler and the collapse of his 'Thousand Year Reich' marked the beginning of the end of fascism as a substantial domestic threat, but at the time there was no such certainty. It was this fear of a resurgence of extreme right-wing and anti-Semitic sentiment which caused at least some sections of MI5 to argue for the continuation of the Jack King entrapment scheme.

> It should be emphasised that the winding up of the S.R. case would deprive the section [F3, counter-subversion] of the confidence which it now enjoys that no underground Fascist or pro-German would be likely to grow up in this country without our knowledge and outside our control.[3]

However reluctantly, Security Service section chiefs evidently heeded this warning, since reports from King and other agents inside the now-fractured fascist underground were filed for at least two years. Although only a handful have survived (or have been declassified), pieced together they provide a snapshot of post-war activities of at least some of the men and women who had sought – sometimes successfully – to betray their country.

Marita Perigoe had somehow – the files on her and her colleagues do not contain any explanation – made her way to Switzerland. Her absence from Britain was, however, expected to be temporary, since Rothschild noted in 1946 that on her return to the Jack King network her weekly stipend was to be reduced to £2.

That the undercover operation remained in business is further evidenced by the dossier on Eileen Gleave. She, too, was being paid, at the rate of £1 every week, on the grounds that she had 'returned to Fascist circles and is in a position to give us a certain amount of useful information'.[4]

By the middle of 1946 she was working as a book-keeper and sharing a substantial six-bedroomed flat on Talgarth Road, near Barons Court tube station, with the returned Marita Perigoe and Oliver Conway Gilbert. Gilbert, in particular, was closely monitored, and memos filed by (unidentified) MI5 informants showed that he appeared to present a continuing threat of violence; the end of the first war crimes trial at Nuremberg, on October 1, 1946, appears to have tipped him over the edge. A report, by an agent codenamed A.B. 20, on October 24 noted:

> Gilbert ... said that something must be done to avenge Nuremberg, amplifying his statement by saying that F-M [Field Marshal] Montgomery[5] had a flat in Latymer Court where it might be possible to make an attempt on his life.
>
> Gilbert considered that the Christmas holidays would be the most likely time to catch him at home, and he proposed that a girl, who would draw less attention than a man, should take what looked like a bundle of laundry and leave it in the corridor outside the flat. The bundle should contain a time bomb. Gilbert in the meantime would provide the necessary alibi if any questions were asked. It was thought that Gilbert was reliable and that under different circumstances he would have the guts to do the job himself.[6]

Subsequent news of the hanging of ten of the twelve Nazi chiefs sentenced to death* further exacerbated Gilbert's anger.

---

* Martin Bormann was tried and sentenced *in absentia*; Hermann Goering committed suicide before he could be executed.

Gilbert is reported to be in an hysterical fury over the Nuremberg executions, and he is alleged to have said that if he had an automatic in his possession he would go down to the East End and shoot up a few Jews. He then babbled about the possibility of killing Montgomery, Churchill and Attlee. It is felt certain that if Gilbert had the desired weapon placed in his hands and told to go ahead, he would have done so without hesitating.[7]

Eileen Gleave, meanwhile, was working on a rather more practical scheme to aid the dying cause by taking an interest in the welfare of German prisoners of war, then still held in camps dotted across the country.

In the immediate aftermath of the D-Day landings, Allied forces had captured thousands of German prisoners. Under a remarkably arbitrary scheme, those whose names began with a letter in the first half of the alphabet were sent to the United States where they were held in mass internment camps. (The remainder were imprisoned in camps in Britain or the parts of Europe liberated by the Allies.) In the middle of 1946, the American government began repatriating its prisoners; most were returned to Germany, but 130,000 were sent – ostensibly temporarily – to Britain.

Among them was a 37-year-old Wehrmacht corporal, Joachim Kirmse; he was taken to a PoW camp at Shepherd's Bush, less than two miles from Gleave's home. The camp's regime was evidently relaxed; visits from neighbouring residents to inmates were allowed and, as Christmas approached, the authorities encouraged arrangements for prisoners to enjoy the festivities in local homes. In the third week in December Eileen Gleave presented herself at the camp gates and was introduced to Kirmse. He duly spent the Christmas period in her flat and, by their own accounts, over the ensuing months the couple became romantically involved. Then, in late April 1947, Kirmse walked out of the camp and caught a bus to Barons Court; for three months Gleave harboured him in her room.

At 7.00am on July 28 their idyll was interrupted by the arrival of Special Branch officers. They searched the rooms, eventually discovering Kirmse hiding, naked, in Gleave's wardrobe.[8] Both were arrested and Gleave was summoned to appear at West London Magistrates' Court; on August 20 she was convicted and bound over for twelve months. The relatively lenient sentence seems to have been informed by the couple's emotional declarations of love. Kirmse told his interrogators: 'What I have done and shall do in the future is done only so that I should not lose Mrs Eileen Gleave, whom I love and esteem and whom I shall marry when my personal affairs are cleared up';[9] while Gleave promised to support them both on the strength of her weekly £3 17s wages.

There was, however, good reason to doubt the honesty of this touching love story. Gleave's past history aside, Joachim Kirmse was very far from the humble army corporal he pretended to be; in reality, he was already married and had five children waiting for him in Berlin. More importantly, his record, held in the Allied war crimes unit, showed him to be a former Gestapo agent who had joined the SS and risen to the rank of Sturmbannfuehrer – the Nazi equivalent to Major. Kirmse had taken part in the 1943 parachute landings on Crete, and his unit was involved in the mass execution of anti-Nazi partisans – an event which led him to assume thereafter the identity of a fallen infantry soldier.[10] Since, at the time of his arrest in Gleave's flat, 24 officers from his Einsatzgruppen unit were awaiting trial at Nuremberg, Kirmse had every reason to maintain his fictional identity and prolong his stay in Britain.*

Whether he did so, and what became of Eileen Gleave is unknown; the files on all the Jack King network conspirators end at the date of her sentence. But she was not the only Fifth Columnist convicted of harbouring escaped PoWs. In March 1947, Arnold Leese – leader of the Imperial Fascist League, now running what he termed a 'Jewish Information Bureau' – was brought to the Old Bailey. He, together with seven of his former IFL colleagues, was charged with conspiring to aid the escape of two Waffen SS officers from the internment camp at Kempton Park racecourse near London.

---

* The Einsatzgruppen (literally: 'operation group') Trial was the ninth of the twelve war crimes proceedings heard at Nuremberg. It lasted from September 1947 to April 1948. All the defendants were convicted; four were executed and the remainder sentenced to lengthy terms of imprisonment.

Since Leese's previous appearance in the dock had been for advocating the mass extermination of Jews by gassing – something for which the Waffen SS had gained notoriety – there was at least some sense of circularity in the case. He and his co-defendants were each sent to prison for twelve months and given a stern lecture by the judge, Sir Gerald Dodson.

'People are entitled to their political opinions so long as they do not take the law into their own hands. That only leads to confusion, anarchy and disorder ... You have been led into this by your opinion. Now you are broken on the rocks of your own foolishness.'[11]

Other prominent anti-Semites and Nazi sympathisers were dealt with rather more leniently. Robert Gordon-Canning, the well-connected and wealthy fascist who once boasted of his willingness to assist German submarine crews, had not allowed the restrictions covering his release from internment to interfere with his political activity. In the immediate post-war years MI5's files noted that he remained 'a close friend of Arnold Leese, Captain Ramsay, Anna Wolkoff, Admiral Domvile and other well-known British National Socialists, and shares in full measure their anti-Jewish obsession'.[12]

Gordon-Canning demonstrated this devotion to National Socialism in November 1945 by paying £500 – equivalent to almost £15,000 today – to secure a granite bust of Hitler being sold at auction in London.[13] He did so, according to a letter he sent to the right-wing weekly magazine, *Truth*, 'to prevent a historical work of art falling into the hands of iconoclasts, to preserve it as an *objet d'art* [and] to return the sculpture to the German nation at the opportune hour'. Lest there be any doubt about his loyalties, he assured the journal's readers that:

When the history of the twentieth century comes to be written, the historians will base their work upon facts and not upon wartime propaganda. Thus Adolf Hitler will take rank with the great figures in the past history of mankind.[14]

Archibald Ramsay, once the would-be leader of a fascist uprising, shared Gordon-Canning's assessment. He remained in the House of

Commons until July 1945, when he lost his seat in the general election which gave Clement Attlee's Labour Party a landslide victory; Ramsay's last political act, in June, was an (unsuccessful) attempt to reintroduce the medieval Statute of the Jewry.*[15] Ejection from Parliament, however, did nothing to temper his rabid beliefs; in April 1946 one of Rothschild's undercover agents filed a report of a conversation with the erstwhile Right Club founder.

> Ramsay says that ... he takes the view that the only possible way of dealing with the Jewish problem is to concentrate on awakening the public by 'any and every means and trick' to the menace of Jewry, and to encourage a state of mind where the public would forget sentimentality and appreciate that extermination by lethal and humane means is the only solution.
>
> He is not in favour of torture or cruelty, but he thinks that the Nazis were fully justified in their methods ... Ramsay speaks very warmly in favour of National Socialist Germany and ... he expresses the belief that Nazism will have to be 'taken back to Germany' as there will be no chance of revival during military occupation. The only way of doing this in Ramsay's view is to fight for National Socialism until victory is secured.[16]

Ramsay's own contribution to this fight was to issue, through a far-right fringe publisher, his autobiography. *The Nameless War: A History of Events Leading up to the Second World War* included his justification for forming a secret society: 'The main object of the Right Club was to oppose and expose the activities of Organised Jewry, in the light of the evidence which came into my possession in 1938. Our first objective was to clear the Conservative Party of Jewish influence, and the character of our membership and meetings were strictly in keeping with this objective.'[17]

---

* The Statute of the Jewry was issued by Edward I in 1253. It required Jews above the age of seven to wear a yellow badge on their clothing, imposed restrictions on where they could live, and outlawed 'usury' or money-lending.

Ramsay died in 1955, three years after the book was published. His legacy lived – and still lives – on after him, however. *The Nameless War* has been regularly reprinted in the decades since his death; the most recent (2018) edition is distributed by an American neo-Nazi mail-order publisher.

Anna Wolkoff, Ramsay's self-styled chief of staff, was released from prison in June 1947, after serving seven of the ten years she received for espionage. She was, by then, penniless and had been stripped of her British citizenship; for the next sixteen years she eked out a living as a jobbing seamstress in south London, before going to Spain to stay with her Right Club comrade and former racing driver, Enid Riddell. On August 2, 1973, Riddell crashed the car in which they were travelling; she survived but Wolkoff was killed.

Tyler Kent, Wolkoff's co-defendant, was sent back to the United States when the war ended. After a brief period of celebrity, he married a wealthy widow and became the publisher of a pro-segregationist newspaper closely tied to the Ku Klux Klan. The venture was ultimately unprofitable: Kent spent his last years in a Texas trailer park, dying in poverty in 1988.

None of the remaining members of the Right Club lived to see their involvement in its machinations exposed. The membership ledger remained a closely guarded secret until it was given to the Wiener Institute in 2000. There is no indication in any publicly released official file that any of the largely privileged or aristocratic names it contained were monitored in the post-war period. Other fascists and fellow-travellers, however, were kept under surveillance.

The Duke of Bedford continued to attract the attention of MI5 – not least since he associated with fellow Nazi sympathisers such as Arnold Leese. Much of the contents of Ramsay's once-extensive file in the Security Service Registry were destroyed in the 1950s – no reason is shown and the authorising signatory is impossible to decipher – but from notes on the Registry Minute Sheets (essentially a narrative index) at the front of the dossier it is clear that a Home Office warrant to intercept his mail was in place until February 10, 1949. The same sheets also record a succession of meetings with other members of the former fascist underground, as well as the regular injections of funding he gave to their attempts to form post-war groups. One name in particular cropped up regularly.

John Beckett, along with his fellow conspirator Ben Greene, had been released from internment on undertakings that they would not engage in any further fascist activity: neither man kept his promise, and backed by Bedford's wealth they restarted the British People's Party. A note filed by MI5's F3 section in June 1945 reported information derived from one of its undercover informants.

> Ben says that Beckett ... had made the utterly fantastic statement that the Duke of Bedford was putting up half a million pounds for a new party, that Ben was on its committee as treasurer, and that the new party was planning to 'set up a sort of armed force to hold a meeting in Queens Hall and take over the government of this country'.[18]

Greene and Beckett evidently fell out very quickly, and Ben left the BPP to form a new right-wing group. This organisation – The National Front After Victory – drew on the dregs of the old English Nationalist Association but, although it also attracted the support of Major General Fuller, did very little to trouble the Security Service. Greene died in 1978, still convinced that fascism was nothing more than a bogeyman, dreamed up by the leaders of international communism.

Beckett's admiration for Hitler and the Third Reich remained undimmed. Although each post-war year revealed further – and worse – evidence of Nazi atrocities, the man who would have replaced Churchill's government with a Quisling administration under Bedford, continued to argue that the Reich had been wilfully misunderstood. A letter he sent to a supporter in October 1945 – intercepted by the continuing Home Office warrant on his correspondence – set out his case.

> Our view on the causes of the war is that even if the stories about the Hitler regime were true – and as we know most of them to have been [sic] propaganda – they would not have justified the war and were in fact not the cause of it. The Axis broke the rules of the game by going off the gold standard and introducing barter. They also broke the Jewish control of their industries and therefore, had they been the

best and finest regimes of the world, they had to be crucified as the enemies of gold and usury have been for the past two thousand years.[19]

With little left of his former political base, Beckett's efforts on behalf of the BPP produced no discernible reward. Its solitary attempt at winning public support, in the March 1946 by-election for the Combined English Universities constituency, ended with the party polling just 239 votes.*

As the BPP gradually wilted, Beckett turned his energies towards campaigning for what he saw as justice for his former comrade-in-arms, William Joyce. Lord Haw-Haw had been captured by British troops in Flensburg, the Third Reich's last and short-lived capital, in May 1945.

Four months later he was tried at the Old Bailey on three counts of High Treason; each cited his broadcasts from Berlin, alleging that 'as a person owing allegiance to our Lord the King, and while a war was being carried on by the German realm against our King [he] did traitorously adhere to the King's enemies in Germany, by broadcasting propaganda'. In truth, the legal basis for the charge was somewhat flimsy. Joyce was technically an American citizen, and thus owed no allegiance to the British monarch; he had, however, obtained a British passport by lying about his nationality – a fact which persuaded the court that he was covered by the law of High Treason.

On 19 September he was convicted on all counts and sentenced to death; two appeals – to the Court of Appeals and the House of Lords – were rejected and by the middle of December Joyce awaited his fate in the condemned cell at Brixton prison. It was to this address that Beckett sent a farewell note to his fellow fascist: it said simply, 'Goodbye, William, it's been good to know you and there are few things in my life I am prouder of than our association.'[20]

Joyce was hanged on the morning of January 3, 1946. He went to his death unrepentant and proclaiming his belief in National Socialism, and was not noticeably mourned by those who had endured Lord Haw-Haw's sneering propaganda broadcasts. His case, though,

---

* The British People's Party finally disbanded in 1954, a year after the Duke of Bedford died and its funding ceased. Beckett died in 1964.

did highlight an uncomfortable truth about the ongoing disparities in the way justice was meted out to those who had betrayed – or sought to betray – their country to Germany.

Of at least fourteen British citizens tried in English courts (or military courts martial) for having made propaganda broadcasts on behalf of the Nazis, only two – Joyce and John Amery* – were executed; the remainder received sentences ranging from life imprisonment to just six months. There is no logical – or legal – explanation for this, since the number and frequency of broadcasts was irrelevant to the crime. In addition, one of the convicted traitors was Norman Baillie-Stewart, the pre-war spy who had served a lengthy prison term for selling military secrets to Germany; under the circumstances, the inexplicably lenient five-year prison term he was given in January 1946 emphasised the wildly inconsistent treatment of what the Home Office files term 'renegades'.

These post-war cases repeat a theme to be found throughout the MI5, Home Office, Treasury department and Cabinet files on the men and women who made up the Fifth Column. Justice, if it was done at all, was often rough at best. Was George Johnson's fumbling effort at espionage any worse than that of Serocold Skeels? Why was he hanged while Skeels received only a relatively short term of imprisonment? Why did Dorothy O'Grady merit clemency when Duncan Scott-Ford did not? And why were aristocratic traitors such as the Duke of Bedford and Lord Sempill afforded protection?

There is no easy or definitive answer to these troubling questions – although it would not be unreasonable to draw the inference that archaic attitudes to class and gender played a significant part. The lack of absolute certainty, however, is due to the lengthy suppression of

---

* Between 1942 and 1944, John Amery, the son of a Conservative MP and wartime government minister, made a succession of Nazi propaganda broadcasts from Berlin. He travelled to Italy in late 1944 to support Mussolini's fascist regime; in the final weeks of the war he was captured by Italian partisans and handed over to British forces. In November 1945 he appeared at the Old Bailey, charged with eight counts of treason; after initially contesting the charges, he pleaded guilty despite being warned that he would be executed. He was hanged at Wandsworth prison on December 19, 1945. National Archives file KV 2/78-84; declassified September 9, 1999.

official dossiers on British Fifth Columnists, and the heavy-handed official weeding of those which have been released. File after file shows that thousands of original documents were either destroyed or removed before their release to the National Archives. And the manner of that release – belated, haphazard and spread over a period of almost twenty years – has greatly hindered a clear understanding of the true scale of the threat posed by domestic British fascists.

But pieced together and cross-referenced, the scores of individual volumes and many thousands of documents which have been released tell an unmistakable story. Throughout the six years Britain was at war with Nazi Germany – and during some of her darkest hours – hundreds of her citizens willingly betrayed their country to the enemy. They were, in the words of Marcus Tullius Cicero, 'the enemy within the gates' and they spoke, as he predicted, 'in accents familiar'. They were, in short, Hitler's British Traitors.

Afterword

'Those who cannot remember the past are condemned to repeat it.'
George Santayana, philosopher and writer[1]

This book tells the stories of people and events from more than 70 years ago. Looking back at them can sometimes feel like staring at another world, its contours, accents and rhythms very different to the 21st century.

But this is deceptive. The same ethical dilemmas which troubled politicians, civil servants and the Security Service before and during the Second World War have not gone away. How far away from the fundamental principles of a democracy – the individual's right to hold and express beliefs which the majority of the country would find abhorrent – should a democracy go to protect itself? If, as Benjamin Franklin warned the Pennsylvania Assembly in 1755, 'Those who can give up essential Liberty to obtain a little temporary Safety, deserve neither Liberty nor Safety', how is society to deal with those for whom personal freedom is anathema?

If we look closely, the story of the spies, saboteurs and Fifth Columnists who made up Hitler's British Traitors offers a parallel to the way 21st-century Britain perceives and reacts to the threat from terrorism.

Initially, at least, much of the effort against the Fifth Column was directed at the assumed threat from 'alien nationals' – immigrants who, for the most part, sought sanctuary in Britain; yet, in reality, the greatest danger was from domestic fascists and Nazi sympathisers. Fast forward seven decades and observe the same press-driven public suspicion of refugees from predominantly Islamic countries, riven by wars which, to some extent, the West has created; then contrast this with the overwhelming evidence that the vast majority of terrorist attacks are carried out by those who have grown up in this country, but who have been 'radicalised' by others. For the 7/7 or 2017 Manchester bombers – British citizens all – read the foot-soldiers of the fascist movement told by their leaders that Jews were the problem and Hitler the solution.

Similarly, the anxiety over MI5's sometimes ethically-dubious methods of investigating and defusing the danger of Nazi sympathisers is the direct precursor to today's debate about how to respond to modern terrorist threats. Since the end of the Second World War, Britain has not succumbed to the seemingly easy option of mass detention without trial (the brief and deeply shameful attempt at internment during the Irish Troubles of the 1970s aside).

Yet today we have its 21st-century variant. TPIMs – Terrorist Prevention and Investigation Measures – were signed into law in 2011 and reaffirmed in 2016. While they do not provide for full (let alone mass) internment, they do enable temporary control orders, including *de-facto* house arrest, for those whom Her Majesty's government describes as 'individuals who pose a real terrorist threat, but whom we cannot prosecute or, in the case of foreign nationals, deport'.[2] There is no difference in principle between TPIMs and Defence Regulation 18B – and very little variance in practice.

Much as in the years leading up to the Second World War, we have arrived at this position without any real public discussion; decisions have been taken, corners are cut and regulations issued under delegated powers without substantive scrutiny by Parliament. And yet there are fundamental issues at stake. How draconian do we, as citizens, want the security apparatus of the state to be? Are we prepared to pay the price – financial and moral – of protecting the country and its citizens from those who would do them harm? Can internment – or even 'internment-lite' – without due process of trial ever be justified?

Beyond that, how do we expect the Security Service to investigate and foil the perceived threat? Are we comfortable with the *agent provocateur* tactics developed by Maxwell Knight and then Lord Rothschild, now repeated by their 21st-century equivalents? And what of torture? Is there a difference in principle between the alleged methods used against German spies and British traitors at Camp 020, and the 'enhanced interrogation techniques' deployed at Abu Ghraib, Camp Bastion or Guantánamo Bay? And on an apparently smaller scale, were not the actions of Jack Bingham and Eric Roberts in playing on the emotions – however chastely and without consummation – of Irma Stapleton and Dorothy Wegener a forerunner to the much-criticised tactics of the Metropolitan Police in sending officers to live with and seduce activists and dissenters in modern Britain?

These are big, serious questions, but they resolve into one over-riding challenge: does the long-term goal – safety and security for the greatest number of people – ever excuse the wholesale trampling of an individual's human rights, which is the inevitable by-product of deception, entrapment and *agent provocateur* schemes? And if it did, in principle, justify those actions almost 80 years ago, is that only because the nation faced a genuine existential threat?

I do not have an answer – at least not a firm answer – to those questions. In the two years it has taken to research and write this book my conclusions have changed from one day to the next. What I do know is that this is a debate which needs to take place.

It is surely irresponsible to demand that the Security Service guarantee our safety without accepting the corresponding duty on every citizen to decide where the ethical line must be drawn. In the Second World War this issue was fudged, causing injustice to MI5 agents and to those whom they investigated alike. Their story was hidden for too long behind a wall of official secrecy.

That wall has now been breached: if the secret history of Hitler's British Traitors does nothing else, I hope it will lead to an honest and open debate about our past and our future.

Tim Tate
Wiltshire, April 2018

Acknowledgements

The files from which this book is largely drawn are held at the National Archives at Kew. The staff there were extremely helpful, and the Archives' policy of making an increasing number of files available as digital downloads greatly eased the research process.

Particular thanks are due to Duncan Heath and all at Icon Books for their support and hard work; Duncan's thorough and careful editing greatly improved the manuscript.

I'm also grateful to Hampstead historian Dick Weindling for unearthing the death certificate for the unfortunate Mrs Else Duncombe.

I owe an enormous debt to my agent, the indefatigable Andrew Lownie; his encouragement and enthusiasm – as well as his exemplary representation – were vital throughout what turned out to be a much larger project than originally envisaged.

And finally, a heartfelt apology is due to my partner, Mia Pennal, who cheerfully put up with my near-total disappearance within the vast mountain of files for more than a year; her love and quiet patience are – always – an inspiration.

Selected Bibliography

Alanbrooke, Field Marshal Lord. *War Diaries, 1939–1945* (University of California Press, 1998)

Andrew, Christopher. *The Defence of the Realm: The Authorized History of MI5* (Allen Lane, 2009)

Beckett, Francis. *The Rebel Who Lost His Cause* (London House, 1999)

Briscoe, Paul (with Michael McMahon). *My friend, the enemy: an English boy in Nazi Germany* (Aurum Press, 2007)

Farago, Ladislas. *The Game of the Foxes* (David McKay & Co., 1971)

Gillman, Peter and Leni. *Collar the Lot! How Britain interned and expelled its wartime refugees* (Quartet, 1980)

Griffiths, Richard. *Patriotism Perverted: Captain Ramsay, the Right Club and British Anti-Semitism, 1939–40* (Constable, 1998)

Hayward, James. *Hitler's Spy: the true story of Arthur Owens, Double Agent Snow* (Simon & Schuster, 2012)

Hemming, Henry. *Maxwell Knight, MI5's Greatest Spymaster* (Preface, 2017)

Hinsley, F.H., and Simkins, C.A.G. *British Intelligence in the Second World War* (HMSO, 1990)

Masters, Anthony. *The Man Who Was M* (Blackwell, 1984)

Miller, Joan. *One Girl's War* (Brandon Books, 1986)

Pugh, Martin. *Hurrah for the Blackshirts! Fascists and Fascism in Britain Between the Wars* (Jonathan Cape, 2005)

Simpson, A.W.B. *In the Highest Degree Odious: Detention Without Trial in Wartime Britain* (Clarendon Press, 1992)

Thurlow, Richard. *Fascism in Britain* (Blackwell, 1987)

Willetts, Paul. *Rendezvous at the Russian Tea Rooms* (Constable, 2015)

Notes

Introduction

1. A.W.B. Simpson, *Rhetoric, Reality, and Regulation 18B* (1988), and *The Judges and the Vigilant State* (1989). Both available at *The Denning Law Journal*.

2. Richard Thurlow, 'The Evolution of the Mythical British Fifth Column'. *Twentieth Century History*, Vol. 10, No. 4, pp. 477–98. Oxford University Press, 1999.

3. F.H. Hinsley and C.A.G. Simkins, *British Intelligence in the Second World War*, Chapter 3: 'The Fifth Column Panic', pp. 47–64. HMSO, 1994.

4. Christopher Andrew, *The Defence of the Realm: The Authorized History of MI5*, p. 224. Allen Lane, 2009.

5. Winston Churchill, speech in the House of Commons, May 17, 1916.

Chapter 1

1. Signed statement of Norman Baillie-Stewart, April 15, 1933. National Archives files KV 2/178.

2. Report on Lt. Norman Baillie-Stewart, October 17, 1932. National Archives files KV 2/174.

3. MI5 file note, October 1, 1932. Ibid.

4. Signed statement of Norman Baillie-Stewart, April 15, 1933. National Archives files KV 2/178.

5. 'Charges Against "Officer In The Tower" – Sold his Country for Sake of £50'. *The Citizen*, March 20, 1933.

6. Christopher Andrew, *The Defence of the Realm: The Authorized History of MI5*, p. 56. Allen Lane, 2009.

7. 'Sentence on The Officer In The Tower'. *Evening News*, April 13, 1933.

8. *Hansard*, November 14 and November 23, 1933.

9. Ibid.

10. 'The German Intelligence Service in World War Two, Vol. 3'. US intelligence report, July 30, 1946. Declassified 2007. CIA Library.

11. 'My Amazing Life by Mrs Jordan: Part One'. *Sunday Mail*, May 29, 1938.

12. Ibid.

13. At some point Jessie also gave birth to a son, Werner, though since local records give his surname as Tillkes it seems likely that she too had an extra-marital affair.

14. 'My Amazing Life by Mrs Jordan: Part Three'. *Sunday Mail*, June 12, 1938.

15. Memo from MI6 to Colonel William Hinchley-Cooke, MI5, April 29, 1938. National Archives file KV 2/193.

16. 'My Amazing Life by Mrs Jordan: Part Three'. *Sunday Mail*, June 12, 1938.

17. Alphabetical List Showing Points of Considerable Importance. National Archives file KV 2/192.

18. 'My Amazing Life by Mrs Jordan: Part Three'. *Sunday Mail*, June 12, 1938.

19. Precognition [pre-trial statement] by Col. William Hinchley-Cooke, MI5. National Archives file KV 2/3534: declassified 2011.

20. Goertz was convicted of espionage in 1936 and jailed for four years. He was deported to Germany in February 1939, but parachuted into the Republic of Ireland in the summer of 1940. He was arrested and imprisoned the following year and spent the remainder of the war in Irish custody. National Archives file KV 2/1319–1323.

21. Ibid.

22. File note by MI5, B.2. Division, January 12, 1938. National Archives file KV 2/193.

23. 'Jessie Jordan or Wallace: Suspected Espionage'. Report by Insp. John Carstairs, Dundee City Police, November 29, 1937. National Archives file KV 2/193.

24. £350 in 1937 is equivalent to approximately £23,000 today.

25. Letter from Chief Constable, Dundee City Police to MI5, December 8, 1937. National Archives file KV 2/193.

26. MI5 file note, March 8, 1938. National Archives file KV 2/193.

27. Letter from 'Crown', sent to Jessie Jordan, January 17, 1938. National Archives file KV 2/193.

28. Memorandum for US Military Attaché, January 29, 1938. National Archives file KV 2/193.

29. In December 1938, Hoffman, Rumrich, Otto Voss and Erich Glaser were

convicted and given prison sentences of between two and six years. National Archives file KV 2/3421.

30. 'Woman Spy Sentenced'. *Yorkshire Post*, May 17, 1938.

31. 'Unconcern of Mrs Jordan at Four Years' Sentence'. *Dundee Courier*, May 17, 1938.

32. The sentence of penal servitude involved hard labour as well as incarceration. It was abolished in England and Wales in 1948; Scotland followed suit two years later.

33. *R. v. Jordan*, May 16, 1938.

34. Convicts sentenced to penal servitude were required to perform harsh, often pointless, physical labour including hours on a treadmill or endlessly turning a heavy iron crank.

35. *Daily Express*, May 18, 1938.

36. MI5 file note, November 21, 1940. National Archives file KV 2/193.

37. Ibid.

38. Letter from the Lord Advocate to Sir Vernon Kell, MI5, July 26, 1938. National Archives file KV 2/194.

39. *Dundee Courier*, May 17, 1938.

Chapter 2

1. Death Certificate No. 9545614-1 of Else Klara Emma Duncombe: 'Narcotic poisoning (probably aspirin). Did kill herself while of unsound mind.' March 5, 1938.

2. Mrs Duncombe appears to have warranted her own MI5 file, referred to in the papers of German agents whom she served as PF 45152. There is, however, no trace of any such file in the National Archives.

3. MI5's eleven-volume analysis of the Siemens-Halske-Schuckert Combine. National Archives file KV 2/3314–3316; declassified August 26, 2010.

4. MI5 memorandum, 'Siemens-Schuckert', November 19, 1941. National Archives file KV 2/3800; declassified February 28, 2014.

5. MI5's eleven-volume analysis of the Siemens-Halske-Schuckert Combine. National Archives file KV 2/3314–3316; declassified August 26, 2010.

6. 'The German Intelligence Service in World War Two, Vol. 3'. US intelligence report, July 30, 1946. Declassified 2007. CIA Library.

7. Equivalent to approximately £1,200 today.

8. 'The German Intelligence Service in World War Two, Vol. 3'. US intelligence report, July 30, 1946. Declassified 2007. CIA Library.

9. 'Rudolph Gottfried Rosel'. National Archives files KV 2/3187–3189; declassified March 8, 2010.

10. MI5 memo on Rudolph Gottfried Rosel. National Archives files KV 2/3187–3189; declassified March 8, 2010.

11. Letter from MI5 to Gladwyn Jebb, Foreign Office, February 23, 1939. National Archives files KV 2/3187–3189; declassified March 8, 2010.

12. 'Arnold Littmann'. National Archives files KV 2/2837–2838; declassified August 30, 2008.

13. Report of Insp. Charles Allen, Special Branch, Metropolitan Police; April 9, 1939. In MI5 file on Carl Kullmann. National Archives files KV 2/2842–2843; declassified August 30, 2008.

14. The network was broken up by the FBI in 1941. 'Carl Kullmann'. National Archives files KV 2/2842–2843; declassified August 30, 2008.

15. 'Paul Borchardt'. National Archives files KV 2/2429–2430; declassified March 2, 2007.

16. Borchardt was finally caught and tried for 'treasonable conspiracy and espionage' in December 1941. A federal court sentenced him to twenty years in prison.

17. 'Rudolph Gottfried Rosel'. National Archives files KV 2/3187–3189; declassified March 8, 2010.

18. 'Hermann Walter Christian Simon'. National Archives files KV 2/1293; declassified September 26, 2003.

19. Equivalent to £900 approx. today.

20. 'Josephine "My" Eriksson'. National Archives files KV 2/535–539; declassified October 30, 2001.

21. Statement of Lady Elveden (undated). National Archives file KV 2/536; declassified October 30, 2001.

22. From his base in 'Nest Hamburg', Ritter ran agents in Britain and the United States. These included Jessie Jordan and the Guenther Rumrich/Crown network, Paul Borchardt, as well as several of the 'Last Spies of Peace' (detailed in Chapter 5). 'Nikolaus Adolf Fritz Ritter'. National Archives files KV 2/85–88; declassified September 9, 1999.

23. MI5, 'Summary of Case against Mrs Eriksson', March 13, 1941. National Archives file KV 2/537; declassified October 30, 2001.

24. 'Hermann Walter Christian Simon'. National Archives files KV 2/1293; declassified September 26, 2003.

25. Undated MI5 memo on Hermann Simon and his British contacts. National Archives file KV 2/1293; declassified September 26, 2003.

26. George Billings subsequently joined the RAF where MI5 noted that 'he is doing well'. There is no further trace of him in any MI5 file in the National Archives.

27. 'Edward Harry Bernard Durrant'. National Archives files KV 2/3759–3760; declassified February 28, 2014.

28. Undated post-war report on Hermann Simon by the Irish Intelligence Service. National Archives file KV 2/1293; declassified September 26, 2003.

29. Transcript of interrogation of Josephine 'My' Eriksson by Col. William Hinchley-Cooke, New Scotland Yard, December 17, 1939. National Archives files KV 2/535–539; declassified October 30, 2001.

30. 'Josephine "My" Eriksson'. National Archives files KV 2/535–539; declassified October 30, 2001.

31. F.H. Hinsley and C.A.G. Simkins, *British Intelligence in the Second World War*, p. 13. HMSO, 1990. This was an official history of MI5 and MI6's activities during the Second World War: both services, and their parent government departments, gave what the authors described as 'free access to official documents'.

32. Ibid.

33. Ibid., pp. 11–12.

Chapter 3

1. 'Franco's Secret Army Scares Madrid: Hundreds Arrested'. *Daily Express*, October 5, 1936.

2. William P. Carney, 'Madrid Rounds Up Suspected Rebels'. *New York Times*, October 16, 1936.

3. Ernest Hemingway, *The Fifth Column and The First Forty-Nine Stories*. Scribner, 1938.

4. Ernst Forsthoff, *Der Totale Staat*. Hamburg: Hanseatische Verlagsanstalt, 1933.

5. Erich Ludendorff, *Der Totale Krieg*. Munich: Verlag GmbH, 1935.

6. Both Ludendorff and Forsthoff quarrelled with Hitler; the Gestapo banned the latter from university teaching posts until 1943.

7. Anthony Eden, 'The German Danger: A Collection of reports from His Majesty's Embassy at Berlin between the accession of Herr Hitler to power in the spring of 1933 and the end of 1935'. Paper for the Cabinet, January 17, 1936. National Archives file CAB 24/259/13.

8. General Hastings Ismay, Secretary of the Committee of Imperial Defence, 'Memo to the Cabinet', September 20, 1938. National Archives file CAB 21/544.

9. Defence Regulation 14B, June 10, 1915.

10. William Blackstone, *Commentaries on the Laws of England*, Vol. 1, Chapter 1. 1765–69.

11. Home Office Memorandum to the Cabinet, December 11, 1936. National Archives file CAB 52/4.

12. 2,000 German nationals were allowed – more accurately, encouraged – to leave voluntarily.

13. F.H. Hinsley and C.A.G. Simkins, *British Intelligence in the Second World War*, p. 5. HMSO, 1990.

14. Sir Maurice Hankey, 'Investigation into the Method of Operation and Organisation of the Security Service', May 1940. National Archives file CAB 127/383.

15. 'Work of the Registry MI5 H2'. National Archives file KV 1/55.

16. Christopher Andrew, *The Defence of the Realm: The Authorized History of MI5*, p. 122. Allen Lane, 2009.

17. Maxwell Knight, 'Report on the work of MS (recruitment and operation of agents) during the Second World War'. National Archives files KV 4/227–228; declassified March 30, 2004.

18. Christopher Andrew, quoting a still-classified document in the Security Service Archives. *The Defence of the Realm: The Authorized History of MI5*, p. 123. Allen Lane, 2009.

19. Ibid., p. 124.

20. Ibid., p. 128.

21. In March 1938, Percy Glading, a founder member of the Communist Party of Great Britain, was convicted, largely on the evidence of Knight's undercover informants, along with two employees at Woolwich Arsenal, of stealing classified military information for the Soviet Union. He was sentenced to six years in prison. 'Percy Eded Glading'. National Archives file KV 2/1020–1023; declassified October 31, 2002.

22. 'Policy re: Study and Investigation of Fascism and other right wing or kindred movements'. National Archives file KV 4/331; declassified June 26, 2006.

23. Maxwell Knight, 'Report on the work of MS (recruitment and operation of agents) during the Second World War'. National Archives files KV 4/227–228; declassified March 30, 2004.

24. Ibid.

25. Joan Miller, *One Girl's War*, p. 42. Brandon Books, 1983. Miller's short memoir was not well received by the Security Service which tried to ban its publication.

26. Christopher Andrew, *The Defence of the Realm: The Authorized History of MI5*, p. 132. Allen Lane, 2009.

27. Ibid., p. 133.

28. Ibid., p. 127.

29. 'Robert Harry Mayes'. National Archives file DPP 2/624; declassified December 1, 2000.

30. 'Walter Whiting Moore'. National Archives file DPP 2/632; declassified December 1, 2000.

31. It is unclear whether this refers to Simmonstown near Dublin, or Simonstown, South Africa.

32. 'Michael Riorden'. National Archives file DPP 2/712; declassified December 1, 2000.

33. Christopher Andrew, *The Defence of the Realm: The Authorized History of MI5*, p. 128. Allen Lane, 2009.

Chapter 4

1. Joseph Goebbels, radio address to the German people. April 20, 1939.

2. 'George VI Sends Hitler Congratulatory Message', UPI report (in *The Pittsburgh Press*, inter alia), April 20, 1939.

3. MI5 compiled a file on Brocket, referred to as PF 47996 (PF was the original classification of MI5 files) in Security Service reports on Rudolph Rosel. However, there is no trace of it in the National Archives.

4. Maj. Gen. J.F.C. Fuller, 'The Cancer of Europe'. *Fascist Quarterly*, Vol. 2, Iss. 1, pp. 65–81, London, 1935.

5. Max Boot, *War Made New: Technology, Warfare and the Course of History, 1500 to Today*. Gotham Books, 2006.

6. Hermann Rauschning, 'Gespräche mit Hitler' (Conversations with Hitler). Rauschning quarrelled with Hitler and the Nazi Party in 1934, fleeing – by stages – to Poland, Switzerland, England and finally the United States. His book was published in Britain shortly before the outbreak of war. *Hitler Speaks – A series of political conversations with Adolf Hitler on his real aims (between 1932–1934)*. Thornton Butterworth, London, 1939.

7. 'Otto Karl Ludwig'. National Archives files KV 2/350–352; declassified May 11, 2001.

8. 'Fritz Thassilo Krug Von Nidda'. National Archives files KV 2/2431–2432; declassified March 2, 2007.

9. List of Von Nidda's British contacts, found in the Reichsluftfahrt Ministerium, Berlin-Charlottenburg, and sent to MI5, December 31, 1946. National Archives file KV 2/2432; declassified March 2, 2007.

10. There is no suggestion that Hall was a willing – or even witting – agent of influence. In fact his name appears in the so-called 'Black Book', the Nazis' 'Special Wanted Arrest List' of British leaders to be captured and

interrogated by the Gestapo after the planned German invasion in 1940. 'Hitler's Black Book', Imperial War Museum: https://www.forces-war-records.co.uk/hitlers-black-book/person/1296/sir-reginald-hall/

11. 'The Dowager Viscountess Downe'. National Archives file KV 2/2146, declassified February 3, 2006.

12. *Torquay Times*, April 7, 1939.

13. Note on the Registry Minute Sheet by MI5's F3 Branch, October 12, 1943. 'The Dowager Viscountess Downe'. National Archives file KV 2/2146, declassified February 3, 2006.

14. Case summary, George Pitt-Rivers. February 9, 1942. 'George Henry Lane-Fox Pitt-Rivers'. National Archives file KV 2/831; declassified May 1, 2002. This MI5 file, like many of those relating to wealthy and well-connected British Nazi fellow-travellers, has been extensively weeded, with many of its original contents destroyed.

15. *Confessions of an anti-Feminist: The Autobiography of Anthony M. Ludovici*, ed. John V. Da, Ch. 5. Counter-Currents Publishing, 2008.

16. Anthony M. Ludovici, 'Hitler and the Third Reich'. *The English Review*, No. 63, pp. 35–41, 1936.

17. Anthony M. Ludovici (writing as 'Cobbett'), *Jews and The Jews in England*. Boswell Publishing Co., London, 1938.

18. Companion of the Order of the Bath is an order of chivalry, founded in 1725, and awarded for service to the Crown 'of the highest calibre'. The Order of St Michael and St George was founded by King George III in 1818; Companionship is bestowed 'for extraordinary and important services abroad or in the Commonwealth'.

19. 'Admiral Sir Barry Domvile'. National Archives files KV 2/834–838; declassified May 1, 2002.

20. Dachau – described by Himmler as 'the first concentration camp for political prisoners', which could hold 5,000 inmates – opened on March 22, 1933. From the outset prisoners were used as forced labour for a local munitions factory.

21. The 1936 event (September 8–14) was the Eighth Nazi Party Conference, and was known as 'The Rally of Honour'. Attended by approximately 800,000 people, the rally had three key themes: The evils of Bolshevism, Germany's need to be independent of foreign sources of raw materials, and its demands to reclaim the colonies it lost after the First World War.

22. MI5 report on Admiral Sir Barry Domvile, KBE, CB, CMG by Marjorie Robert, F3 Branch; March 6, 1944. National Archives file KV 2/836; declassified May 1, 2002.

23. Barry Domvile, Letter to Reichsfuehrer Heinrich Himmler, March 21, 1938. National Archives file KV 2/834; declassified May 1, 2002.

24. 'Admiral Sir Barry Domvile'. National Archives files KV 2/834–838; declassified May 1, 2002. There is no MI5 file on Carroll himself – despite references to it in Domvile's files.

25. 'Admiral Sir Barry Domvile'. National Archives files KV 2/834–838; declassified May 1, 2002.

26. Ibid.

27. *Hansard*, August 3, 1939. 'German Propaganda'.

28. William J. Donovan and Edgar Mowrer, *Fifth Column Lessons for America*. American Council on Public Affairs, 1940.

Chapter 5

1. *London Evening Standard*, July 14, 1939.

2. *Daily Mail*, July 15, 1939.

3. *News Chronicle*, July 15, 1939.

4. *Daily Mail*, September 26, 1939.

5. His four-year-old daughter had spent several months in the local isolation hospital being treated for diphtheria.

6. 'Joseph Patrick Kelly'. National Archives files KV 2/359–360; declassified May 11, 2001.

7. Lt. Col. William Hinchley-Cooke, 'Interview with Jan Johannes Barendrecht', May 3, 1939. National Archives file KV 2/359; declassified May 11, 2001.

8. Letter from Jan Johannes Barendrecht to His Excellency, The British Minister, March 18, 1939. National Archives file KV 2/359; declassified May 11, 2001.

9. Memo from MI6 to Lt. Col. Hinchley-Cooke, MI5, April 25, 1939.

10. 'Reprisals for Ban on Nazi'. *Daily Mirror*, June 15, 1939.

11. Letter from Governor, Manchester prison to the Chief Constable, Preston Constabulary, March 29, 1939. National Archives file KV 2/359; declassified May 11, 2001.

12. Like most of the espionage prosecutions before and during the war, Kelly's trial was held largely *in camera*.

13. 'Stole Secret Plans: Ten Years' Sentence'. *Liverpool Daily Post*, May 20, 1939.

14. 'William Wishart'. National Archives files KV 2/361–362; declassified May 11, 2001.

15. Report of Sgt. Daniel, Special Branch, Port of Grimsby, March 11, 1939. National Archives files KV 2/361–362; declassified May 11, 2001.

16. Crime indexes were then maintained by individual police forces, with little or no coordination between them. Wishart's court martial had been held at Dover and would have been recorded only by Kent Police.

17. 'Statement of Case Against William Wishart'. B10 Branch, MI5, September 22, 1939. National Archives files KV 2/361–362; declassified May 11, 2001.

18. 'Edwin Fuller Heath'. National Archives files KV 2/2104–2105; declassified February 3, 2006.

19. Special Branch report on Edwin Fuller Heath, February 16, 1940. National Archives files KV 2/2104–2105; declassified February 3, 2006.

20. Subsequent enquiries with the Bank of England showed that the two £5 notes sent by 'Barlen' had been part of a consignment of notes shipped to a bank in Rio de Janeiro – evidence that the Abwehr was able to lay its hands on British currency from sources around the world.

21. Memo from MI5 to the Home Office, November 8, 1943. National Archives files KV 2/2104–2105; declassified February 3, 2006.

22. Special Branch report on Edwin Fuller Heath, February 16, 1940. National Archives files KV 2/2104–2105; declassified February 3, 2006.

23. Letter from Edwin Heath to 'The Commissioner of Police, New Scotland Yard', June 19, 1939. National Archives files KV 2/2104–2105; declassified February 3, 2006.

24. Letter from Edwin Heath to 'The Commissioner of Police, New Scotland Yard', July 2, 1939. National Archives files KV 2/2104–2105; declassified February 3, 2006.

25. Undated MI5 file note, 'Edwin Heath'. National Archives files KV 2/2104–2105; declassified February 3, 2006.

26. Heath was eventually released, with restrictions on his movements, in November 1943.

27. 'Donald Owen Reginald Adams'. National Archives files KV 2/290–293; declassified November 10, 2000.

28. Letter from H.L Rabino, British Consulate, Cairo, to the British Foreign Secretary, May 30, 1924. National Archives files KV 2/290–293; declassified November 10, 2000.

29. Memo from MI5 to MI6, July 8, 1939. National Archives files KV 2/290–293; declassified November 10, 2000.

30. MI5 memo, April 30, 1944. National Archives files KV 2/290–293; declassified November 10, 2000.

31. Registry Minute Sheet entry, June 23, 1939.

32. Deposition of Lt. Col. William Hinchley-Cooke, July 14, 1939, Exhibit 14. *R. v. Adams*. Central Criminal Court, September 1939.

33. 'Man Named as "Paid Nazi Agent"'. *Daily Mail*, July 15, 1939.

34. Deposition of Lt. Col. William Hinchley-Cooke, July 14, 1939, Exhibit 40. *R. v. Adams*. Central Criminal Court, September 1939.

35. Report sent by Donald Adams, June 19, 1939. National Archives files KV 2/290–293; declassified November 10, 2000.

36. Special Branch report on the arrest of Donald Adams, June 30, 1939. National Archives files KV 2/290–293; declassified November 10, 2000.

37. 'Spy "Worse Than Killer"'; *Daily Mirror*, September 26, 1939.

Chapter 6

1. 'Guy Liddell Diaries', Vol. 1. October 24, 1939. National Archives file KV 4/185; declassified November 1, 2002.

2. The Combined Scottish Universities had a seat in the House of Commons from 1918 to 1950 when the constituency was abolished.

3. Peter and Leni Gilman, *Collar The Lot*, p. 40. Quartet, 1980.

4. By January 1940, MI5 directly employed 102 officers.

5. Sir David Petrie, 'Director-General's Report on the Security Service, February 1941'. National Archives file KV 4/88; declassified April 12, 2000.

6. Christopher Andrew, *The Defence of the Realm: The Authorized History of MI5*, pp. 217–18. Allen Lane, 2009.

7. Home Office memorandum, June 1938. Quoted in F.H. Hinsley and C.A.G. Simkins, *British Intelligence in the Second World War*, p. 29. HMSO, 1990.

8. Ibid., p. 30.

9. Ibid., p. 32.

10. Christopher Andrew, *The Defence of the Realm: The Authorized History of MI5*, p. 222. Allen Lane, 2009.

11. Guy Liddell minute, 1943, in 'D.G. White Lecture Notes re: Counter-Espionage Investigations and Organisation'. National Archives file KV 4/170; declassified November 1, 2002.

12. There is no trace of a file on 'Raydt' in the National Archives.

13. 'Guy Liddell Diaries', Vol. 1. National Archives file KV 4/185; declassified November 1, 2002.

14. 'William Frederick Craven'. National Archives files KV 2/486–488; declassified May 11, 2001.

15. 'Statement under caution of William Craven', December 22, 1942. National Archives files KV 2/486–488; declassified May 11, 2001.

16. 'William Craven: Transcript of Advisory Committee testimony'.

September 25, 1939. National Archives files KV 2/486–488; declassified May 11, 2001.

17. Intercepted letter from William Craven to German Intelligence, May 3, 1938. National Archives files KV 2/486–488; declassified May 11, 2001.

18. 'William Craven: Transcript of Advisory Committee testimony'. September 25, 1939. National Archives files KV 2/486–488; declassified May 11, 2001.

19. 'Selected Historical Papers from the SNOW case'. National Archives files KV 2/444–453; declassified May 11, 2001.

20. After a succession of increasingly bizarre 'missions', Owens was eventually interned under Defence Regulation 18B and detained until September 1944.

21. Lt. J.R. Stopford, 'Notes re: Snow's £5 notes'. November 19, 1939. 'Mathilde Caroline Marie Krafft'. National Archives files KV 2/701–706; declassified May 1, 2002.

22. 'Notes on the visit of Mr T.A. Robertson and Mr Stopford to Bournemouth on 5.12.39'. 'Mathilde Caroline Marie Krafft'. National Archives files KV 2/701–706; declassified May 1, 2002.

23. Equivalent to approximately £1,100 today.

24. 'Notes on the visit of Mr T.A. Robertson and Mr Stopford to Bournemouth on 5.12.39'. 'Mathilde Caroline Marie Krafft'. National Archives files KV 2/701–706; declassified May 1, 2002.

25. 'Note by Lt. J.R. Stopford on Identification of Mrs Krafft on 7.12.39'. 'Mathilde Caroline Marie Krafft'. National Archives files KV 2/701–706; declassified May 1, 2002.

26. 'Guy Liddell Diaries', Vol. 1. January 19, 1940. National Archives file KV 4/185; declassified November 1, 2002.

27. 'Editha Ilsa Hilda Dargel'. National Archives files KV 2/916; declassified October 31, 2002.

28. 'Guy Liddell Diaries', Vol. 1. December 3, 1939. National Archives file KV 4/185; declassified November 1, 2002.

29. 'Guy Liddell Diaries', Vol. 1. December 7, 1939. National Archives file KV 4/185; declassified November 1, 2002.

30. 'Alexandra Wolkoff'. National Archives file KV 2/1117; declassified October 31, 2002.

Chapter 7

1. Carl Schorske, 'Two German Ambassadors: Dirksen and Schulenburg', in Gordon Craig and Felix Gilbert, *The Diplomats 1919–1939*, pp. 477–511. Athanaeum, 1965.

2. 'Dirksen dispatch', July 19, 1939. In 'British Anti-Semitism was Hitler's Hope'. Wiener Library Bulletin, p. 17, Issue XVI, Vol. 1, 1962.

3. Herbert von Dirksen, *Moscow, Tokyo, London: Twenty years of German Foreign Policy*. Hutchinson, 1951.

4. Mass-Observation, *War Begins at Home*, pp. 421–2. London, 1940.

5. *Hansard*, March 9, 1933.

6. *Glasgow Herald*, March 10, 1938.

7. *Blackshirt*, November 14, 1936, p. 2.

8. *Action*, April 2, 1936, p. 11.

9. Christopher Andrew, *The Defence of the Realm: The Authorized History of MI5*, p. 191. Allen Lane, 2009.

10. F.H. Hinsley and C.A.G. Simkins, *British Intelligence in the Second World War*, p. 15. HMSO, 1990.

11. Christopher Andrew, *The Defence of the Realm: The Authorized History of MI5*, p. 191. Allen Lane, 2009.

12. 'Metropolitan Police report regarding accounts at Westminster Bank in the names of Allen, Dundas and Tabor'. National Archives file HO 283/10.

13. Christopher Andrew, *The Defence of the Realm: The Authorized History of MI5*, p. 191. Allen Lane, 2009.

14. G.C. Webber, 'Patterns of Membership and Support for the British Union of Fascists', *Journal of Contemporary History*, 19, pp. 575–606, 1984.

15. 'Arnold Spencer Leese'. National Archives file KV 2/1365–1367; declassified September 26, 2003.

16. 'Intelligence Report: Imperial Fascist League', April 15, 1937. Board of Deputies of British Jews.

17. William Joyce, *National Socialism Now*. National Socialist League, London, 1937.

18. Ibid.

19. 'Disturbances: National Socialist League, formation and closure by William Joyce and John Beckett'. National Archives file HO 144/21247.

20. 'Nordische Gesellschaft'. National Archives file GFM 33/1396/3516.

21. 'Disturbances: Jew Baiting by Fascists, 1936–1937'. National Archives file HO 144/21379.

22. 'Intelligence Report C6/10/29'. Board of Deputies of British Jews.

23. National Archives file HO 144/22454.

24. 'Disturbances: Jew Baiting by Fascists, 1936–1937'. National Archives file HO/144/21379.

25. 'Disturbances: Jew Baiting by Fascists, 1938–1939'. National Archives file HO/144/21381.

26. 'Disturbances: Jew Baiting by Fascists, 1936–1937'. National Archives file HO/144/21379.

27. 'Disturbances: Fascist Organisations, 1939–1944'. National Archives file HO/144/22454.

28. 'Disturbances: Jew Baiting by Fascists, 1936–1937'. National Archives file HO/144/21379.

29. A region of Bavaria which included the Nazis' spiritual home of Nuremberg.

30. 'Defence Regulation 18B Detainees: Cecil Serocold Skeels'. National Archives file HO 45/25746; declassified August 5, 2005.

31. 'New Fascist Group Formed in Britain'. Jewish Telegraphic Agency, January 16, 1934.

32. 'Defence Regulation 18B Detainees: Cecil Serocold Skeels'. National Archives file HO 45/25746; declassified August 5, 2005.

33. 'Disturbances: Jew Baiting by Fascists, 1936–1937'. National Archives file HO 144/21379.

34. 'Defendants: David Esme Vaughan and Cyril Serocold Skeels. Offences contrary to the Defence (General) Regulations 1939'. National Archives file CRIM 1/1278.

35. 'Memo on information relating to Capt. Maule Ramsay', June 8, 1939. 'Archibald Maule Ramsay'. National Archives file KV 2/677; declassified October 30, 2001.

36. Registry Minute Sheet note from MI5 B2f Branch, November 18, 1939. 'Oliver Conway Gilbert'. National Archives file KV 2/1343; declassified September 26, 2003.

37. 'Oliver Conway Gilbert'. National Archives files KV 2/1343–1344; declassified September 26, 2003.

38. 'Disturbances: Jew Baiting by Fascists, 1938–1939'. National Archives file HO 144/21381.

39. Extract of report by 'Agent M/F', September 23, 1939. 'Oliver Conway Gilbert'. National Archives files KV 2/1343–1344; declassified September 26, 2003.

40. Gilbert subsequently told the Home Office Advisory Committee that he kept the loaded weapon, for which he had a licence, 'because he had been threatened several times with personal violence because he was doing anti-Jewish work and he thought the communists might attack him'.

41. 'Archibald Maule Ramsay MP'. National Archives file KV 2/677–679; declassified October 30, 2001.

42. 'Report made on a speech by Captain Ramsay'. March 8, 1939. 'Archibald Maule Ramsay MP'. National Archives file KV 2/677; declassified October 30, 2001.

43. 'Report by Oswald Harker, Deputy Director, MI5, of meeting with Capt. Archibald Ramsay', June 8, 1939. 'Archibald Maule Ramsay MP'. National Archives file KV 2/677; declassified October 30, 2001.

44. 'Report on Nordic league meeting', MI5 B5b Branch, June 8, 1939. National Archives file KV 2/677; declassified October 30, 2001.

45. Ibid.

46. Allowing for inflation, the most expensive joining fee equates to around £1,100 today.

47. Letter from George Ramsay to Col. Thompson, July 20, 1939. 'Archibald Maule Ramsay MP'. National Archives file KV 2/677; declassified October 30, 2001.

Chapter 8

1. *New Pioneer*, October, November and December 1939.

2. Letter from the Duke of Buccleuch to Arthur Bryant, 10 November 1939. Sir Arthur Bryant Papers C 111/4, held at the Liddell Hart Centre for Military Archives, King's College, London.

3. Leslie Fields, *Bendor, The Golden Duke of Westminster*, pp. 260–64. Weidenfeld & Nicholson, 1983.

4. Letter to Lord Halifax, September 30, 1939. Duke of Hamilton Papers, Item 5001/7, Scottish National Archives.

5. Note by 'B' (Oswald Harker), January 12, 1926. 'Lord William Francis Forbes-Sempill'. National Archives files KV 2/871–873; declassified May 1, 2002.

6. 'Tabulated Statement by Mr Harker of information supplied by Sempill to Toyoda'. April 29, 1926. 'Lord William Francis Forbes-Sempill'. National Archives files KV 2/871–873; declassified May 1, 2002.

7. Note on Sempill case by Major Ball (MI5), April 22, 1926.

8. Letter from William Forbes-Sempill to the Secretary of the Air Ministry, May 7, 1926. 'Lord William Francis Forbes-Sempill'. National Archives files KV 2/871–873; declassified May 1, 2002.

9. Note by 'B' (Oswald Harker), January 12, 1926. 'Lord William Francis Forbes-Sempill'. National Archives files KV 2/871–873; declassified May 1, 2002.

10. Registry Minute Sheet note, August 20, 1937.

11. Letter from S. Yashima, Mitsubishi Heavy Industries, Tokyo, to Manager, London Branch of Mitsubishi Shoji Kaisha, Plantation House, Fenchurch

Street, London EC3, February 27, 1940. 'Lord William Francis Forbes-Sempill'. National Archives files KV 2/871–873; declassified May 1, 2002.

12. Letter from Mitsubishi Heavy Industries Ltd to S. Yamagata, HQ, Naval Air Force; 'Subject: Honorarium paid to Lord Sempill', February 29, 1940. 'Lord William Francis Forbes-Sempill'. National Archives files KV 2/871–873; declassified May 1, 2002.

13. 'Connections with Mitsubishi'. Report by B1F Branch, December 17, 1941. 'Lord William Francis Forbes-Sempill'. National Archives files KV 2/871–873; declassified May 1, 2002.

14. Letter from Lord Sempill to the Department of Air Matériel, September 30, 1940. 'Lord William Francis Forbes-Sempill'. National Archives files KV 2/871–873; declassified May 1, 2002.

15. Telegram from Lord Sempill to Kawamura, Mitsubishi Heavy Industries, Tokyo, August 5, 1941. 'Lord William Francis Forbes-Sempill'. National Archives files KV 2/871–873; declassified May 1, 2002.

16. 'Contents of Despatch Case' (undated). 'Lord William Francis Forbes-Sempill'. National Archives files KV 2/871–873; declassified May 1, 2002.

17. Letter from the Prime Minister to the Foreign Secretary, September 20, 1941. 'Lord William Francis Forbes-Sempill'. National Archives files KV 2/871–873; declassified May 1, 2002.

18. Hinchley-Cooke prepared an 18B arrest warrant on December 13, 1941. There is no indication that it was ever served. 'Lord William Francis Forbes-Sempill'. National Archives files KV 2/871–873; declassified May 1, 2002.

19. Letter from the Prime Minister to the Foreign Secretary, September 20, 1941. 'Lord William Francis Forbes-Sempill'. National Archives files KV 2/871–873; declassified May 1, 2002.

20. Edward Blanshard Stamp, F3 Branch, MI5. Memo on the Duke of Bedford, December 5, 1941. 'The Duke of Bedford'. National Archives files KV 2/793–795; declassified May 1, 2002.

21. Stamp would go on to become a High Court judge in the Chancery Division, a Lord Justice of Appeal and a member of the Privy Council (both 1971).

22. Edward Blanshard Stamp, F3 Branch, MI5. Memo on the Duke of Bedford, December 5, 1941. 'The Duke of Bedford'. National Archives files KV 2/793–795; declassified May 1, 2002.

23. Ibid.

24. Guy Aldred, an anti-war activist and 'proponent of anarchist aims'. He was imprisoned in 1909 for sedition and again in 1916 as a conscientious

objector. 'Guy A. Aldred'. National Archives file KV 2/792; declassified
May 1, 2002.

25. MI5 note of Special Branch report, February 29, 1940. 'John Beckett'.
National Archives file KV 2 1508; declassified March 30, 2004.

26. 'John Beckett'. National Archives file KV 2/1508; declassified March 30,
2004.

27. Memo by Edward Blanshard Stamp, December 5, 1941. 'The Duke of
Bedford', National Archives file KV 2/793; declassified May 1, 2002.

28. Report by Agent 'M/D', February 27, 1940. 'John Beckett'. National
Archives file KV 2 1508; declassified March 30, 2004.

29. Sir Edward Louis Spears had served as liaison with French forces during
the First World War. Close to Churchill, he argued for a hawkish policy
towards Germany. During the Phoney War he complained that Britain and
France were not doing 'anything more warlike than dropping leaflets'.

30. George Strauss was a long-serving Labour backbencher. Having
experienced anti-Semitic bullying throughout his education at Rugby
School, he became a lifelong campaigner for racial equality.

31. *Hansard*, House of Commons, March 4, 1940, Vol. 358, cc. 2–42.

32. Letter from Lord Tavistock to Brigadier General Edward Spears MP,
March 9, 1940. 'The Duke of Bedford', National Archives file KV 2/793;
declassified May 1, 2002.

33. Summary of case against Hastings William Sackville Russell, 12th Duke of
Bedford, December 7, 1941. 'The Duke of Bedford', National Archives file
KV 2/793; declassified May 1, 2002.

34. Report on James Lonsdale Bryans by Edward Blanshard Stamp, March 27,
1941. 'James Lonsdale Bryans'. National Archives file KV 2/2839;
declassified August 30, 2008.

35. Letter from Oswald Harker, Deputy Director General, MI5, to
Sir Alexander Cadogan, Permanent Under-Secretary for Foreign Affairs,
December 13, 1940. 'James Lonsdale Bryans'. National Archives file
KV 2/2839; declassified August 30, 2008.

36. Andersen was pulled off a Portugal-bound boat on the orders of MI6 in
December 1940. He was found to be carrying letters, given to him by
Bryans, from Lord Brocket and the Duke of Buccleuch.

37. Report of interrogation of Ole Erik Andersen, December 17, 1940.
'James Lonsdale Bryans'. National Archives file KV 2/2839; declassified
August 30, 2008.

38. Memo by Edward Blanshard Stamp, March 14, 1941. 'James Lonsdale
Bryans'. National Archives file KV 2/2839; declassified August 30, 2008.

Chapter 9

1. To a degree, the military disaster unfolding in Norway was of Churchill's own making, since he had masterminded Britain's hasty and ill-prepared campaign.

2. Frank Newsam was Assistant Under-Secretary of State at the Home Office and had a lifelong reputation as a man of strong personality and intolerant of those who disagreed with him.

3. Guy Liddell, diary entry, January 15, 1940. 'Guy Liddell Diaries', Vol. 1. National Archives file KV 4/185; declassified November 1, 2002.

4. 'Prison for Two Fascists'. *Daily Mirror*, January 31, 1940.

5. Guy Liddell, diary entry, January 30, 1940. 'Guy Liddell Diaries', Vol. 1. National Archives file KV 4/185; declassified November 1, 2002.

6. Guy Liddell, diary entry, May 12, 1940. 'Guy Liddell Diaries', Vol. 1. National Archives file KV 4/185; declassified November 1, 2002.

7. Christopher Andrew, *The Defence of the Realm: The Authorized History of MI5*, p. 223. Allen Lane, 2009.

8. Report on Security Service by Lord Hankey, May 1940. National Archives file CAB 63.

9. Ibid.

10. Ibid.

11. Tom Dale and Robert Ingram, 'The Lord Chancellor Who Never Was'. *Journal of Liberal Democrat History*, No. 36, Autumn 2002.

12. Interim report on Security Service by Lord Hankey, May 1940. National Archives file CAB 63.

13. Ibid.

14. 'Mitzi Smythe'. National Archives file KV 2/1341; declassified September 26, 2003.

15. 'Statement of Ronald Dines', May 14, 1938. 'Mitzi Smythe'. National Archives file KV 2/1341; declassified September 26, 2003.

16. 'Statement of Case Against Mitzi Smythe', January 23, 1941. 'Mitzi Smythe'. National Archives file KV 2/1341; declassified September 26, 2003.

17. The officer in question was a Lieutenant Commander in Naval Intelligence.

18. 'Statement of Case Against Mitzi Smythe', January 23, 1941. 'Mitzi Smythe'. National Archives file KV 2/1341; declassified September 26, 2003.

19. Ibid.

20. Report by Ramsgate Police, June 7, 1940. 'Mitzi Smythe'. National Archives file KV 2/1341; declassified September 26, 2003.

21. Report on the interrogation of Mitzi Smythe, October 12, 1940.
22. Sir Nevile Bland, 'Fifth Column Menace'. National Archives file FO 371/25189.
23. Prof. A.W. Brian Simpson, *In The Highest Degree Odious*, p. 107. Clarendon Press, 1992.
24. 'Margaret Elizabeth Newitt, *née* Winter'. National Archives files KV 2/3326–3327; declassified August 26, 2010.
25. Mrs Newitt was interned under Regulation 18B until 1945. She made repeated – and unsuccessful – attempts during her detention to have the employment agency returned to her.
26. War Cabinet Minutes, May 15, 1940. National Archives file CAB 67/7.
27. Guy Liddell, diary entry, April 20, 1940. 'Guy Liddell Diaries', Vol. 2. National Archives file KV 4/186; declassified November 1, 2002.
28. 'Act! Act! Act! – Do It Now!'. *Daily Mail*, May 24, 1940.
29. Sir Nevile Bland, BBC Radio address, May 30, 1940. Quoted in Peter and Leni Gilmann, *Collar The Lot*, pp. 110–11. Quartet Books, 1980.
30. Sir Charles Peake was chief press advisor at the Ministry of Information.
31. Field Marshal Alan Brooke was Chief of the Imperial General Staff – essentially the head of the British Army.
32. War Cabinet Minutes, May 22, 1940. National Archives file CAB 65/7.
33. Guy Liddell, diary entry, May 25, 1940. 'Guy Liddell Diaries', Vol. 2. National Archives file KV 4/186; declassified November 1, 2002.
34. Benjamin Franklin, Pennsylvania Assembly's 'Reply to the Governor', November 11, 1775.
35. Report on Security Service by Lord Hankey, May 1940. National Archives file CAB 63.

Chapter 10

1. Guy Liddell, diary entry, October 21, 1939. 'Guy Liddell Diaries', Vol. 1. National Archives file KV 4/185; declassified November 1, 2002.
2. *Sunday Times*, June 9, 1940.
3. Christopher Andrew, *The Defence of the Realm: The Authorized History of MI5*, p. 223. Allen Lane, 2009
4. Guy Liddell, diary entry, July 3, 1940. 'Guy Liddell Diaries', Vol. 2. National Archives file KV 4/186; declassified November 1, 2002.
5. Ibid.
6. Home Intelligence report, June 5, 1940. Ian McLaine, *Ministry of Morale – Home Front Morale and the Ministry of Information in World War Two*, p. 74. Allen & Unwin, 1979.

7. Statement by Wanda Penlington, June 14, 1940. 'Sabotage: Wanda Penlington and William Gutheridge'. National Archives file CRIM 1/1211.

8. Ibid.

9. Statement by William Anthony Gutheridge, June 17, 1940. 'Sabotage: Wanda Penlington and William Gutheridge'. National Archives file CRIM 1/1211.

10. Statement by Wanda Penlington, June 14, 1940. 'Sabotage: Wanda Penlington and William Gutheridge'. National Archives file CRIM 1/1211.

11. '19, Had Gun, List of 'Dromes: Three months'. *Daily Mirror*, June 8, 1940.

12. 'Thomas Hubert Beckett'. National Archives files KV 2/363–364; declassified May 11, 2001.

13. 'Statements of Mary Beckett and Mrs Jane Doherty', August 20, 1940. 'Thomas Hubert Beckett'. National Archives files KV 2/363–364; declassified May 11, 2001.

14. 'Three Years for Ministry Architect'. *Dundee Courier*, November 8, 1940.

15. MI5 Summary of case against Frederick Roesch (undated); 'Frederick Roesch'. National Archives files KV 2/710–711; declassified May 1, 2002.

16. Sir Dick White would rise to become MI5 Director General from 1953–56.

17. Registry Minute Sheet note by Dick White, B.2 Branch, June 26, 1941. 'Frederick Roesch'. National Archives file KV 2/710; declassified May 1, 2002.

18. Statement of Cecil Rashleigh (undated). 'William Swift and Marie Louisa Ingram'. National Archives file KV 6/49; declassified February 7, 2005.

19. Ibid.

20. Baron's first name and all details of his unit have been redacted in the file released to the National Archives.

21. Statement of Cecil Rashleigh (undated). 'William Swift and Marie Louisa Ingram'. National Archives file KV 6/49; declassified February 7, 2005.

22. Statement of Corporal Baron (undated). 'William Swift and Marie Louisa Ingram'. National Archives file KV 6/49; declassified February 7, 2005.

23. Guy Liddell, diary entry, June 9, 1940. 'Guy Liddell Diaries', Vol. 2. National Archives file KV 4/186; declassified November 1, 2002.

24. *Hansard*, July 24, 1940. Vol. 363, cc. 800–1800.

25. Guy Liddell, diary entry, September 8, 1939. 'Guy Liddell Diaries', Vol. 1. National Archives file KV 4/185; declassified November 1, 2002.

26. Guy Liddell, diary entry, October 4, 1939. 'Guy Liddell Diaries', Vol. 1. National Archives file KV 4/185; declassified November 1, 2002.

27. Guy Liddell, diary entry, December 8, 1939. 'Guy Liddell Diaries', Vol. 1. National Archives file KV 4/185; declassified November 1, 2002.

28. Guy Liddell, diary entry, March 18, 1940. 'Guy Liddell Diaries', Vol. 2. National Archives file KV 4/186; declassified November 1, 2002.

29. Treachery Act, Section 1, 1940.

30. *Hansard*, July 24, 1940. Vol. 363, cc. 800–1800.

31. Ibid.

32. Reports on British Union of Fascists, 1940: National Archives file HO 45/24895.

33. Recommendation by MI5 for the detention of Charles Stephen Geary; August 8, 1940. 'Charles Stephen Geary'. National Archives file HO 45/23775; declassified May 5, 2006.

34. Ibid.

35. It was the Camp 020 regime to which MI5 had briefly considered sending Mitzi Smythe as a means to make her talk.

36. Ian Cobain, *Cruel Britannia – A Secret History of Torture*. Portobello Books, 2012.

37. 'List of cases investigated by Camp 020'. National Archives file KV 2/2593; declassified March 2, 2007.

38. 'Charles Stephen Geary'. National Archives file HO 45/23775; declassified May 5, 2006.

39. Guy Liddell, diary entry, August 30, 1940. 'Guy Liddell Diaries', Vol. 2. National Archives file KV 4/186; declassified November 1, 2002.

40. This was a book of the Leader's collected speeches, published by the BUF itself.

41. Letter from Chief Constable, Cumberland and Westmorland Police, to Chief Constable, West Riding Constabulary, September 16, 1940. 'John Ellis', 18B Detainee, National Archives file HO 45/25726.

42. New Defence Regulations, issued that month and aimed at easing the burden on the Home Office, devolved some of the Home Secretary's internment powers on a network of Regional Commissioners.

43. Order for the detention of John Ellis, under Defence Regulation 18B, June 25, 1940. 'John Ellis', 18B Detainee, National Archives file HO 45/25726.

44. Statement of John Ellis to Home Office Advisory Committee, August 1940. 'John Ellis', 18B Detainee, National Archives file HO 45/25726.

45. Ibid.

46. Letter from Advisory Committee to the Home Secretary, September 5, 1940. 'John Ellis', 18B Detainee, National Archives file HO 45/25726.

47. Letter from Edward Blanshard Stamp, MI5 to the Home Office, August 31, 1940. 'John Ellis', 18B Detainee, National Archives file HO 45/25726.

48. Letter from Lord Harlech, Regional Commissioner (Civil Defence) North-East, to Sir Alexander Maxwell, Permanent Under-Secretary, the Home Office, October 8, 1940. 'John Ellis', 18B Detainee, National Archives file HO 45/25726.

49. The legislation which established the Advisory Committees specifically required the Home Secretary to view their conclusions as non-binding recommendations only.

50. Letter from Sir Alexander Maxwell, PUS, Home Office, to Lord Harlech, Regional Commissioner, October 11, 1940. 'John Ellis', 18B Detainee, National Archives file HO 45/25726.

51. 'John Ellis', 18B Detainee, National Archives file HO 45/25726.

Chapter 11

1. 'Brown Paper and Locked Doors'. *Daily Express*, November 6, 1940.

2. Letter from Oswald Harker, Deputy Director General MI5, to Sir Edward Tindal Atkinson, DPP, November 4, 1940.

3. 'Secrets Case Ended'. *The Times*, November 8, 1940.

4. Maxwell Knight, 'Report on the work of MS (recruitment and operation of agents) during the Second World War', April 4, 1945. National Archives file KV 4/227; declassified March 30, 2004.

5. Ibid.

6. Statement of 'M/Y' (Marjorie Amor), New Scotland Yard, February 5, 1941. 'Anna Wolkoff'. National Archives file KV 2/841; declassified May 1, 2002.

7. Ibid.

8. 'Special Report', September 23, 1939. 'Archibald Maule Ramsay'. National Archives file KV 2/677; declassified October 30, 2001.

9. Special Branch report, November 9, 1939. 'Admiral Sir Barry Domvile'. National Archives file KV 2/834; declassified May 1, 2002.

10. Report of the Advisory Committee on Capt. Archibald Ramsay, July 18, 1940. 'Archibald Maule Ramsay'. National Archives file KV 2/677; declassified October 30, 2001.

11. Weekly Summary of Report by Agent 'M/Y'. 'Archibald Maule Ramsay'. National Archives file KV 2/677; declassified October 30, 2001.

12. MI5 Memorandum (undated). 'Anna Wolkoff'. National Archives file KV 2/841; declassified May 1, 2002.

13. Report of Agent 'M/Y', May 3, 1940. 'Archibald Maule Ramsay'. National Archives file KV 2/677; declassified October 30, 2001.

14. 'Admiral Sir Barry Domvile'. National Archives file KV 2/836; declassified May 1, 2002.

15. Weekly Summary of Report by Agent 'M/Y'. 'Archibald Maule Ramsay'. National Archives file KV 2/677; declassified October 30, 2001.

16. Ibid.

17. 'Alexandra Wolkoff'. National Archives file KV 2/1117; declassified October 31, 2002.

18. 'Frances Helen [Fay] Taylour'. National Archives files KV 2/2143–2144; declassified February 3, 2006.

19. MI5 report on speech by John Beckett at Kingsway Hall, London, April 8, 1940. 'John Beckett'. National Archives file KV 2/1510; declassified March 30, 2004.

20. Joan Miller, *One Girl's War*, p. 26. Brandon Books, 1986.

21. 'Enid Mary Riddell'. National Archives file KV 2/839; declassified May 1, 2002.

22. Joan Miller, *One Girl's War*, p. 33. Brandon Books, 1986.

23. Report on Right Club by B5b Branch, MI5, April 14, 1940. 'Anna Wolkoff'. National Archives file KV 2/840; declassified May 1, 2002.

24. Ibid.

25. Joan Miller, *One Girl's War*, p. 24. Brandon Books, 1986.

26. Maxwell Knight, Statement of Evidence, *R. v Kent & Others*, June 30, 1940. 'Anna Wolkoff'. National Archives file KV 2/841; declassified May 1, 2002.

27. 'Archibald Maule Ramsay'. National Archives file KV 2/677; declassified October 30, 2001.

28. Maxwell Knight, 'Report on the work of MS (recruitment and operation of agents) during the Second World War', April 4, 1945. National Archives file KV 4/227; declassified March 30, 2004.

29. Statement of Hélène de Munck, New Scotland Yard, June 24, 1940. 'Anna Wolkoff'. National Archives file KV 2/841; declassified May 1, 2002.

30. MI5 memo on the Right Club (undated). 'Archibald Maule Ramsay'. National Archives file KV 2/677; declassified October 30, 2001.

31. Ibid.

32. Ibid.

33. Report by Agent 'M/Y', May 3, 1940. 'Anna Wolkoff'. National Archives file KV 2/840; declassified May 1, 2002.

34. Guy Liddell, diary entry, May 31, 1940. 'Guy Liddell Diaries', Vol. 2. National Archives file KV 4/186; declassified November 1, 2002.

35. MI5 memo (undated). 'Archibald Maule Ramsay'. National Archives file KV 2/677; declassified October 30, 2001.

36. Ibid.
37. File note by Maxwell Knight, June 28, 1940. 'Anna Wolkoff'. National Archives file KV 2/840; declassified May 1, 2002.
38. Ibid.
39. Birkett's role in this unseemly saga was, to say the least, strange: notionally he was independent of the Home Office, advising it at arm's length on whether or not to release interned fascists. Yet the correspondence clearly shows that he was deeply involved in the political decision on whether to prosecute Ramsay.
40. Letter from R.H. Carter, Admiralty Intelligence Officer, to Sir Alexander Maxwell, June 20, 1940. 'Sir Barry Domvile'. National Archives file KV 2/834; declassified May 1, 2002.
41. Field Marshal Lord Alan Brooke, November 20, 1940. *War Diaries 1939–1945*, p. 201. Weidenfeld & Nicholson, 2001.

Chapter 12

1. Special Branch report on John Beckett, May 17, 1940. 'John and Anne Beckett'. National Archives file KV 2/1511; declassified March 30, 2004.
2. Francis Beckett, *The Rebel Who Lost His Cause – The Tragedy of John Beckett MP*, pp. 18–19. London House, 1999.
3. *Hansard*, House of Commons debate, July 17, 1930.
4. Francis Beckett, *The Rebel Who Lost His Cause – The Tragedy of John Beckett MP*, pp. 140–41. London House, 1999.
5. File Note by Maxwell Knight's B5b Branch, February 29, 1940. 'John and Anne Beckett'. National Archives file KV 2/1508; declassified March 30, 2004.
6. 'John Beckett; Brief Summary of Activities to February 1940'. 'John and Anne Beckett'. National Archives file KV 2/1508; declassified March 30, 2004.
7. 'Friedrich Hugo Bernard Theodore Lieber, alias Dr Bauer'. National Archives file KV 2/392; declassified May 11, 2001.
8. Francis Beckett, *The Rebel Who Lost His Cause – The Tragedy of John Beckett MP*, p. 156. London House, 1999.
9. BPP advertisement in *The New Pioneer*, June 1939.
10. Lord Tavistock, letter in *New English Weekly*, March 24, 1938.
11. Royden, the daughter of Sir Thomas Bland Royden, 1st Baronet of Frankby Hall, Birkenhead, was a celebrated suffragette and social campaigner. A dedicated pacifist, she renounced that position late in 1939, believing Hitler to be a greater evil than war.

12. *Sunday Express*, October 15, 1939.

13. Extract from Jimmy Dickson's report on meeting of British Council for Christian Settlement in Europe held on October 14, 1939. 'Benjamin Greene'. National Archives file, KV 2/491; declassified May 11, 2001.

14. Maude Royden, *Sunday Express*, October 22, 1939.

15. The 'Rif War' was a long-running revolutionary conflict fought between 1922 and 1927 by the Berber tribes of Morocco's Rif Mountains to oust the Colonial powers of Spain and France.

16. Registry Minute Sheet note from B.2.c. Branch, March 28, 1938. 'Captain Robert Cecil Gordon-Canning'. National Archives files KV 2/877; declassified October 31, 2002.

17. Robert Gordon-Canning; transcript of testimony to the Home Office Advisory Committee, August 14, 1941. 'Captain Robert Cecil Gordon-Canning'. National Archives files KV 2/877; declassified October 31, 2002.

18. Letter from Home Office Advisory Committee to MI5, October 26, 1940. 'Captain Robert Cecil Gordon-Canning'. National Archives files KV 2/877; declassified October 31, 2002.

19. Extract from intelligence report, April 14, 1937. 'Captain Robert Cecil Gordon-Canning'. National Archives files KV 2/877; declassified October 31, 2002.

20. Letter from S.H. Noakes, MI5 legal section, to the Home Office Advisory Committee, November 13, 1940. 'Captain Robert Cecil Gordon-Canning'. National Archives files KV 2/877; declassified October 31, 2002.

21. John Maude was a barrister and former War Office bureaucrat. After the war he sat as Conservative MP for Exeter, and subsequently served as a judge at the City of London and Central Criminal Courts.

22. File note by John Maude, May 23, 1940. 'Captain Robert Cecil Gordon-Canning'. National Archives files KV 2/877; declassified October 31, 2002.

23. 'Statement of Case Against Benjamin Greene', June 3, 1941. 'Benjamin Greene', National Archives file KV 2/489; declassified May 11, 2001.

24. The referendum on territorial status of the Saar Basin was held on January 13, 1935. The area concerned lay between France and Germany and had been administered by the League of Nations from the end of the First World War. In the plebiscite, more than 90 per cent of voters opted for reunification with Germany.

25. 'The Greene family: Summary of Activities to February 1940'. 'John and Anne Beckett'. National Archives file KV 2/1508; declassified March 30, 2004.

26. Ernst Wilhelm Bohle was head of the NSDAP Auslands Organisation. In April 1949 he was convicted in the War Crimes Trials at Nuremberg and sentenced to five years in prison, but was pardoned by the US High Commissioner for Germany eight months later.

27. 'The Greene family: Summary of Activities to February 1940'. 'John and Anne Beckett'. National Archives file KV 2/1508; declassified March 30, 2004.

28. 'Mrs Beckett' was, more accurately, Anne Cutmore, a former BUF member with whom Beckett – then still married to his second wife – lived. Although the couple lived as man and wife, they were not married.

29. Charles Graves, 'These Men Are Dangerous'. *Sunday Dispatch*, February 25, 1940.

30. Report of Agent M/B, January 13, 1940. 'John and Anne Beckett'. National Archives file KV 2/1508; declassified March 30, 2004.

31. Letter from B.7 Branch, MI5, to Foreign Office official Gladwyn Jebb, February 21, 1940. 'John and Anne Beckett'. National Archives file KV 2/1508; declassified March 30, 2004.

32. Hastings Russell, Lord Tavistock, 'The Fate of a Peace Effort', BCCSE, March 1940.

33. Since this was written in March 1940, when the war had been going on for just under seven, not ten, months, Beckett appears to have been exaggerating slightly.

34. Report of 'Agent M/D' on the British Council for Christian Settlement in Europe, March 21, 1940. 'John and Anne Beckett'. National Archives file KV 2/1508; declassified March 30, 2004.

35. Noel Noel-Buxton, 1st Baronet Noel-Buxton, was a politician and MP; initially a Liberal, he joined the Labour Party and twice served as Minister of Agriculture and Fisheries under Ramsay MacDonald, before being raised to the peerage.

36. Statement of Harald Kurtz (undated, but filed on January 23, 1942). 'Benjamin Greene', National Archives file KV 2/491; declassified May 11, 2001.

37. Ibid.

38. Ibid.

39. Ibid.

40. John McGovern was a long-time peace activist and conscientious objector. He flirted with communism and anarchism in the early 1920s; he was elected as a Labour MP in 1930 before being expelled from the Party and becoming an ILP MP the following year.

41. This was a 1939 anti-fascist booklet, subtitled 'Fifty Facts'; priced at 3d, it was published by War Facts Press, 149 Fleet Street, EC4.

42. 'John Beckett's Meeting at Kingsway Hall', MI5 B5b Branch memo, April 8, 1940. 'John and Anne Beckett'. National Archives file KV 2/1510; declassified March 30, 2004.

43. Statement of Harald Kurtz (undated, but filed on January 23, 1942). 'Benjamin Greene', National Archives file KV 2/491; declassified May 11, 2001.

44. Statement of Friedl Gaertner (undated). 'Benjamin Greene', National Archives file KV 2/491; declassified May 11, 2001.

45. Ibid.

46. Ibid.

47. Statement of Harald Kurtz (undated, but filed on January 23, 1942). 'Benjamin Greene', National Archives file KV 2/491; declassified May 11, 2001.

48. Transcript of John Beckett's evidence before the Home Office Advisory Committee, October 6, 1941. 'John and Anne Beckett'. National Archives file KV 2/1514; declassified March 30, 2004.

49. MI5 B5b Branch file note, May 18, 1940. 'John and Anne Beckett'. National Archives file KV 2/1511; declassified March 30, 2004.

50. MI5 B5b Branch supplementary file note, May 18, 1940. 'John and Anne Beckett'. National Archives file KV 2/1511; declassified March 30, 2004.

51. Ibid.

52. Report of information from 'Agent M/M', May 27, 1940. 'John and Anne Beckett'. National Archives file KV 2/1511; declassified March 30, 2004.

53. John Beckett, letter to Lord Tavistock, May 22, 1940. 'John and Anne Beckett'. National Archives file KV 2/1511; declassified March 30, 2004.

54. During a debate in the House of Lords in December 1939, Arnold denounced Churchill as a warmonger and asserted that 'there were grounds for thinking that Hitler would be prepared to make great concessions to secure peace'. *The Times*, December 14, 1939.

55. 31 of the men listed as senior or junior ministers have a file number beside their names. Of these, just ten are the subject of files released to the National Archives.

56. John Beckett, letter to Lord Tavistock, May 22, 1940. 'John and Anne Beckett'. National Archives file KV 2/1511; declassified March 30, 2004.

57. Report of Agent M/M, June 1, 1940. 'John and Anne Beckett'. National Archives file KV 2/1511; declassified March 30, 2004.

Chapter 13

1. 'Defence Regulation 18B: claim by Dr Leigh Vaughan-Henry for damages for wrongful arrest and for breach of statutory duty'. National Archives file TS 27/533.

2. The Gorsedd Beirdd Ynys Prydain was the most famous community of druids and bards, dedicated to keeping alive ancient Welsh rituals through music and poetry.

3. 'Hans Wilhelm Thost'. National Archives files KV 2/952–954: declassified 2002.

4. 'Defence Regulation 18B: claim by Dr Leigh Vaughan-Henry for damages for wrongful arrest and for breach of statutory duty'. National Archives file TS 27/533.

5. Between 1937 and 1938 Bene was briefly the head of the Nazi Party Landesgruppe in Britain. A commissioned SS Standartenfuehrer, he was posted to Amsterdam after the German conquest of Holland and was deeply involved in the deportation of Dutch Jews. After the war he was imprisoned in the Netherlands until 1948.

6. 'Statement of Case Against Leigh Vaughan-Henry', November 28, 1940. 'Defence Regulation 18B: claim by Dr Leigh Vaughan-Henry for damages for wrongful arrest and for breach of statutory duty'. National Archives file TS 27/533.

7. Ibid.

8. Originally founded in 1919 as the Middle Class Union to represent the interests of small traders and clerical workers against what it perceived to be the threat of the organised working class, two years later it changed its name to the National Citizens Union and began drifting further towards right-wing extremism.

9. Aubrey T.O. Lees was a Colonial Office civil servant, who was brought back to the UK from Palestine by the Foreign Office in December 1938 because he had been engaged in anti-Semitic propaganda. He joined the BU, British People's Party, Right Club and the Nordic League. He was interned from June to September 1940, then released under a restriction order which lasted until 1944.

10. 'Statement of Case Against Leigh Vaughan-Henry', November 28, 1940. 'Defence Regulation 18B: claim by Dr Leigh Vaughan-Henry for damages for wrongful arrest and for breach of statutory duty'. National Archives file TS 27/533.

11. Ibid.

12. 'John Alban Webster, alias "Jock of London"'. National Archives files KV 2/4170–4174; declassified October 23, 2015.

13. E-mail from MI5 to author; November 8, 2018.

14. Christopher Andrew, *The Defence of the Realm: The Authorized History of MI5*, p. 231. Allen Lane, 2009.

15. 'Statement of Case Against Leigh Vaughan-Henry'. 'Defence Regulation 18B: claim by Dr Leigh Vaughan-Henry for damages for wrongful arrest and for breach of statutory duty'. National Archives file TS 27/533.

16. Special Branch memo by Insp. Arthur Cain, June 13, 1940. 'Defence Regulation 18B: claim by Dr Leigh Vaughan-Henry for damages for wrongful arrest and for breach of statutory duty'. National Archives file TS 27/533.

17. Approximately £15,000 today.

18. 'John and Anne Beckett'. National Archives file KV 2/1511: declassified 2004.

19. Special Branch memo by Insp. Arthur Cain, June 13, 1940. 'Defence Regulation 18B: claim by Dr Leigh Vaughan-Henry for damages for wrongful arrest and for breach of statutory duty'. National Archives file TS 27/533.

20. 'Statement of Case Against Leigh Vaughan-Henry'. National Archives file TS/27/533; op. cit.

21. Special Branch memo by Insp. Arthur Cain, June 13, 1940. National Archives file TS/27/533; op. cit.

22. 'Statement of Case Against Leigh Vaughan-Henry'. National Archives file TS/27/533; op. cit.

23. 'Cecil Serocold Skeels, member of the Nordic League'. National Archives file HO 45/25746; declassified August 5, 2005.

24. 'Report by M/W of meeting on May 28, 1940', June 2, 1940. National Archives file KV 2/1511, p. 67; declassified 2004.

25. William Edmund Ironside, journal entry for September 8, 1939. *The Ironside Diaries 1937–1940*. Constable, 1962.

26. Richard Thurlow, 'The Evolution of the Mythical Fifth Column'. *Twentieth Century British History*, Vol. 10, No. 4, p. 488. Oxford University Press, 1999.

27. Barry Domvile, diary entry for November 12, 1939. Papers of Admiral Sir Barry Domvile, DOM 56. National Maritime Museum, Greenwich, London.

28. 'Oliver Conway Gilbert, member of the Nordic League'. National Archives file HO 45/25692.

29. 'Report by M/W of meeting on May 28, 1940', June 2, 1940. 'John and Anne Beckett'. National Archives file KV 2/1511: declassified 2004.

30. Ibid.

31. Ibid.

32. Report filed by M/W, June 2, 1940. 'John and Anne Beckett'. National Archives file KV 2/1511: declassified 2004.

33. Report filed by M/M, June 7, 1940. 'John and Anne Beckett'. National Archives file KV 2/1511: declassified 2004.

34. 'Statement of Case Against Leigh Vaughan-Henry'. National Archives file TS/27/533.

35. Report filed by M/M, June 7, 1940. National Archives file KV 2/1511, p. 63: declassified 2004.

36. Transcript of Leigh Vaughan-Henry's evidence to the Home Office Advisory Committee, January 21, 1940. National Archives file TS/27/533.

37. Ibid.

38. Memo on Conduct of Officers who Detained Vaughan-Henry (undated); National Archives file TS/27/533.

39. Memo by Insp. Arthur Cain, Metropolitan Police Special Branch, June 13, 1940. National Archives file TS/27/533.

40. '"Commander" Mary Allen'. National Archives file HO 144/21933; declassified 1984.

41. 'Leigh Vaughan-Henry: Reasons for Internment', November 28, 1940. National Archives file TS/27/533; op. cit.

42. Ibid.

43. Ibid.

44. Report of Insp. Arthur Cain, Metropolitan Police Special Branch, July 16, 1940. National Archives file TS/27/533; op. cit.

45. *Union*, June 19, 1948.

46. Nigel West, *MI5 – British Security Service Operations 1909–1945*, pp. 146–9. Bodley Head, 1981.

47. Robin W.G. Stephens, *Camp 020 – MI5 and the Nazi Spies*. Public Records Office, London, 2000.

48. The CHEKA and OGPU were two branches of the Soviet Secret Police.

49. Transcript of Leigh Vaughan-Henry's evidence to the Home Office Advisory Committee, January 21, 1940. National Archives file TS/27/533; op. cit.

50. List of cases investigated by Camp 020. National Archives file KV 2/2593; declassified March 2, 2007.

51. In 1940, the organisation of B Division was chaotic, with upwards of twenty separate sub-branches often working independently of each other.

52. Letter from 'G.W.' to B.8L Branch, MI5, October 1, 1940. 'William Wishart'. National Archives file KV 2/362; declassified May 11, 2001.

53. Letter from 'G.W.' to B.8L Branch, MI5, October 2, 1940. 'William Wishart'. National Archives file KV 2/362; declassified May 11, 2001.

54. *Leigh-Henry v. Secretary of State (ex-parte)*, February 3, 1944. National Archives file TS/27/533; op. cit.

Chapter 14

1. Prime Minister's Office, Confidential Correspondence and Papers, July 1, 1940–February 28, 1941. PREM 4/39/3.

2. *Hansard*, August 15, 1940. Vol. 364, cc. 957–64.

3. The Home Defence (Security) Executive – later rechristened as the Security Executive – was established on May 28, 1940. Its head, Philip Cunliffe-Lister, Lord Swinton, was tasked with examining 'all questions relating to defence against the Fifth Column'.

4. *Hansard*, August 15, 1940; op. cit.

5. Guy Liddell, diary entry, August 21, 1940. 'Guy Liddell Diaries', Vol. 2. National Archives file KV 4/186; declassified November 1, 2002.

6. 'Trial Heard in "Black-out"', *Daily Herald*, February 15, 1941.

7. Equivalent to £2,800 today.

8. 'Statement of David Esmé Vaughan', December 27, 1940. Defendants: David Esmé Vaughan and Cyril Serocold Skeels. National Archives file CRIM 1/1278. In summer 2018, this file and its companion – HO 45/25746 – was withdrawn for 'review' from public access at the National Archives.

9. Ibid.

10. Ibid.

11. 'Serocold Skeels and David Vaughan: Letter to William Joyce', September 11, 1940. Defendants: David Esmé Vaughan and Cyril Serocold Skeels. National Archives file CRIM 1/1278.

12. 'Statement of David Esmé Vaughan', December 27, 1940. Defendants: David Esmé Vaughan and Cyril Serocold Skeels. National Archives file CRIM 1/1278.

13. 'Letter from David Vaughan to Adolf Hitler, via William Joyce'. Undated, but probably early December 1940. Defendants: David Esmé Vaughan and Cyril Serocold Skeels. National Archives file CRIM 1/1278.

14. 'Statement of Cecil Serocold Skeels', December 27, 1940. Defendants: David Esmé Vaughan and Cyril Serocold Skeels. National Archives file CRIM 1/1278.

15. Sir Frederick Wrottesley was appointed to the High Court in 1937; ten years later he was made a Lord Justice of Appeal and a member of the Privy Council. He died in November 1948.

16. None of the files include the exact sentence passed on David Vaughan.

17. Extract of Summing Up by Mr Justice Wrottesley, *R. v. Vaughan and Skeels*, February 17, 1941. Defence Regulation 18B Detainees: Serocold Skeels. National Archives file HO 45/25746; declassified August 5, 2005.

18. Report of the Home Office Advisory Committee on Cecil Serocold Skeels, January 22, 1943. National Archives file HO 45/25746; declassified August 5, 2005. In summer 2018, this file and its companion – CRIM 1/1278 – was withdrawn for 'review' from public access at the National Archives.

19. *Hansard*, February 25, 1944, Vol. 397, cc. 1115–6W.

20. Leigh Vaughan-Henry, letter to Emil van Loo, June 6, 1939. 'Gertrude Hiscox and Norah Briscoe'. National Archives file KV 2/899; declassified October 31, 2002.

21. Paul Briscoe, *My Friend The Enemy*, p. 63. Aurum Press, 2007.

22. Report by B7 Branch on The Right Club, March 11, 1941. 'Archibald Maule Ramsay'. National Archives file KV 2/677; declassified October 30, 2001.

23. Ibid.

24. Ibid.

25. Ibid.

26. Ibid.

27. Oddly, given the extreme nature of Mogg's threats and alleged history, there is no trace of an MI5 file on him in the National Archives.

28. Report on Hon. Ismay Ramsay, September 23, 1943. 'Archibald Maule Ramsay'. National Archives file KV 2/678; declassified October 30, 2001.

29. Report by 'Special Source' (John Hirst), March 7, 1941. 'Gertrude Hiscox and Norah Briscoe'. National Archives file KV 2/898; declassified October 31, 2002.

30. Ibid.

31. Ibid.

32. Statement of Agent M/H, March 13, 1941. 'Gertrude Hiscox and Norah Briscoe'. National Archives file KV 2/898; declassified October 31, 2002.

33. Ibid.

34. Guy Liddell, diary entry, March 17, 1941. 'Guy Liddell Diaries', Vol. 3. National Archives file KV 4/187; declassified November 1, 2002.

35. Guy Liddell, diary entry, December 19, 1940. 'Guy Liddell Diaries', Vol. 3. National Archives file KV 4/187; declassified November 1, 2002.

36. Statement of 'Agent M/Y', New Scotland Yard, February 5, 1941. 'Christabel Sybil Caroline Nicholson'. National Archives file KV 2/902; declassified October 31, 2002.

37. Statement of Catherine Emily Welberry, June 20, 1940. 'Christabel Sybil Caroline Nicholson'. National Archives file KV 2/902; declassified October 31, 2002.

38. Statement of Major Maxwell Knight, November 15, 1940. 'Christabel Sybil Caroline Nicholson'. National Archives file KV 2/902; declassified October 31, 2002.

39. Additional statement of Catherine Emily Welberry, November 15, 1940. 'Christabel Sybil Caroline Nicholson'. National Archives file KV 2/902; declassified October 31, 2002.

40. Memo from (unknown) Special Branch Superintendent to MI5 B5(b), May 8, 1941. 'Christabel Sybil Caroline Nicholson'. National Archives file KV 2/902; declassified October 31, 2002.

41. Guy Liddell, diary entry, May 7, 1941. 'Guy Liddell Diaries', Vol. 3. National Archives file KV 4/187; declassified November 1, 2002.

42. Memorandum by Maxwell Knight, June 17, 1941. 'Gertrude Hiscox and Norah Briscoe': National Archives file KV 2/899; declassified October 31, 2002.

43. 'Women Get 5 Years for Treason', *Daily Mirror*, June 17, 1941.

44. Memorandum by Maxwell Knight, June 17, 1941. 'Gertrude Hiscox and Norah Briscoe'. National Archives file KV 2/899; declassified October 31, 2002.

45. 'Women Told Secrets: Sent to Jail', *Daily Herald*, June 17, 1941.

46. Sir Cyril Asquith was a Conservative-leaning judge; after the war he was appointed to the Appeal Court and the Privy Council, before being ennobled as Baron Asquith of Bishopstone.

47. 'Women Get 5 Years for Treason', *Daily Mirror*, June 17, 1941.

Chapter 15

1. 'Underground broadcasting stations: Locations, descriptions and reports, 1940–1945'. National Archives file FO 898/52.

2. In Britain, the Political Warfare Executive, a department of the Ministry of Economic Warfare, broadcast regularly to Germany under 'false flags' throughout the war.

3. Banning subsequently fell out with his employers and spent five months in a labour camp. This did not save him from prosecution when he returned to Britain after the war. On January 22, 1946 he was tried at the Old Bailey on seven counts of assisting the enemy by making propaganda broadcasts; he was sentenced to ten years' penal servitude. 'Leonard Banning, alias John Brown'. National Archives file KV 2/432–433; declassified May 11, 2001.

4. Compilation of NBBS transmissions, 1940. https://www.youtube.com/watch?v=pZ-65U_LdZk

5. *Hansard*, March 20, 1940. Vol. 358 cc. 1970–1.

6. Guy Liddell, diary entry, May 22, 1940. 'Guy Liddell Diaries', Vol. 2. National Archives file KV 4/186; declassified November 1, 2002.

7. F.H. Hinsley and C.A.G. Simkins, *British Intelligence in the Second World War*, Vol. 4, p. 67n. HMSO, 1990.

8. 'Defendant: Violet Lillian Freeman and Rex Wilfred Freeman. Charge: Assisting the enemy'. National Archives file CRIM 1/1202.

9. '7 Years for Fascist and 12 Months for Mother', *Birmingham Daily Gazette*, July 6, 1940.

10. *Daily Record*, July 4, 1940.

11. 'A "British" Radio Station', *Yorkshire Post*, June 7, 1940.

12. 'Defendant: William Saxon-Steer'. National Archives file CRIM 1/1203.

13. 'Olive Evelyn Baker'. National Archives file KV 6/51; declassified June 27, 2005.

14. 'Bath Woman on "Fifth Column" Charge', *Bath Weekly Chronicle and Herald*, May 25, 1940.

15. Letter dated April 28, 1940. 'Olive Evelyn Baker'. National Archives file KV 6/51; declassified June 27, 2005.

16. Letter from Admiral Sir Barry Domvile to Olive Baker, April 1, 1940. 'Olive Evelyn Baker'. National Archives file KV 6/51; declassified June 27, 2005.

17. Ibid.

18. Letter from Lady Alexandrina Domvile to Olive Baker, April 22, 1940. 'Olive Evelyn Baker'. National Archives file KV 6/51; declassified June 27, 2005.

19. 'An Admirer of Hitler – Woman in Bath Fifth Column Case', *Bath Weekly Chronicle and Herald*, July 6, 1940.

20. These, referred to in her MI5 dossier as serial number HO 833594, were once evidently substantial and ran to at least four volumes. There is, however, no trace of them in the National Archives.

21. Extract from Home Office file HO 833594, June 10, 1941. 'Olive Evelyn Baker'. National Archives file KV 6/51; declassified June 27, 2005.

22. Extract from Home Office file HO 833594, January 2, 1942. 'Olive Evelyn Baker'. National Archives file KV 6/51; declassified June 27, 2005.

23. Extract from Home Office file HO 833594, January 9, 1942. 'Olive Evelyn Baker'. National Archives file KV 6/51; declassified June 27, 2005.

24. '"Pro-British" Fascist for Trial', *Newcastle Journal*, June 27, 1940.

25. Sir Fenton Atkinson.

26. 'Gaol for Boosting Nazi Radio', *Daily Mirror*, July 25, 1940.

27. *Hansard*, July 31, 1941. Vol. 373, cc. 1509–10.

28. Edward Blanshard Stamp, F3 Branch, Memorandum on the Duke of Bedford, December 5, 1941. 'The Duke of Bedford', National Archives file KV 2/793; declassified May 1, 2002.

29. 'The Uncensored News Bulletin', Vol. 1, No. 2, July 25, 1940. 'Defendant Ray Leonard Townsend Day'. National Archives file CRIM 1/1233.

30. 'The Uncensored News Bulletin', Vol. 1, No. 4, August 7, 1940. 'Defendant Ray Leonard Townsend Day'. National Archives file CRIM 1/1233.

31. 'Threw Leaflets at Sentry – Gaoled', *Daily Mirror*, June 22, 1940.

32. 'Sentences Completely Inadequate', *The People*, July 7, 1940.

33. 'Five Years for Woman Teacher', *Yorkshire Post*, June 25, 1941.

34. There is a Home Office file on Elsie Orrin but, curiously, this remains closed to public scrutiny until January 1, 2047. 'Criminal Cases: Elsie Sarah Constance Orrin'. National Archives file (closed) HO 144/2708.

35. 'Defendant: Cyril Desmond Stephens'. National Archives file CRIM 1/1205.

36. 'Six Years For Radio Engineer', *Birmingham Daily Gazette*, September 20, 1940.

37. 'George Mace Wall'. National Archives file DPP 2/766; declassified December 1, 2000.

38. Statement of Albert Munt, Tottenham police station, September 25, 1940. 'Defendant: Albert Victor Munt'. National Archives file CRIM 1/1237.

39. Report of A.P. Rossiter Lewis, October 8, 1940. 'Defendant: Albert Victor Munt'. National Archives file CRIM 1/1237.

40. 'Boy Fired Houses to Light Way for Raiders', *Manchester Evening News*, October 16, 1940.

41. Evidence of Sgt. John H. Dodridge, *R. v. Revill*, December 11, 1940. Quoted in 'Boy Sketched Secret Aircraft; 19, Gets 4 Years Penal Servitude', *Birmingham Gazette*, December 12, 1940.

42. Registry Minute Sheet entry, September 12, 1939. 'Louise and Peter Revill'. National Archives file KV 2/1211; declassified April 4, 2003.

43. Registry Minute Sheet entry, September 29, 1939. 'Louise and Peter Revill'. National Archives file KV 2/1211; declassified April 4, 2003.

44. HO 144/21843. 'War: Peter Revill (sentenced to four years penal servitude under the OSA); position under Defence Regulation 18b'.

45. 'War Plane Plans. German's son gaoled for "Treachery"', *News of the World*, December 15, 1940.

46. Letter from S.H. Sargant to Flight Officer E.M. Shippard, Air Ministry, August 29, 1943. 'Louise and Peter Revill'. National Archives file KV 2/1211; declassified April 4, 2003.

47. Letter from G.E. Wakefield (a barrister working in MI5's legal section) to Capt. D.B. Dykes in MI5's Birmingham office, July 28, 1943. 'Louise and Peter Revill'. National Archives file KV 2/1211; declassified April 4, 2003.

Chapter 16

1. 'Spy Carried Secret to Grave', *Daily Herald*, July 10, 1941.

2. 'Criminal cases: Kieboom, Meier and Waldberg'. National Archives file HO 144/21472; declassified March 22, 2007.

3. National Archives files KV 2/1701–1706: declassified 2005.

4. National Archives file KV 2/24–27: declassified 1999.

5. National Archives file KV 2/30–32: declassified 1999.

6. National Archives file KV 2/3854–3856: declassified 2014.

7. National Archives file HO 45/25605; declassified January 1, 2001.

8. National Archives file HO 45/25606; declassified July 11, 2014.

9. National Archives file HO 144/22028; declassified November 11, 2016.

10. National Archives file HO 144/22039; declassified March 9, 2007.

11. National Archives file HO 144/22739; declassified January 6, 2017.

12. Psychological report by medical staff at Aylesbury prison, June 21, 1945. 'Dorothy Pamela O'Grady'. National Archives file PCOM 9/1497; declassified February 19, 2007.

13. Quoted in *Dotty Dorothy – The Perfect Spy*, Andrew Bradford, 2012; http://www.andrewbradfordauthor.com

14. Prison Governor's report on Pamela Arland, January 2, 1918. 'Dorothy Pamela O'Grady'. National Archives file PCOM 9/1497; declassified February 19, 2007.

15. 'Treason: Dorothy Pamela O'Grady'. National Archives file HO 45/25408; declassified January 1, 2006, recorded as lost October 7, 2010.

16. 'Woman says she had herself sentenced to death as "a huge joke"', *Daily Express*, March 5, 1950.

17. Ibid.

18. Ibid.

19. Guy Liddell diary entries, September 12 and September 17, 1940. 'Guy Liddell Diaries', Vol. 2. National Archives file KV 4/186; declassified November 1, 2002.

20. 'Woman to Die For Treachery', *Western Mail*, December 18, 1940.

21. *Daily Express*, March 5, 1950; op. cit.

22. 'O'Grady Not To Die, Gets 14 Years', *Daily Mirror*, February 11, 1941

23. She was released on February 24, 1950. 'Dorothy Pamela O'Grady'. National Archives file PCOM 9/1497; declassified February 19, 2007.

24. Criminal record of George Johnson Armstrong. 'George Johnson Armstrong'. National Archives file PCOM 9/900; declassified February 6, 2008.

25. Transcript of interview with George Johnson Armstrong by Lt. Col. William Hinchley-Cooke, New Scotland Yard, March 2, 1941. 'Defendant: George Johnson Armstrong'. National Archives file CRIM 1/1300.

26. Ibid.

27. Ibid.

28. Ibid.

29. Transcript of interview with George Johnson Armstrong by Lt. Col. William Hinchley-Cooke, New Scotland Yard, March 2, 1941. 'Defendant: George Johnson Armstrong'. National Archives file CRIM 1/1300.

30. Statement of Lt. Col. William Hinchley-Cooke, March 19, 1941. 'Defendant: George Johnson Armstrong'. National Archives file CRIM 1/1300.

31. Second statement of George Johnson Armstrong, March 3, 1941. 'Defendant: George Johnson Armstrong'. National Archives file CRIM 1/1300.

32. Third statement of George Johnson Armstrong, March 2, 1941. (For unexplained reasons this document is dated the day before his previous

statement.) 'Defendant: George Johnson Armstrong'. National Archives file CRIM 1/1300.

33. Extract of evidence by George Johnson Armstrong, Central Criminal Court, May 7, 1941. 'Criminal Cases: George Johnson Armstrong'. National Archives file HO 144/21558; declassified December 29, 2006.

34. Extract of ruling by Lord Caldecote, Court of Criminal Appeal, June 23, 1941. 'George Johnson Armstrong'. National Archives file HO 144/21558; declassified December 29, 2006.

35. Report on Duncan Scott-Ford by Edward Blanshard Stamp, Legal Section, January 22, 1943. 'Duncan Alexander Croall Scott-Ford'. National Archives file KV 2/57; declassified January 21, 1999.

36. Statement of Duncan Scott-Ford, Salford City police station, August 20–21, 1942. 'Duncan Alexander Croall Scott-Ford'. National Archives file KV 2/57; declassified January 21, 1999.

37. 'Liquidation Report on Scott-Ford case', Camp 020, October 27, 1942. 'Duncan Alexander Croall Scott-Ford'. National Archives file KV 2/57; declassified January 21, 1999.

38. Statement of Duncan Scott-Ford, in 'Liquidation Report on Scott-Ford case', Camp 020, October 27, 1942. 'Duncan Alexander Croall Scott-Ford'. National Archives file KV 2/57; declassified January 21, 1999.

39. Ibid.

40. A handwritten file note by Colonel Robin 'Tin Eye' Stephens on August 28, 1942 identifies 'Henley' as a middle-aged German intelligence officer and former sea captain named 'Schubert'. There are two likely candidates for this: Henry Schubert, a dual British and German national resident in Berlin before the war who was forced to serve in the German navy (National Archives file KV 2/3438; declassified April 2, 2011); and Theodor Schubert, alias Schade, an Abwehr officer thought to have been based in Spain from 1942–45 (National Archives file KV 2/1974; declassified June 23, 2005).

41. Statement of Duncan Scott-Ford, Salford City police station, August 20–21, 1942. 'Duncan Alexander Croall Scott-Ford'. National Archives file KV 2/57; declassified January 21, 1999.

42. Ibid.

43. Approximately £635 today.

44. 'Liquidation Report on Scott-Ford case', Camp 020, October 27, 1942. 'Duncan Alexander Croall Scott-Ford'. National Archives file KV 2/57; declassified January 21, 1999.

45. Ibid.

46. Report on Duncan Scott-Ford by Edward Blanshard Stamp, Legal Section, January 22, 1943. 'Duncan Alexander Croall Scott-Ford'. National Archives file KV 2/57; declassified January 21, 1999.

47. Report of Regional Security Officer, August 18, 1942. 'Duncan Alexander Croall Scott-Ford'. National Archives file KV 2/57; declassified January 21, 1999.

48. 'Liquidation Report on Scott-Ford case', Camp 020, October 27, 1942. 'Duncan Alexander Croall Scott-Ford'. National Archives file KV 2/57; declassified January 21, 1999.

49. MI5 Legal Section report on the trial of Duncan Scott-Ford, October 16, 1942. 'Duncan Alexander Croall Scott-Ford'. National Archives file KV 2/57; declassified January 21, 1999.

50. From November 1941, Norman Birkett KC combined his role as a High Court judge with that of *de-facto* head of the Home Office Advisory Committee panels hearing appeals against internment.

51. Letter from Gunner Philip Jackson. Undated, but posted in late September 1941. 'Philip Jackson'. National Archives file KV 2/3319; declassified August 26, 2010.

52. Since MI19 was responsible for obtaining information from German prisoners of war and MI11 charged with protecting British military personnel from enemy agents, there was no reason for either department to have been involved.

53. Letter from 'John Browne' to Gunner Philip Jackson, October 28, 1941. 'Philip Jackson'. National Archives file KV 2/3319; declassified August 26, 2010.

54. 'Eric Arthur Roberts'. National Archives file KV 2/3874; declassified October 24, 2014.

55. Major Jock Whyte, 'Additional Notes for Mr Roberts', December 2, 1941. 'Philip Jackson'. National Archives file KV 2/3320; declassified August 26, 2010.

56. Letter from Bedford to Gunner Philip Jackson, October 29, 1941. 'Philip Jackson'. National Archives file KV 2/3320; declassified August 26, 2010.

57. Transcript of interview with Philip Jackson, Woolpack Hotel, Birmingham, December 4, 1941. 'Philip Jackson'. National Archives file KV 2/3321; declassified August 26, 2010.

58. Ibid.

59. Letter from J.S. Badeley, Legal Branch to MI5's Regional Officer, Nottingham, June 10, 1942. 'Philip Jackson'. National Archives file KV 2/3322; declassified August 26, 2010.

Chapter 17

1. Memorandum by Alexander Maxwell, Home Office, October 6, 1939. 'Defence Regulation 18B: Appointments to Membership of Advisory Committee'. National Archives file HO 45/25114.

2. The top-level internal conference of MI5 section chiefs.

3. Gonne St Clair 'Toby' Pilcher was one of the barristers brought in to MI5's legal section to handle liaison with the Home Office and the Advisory Committee. He later became a High Court judge.

4. 'Guy Liddell Diaries', Vol. 2, August 13, 1940. National Archives file KV 4/186; declassified November 1, 2002.

5. 'Note on the case of William Frederick Craven', MI5 Legal Branch, August 5, 1941. 'William Frederick Craven'. National Archives files KV 2/488; declassified May 11, 2001.

6. Petrie replaced Sir Vernon Kell in April 1941.

7. Letter from Alexander Maxwell, Home Office, to Sir David Petrie, MI5, July 25, 1941. 'William Frederick Craven'. National Archives files KV 2/488; declassified May 11, 2001.

8. Letter from Sir David Petrie, MI5 to Alexander Maxwell, Home Office, August 7, 1941. 'William Frederick Craven'. National Archives files KV 2/488; declassified May 11, 2001.

9. Extract from Home Office files for W.F. Craven, in 'William Frederick Craven'. National Archives files KV 2/486; declassified May 11, 2001.

10. 'Disturbances: Activities of the British National Party, 1942–1943'. National Archives file HO 144/21845.

11. Letter from William Craven to Home Secretary Herbert Morrison, November 8, 1942. 'William Frederick Craven'. National Archives files KV 2/486; declassified May 11, 2001.

12. Signed statement of William Frederick Craven to Det. Sgt. Victor Tuffley, Special Branch, Horsely Priory, Stroud, December 22, 1942. 'Extract from Home Office files for W.F. Craven', in 'William Frederick Craven'. National Archives files KV 2/486; declassified May 11, 2001.

13. This was untrue: Craven had once planned to join pro-Nazi Finnish forces but had never done so.

14. Letter from William Craven to 'The Leader, Swedish National Socialist Party, Stockholm', February 7, 1943. 'William Frederick Craven'. National Archives files KV 2/488; declassified May 11, 2001.

15. Letter to German Legation, Dublin, February 24, 1943. 'William Frederick Craven'. National Archives files KV 2/488; declassified May 11, 2001.

16. 'Fascist who wrote to Huns gaoled for life', *Daily Mirror*, April 7, 1943.

17. 'Guy Liddell Diaries', Vol. 7, April 9, 1943. National Archives file KV 4/191; declassified November 1, 2002.

18. Transcript of appeal to the Home Office Advisory Committee by Mrs Christabel Nicholson, October 14, 1941. 'Christabel Sybil Caroline Nicholson'. National Archives file KV 2/902; declassified October 31, 2002.

19. Home Office Advisory Committee report on Mrs Christabel Nicholson, October 29, 1941. 'Christabel Sybil Caroline Nicholson'. National Archives file KV 2/902; declassified October 31, 2002.

20. Report of the Home Office Advisory Committee on Captain Ramsay, July 18, 1940. 'Archibald Maule Ramsay'. National Archives file KV 2/677; declassified October 30, 2001.

21. Ibid.

22. Ibid.

23. Ibid.

24. *New York Times*, August 22, 1940.

25. William ('Wild Bill') Donovan was a US Army veteran of the First World War. An outspoken voice warning of the dangers posed by Nazi Germany, in 1940 Roosevelt appointed him as his unofficial intelligence emissary to Europe. Donovan regularly met with Churchill and other members of the War Cabinet. After America joined the war in 1941, he set up the Office of Strategic Services – the forerunner of the CIA.

26. Memorandum by S.H. Noakes, April 7, 1941. 'Archibald Maule Ramsay'. National Archives file KV 2/677; declassified October 30, 2001.

27. 'Ramsay: Friend to Hitler', *Daily Mirror*, August 1, 1941.

28. Memorandum on Ramsay by Marjorie Roberts, F3 Branch, MI5, July 13, 1945. 'Archibald Maule Ramsay'. National Archives file KV 2/679; declassified October 30, 2001.

29. Transcript of evidence by Robert Gordon-Canning to the Home Office Advisory Committee, August 28, 1940. 'Captain Robert Cecil Gordon-Canning'. National Archives file KV 2/877; declassified October 31, 2002.

30. Ibid.

31. Observations on the proposal of the Home Office Advisory Committee to release Robert Cecil Gordon-Canning. Edward Blanshard Stamp, MI5 Legal Section, September 19, 1940. 'Captain Robert Cecil Gordon-Canning'. National Archives file KV 2/876-877; declassified October 31, 2002.

32. Home Office Advisory Committee letter to MI5, October 26, 1940. 'Captain Robert Cecil Gordon-Canning'. National Archives file KV 2/877; declassified October 31, 2002.

33. Letter from S.H. Noakes, MI5 Legal Section, to the Advisory Committee, November 9, 1940. 'Captain Robert Cecil Gordon-Canning'. National Archives file KV 2/877; declassified October 31, 2002.

34. Transcript of evidence by Robert Gordon-Canning to the Home Office Advisory Committee, August 14, 1941. 'Captain Robert Cecil Gordon-Canning'. National Archives file KV 2/877; declassified October 31, 2002.

35. Report of the Home Office Advisory Committee, August 25, 1941. 'Captain Robert Cecil Gordon-Canning'. National Archives file KV 2/877; declassified October 31, 2002.

36. Ibid.

37. Letter from S.H. Noakes, MI5 Legal Section, to the Home Office, October 6, 1941. 'Captain Robert Cecil Gordon-Canning'. National Archives file KV 2/877; declassified October 31, 2002.

38. File note by Edward Blanshard Stamp, MI5 Legal Section, December 15, 1941. 'Captain Robert Cecil Gordon-Canning'. National Archives file KV 2/877; declassified October 31, 2002.

39. Letter from Duff Cooper, Chancellor of the Duchy of Lancaster, to Sir David Petrie, Director General, MI5, January 5, 1943. 'Captain Robert Cecil Gordon-Canning'. National Archives file KV 2/877; declassified October 31, 2002.

40. Report of the Home Office Advisory Committee on the Case of John Beckett, July 30, 1940. 'John and Anne Beckett'. National Archives file KV 2/1511; declassified March 30, 2004.

41. Ibid.

42. Ibid.

43. Report of Home Office Advisory Committee in the Case of Benjamin Greene, August 30, 1940. 'Benjamin Greene'. National Archives file KV 2/489; declassified May 11, 2001.

44. Letter from Legal Section, MI5, to the Home Office Advisory Committee, August 20, 1940. 'Benjamin Greene'. National Archives file KV 2/489; declassified May 11, 2001.

45. *The Times Law Report*, July 31, 1941.

46. The House of Lords subsequently upheld the Court of Appeal's decision.

47. Hickson was retained by many British fascists seeking to challenge 18B internment orders. He was not himself remotely right-wing, but was a passionate believer in human rights and the rule of law.

48. Letter from S.H. Noakes, MI5 Legal Section, to Home Office Advisory Committee, July 1, 1941. 'Benjamin Greene'. National Archives file KV 2/489; declassified May 11, 2001.

49. Statement of Harald Kurtz, October 21, 1941. Ibid.

50. Ibid.

51. 'Document handed to Kurtz by Oswald Hickson', October 21, 1941. 'Benjamin Greene'. National Archives file KV 2/489; declassified May 11, 2001.

52. 'Guy Liddell Diaries', Vol. 4, October 23, 1941. National Archives file KV 4/188; declassified November 1, 2002.

53. Letter from Sir David Petrie, Director General, MI5, to Sir Alexander Maxwell, Permanent Under-Secretary of State, the Home Office, October 23, 1941. 'Benjamin Greene'. National Archives file KV 2/489; declassified May 11, 2001.

54. Supplementary report of the Home Office Advisory Committee on the case of Ben Greene, December 16, 1941. 'Benjamin Greene'. National Archives file KV 2/490; declassified May 11, 2001.

55. Ibid.

56. Edward Blanshard Stamp, MI5 Legal Section, 'Observations in the case of Ben Greene', December 23, 1941. 'Benjamin Greene'. National Archives file KV 2/490; declassified May 11, 2001.

57. Letter from Sir David Petrie, Director General MI5, to Sir Alexander Maxwell, January 6, 1942. 'Benjamin Greene'. National Archives file KV 2/491; declassified May 11, 2001.

58. *Hansard*, House of Commons debate, February 5, 1942. Vol. 377, cc. 1255-7.

59. 'Guy Liddell Diaries', Vol. 5, January 18, 1942. National Archives file KV 4/189; declassified November 1, 2002.

Chapter 18

1. 'Report on the Work of MS (Agents) During the War', Maxwell Knight, April 4, 1945. National Archives file KV 4/227; declassified March 30, 2004.

2. Joan Miller, *One Girl's War*, p. 53. Brandon Books, 1986.

3. Transcript of meeting between Irma Stapleton and John Bingham, Cumberland Hotel, November 14, 1941. 'Irma Sophie Gertrude Stapleton'. National Archives file KV 2/945; declassified October 31, 2002.

4. Equivalent to more than £600 today.

5. Naturalisation Certificate: Helmut Eduard Husgen, January 6, 1948. National Archives file HO 334/200/37047.

6. 'The Stapleton Case: Digest of Activity to Be Included in the Intelligence Summary', May 1942. 'Irma Sophie Gertrude Stapleton'. National Archives file KV 2/945; declassified October 31, 2002.

7. Ibid.

8. The document itself is badly damaged in the surviving files, its pages tattered and missing corners which obscure some of Stapleton's incriminating statements.

9. Transcript of meeting between Irma Stapleton and 'John Brunner' (John Bingham), Cumberland Hotel, November 14, 1941. 'Irma Sophie Gertrude Stapleton'. National Archives file KV 2/945; declassified October 31, 2002.

10. Ibid.

11. 'The Stapleton Case: Digest of Activity to Be Included in the Intelligence Summary', May 1942. 'Irma Sophie Gertrude Stapleton'. National Archives file KV 2/945; declassified October 31, 2002.

12. 'Guy Liddell Diaries', Vol. 4, November 18, 1941. National Archives file KV 4/188; declassified November 1, 2002.

13. Ibid.

14. 'The Stapleton Case: Digest of Activity to Be Included in the Intelligence Summary', May 1942. 'Irma Sophie Gertrude Stapleton'. National Archives file KV 2/945; declassified October 31, 2002.

15. Memorandum by Guy Liddell to Sir David Petrie, November 20, 1942. 'Irma Sophie Gertrude Stapleton'. National Archives file KV 2/945; declassified October 31, 2002.

16. Registry Minute Sheet note by Jock Whyte, November 14, 1941. 'Irma Sophie Gertrude Stapleton'. National Archives file KV 2/945; declassified October 31, 2002.

17. '10 years for Typist in Old Bailey Trial', *Daily Mirror*, February 10, 1942.

18. Stapleton's appeal against conviction and sentence was turned down in March 1942; she remained in prison until 1948.

19. Letter from Sir David Petrie to Lord Swinton, February 12, 1942. 'Irma Sophie Gertrude Stapleton'. National Archives file KV 2/945; declassified October 31, 2002.

20. 'Guy Liddell Diaries', Vol. 4, September 15, 1941. National Archives file KV 4/188; declassified November 1, 2002.

21. 'Ibid.

22. Jimmy Dickson, Knight's protégé, made a succession of complaints to Guy Liddell. 'Guy Liddell Diaries', Vols 8–9, October–December 1943. National Archives file KV 4/192–193; declassified November 1, 2002.

23. 'Guy Liddell Diaries', Vol. 5, March 25, 1942. National Archives file KV 4/189; declassified November 1, 2002.

24. Henry Hemming, *Maxwell Knight, MI5's Greatest Spymaster*, pp. 152–8. Preface Publishing, 2017.

25. Francis Aitken-Sneath, Request to appoint Eric Roberts, May 31, 1940. 'Eric Arthur Roberts, alias Jack King'. National Archives file KV 2/3874; declassified October 24, 2014.

26. Letter from R.W. Jones, Westminster Bank, to Oswald Harker, MI5, June 11, 1940. 'Eric Arthur Roberts, alias Jack King'. National Archives file KV 2/3874; declassified October 24, 2014.

27. MI5 website: https://www.mi5.gov.uk/ERIC-ROBERTS -UNDERCOVER-WORK-IN-WORLD-WAR-II

28. 'The "S.R." Case', MI5 Memo, September 9, 1945. 'Mary Marita Perigoe, alias Brahe'. National Archives file KV 2/3800; declassified February 28, 2014.

Chapter 19

1. Correspondence between Dorothy Wegener and 'Jack King', summer–autumn 1940. 'Mary Marita Perigoe, alias Brahe'. National Archives file KV 2/3800; declassified February 28, 2014.

2. Ibid.

3. Further Observations of MI5 on Walter Ernest Oscar Wegener, June 8, 1942. 'Walter Ernest Oscar Wegener'. National Archives file KV 2/540; declassified October 30, 2001.

4. 'Extract of reports from Source S.R.', April 4, 1944. 'Walter Ernest Oscar Wegener'. National Archives file KV 2/540; declassified October 30, 2001. Wegener's handler appears to have been Hans Paul Kruger, alias Kruse. 'A Wehrmacht officer in charge of Abwehr operations in Tangiers, specializing in espionage and sabotage.' National Archives file KV 2/525; declassified October 30, 2001.

5. 'Memorandum of the firm of Siemens Schuckert Ltd [and] Minutes of Meeting with the Director General on the Agent provocateur Scheme', November 19, 1941. 'Mary Marita Perigoe, alias Brahe'. National Archives file KV 2/3800; declassified February 28, 2014.

6. In 'Minutes of Meeting with the Director General on the Agent provocateur Scheme', November 19, 1941. 'Mary Marita Perigoe, alias Brahe'. National Archives file KV 2/3800; declassified February 28, 2014.

7. He was arrested under DR 18B on May 26, 1940.

8. In 'Minutes of Meeting with the Director General on the Agent provocateur Scheme', November 19, 1941. 'Mary Marita Perigoe, alias Brahe'. National Archives file KV 2/3800; declassified February 28, 2014.

9. Ibid.

10. Ibid.

11. 'Guy Liddell Diaries', Vol. 4, October 8, 1941. National Archives file KV 4/188; declassified November 1, 2002.

12. 'Guy Liddell Diaries', Vol. 5, December 2, 1941. National Archives file KV 4/189; declassified November 1, 2002.

13. 'Guy Liddell Diaries', Vol. 5, February 14, 1942. National Archives file KV 4/189; declassified November 1, 2002.

14. Report of the Home Office Advisory Committee on Walter Wegener, January 15, 1941. 'Walter Ernest Oscar Wegener'. National Archives file KV 2/540; declassified October 30, 2001.

15. Report of the Home Office Advisory Committee on Walter Wegener, June 19, 1942. 'Walter Ernest Oscar Wegener'. National Archives file KV 2/540; declassified October 30, 2001.

16. In 'Minutes of Meeting with the Director General on the Agent provocateur Scheme', November 19, 1941. 'Mary Marita Perigoe, alias Brahe'. National Archives file KV 2/3800; declassified February 28, 2014.

17. Ibid.

18. 'Mary Marita Perigoe, alias Brahe'. National Archives file KV 2/3800; declassified February 28, 2014.

19. Bernard Perigoe was interned, under Regulation 18B, early in the Second World War and was one of the last British fascists to be released from detention. National Archives file HO 283/41. He divorced Marita after the war and by 1949 was married to someone with no connection to fascism.

20. 'Minutes of Meeting with the Director General on the Agent provocateur Scheme', November 19, 1941. 'Mary Marita Perigoe, alias Brahe'. National Archives file KV 2/3800; declassified February 28, 2014.

21. Ibid.

22. Ibid.

23. Helen Fry, *The M Room – Secret Listeners Who Bugged the Nazis.* CreateSpace Publishing, 2012.

24. 'The "SR" Case'. Memorandum by Gonne St C. Pilcher, MI5 Legal Section, September 9, 1945. 'Mary Marita Perigoe, alias Brahe'. National Archives file KV 2/3800; declassified February 28, 2014.

Chapter 20

1. Transcript of recording, May 5, 1943. 'Eric Arthur Roberts, alias Jack King'. National Archives file KV 2/3874; declassified October 24, 2014.

2. Equivalent to £90 today; the payment was increased to £5 (approximately £200 today) in January 1944.

3. 'Memorandum on Fifth Column organisation', July 10, 1942. 'Mary Marita Perigoe, alias Brahe'. National Archives file KV 2/3800; declassified February 28, 2014.

4. The Petroleum Board was formed by British oil companies on the outbreak of war; on behalf of the government it had a monopoly on controlling and distributing petrol stocks throughout the country.

5. Memorandum on Fifth Column organisation', July 10, 1942. 'Mary Marita Perigoe, alias Brahe'. National Archives file KV 2/3800; declassified February 28, 2014.

6. Ibid.

7. 'Hilda Marian Agnes Leech'. National Archives file KV 6/119; declassified February 28, 2014.

8. Transcript of recording, August 29, 1942. 'Eric Arthur Roberts, alias Jack King'. National Archives file KV 2/3874; declassified October 24, 2014.

9. S.R. Case report, April 18, 1943. In 'Post-war Applications of the Case', 1943. 'Mary Marita Perigoe, alias Brahe'. National Archives file KV 2/3800; declassified February 28, 2014.

10. Registry Minute Sheet note, January 31, 1941. 'Eileen Lesley Gleave'. National Archives file KV 2/2677; declassified September 3, 2007.

11. Memo by Lord Rothschild to Sir David Petrie, MI5 Director General, September 8, 1942. 'Eileen Lesley Gleave'. National Archives file KV 2/2677; declassified September 3, 2007.

12. Transcript of recording, September 4, 1943. 'Eric Arthur Roberts, alias Jack King'. National Archives file KV 2/3874; declassified October 24, 2014.

13. 'Memorandum on Fifth Column organisation', July 10, 1942. 'Mary Marita Perigoe, alias Brahe'. National Archives file KV 2/3800; declassified February 28, 2014.

14. Ibid.

15. Transcript of recording, August 29, 1942. 'Eric Arthur Roberts, alias Jack King'. National Archives file KV 2/3874; declassified October 24, 2014.

16. Transcript of recording, May 17, 1943. 'Eric Arthur Roberts, alias Jack King'. National Archives file KV 2/3874; declassified October 24, 2014.

17. 'S.R. Case Report', July 11, 1943. 'Eileen Lesley Gleave'. National Archives file KV 2/2677; declassified September 3, 2007.

18. 'S.R. Case Report', April 21, 1942. 'Eileen Lesley Gleave'. National Archives file KV 2/2677; declassified September 3, 2007.

19. Letter from Edgar Thoreau Bray to Dr Hans Thost, September 12, 1933. 'Edgar Bray, alias Whitehead and Sophia Bray, alias Voznesennsky'. National Archives file KV 2/3799; declassified February 28, 2014.

20. 'S.R. Case Report', June 27, 1942. 'Edgar Bray, alias Whitehead and Sophia Bray, alias Voznesennsky'. National Archives file KV 2/3799; declassified February 28, 2014.

21. 'Memorandum on the Fifth Column Organisation', July 10, 1942. 'Mary Marita Perigoe, alias Brahe'. National Archives file KV 2/3800; declassified February 28, 2014.

22. 'S.R. Case Report', July 7, 1942. 'Edgar Bray, alias Whitehead and Sophia Bray, alias Voznesennsky'. National Archives file KV 2/3799; declassified February 28, 2014.

23. 'S.R. Case Report', July 31, 1942. 'Edgar Bray, alias Whitehead and Sophia Bray, alias Voznesennsky'. National Archives file KV 2/3799; declassified February 28, 2014.

24. 'S.R. Case Report', October 20, 1942. 'Edgar Bray, alias Whitehead and Sophia Bray, alias Voznesennsky'. National Archives file KV 2/3799; declassified February 28, 2014.

25. Transcript of recording, January 7, 1943. 'Eric Arthur Roberts, alias Jack King'. National Archives file KV 2/3874; declassified October 24, 2014.

26. 'Hans Kohout'. National Archives file KV 6/118; declassified February 28, 2014.

27. 'Memorandum on Fifth Column organisation', July 10, 1942. 'Mary Marita Perigoe, alias Brahe'. National Archives file KV 2/3800; declassified February 28, 2014.

28. Transcript of recording, August 29, 1942. 'Eric Arthur Roberts, alias Jack King'. National Archives file KV 2/3874; declassified October 24, 2014.

29. Transcript of recording, September 5, 1942. 'Eric Arthur Roberts, alias Jack King'. National Archives file KV 2/3874; declassified October 24, 2014.

30. Transcript of recording, October 8, 1942. 'Eric Arthur Roberts, alias Jack King'. National Archives file KV 2/3874; declassified October 24, 2014.

31. Transcript of recording, October 20, 1942. 'Eric Arthur Roberts, alias Jack King'. National Archives file KV 2/3874; declassified October 24, 2014.

32. Guy Liddell, diary entry, August 24, 1943. 'Guy Liddell Diaries', Vol. 8. National Archives file KV 4/192; declassified November 1, 2002.

33. Guy Liddell, diary entry, October 4, 1943. 'Guy Liddell Diaries', Vol. 8. National Archives file KV 4/192; declassified November 1, 2002.

34. 'Note for meeting with D.B. [Guy Liddell, Director, B Division]', Victor Rothschild, January 25, 1944. 'Mary Marita Perigoe, alias Brahe'. National Archives file KV 2/3800; declassified February 28, 2014.

35. Thomas M. Shelford, 'Memorandum on the Fifth Column Case', September 23, 1944. 'Mary Marita Perigoe, alias Brahe'. National Archives file KV 2/3800; declassified February 28, 2014.

36. Although Donko appears throughout the Alwina Thies file, there is no record of her in the National Archives.

37. 'S.R. Case Report', January 19, 1944. 'Alwina Pauline Thies'. National Archives file KV 2/3801; declassified February 28, 2014.

38. 'S.R. Case Report', January 21, 1944. 'Alwina Pauline Thies'. National Archives file KV 2/3801; declassified February 28, 2014.

39. 'S.R. Case Report', March 18, 1944. 'Alwina Pauline Thies'. National Archives file KV 2/3801; declassified February 28, 2014.

40. 'Post-war Applications of a Case Involving a Group of Disloyal Persons in Great Britain', August 1943. 'Mary Marita Perigoe, alias Brahe'. National Archives file KV 2/3800; declassified February 28, 2014.

41. 'The S.R. Case – Top Secret'. Gonne St C. Pilcher, September 1945. 'Mary Marita Perigoe, alias Brahe'. National Archives file KV 2/3800; declassified February 28, 2014.

42. Ibid.

43. Ibid.

Chapter 21

1. *The Word*, June 1945, pp. 128–9.

2. 'Report by Source S.R. 60', May 3, 1945. 'Oliver Conway Gilbert'. National Archives files KV 2/1343–1344; declassified September 26, 2003.

3. 'The S.R. Case – Top Secret'. Memorandum by Gonne St Clair Pilcher, September 9, 1945. 'Mary Marita Perigoe, alias Brahe'. National Archives file KV 2/3800; declassified February 28, 2014.

4. Registry Minute Sheet note by Theresa Clay, May 1, 1945. 'Eileen Lesley Gleave'. National Archives file KV 2/2677; declassified September 3, 2007.

5. Field Marshal Bernard Montgomery was Britain's most senior Army commander in the last days of the Second World War. He accepted the German surrender and went on to become Chief of the Imperial General Staff in 1946.

6. 'Report of Source A.B. 20', October 24, 1946. 'Oliver Conway Gilbert'. National Archives files KV 2/1343–1344; declassified September 26, 2003.

7. 'Report of Source A.B. 21', October 30, 1946. 'Oliver Conway Gilbert'. National Archives files KV 2/1343–1344; declassified September 26, 2003.

8. Statement of Inspector George Smith, Metropolitan Police Special Branch, July 28, 1947.

9. Statement of Joachim Kirmse (undated). Eileen Lesley Gleave. National Archives file KV 2/2677; declassified September 3, 2007.

10. 'Report of the interrogation of Joachim Kirmse, Wormwood Scrubs Prison' (undated but probably June 1947). 'Eileen Lesley Gleave'. National Archives file KV 2/2677; declassified September 3, 2007.

11. 'Seven Jailed For Helping Escaped P.O.W.s', *Dundee Evening Telegraph*, March 31, 1947.

12. 'Report by MI5 to British Army on the Rhine Intelligence', February 27, 1950. 'Captain Robert Cecil Gordon-Canning'. National Archives file KV 2/878; declassified October 31, 2002.

13. '18B Man pays £500 for Bust of Hitler', *News Chronicle*, November 28, 1945.

14. *Truth* magazine, January 9, 1946.

15. 'MP's "Statute of Jewry" Motion', *Manchester Guardian*, June 2, 1945. 'Eileen Lesley Gleave'. National Archives file KV 2/2677; declassified September 3, 2007.

16. 'Report from Source A.B. 21', April 17, 1946. 'Oliver Conway Gilbert'. National Archives file KV 2/1344; declassified September 26, 2003.

17. Captain Archibald H. Maule Ramsay, *The Nameless War*. The Britons Publishing Society, 1952.

18. Extract from F3/1588 Report, June 8, 1945. 'John and Anne Beckett'. National Archives file KV 2/1518; declassified March 30, 2004.

19. Letter from John Beckett to Major McDonagh, October 9, 1945. 'John and Anne Beckett'. National Archives file KV 2/1519; declassified March 30, 2004.

20. Letter from John Beckett to William Joyce, December 19, 1945.

Afterword

1. In *The Life of Reason*, Vol. 1, 'Reason In Commonsense'. Constable, 1905.

2. https://www.gov.uk/government/collections/terrorism-prevention-and-investigation-measures-act

Index

Entries in **bold** appear in the photographic plate section